Law in the Ancient World

Law in the Ancient World

Russ VerSteeg

CAROLINA ACADEMIC PRESS
Durham, North Carolina

Library of Congress Cataloging-in-Publication Data

VerSteeg, Russ.
   Law in the ancient world / Russ VerSteeg.
      p. cm.
   Includes bibliographical references and index.
   ISBN 0-89089-976-2
      1. Law, Ancient. 2. Law--History. I. Title.

   K590 .V47 2001
   340.5'3--dc21

                                                        2001052798

CAROLINA ACADEMIC PRESS
700 Kent Street
Durham, North Carolina 27701
Telephone (919) 489-7486
Fax (919) 493-5668
E-mail: cap@cap-press.com
www.cap-press.com

Printed in the United States of America.

For Christina Elliott Sorum

Contents

Unit II
Law in Ancient Egypt

Unit III
Law in Classical Athens

Unit IV
Law in Ancient Rome

Preface

The primary goal of the present volume is simple. I wish to provide a modern introduction to ancient law. It is common for undergraduate students of ancient history to focus their attention on four great civilizations: the Mesopotamians; Egyptians; Greeks; and Romans. Admittedly, this syllabus ignores other worthy civilizations such as the Hebrews, Chinese, and those peoples who inhabited the Indus River Valley. With the understanding that the traditional (*i.e.,* Mesopotamian, Egyptian, Greek, and Roman) approach has shortcomings, I, nevertheless, have chosen to follow that traditional model. There are many books that give excellent introductions to Roman law. There are significantly fewer books devoted to Athenian law. And there are only a handful that relate to law in ancient Mesopotamia and Egypt. There is, I believe, need for a single-volume survey that offers an overview of law and the legal systems in these four great civilizations.

This book contains four units. Unit I explores early law in ancient Mesopotamia. Unit II addresses law in ancient Egypt. Unit III is devoted to law in Classical Athens. And Unit IV provides a survey of Roman law. Each unit contains three chapters. The first chapter in each unit presents an overview. It gives essential historical background material and explains the origins of law. These chapters also probe the meaning of law in the abstract and acquaint the reader with the jurisprudential foundations of law. The second chapter in each unit examines the legal system and its structures and procedures. In particular the middle chapters describe the court systems, judges, and jurors. These chapters also discuss legal procedure and the law of evidence. The final chapter in each unit considers substantive law (*i.e.,* personal status, family law, inheritance, property, torts, criminal law, and contracts). In order to make this information more understandable to modern readers, these chapters explain the ancient laws using contemporary legal categories. As one might presume, it is this final chapter in each unit that is the longest.

A great deal that has been written about ancient law has been written by specialists in Assyriology, Egyptology, and Classics. I am neither an Assyriologist nor Egyptologist. I am something of a Classicist, however. I majored in Latin in college at the University of North Carolina at Chapel Hill. And I taught high school Latin and Ancient History for five years after my college graduation (1979–1984). I studied Egyptology under Dr. Edmund Meltzer at UNC-CH while I was teaching high school, and I briefly (for 4–5 years) considered attending graduate school in Egyptology. During that same time, I took a summer school course (*The Cultures of the Ancient Near East*) under Dr. Jack Sasson at UNC-CH. I attended the University of Connecticut School of Law (1984–1987) and studied Roman Law there. I practiced law for two years in Hartford, Connecticut prior to beginning my career as a law professor. Thus, my training has been a mixture of ancient languages, literature, history, civilization, and law. As such, I hope that I am able to offer an organization, approach, perspective, and insight that will help readers appreciate law and its role in these magnificent and dynamic ancient civilizations.

I have a long list of individuals whom I would like to thank. First and foremost, I've dedicated the book to Dr. Christina Elliott Sorum. Christie taught me seven classes during my Freshman and Sophomore years in college. She was my first Latin and Greek professor and also taught me *Greek Tragedy*. She did her best to sharpen my critical thinking skills, to improve my prose style, and to force me to take myself a little less seriously. Her energetic teaching and thought-provoking lectures sparked my interest and inspired me to continue studying Classics. It is difficult for me to imagine what I'd be doing today had she not been there. Christie, from the bottom of my heart, I thank you for making a difference in my life.

Unit I is essentially a condensed version of my book, *Early Mesopotamian Law*. Dr. Martha Roth at the Oriental Institute, University of Chicago, Dr. Raymond Westbrook at John Hopkins University, and Dr. Ronald Sack at North Carolina State University read and commented on an early draft of that manuscript, and thus contributed to Unit I of the present work. Similarly, Unit II is a condensed version of my book, *Law in Ancient Egypt*. Dr. Janet Johnson at the Oriental Institute, University of Chicago and Dr. Richard Jasnow at Johns Hopkins University read and commented on an early draft of that manuscript, and thus contributed to Unit II of the present volume. My father, Bob VerSteeg, read that manuscript when it was near completion and gave me valuable advice regarding style, grammar, spelling, and punctuation. So Dad, thanks for making Unit II read more smoothly and correctly. Dr. Ed Carawan at Southwest Missouri State University read Unit III in an early iteration and then read it again when it was near completion. Ed's comments and suggestions clarified a number of issues for me, helped me better understand some of the nuances of Athenian law, and generally improved that Unit. Dr. Kathryn Williams at the University of North Carolina at Greensboro read and commented on Unit IV. Her criticisms and recommendations greatly enhanced the accuracy of those chapters. My wife, Nina Barclay (B.A. Classics, Brown University; M.A. Latin, University of North Carolina at Chapel Hill), who teaches Latin and Greek at the Norwich Free Academy in Norwich, Connecticut read pretty much everything at one stage or another. As always, her common sense suggestions and perceptive analysis made this a better book both microscopically and macroscopically. Thanks are also due to the students in my Roman Law Class at the University of Malta during the summer of 2001 who offered a number of helpful suggestions for chapters 10–12. All errors and omissions are, of course, my responsibility and should not be attributed to these generous people who unselfishly gave their time and energy to help improve my work.

John F. O'Brien, Dean of New England School of Law and the Board of Trustees offered their support for this project by giving me funding through the Honorable James R. Lawton Summer Research Stipend program. In particular, I wrote the initial drafts of Unit III (1996) and Chapter 5 (2000) pursuant to James R. Lawton Summer Research Stipends. I wrote a significant amount of Units II and IV while on Sabbatical at the Institute of Advanced Legal Studies at the University of London (Fall 1999). My hosts in London and the library staff at the IALS were very helpful.

I would also like to thank the Carolina Academic Press. I am genuinely indebted to Keith Sipe, the Publisher. Keith encouraged me to undertake this project six years ago when it was nothing more than an idea casually raised over dinner. His support, enthusiasm, warmth, and sense of humor have made the path easier to travel. Tim Colton and Kasia Krzysztoforska, my editors, have kept their wits about them and endured numerous unreasonable demands that I've placed on them. Thank you for your patience with me, Tim and Kasia.

I've tried to keep the number of footnotes down. Because there are very few general works on either Mesopotamian or Egyptian law, I've footnoted those units more generously than the units on Athenian and Roman law. For the sake of consistency and simplicity, I have standardized most ancient spellings and proper names (*e.g.,* Thutmose not Thutmosis) and I've liberally changed them even in quoted material and titles.

R.V.
Boston, October 2001

Unit I

Early
Mesopotamian Law

CHAPTER 1

Background and Beginnings
of Mesopotamian Law

§ 1.01 INTRODUCTION

This Unit considers law in ancient Mesopotamia from its beginnings (roughly 3000 B.C.) to about 1600 B.C. There are numerous law collections (the so-called "codes") as well as other legal documents that have survived from the period before 1600 B.C. Assyriologists refer to the period around 1600 B.C. (about 150 years after Hammurabi) as the end of the "First Dynasty of Babylon," and generally consider this one of the "landmarks of ancient history."[1] It represents a significant break in Mesopotamian civilization, for it was in 1595 B.C. that the Hittite king, Mursilis I, sacked both Mari and Babylon. After his departure, a Kassite invasion hobbled much of Mesopotamia.

In general, our sources for Mesopotamian law—from Sumerian to Neo-Babylonian—include a number of law collections (or "codes"), *mīsarum* edicts[2] (written advice given by the king regarding specific legal topics),[3] and private and public legal documents such as letters, contracts, adoption documents, loans, boundary markers, administrative texts, and international agreements. Luckily, many traditional texts changed very little over the course of time. This may also have been true of the law collections. Thus, once "frozen," a text was likely to reflect law and society from an early time; not the age of scribal copying, but rather the age of original composi-

---

1. H.W.F. SAGGS, THE GREATNESS THAT WAS BABYLON 74 (1962) [hereinafter "SAGGS, BABYLON"].
2. *See infra* § 1.10.
3. *See generally* Sophie Lafont, *The Ancient Near Eastern Laws: Continuity and Pluralism* in THEORY AND METHOD IN BIBLICAL AND CUNEIFORM LAW 91, 97–100 (Bernard M. Levinson ed., 1994) [hereinafter "Lafont, *Continuity and Pluralism*"].

tion and standardization. This makes the law collections especially useful tools for studying Mesopotamian law. As a rule, the law collections are relatively easy to understand; and most of the "law" described in this Unit is based on the "law" as it is presented in these law collections. The structural patterns of the Mesopotamian laws in the law collections (codes) tend to be similar. Each provision begins with a protasis ("if" clause) and concludes with an apodasis ("then" clause). The protasis establishes the conduct or circumstance that requires an application of law. The apodasis, then, articulates the legal result. The records and documents used on a daily basis, however, pose significant problems even for the scholars who work with closely with them.

§ 1.02 OVERVIEW OF THE LAW COLLECTIONS

Without doubt, the great law collections (codes) are among the most important sources for any study of Mesopotamian law. Today most scholars refer to these as "collections" not as "codes" because the word "code" suggests a comprehensive treatment of law—something that the Mesopotamian collections clearly are not.[4] To a certain degree, the codifications expressed a king's interest in the welfare of his citizens and his desire to change their lives for the better. Most Mesopotamian legal scholars have concluded, however, that it is unlikely that these collections ever received practical application in daily life.[5] There are many theories about the nature of the collections. Edwin Good summarizes the debate as follows:

---

4. SAMUAL GREENGUS, *Legal and Social Institutions of Ancient Mesopotamia, in* 1 CIVILIZATIONS OF THE ANCIENT NEAR EAST, at 469, 471 ("These ancient law collections are often referred to as 'codes,' but the modern term can be misleading. The collections are not 'codes' in the modern, comprehensive sense of that term because they convey only a part of all of the operative laws at that time."). According to Driver & Miles, the convention of referring to these legal documents as "codes" goes back to the early translator named Scheil. G.R. DRIVER & JOHN C. MILES, THE BABYLONIAN LAWS (VOL. I: LEGAL COMMENTARY 1952) [hereinafter "DRIVER & MILES, BABYLONIAN LAWS"] 45, n. 1. *See also* Martha T. Roth, *The Law Collection of King Hammurabi: Toward an Understanding of Codification and Text.* Strasbourg Codification Conference (1997) 2 [hereinafter "Roth, *The Law Collection of King Hammurabi*"] ("Although Schiel, who edited and published the editio princeps of the text on the stela excavated in 1902, labeled the text as a 'code de lois,' subsequent scholars have had trouble with the label 'code.'") (footnote omitted).

5. *See e.g.,* Lafont, *Continuity and Pluralism* 94; A. LEO OPPENHEIM, ANCIENT MESOPOTAMIA: PORTRAIT OF A DEAD CIVILIZATION 231–232 (revised ed. completed by Erica Reiner 1977).

Scholars of the ancient Near Eastern cultures have debated the question whether any of these codes actually represents legislation which was intended to be enforced. Some scholars hold that most or all of the codes are simply compilations of precedents brought together to guide judges in what had been done before in similar cases but not necessarily to bind them. Others hold that the codes are statements of the ideal, describing in legal terms what the desired society would be, utopian in the strict sense of the term.[6]

The debate about the purpose of the law collections has often focused on the most extensive collection of laws—the Laws of Hammurabi. In short, the questions most often asked are these: Were these laws statutes intended to be applied to given situations? Were they statements of abstract principles? Were they summaries of actual decisions? Or were they something else? According to Westbrook, Hammurabi's Law Collection was "neither a comprehensive digest of the contemporary law, nor even a statute—whether reforming or codifying—in the modern sense."[7]

The epilogue of Hammurabi's Laws is potentially helpful in understanding what these collections represent. In the epilogue, he refers to his "laws" as "just decisions."[8] The phrase "just decisions" suggests that, perhaps, these laws are summaries of actual cases that were decided under Hammurabi's

---

6. Edwin M. Good, *Capital Punishment and Its Alternatives in Ancient Near Eastern Law*, 19 Stan. L. Rev. 947, 949 (1967) (footnotes omitted). For more on the question regarding the purpose and nature of the Mesopotamian law collections ("codes"), *see* B.L. Eichler, *Literary Structure in the Laws of Eshnunna*, in Language, Literature, and History: Philosophical and Historical Studies Presented to Erica Reiner, Vol. 67, American Oriental Series (Francesca Rochberg-Halton ed., 1987), 71 n. 1 (Citing especially the work of F.R. Kraus and JJ. Finkelstein); Raymond Westbrook, *Biblical and Cuneiform Law Codes*, 92 Revue Biblique 248, 254 (1985) ("We suggest that the compiling of lists of legal decisions served... [as] ... a reference work for consultation by judges when deciding difficult cases.") and *Id.* at 257–58 ("To summarize: in our view the Ancient Near Eastern law codes derive from a tradition of compiling series of legal precedents in the same manner as omens, medical prognoses and other scientific treatises. The purpose of these series to act was as reference works for the royal judges in deciding difficult cases. Probably this began as an oral tradition and only gradually became a systematic written corpus.") (footnote omitted).

7. Westbrook, Old Babylonian Marriage Law 2 (footnote omitted).

8. Samual Greengus, *Legal and Social Institutions of Ancient Mesopotamia*, in 1 Civilizations of the Ancient Near East at 469, 472; Roth, Law Collections 133. *Also see* Bottéro, Writing, Reasoning, and the Gods 164. *Also see* Driver & Miles, Babylonian Laws 48 ("On the face of them, the Laws are a collection of decisions on the facts of a number of isolated cases. * * * * The sections are somewhat like the headnotes to a reported case, and the whole may in some respects be compared with a Digest of Case-law or a collection of records.").

authority. Similarly, his epilogue implies that his Laws were, indeed, nutshell versions of cases that he actually decided: "[M]ay that stela reveal... the traditions, the proper conduct, [and] the judgments of the land that I rendered...."[9] Although modern scholars have concluded that it is unlikely that Hammurabi's Laws were ever used as precedent for an actual case in ancient Babylon, the epilogue also suggests that that may have been his intention: "Let any wronged man who has a lawsuit come before the statue of me, the king of justice, and let him have my inscribed stela read aloud to him, thus may he hear my precious pronouncements and let my stela reveal the lawsuit for him; may he examine his case, may he calm his (troubled) heart...."[10] Hammurabi also implores future rulers to follow his decisions: "May any king who will appear in the land in the future, at any time, observe the pronouncements of justice that I inscribed upon my stela. May he not alter the judgments that I rendered and the verdicts that I gave...."[11] In addition, Hammurabi implies that one of his goals is to influence future decision-making. He expresses his desire that judges in the future will use his Laws to render judgments and verdicts, and to "eradicate the wicked and the evil from this land" and to "enhance the well-being of...[the] people."[12]

Opinions continue to differ and we may never completely resolve the question of the nature of the Mesopotamian law collections. Nevertheless, given their prominence, it seems wise to treat them as valid sources for studying the law of ancient Mesopotamia.

---

9. MARTHA T. ROTH, LAW COLLECTIONS FROM MESOPOTAMIA AND ASIA MINOR 135 (1995) [hereinafter "ROTH, LAW COLLECTIONS"]. Dr. Roth has translated the major law collections (*i.e.*, Hammurabi, Ur-Nammu, Lipit-Ishtar, and Eshnunna) as well as other less extensive and less complete collections: 1) the laws of X (*c.* 2050–1800 B.C.) (Origin unknown—perhaps belonging to Ur-Nammu's Laws); 2) Laws about Rented Oxen (*c.* 1800 B.C.); 3) Sumerian Laws Exercise Tablet (*c.* 1800 B.C.); and, 4) Sumerian Laws Handbook of Forms (*c.* 1700 B.C.). Unless otherwise noted, all translations from ancient Mesopotamian law collections in this book are from ROTH, LAW COLLECTIONS. For convenience, I cite them by the name of the relevant collection (*e.g.*, Hammurabi ¶__, Ur-Nammu ¶__, Lipit-Ishtar ¶__, etc.

10. *Id.* at 134. *See* Raymond Westbrook, *Cuneiform Law Codes and the Origins of Legislation*, 79 ZEITSCHRIFT FÜR ASSYRIOLOGIE UND VORDERASIATISCHE ARCHÄOLOGIE 201, 202 (1989) ("[C]ertain remarks in the epilogue to CH are taken to show that the text of the code was intended to be cited in court." (footnote omitted)). For an interesting discussion of this statement in the epilogue, *see* Roth, *The Law Collection of King Hammurabi* 10–12. Roth interprets the "wronged man" as someone "who has already lost a case—not one who is about to enter into a lawsuit." *Id.* at 11.

11. ROTH, LAW COLLECTIONS 135.

12. *Id.*

Of course, the most famous and extensive law collection is that attributed to the Babylonian king, Hammurabi (c. 1792–1750 B.C.). But there are about a half-dozen additional, extant law collections that predate Hammurabi. Of these the three most significant (or "major") collections are, in chronological order: 1) The Laws of Ur-Nammu (c. 2100 B.C.); 2) The Laws of Lipit-Ishtar (c. 1930 B.C); and 3) The Laws of Eshnunna (c. 1770 B.C.). In addition to the collections, the "Reforms of Urukagina" (who is now ordinarily referred to as "Uru-inimgina") represent the earliest written legal text from Mesopotamia of appreciable length and breadth. And even though Urukagina's (Uru-inimgina's) Reforms cannot be classified as a "collection," it is necessary at least to mention this text due to its primacy in chronology.

§ 1.03 URUKAGINA'S (URU-INIMGINA'S) REFORMS

Among the earliest writings that purport to have had legal significance in Mesopotamia are Urukagina's (Uru-inimgina's) "Reforms." Urukagina (Uru-inimgina) was the ruler of Lagash around 2400 B.C. Apparently the main purpose of his Reforms was to decrease taxes and lend assistance to the poor. His inscription, which lists his changes, does not really rise to the level of organization and complexity necessary to call it a "code" or "collection" on par with the later collections.

§ 1.04 UR-NAMMU

The oldest of the ancient Mesopotamian law collections is that ascribed to king Ur-Nammu (2112–2095 B.C.) (who founded the Third Dynasty of Ur (Ur III), uniting Sumer and Akkad in about 2100 B.C.) or his son Shulgi (2094–2047 B.C.). This collection contains a prologue plus about forty laws. In the prologue, Ur-Nammu claims to have received his authority from the gods. He takes credit for having "established justice in the land" and freedom for Akkadians and foreigners, and "for those conducting foreign maritime trade."[13] He declares that he has standardized weights and measures—an immensely important step for an efficient economy—and

---

13. ROTH, LAW COLLECTIONS 15.

that he has regulated riverboat traffic on the Tigris and Euphrates. Boldly he asserts: "I eliminated enmity, violence, and cries for justice in the land."[14] One striking feature of this most ancient of law collections is its apparent civility. Imprisonment is a penalty for only one offense—detaining another. The death penalty is imposed in only four instances: homicide; rape; adultery; and "lawless" behavior. Thematically speaking, the laws are, for the most part, grouped into small clusters. Occasionally a single law appears to have no theoretical connection to the law that either precedes or follows it.

Ur-Nammu's Laws promote several values and protect a number of interests of the citizenry as a whole. Although, it is clear that the Laws are primarily directed at protecting the interests of the upper class citizens. Laws relating to slaves indicate a sharp difference in treatment for them. Overall, the Laws protect the interests of the family structure, the integrity of an individual's own body and personal freedom, his property, and his authority.

Ur-Nammu's Laws reflect a deep concern for the family. At least one quarter of the provisions deal with family law matters such as marriage, divorce, and fidelity. The Laws protect the reasonable expectations of persons in positions of relative weakness. For example, a man who divorces his "first-ranking wife" must pay her 60 shekels of silver as a settlement. A man must pay 30 shekels of silver to a widow whom he divorces. If a father gives away his daughter to a friend of the man to whom he had originally promised his daughter (*i.e.,* a friend of the "promised" son-in-law—essentially breaking a marriage contract), the breaching father-in-law must pay double the amount of the property value that the promised son-in-law originally brought with him ("twofold (the value of) the prestations [which he (the "promised" son-in-law) brought (when he entered the house)]."(UR-NAMMU ¶15). Thus, the divorcees and the jilted son-in-law, who occupy weaker social positions (*i.e.,* have less power) than the husband and father-in law, gain a certain measure of security through the Laws.

Many laws secure the personal integrity of an individual's body. About half a dozen provisions provide specific damage awards for personal injury. For example, one law requires that someone who cuts off another's nose must pay 40 shekels of silver.

One law defends an individual's freedom of movement—the liberty to go about as one pleases. That law imposes both a 15-shekel fine and imprisonment on a person who detains another. This may be an early version of our modern notion of false imprisonment. Several laws safeguard property rights. One law imposes a 5-shekel penalty on a man who "deflowers"

---

14. *Id. See* S.N. Kramer, *Ur-Nammu Law Code,* 23 ORIENTALIA 40, 41 (1954).

someone else's virgin slave. Another law provides that a slave owner must pay a certain sum as a reward for the return of a runaway slave. There is also a specific rule stating that if one property owner floods another's field, he must pay compensation to the injured landowner based on the amount of acreage damaged by the water.

A slave owner's authority was considered inviolate. One law provides that a female slave will have her mouth scoured with a litre of salt if she curses someone who acts with her mistress's authority. This law is interesting for another reason. Unlike many of the laws designed to remedy damage to a person, his property, or his economic interests, this law is aimed at a purely intangible loss — an affront to the owner's authority.

At least four of the laws appear to promote procedural efficiency. Two laws impose a financial penalty on persons who unsuccessfully accuse others of wrongdoing. In one case a man must pay 20 shekels of silver for accusing another's wife of promiscuity, if "the divine River Ordeal clears her."(UR-NAMMU ¶14). In the other provision of this type, the penalty for the unsuccessful litigant is only 3 shekels, but the text is unclear about the nature of the alleged wrongdoing. Nevertheless, the imposition of financial penalties on unsuccessful prosecutors probably served as a deterrent for those who might otherwise have been inclined to bring unsubstantiated accusations. Since the divine River Ordeal may have been something like a roll of the dice,[15] litigants may have been disinclined to subject themselves to the risk of financial penalties unless they were very certain of the truth of their accusations. Another law that apparently fosters procedural efficiency provides that if a witness refuses to take an oath, he must pay the amount that is disputed in the case. Clearly, this law would encourage witnesses to take the oath and testify, thereby helping the judicial process to run more smoothly.[16] Another law helped advance procedural efficiency by imposing a fine of 15 shekels on a witness who committed perjury.

§ 1.05 LIPIT-ISHTAR

Lipit-Ishtar was the fifth king of the First Dynasty of the city Isin. He ruled for about ten years (1934–1924 B.C.). In addition to nearly fifty laws, Lipit-Ishtar's law collection has also both a prologue and epilogue. But unlike Hammurabi's Laws some 200 years later, one must strain to find any

---

15. *See infra* §2.03.
16. *See infra* §2.03 regarding oaths.

cohesiveness in these laws. There tend to be short groups; sometimes only two or three laws relate to one another.

In terms of policy, Lipit-Ishtar's Laws promote a variety of interests. Perhaps the predominant interest that they protect is an owner's right to property. The Laws of Lipit-Ishtar preserve the rights of an owner in situations where he has bailed his property, rented his property, and had his property damaged or taken by others. These individual property rights are applicable to things as diverse as boats, oxen, orchards, and slaves.

Several laws guard the rights of children. An unmarried daughter was entitled to inherit. Children by a second wife were given a measure of financial security. Children of a slave woman were considered free if their mother's master was their father. Children of a prostitute were considered free and could inherit from their father.

More than one law penalized someone who unsuccessfully accused another. One such law imposed the same penalty on the accuser that the accused would have borne had he been found guilty of the wrong. These laws promoted procedural efficiency by acting as a deterrent to those who might have otherwise brought weak claims.

One interesting point about Lipit-Ishtar's Laws deserves special mention. In generalizing about laws from the ancient Near East, we often assume that the laws were primitive, almost barbaric. Thus, there is a conventional misconception that the death penalty was common. In truth it was not. This is especially noticeable in Lipit-Ishtar's Laws, where the death penalty was only imposed for one offense (striking and killing the pregnant daughter of a man).

§ 1.06 ESHNUNNA

The Laws of Eshnunna come from about 1800 B.C, a time just before the Laws of Hammurabi. They are "the earliest laws in Akkadian" and are inscribed "on two clay tablets found in 1947 at Tell Harmal, a suburb of Baghdad."[17] The laws are attributed to a king of Eshnunna (a city about 120 kilometers north-northeast of Babylon) named Dadusha. It seems somewhat unfair that the three other prominent law collections from Mesopotamia are known by the names of the kings to whom they are ascribed (*i.e.*, Ur-Nammu, Lipit-Ishtar, and Hammurabi), but that the Laws of Eshnunna

---

17. SAMUEL GREENGUS, *Legal and Social Institutions of Ancient Mesopotamia, in* 1 CIVILIZATIONS OF THE ANCIENT NEAR EAST, at 469, 471; JACK M. SASSON, *King Hammurabi of Babylon, in* 2 CIVILIZATIONS OF THE ANCIENT NEAR EAST, at 901, 904.

are known by a city name rather than the king's name. Tradition partly accounts for this, but some scholars also speculate that the Laws are not in fact Dadusha's. In any event, Dadusha was a contemporary of Hammuarabi's, and Hammurabi ultimately overthrew Dadusha.

Although the Eshnunna Laws are similar in certain respects to those in Hammurabi's collection, it is doubtful that either borrowed directly from the other. "Scholars conclude, from a detailed study, that there is no clear evidence of this [*i.e.* direct borrowing] and postulate that the basic material of both was ultimately derived from an older common source."[18] For years, historians have used both the Laws of Eshnunna and the Laws of Hammurabi to gain insight into the stratification of Babylonian society. Although most of the laws in the Eshnunna collection deal with the upper class (*awīlum*), some laws also refer to the commoner-class (*muškēnum*), slaves of free persons (*wardum* and *amtum*) and of the palace (*ekallum*), and a few other categories of persons as well.

These Laws have neither prologue nor epilogue. As was the case with Lipit-Ishtar's Laws, it is difficult to perceive an overall, macroscopic organization or plan to the Laws of Eshnunna. We can, however, discern some groups. But even in the groups, a law here or there is included that to modern eyes relates only tangentially to the rest of the laws in the group.

Most of the Laws of Eshnunna protect the interests of the well-to-do — the upper class people who have financial resources to begin with. For example, the laws that fix commodity prices protect the interests of buyers and sellers, since fixed prices help to avoid irregularities and unexpected surprise in the marketplace. The same can be said for the laws that establish wages or rental prices for oxen, donkeys, wagons, boats, drivers, harvesters, and fullers. In a similar way, laws setting interest rates protect commercial borrowers and the credit system in general. Other provisions operate to protect domestic businesses at the expense of foreigners.

A number of sections protect an owner's property interest. Examples include laws that provide compensation for an owner of property when it is damaged or stolen (*e.g.,* property that is bailed, agricultural fields, oxen, and slaves).

In addition to these individual interests, the Laws also helped promote a number of societal values and public policies, such as family unity, caring for children, marriage (consent of a daughter's parents, a marriage con-

---

18. SAGGS, BABYLON 206; WESTBROOK, OLD BABYLONIAN MARRIAGE LAW 3 ("Both codes therefore appear to be drawing from a common academic legal tradition, a set of standard examples going back to much earlier law-codes.") (footnote omitted).

tract,[19] and a marriage feast[20] were all required), participation in the military (wives and property were protected during soldiers' absence), individual bodily integrity, freedom from abuse by officials, and public safety (*e.g.,* laws encouraging animal owners to control them, laws requiring homeowners to maintain their property).

Thus, on the whole, the Laws of Eshnunna protected the economic interests of the upper class, although many provisions promoted also institutions that we today would consider beneficial to society in general: the family, marriage, children, public safety, and public welfare.

§ 1.07 THE LAWS OF HAMMURABI

[A] INTRODUCTION

Hammurabi, king of Babylon, inherited what was actually a relatively modest kingdom from his father (Sin-Muballit), and over the course of more than forty years (1792–1750 B.C.) gradually conquered and annexed his neighboring cities and towns in southern Mesopotamia. He probably promulgated his collection of laws in the final years of his reign. The collection has 275–300 provisions (the traditional number is 282) arranged according to subject (*e.g.,* procedure, family, inheritance, commerce, personal injury, *etc.*[21]). French archaeologists discovered the most famous and most complete copy of Hammurabi's Laws during a December 1901–January 1902 excavation at Susa, the ancient Elamite capital.[22] The Laws are carved on a cone-shaped black diorite stela that stands over seven feet tall.[23] This

---

19. *See infra* §3.03[B][1].

20. The term translated as "marriage feast" is *kirrum.* According to Westbrook, "[t]he exact meaning of *kirrum* is a matter of dispute, but appears to be a formality involving the drinking of beer which, inter alia, attended various types of contract." WESTBROOK, OLD BABYLONIAN MARRIAGE LAW 30 (footnote omitted).

21. The Louvre stele itself does not indicate any lines or divisions that separate the subject categories. But other copies of the text do divide the laws by lines or spaces to create "sections." DRIVER & MILES, BABYLONIAN LAWS 42.

22. DRIVER & MILES, BABYLONIAN LAWS 28. *See also* BOTTÉRO, WRITING, REASONING, AND THE GODS, 157; Martha T. Roth, *Mesopotamian Legal Traditions and the Laws of Hammurabi,* 71 CHICAGO-KENT L. REV. 13, 21, 23–24 (1995) ("[T]he stela did not leave the Elamite workroom for almost another two thousand years, until A.D. 1901, when the French Archaeological Mission, under the direction of Jacques de Morgan, working in the Acropole in Susa, found it along with other Babylonian trophies brought there in antiquity.").

23. JACK M. SASSON, *King Hammurabi of Babylon, in* 2 CIVILIZATIONS OF THE ANCIENT NEAR EAST, at 901, 908; GEORGES ROUX, ANCIENT IRAQ 191 (2d ed. 1979). *See also* Norman Yoffee, *Context and Authority in Early Mesopotamian Law* 100–101 (Ch.

principal copy is now in the Louvre in Paris. Other less-complete copies and fragments also have been found.[24] It is likely that Hammurabi's Laws existed on at least three stelae in antiquity. Apparently the Elamites carried three back to Susa when they sacked Babylon in the twelfth century B.C. At the top of the stela is an artistic representation of what many believe is Shamash, the god of justice, seated, delivering or dictating the laws to Hammurabi. The laws themselves are arranged in columns of vertical writing that encircle the stela. In addition to the laws, there is also a prologue and an epilogue (both written in poetic form). The prologue recounts many of Hammurabi's accomplishments and enunciates his desire to establish justice. The epilogue articulates Hammurabi's purpose and pronounces curses on anyone who would disobey or deface the stela.

Saggs notes that Hammurabi's Laws have "a much more ordered arrangement" than any other collection of laws from ancient Mesopotamia.[25] For convenience, it is possible to identify 11 groups of laws in the collection: 1) Procedure (¶¶1–5); 2) Property (¶¶6–25); 3) Military (¶¶26–41); 4) Land & Agriculture (¶¶42–65); 5) Miscellaneous Gap Provisions (29 sections, gap ¶¶a–cc); 6) Principal & Agent (¶¶100–112); 7) Debts & Bailment (¶¶113–126); 8) Family Law (¶¶127–195); 9) Personal Injury (¶¶196–214); 10) Professional Wages and Liability (¶¶215–277); and 11) Sale of Slaves

---

5 *in* POLITICAL ANTHROPOLOGY (1988)); Roth, *The Law Collection of King Hammurabi* (Describing the stela as "a physically imposing monument: a 2.25-meter tall black basalt stela...."). Driver & Miles say that the structure is 2.25 meters high, and 1.65 meters circumference at the top and 1.90 meters at the base. DRIVER & MILES, BABYLONIAN LAWS 28.

24. SAMUEL GREENGUS, *Legal and Social Institutions of Ancient Mesopotamia, in* 1 CIVILIZATIONS OF THE ANCIENT NEAR EAST, at 469, 471; DRIVER & MILES, BABYLONIAN LAWS 30; Martha T. Roth, *Mesopotamian Legal Traditions and the Laws of Hammurabi*, 71 CHICAGO-KENT L. REV. 13, 20 (1995) ("Well over fifty manuscripts are known to me, coming originally from law centers in Susa, Babylon, Nineveh, Assur, Borsippa, Nippur, Sippar, Ur, Larsa, and more.").

25. SAGGS, BABYLON 206. Roth says that the Laws of Hammurabi "demonstrate[] the most sophisticated internal organization" of the Mesopotamian law collections. Roth, *The Law Collection of King Hammurabi* 2. *Also see* Martha T. Roth, *Mesopotamian Legal Traditions and the Laws of Hammurabi*, 71 CHICAGO-KENT L. REV. 13, 21 (1995) ("Although Hammurabi's court scribes and scribal schools did not originate the genre of the law collection, they did refine it to a more sophisticated and comprehensive level than it had achieved in the previous centuries. The Laws of Hammurabi then became something of the model for other later collections (none of which attained the sophistication of Hammurabi's), and certainly a staple of the scribal training curriculum for centuries to come."). For an enlightening comparison between the structure of the Laws of Eshnunna with the Laws of Hammurabi, *see* Eichler, *Literary Structure* 83. For more on the order and arrangement of Hammurabi's Laws, *see* DRIVER & MILES, BABYLONIAN LAWS 49.

(¶¶278–282).[26] Like most ancient Mesopotamian law collections, the groups reflect attention to subject matter, not to legal theory.

The procedural laws promoted truth as a value. This was accomplished by punishing false witness and unsubstantiated accusation. These laws also promoted efficiency, because they discouraged the bringing of lawsuits in cases where an accuser had a weak case.

Many of the laws pertaining to property promoted an individual's interest in protecting his property. A number of Hammurabi's Laws were designed to protect the property interests of the palace as well as personal property of individuals such as slaves, oxen, and other chattels. In addition, there are many provisions that protected a property owner's interest in his land and fields. To be sure, economic interests are protected whenever property rights are protected.

It is useful to note that certain types of contracts were considered invalid without witnesses or without observing other formalities for the agreement. These laws apparently protected the interests of both buyers and sellers.

A number of laws protected the interests of children. There was, for example, a law criminalizing kidnapping, and another law penalized a builder if a house that he built collapsed and injured the owner's son. Other laws protected the interests of children in a variety of ways, including prohibiting incest and protecting a child's property rights in inheritance.

In addition to the general laws that protected the interests of property owners, there were laws that protected the interests of slave owners. Some laws even protected the health and well-being of slaves. Many laws safeguarded a slave owner's pure interest in physically retaining his slaves. Some laws rewarded the return of a lost slave, while others punished those who failed to return slaves.

As was true in the Laws of Eshnunna, Hammurabi's Laws promoted an interest in public safety and welfare by creating laws that protected those who engaged in military service. But also in the midst of the military laws, we see provisions that protected individual privacy and freedom by punishing military officers who abused their power.

Quite a number of laws protected the interests of wealthy land owners, such as laws that punished tenants for failing to produce crops and laws that punished defaulting debtors and their families. But the Laws are not completely one-sided in favor of the wealthy. Some laws protected debtors,

---

26. This is roughly the same categorization as described by Driver & Miles and Jean Bottéro. *See* DRIVER & MILES, BABYLONIAN LAWS 43–45; and, BOTTÉRO, WRITING, REASONING, AND THE GODS 159.

too. For example, debtors were, under some circumstances, permitted to pay debts with goods, not just silver, and creditors were legally required to accept these alternative forms of payment. In addition, there were laws that held creditors to their contracts, and other provisions that punished creditors who tried to defraud their debtors. Some laws were intended to keep debtors out of debt-slavery, and one law put a ceiling on the number of years that a family member could be held as a "debt-hostage."

The marriage laws show a strong desire to preserve families and to promote fidelity and the institution of marriage itself. These and other laws also demonstrate an interest in protecting some of the rights of women. This is particularly true in the laws dealing with marriage settlements. Men who divorced their wives without an appropriate reason were legally required to pay a certain amount of money. Several of these laws helped to preserve a wife's interest in marital property and encouraged her husband to treat her fairly. A woman may also have been entitled to divorce her husband.

[B] SUMMARY OF KEY LEGAL PRINCIPLES

When one reads Hammurabi's Laws for the first time, it is striking to notice how contemporary many of the provisions seem. It may be helpful here briefly to summarize—according to modern legal categories—some of the more salient features of the laws and legal principles found in Hammurabi's Laws.

[1] CONTRACTS

1) It is very important—although not absolutely necessary—to have witnesses and written proof of transactions for contracts. This includes bailment and marriage contracts.
2) Several provisions occasionally acknowledge that "acts of god" and force majeure operate to relieve a party of liability. This is basically the same as recognizing failure of a presupposed condition or impossibility in modern contract law.
3) Several provisions grant expectation damages for breach of contract. Some laws also give punitive damages in a number of contract contexts.

[2] SALES

1) The Laws contain some recognition of the concept of a bona fide purchaser for value, but these laws use presumptions different from the modern Uniform Commercial Code.
2) The Laws impose a one year warranty for boat repair.

[3] SOCIAL INSURANCE

1) The Laws provide social insurance for property theft, social insurance for life, and social insurance for prisoners of war.

[4] PROPERTY

1) Property given to soldiers by the king is inalienable.
2) Some provisions in the Laws show that the ancient Mesopotamians recognized the principle of a life estate.
3) The Laws envision the use of dowry and bridewealth as antecedent to marriage.

[5] WOMEN

1) As a rule, women can inherit and own property.
2) On occasion women have some choice in marriage decisions.

[6] TORTS

1) The Laws use compensation as the remedy for negligence in property damage suits when the damage was foreseeable or actually foreseen.
2) There is some recognition of either comparative negligence or assumption of risk (injury in a "brawl").
3) The Laws establish the presumption that an upstream boat is liable for damages in a collision with a downstream boat.
4) The ox-goring provisions limit liability in a manner that is similar to the modern judicial response to new technology and important industry (*e.g.*, railroads and automobiles).
5) The Laws distinguish between injuries that occur through negligence *vs.* unforeseeable "acts of god."
6) The Laws impose damages for theft (conversion) at five-times the value of the property taken.

[7] DEBTS

1) The Laws sanction debt slavery.
2) The maximum that a family member can serve as a debt-slave is three years.
3) The Laws permit a creditor to attach either goods or people ("debt-hostages") to satisfy a debt.

[8] BUSINESS LAW

1) The Laws recognize corporate entities such as partnerships.
2) Under the Laws' provisions, all partners share profits equally (pro-rata).

3) The Laws carefully delineate the duties of agents in principal-agent relationships.

[9] PROCEDURE

1) Hammurabi's Laws make clear the importance of having eyewitnesses for legal proceedings. Oaths are used to establish truth. The River Ordeal is used to make decisions for certain serious crimes.

2) If an accuser fails to prove his allegations, several laws impose on the accuser the same punishment that the charge itself carries.

2) Many laws use the Lex Talionis; retribution in kind as the means of punishment.

[10] INHERITANCE

1) The Laws impose a number of rules for intestate succession (*i.e.,* inheritance in the absence of a will).

2) Under Hammurabi's Laws, bastard children whom a father has acknowledged during his lifetime inherit equally along with legitimate children.

3) The Laws allow parents to disinherit children for cause (*i.e.,* on the second offense).

4) As a rule, the Laws consider children free and capable of inheriting (*i.e.,* not slave) if one parent is slave but the other is free.

§ 1.08 JUSTICE & JURISPRUDENCE: THE ROLE OF LAW

[A] INTRODUCTION

In his book *Writing, Reasoning, and the Gods*, Jean Bottéro explains the Babylonian concept of justice.[27] His explanation is lucid, and it would be difficult to improve upon it by paraphrasing. Thus, I take the liberty of quoting Bottéro's discussion at length:

> The Babylonians used especially two words that we can associate more or less with the word "justice": *kittu* and *mêsaru*, which they often combined: *kittu mêsaru*, and always in this order, as if the second complimented and enclosed the first. *Kittu* by its basic meaning (*kânu: to establish firmly*) evokes something firm, immobile, and is best understood as that which derives its solidity from its confor-

---

27. Bottéro Writing, Reasoning, and the Gods 181–82.

mity to the law (abstracting from the law's presentation, written or unwritten). We translate it best by *honesty* or by *justice* in the narrow sense, depending on the context. *Mêsaru*, derived from *esêru* (*to go straight, in the right way; to be in order*) contains a more dynamic element; one can understand it, depending on the context, as a state or as an activity. As a state it reflects the *good order* of each thing in its place and according to its ways, in other words, its nature and its role (its "destiny" one would have said in Mesopotamia). As a type of activity or of conduct it renders or attributes to each being and to each man that which comes to him by nature or by his place in society: again his "destiny" —*justice* in short.[28]

§ 1.09 MYTHOLOGICAL FOUNDATIONS OF JURISPRUDENCE

The Akkadian word for "justice" literally means "the straight thing."[29] The earliest Mesopotamians considered justice to have been a gift from the gods. According to Sumerian myth, the god Enki got drunk and, in his over-generous, inebriated state, began lavishing gifts upon Innin, the goddess of Erech. Among the gifts that Enki bestowed were justice, truth, and falsehood. Thus, the Sumerians received the foundations of law—justice, truth, and falsehood—from Enki when he was drunk. Although several deities were identified with justice, Shamash was the principal god of justice. He was also the deity who represented the sun. To the Mesopotamians it was logical that Shamash, the sun god, should also serve as the foremost god of justice. The sun god shone his light everywhere and thus could see all. No one could hide a secret from Shamash. He alone had the capacity to discover all truth—the essence of justice. His iconographic symbols were the rod and ring, which signified straightness (right) and completeness (justice). Although Assyriologists differ in opinion on this point, the majority believe that it is Shamash who appears at the top of Hammurabi's stela, giving him the rod and ring, the symbols of justice. In mythology Shamash typically serves as a judge and arbiter. He was the judge of heaven and earth, and, was therefore, the principal figure responsible for protecting those who were poor or those who had been wronged. In addition to

---

28. *Id.* at 182.
29. SAGGS, BABYLON 197.

Shamash, Anu, "the overpowering personality of the sky,"[30] acts in Mesopotamian mythology as arbitrator of disputes. Sin and Gira (the son of Anu) also appear in myth as judges. The gods were responsible both for creating justice as well as administering it. Thus, through their gods, the ancient Mesopotamians perceived an inseparable link to justice.

§ 1.10 MISHARUM

An ancient Mesopotamian institution which helps to provide a more complete understanding of their concept of justice is the *misharum* (*mīšarum*). *Misharum* is the Akkadian word that denotes "the quality of 'equity' in human society, that which is achieved by the king's attempt to bring human affairs into balance with *kittum*, 'natural law.'"[31] Generally speaking the *misharum* was an institution unique to the Old Babylonian period. At the beginning of a king's reign, he pronounced his *misharum*— an edict—which ordinarily comprised various temporary economic reforms intended to alleviate financial hardships created by the previous rulers. It is likely that the king then followed up his *misharum* with a more formal, official text. Kings routinely copied or borrowed from previous *misharums*, so that they were not "reinventing the wheel" each time. One such edict, the edict of Ammisaduqa, addresses such diverse topics as: debtor-creditor law; administration of palace-owned property; crop division between tenant and landowner; tax computations; the law of distraint ("debt-hostages"); laws relating to the *sabītum* (woman inkeeper); and contracts to buy and sell slaves.

§ 1.11 JURISPRUDENCE IN THE LAW COLLECTIONS

The prologues and epilogues of the law collections provide considerable insight into what the ancient Mesopotamians perceived the role of the laws to be—their legal philosophy. Arguably, these prologues and epilogues

---

30. GEORGES ROUX, ANCIENT IRAQ 94 (2d ed. 1979) [hereinafter "ROUX, ANCIENT IRAQ"].

31. Yoffee, *Context and Authority* 106. *See also* Ellickson & Thorland, *Ancient Land Law*, 71 CHICAGO-KENT L. REV. 321, 401–402 (1995); DRIVER & MILES, BABYLONIAN LAWS 23 (definition of *kittum* as "justice").

consolidate the principal elements of justice in ancient Mesopotamia; in them we see goals and aspirations manifest. Prologues and epilogues commonly state that the promulgating ruler established justice. It is *how* they articulate their conceptions of what justice is that is telling. Kings tout the accomplishments that they say have helped them to achieve justice. The prologues and epilogues from the collections suggest that there are at least eight predominant elements that defined "justice" for the ancient Mesopotamians: 1) freedom (especially for the weak and poor, freedom from oppression by the strong and rich); 2) public safety; 3) economic prosperity; 4) peace; 5) order; 6) family security (ensuring that family members cared for one another); 7) truth; and, 8) the existence of a dispute resolution process.

§ 1.12 CHAPTER SUMMARY

Law collections, misharum edicts, and both public and private documents provide most of our information about ancient Mesopotamian law. The law collections, in particular, are especially helpful. Although scholars continue to debate the nature of them, the law collections appear to articulate fundamental policies and accurate statements of ancient legal principles. The most significant collections are: 1) The Laws of Ur-Nammu (*c.* 2100 B.C.); 2) The Laws of Lipit-Ishtar (*c.* 1930 B.C.); 3) The Laws of Eshnunna (*c.* 1770 B.C.); and, 4) The Laws of Hammurabi (*c.* 1750 B.C.). The Laws of Ur-Nammu (there are about 40 of them) protect interests such as property and family. And althougth many serve the interests of the wealthy, some laws offer protection for the poor and weak. Lipit-Ishtar's Laws (almost 50 in number) are largely concerned with securing and protecting property. Several laws defend the rights of children. A number of sections punish persons who bring unsubstantiated lawsuits; thereby discouraging frivolous litigation. The Laws of Eshnunna (over 60 laws) distinguish among different classes of persons in Babylonian society. — *awilum* (upper class), *mushkenum* (commoner), and slave. These laws are concerned especially with promoting the interests of the upper class citizens. Laws protecting property and commercial transactions abound. But the collection also includes laws designed to foster family values and some rights of the individual (whether rich or poor).

Hammurabi's Laws (the traditional number is 282) are the most famous and complete of the Mesopotamian law collections. An extensive prologue and epilogue add a great deal of information about Hammurabi, himself, his interest in justice, and his goals. Among the numerous legal topics addressed in the collection are legal procedure, land and property, the military, family, personal injury, and many different types of laws relating to business and commerce (*e.g.,* debts, agency, and professional liability). Prominent among the interests protected by Hammurabi's Laws are property (including slave ownership), commerce, women, children, and marriage.

Shamash, a solar deity, was the god most closely associated with justice in Meopotamian mythology. For the ancient Mesopotamians, both justice and truth were part of the fabric of religion and myth. The misharum of kings and prologues and epilogues of the law collections help flesh out our understanding of the abstract nauture of justice in ancient Mesopotamia. A number of misharum suggest that forgiveness of debts and taxes was considered just. The law collections show freedom, truth, order, and security as principal aims of justice.

CHAPTER 2

Legal Procedure, Institutions, & Organization

§ 2.01 ORGANIZATION & PERSONNEL

[A] THE ROLE OF THE "ASSEMBLY" AS AN EARLY COURT

One of the most important functions of any government is the administration of a legal system. Most decision-making (even legal decision-making) in the early stages of a civilization rests with either a monarch, a council of elders, or a completely democratic "town meeting" involving all citizens. Sumerologists theorize that the earliest Sumerians governed themselves by means of a "general assembly of all citizens—probably including women as well as men—who came together to decide upon action when some emergency threatened."[32]

The Sumerian myths suggest that, at some early stage of development, a general assembly of all adult men made important decisions.[33] But as early as the Early Dynastic period (c. 2900–2350 B.C.), Sumerian mythology provides an example of an individual (a king)—not the democratic assembly—making legal decisions. The myth of the warrior-god, Nintura, depicts the king functioning as a judge, "redresser of wrongs."[34] In addition to the mythological tradition, there is inscriptional evidence suggesting that an early king of Kish named Me-Silim served as an arbitrator, "settling

---

32. SAGGS, BABYLON 37.
33. *See Id.* at 160 ("the organization of the gods must be a reflection of the organization of a human society within the memory of the time at which that society crystallized."); ROUX, ANCIENT IRAQ 92 (According to Roux, "The divine society was conceived as a relic of the human society of Sumer and organized accordingly.").
34. SAGGS, BABYLON 39.

the terms of peace and setting up a boundary stone between the territories of the two cities...."[35]

The citizen Assembly in early Mesopotamia probably "functioned like a tribal gathering, reaching agreement by consensus under the guidance of the more influential, richer, and older members."[36] Most Assyriologists believe that the Assembly was the original "court" or judicial body in Mesopotamia. According to Saggs: "In Babylonia, although at some periods and places the king or his official alone might settle a case, this was exceptional, and generally speaking the Assembly retained a concern in cases involving private individuals down to the end of the New Babylonian period."[37] It is also likely that the early Mesopotamian Assembly made legal decisions, even in cases involving murder or robbery outside of the city limits (at least within close proximity). According to Driver and Miles, "In ancient times assembly and court were not clearly distinguished and an assembly often exercised the functions of a court."[38] In the Old Babylonian period (c. 2000–1600 B.C.), the judicial Assembly was probably comprised of all adult male citizens.

It is possible that the Assembly met in a place called the *rebitu*, which was just inside the city next to the gate. We also know that a building called the *ekallum* served as the royal palace and administrative governor's residence in most large cities. It was in the *ekallum* that "the king or governor heard the cases brought before him, and it served in some respects as a police-court."[39] Otherwise, we really do not know where the judges held their courts. Paragraph 5 of Hammurabi's Laws mentions the assembly, but contemporary documents indicate that courts convened primarily in local temples, like the temple of Shamash, although other locations are also mentioned.

[B] JUDGES & "COURTS"

Historical sources mention judges at least as early as the time of Sargon of Akkad (c. 2300 B.C.). We know that there were professional judges of some sort at the time of the Old Babylonian period. It is very likely that the king appointed most judges, but on occasion the elders of a community

---

35. *Id.* at 45.
36. OPPENHEIM, ANCIENT MESOPOTAMIA 112.
37. SAGGS, BABYLON 216.
38. DRIVER & MILES, BABYLONIAN LAWS 242 n. 8, 493 (Citing both contemporary Old Babylonian documents as well as Hammurabi's Laws ¶¶126, 142, 251).
39. *Id.* at 492 (footnote omitted).

must have functioned as judges as well. A town's mayor may also have had a hand in judging along with the elders. One of Hammurabi's Laws refers to a judge as maintaining a "judgeship in the assembly" and as "sit[ting] in judgment with the [other] judges." (HAMMURABI ¶5). According to Driver and Miles, the Old Babylonian judges "almost invariably... sat in threes or fours"[40] and judges ordinarily heard cases as part of a college or bench.[41] Greengus states that they "presided in groups from three to six persons."[42]

Scribes learned legal phrases in school in order to serve as scribes for judges, and the judges themselves probably were chosen from these same scribal students. It is likely, therefore, that ancient Mesopotamian judges were a specialized group that sat with the Assembly and gave advice and assistance regarding the technical aspects of law and legal procedure. Later, the judges probably conducted legal proceedings on their own, while the Assembly merely observed.

Hammurabi himself generally preferred to delegate judicial decision-making "to his local governors or to a court of law."[43] The only direct reference to a king rendering legal decisions in Hammurabi's Laws is in ¶129, where the king pardons an adulteress's paramour in cases where the husband pardoned his wife.[44] Records from actual trials for adultery corroborate that the king could play a significant role in determining punishments for adultery. In addition to special cases where the king himself acted as the court, it is possible that, on occasion, Old Babylonian kings "gave a decision on the point of law and remitted the case for a decision on questions of fact to the local judges or authorities."[45] Furthermore, an Old Babylonian king could remand a case completely by sending it back to the local judges.

[C] JURISDICTION OF JUDGES AND ROYAL JURISDICTION

In the Laws of Eshnunna, judges had jurisdiction to decide cases where the amount in controversy was 20 to 60 shekels. Only the king had jurisdic-

---

40. *Id.* at 76–77.
41. *Id.* at 491 ("The judges, since they are almost always mentioned in the plural number, seem normally to have sat as a college or bench....").
42. SAMUEL GREENGUS, *Legal and Social Institutions of Ancient Mesopotamia, in* 1 CIVILIZATIONS OF THE ANCIENT NEAR EAST at 469, 473.
43. JACK. M. SASSON, *King Hammurabi of Babylon, in* 2 CIVILIZATIONS OF THE ANCIENT NEAR EAST at 901, 908; DRIVER & MILES, BABYLONIAN LAWS 490.
44. *See* WESTBROOK, OLD BABYLONIAN MARRIAGE LAW 35, 75. *See also infra* §3.05 [D][2].
45. WESTBROOK, OLD BABYLONIAN MARRIAGE LAW 2.

tion to hear capital cases. In Hammurabi's Laws, a judge was not permitted to reverse his decision once judgment was rendered, a verdict given, or his sealed opinion was deposited. The penalty for doing so was to pay twelve times the amount involved in the case, and he was removed from the bench as well (HAMMURABI ¶5). Presumably, this law, at least in part, was intended to curb judicial bribery. Otherwise, the great law collections, like Hammurabi's "tell us next to nothing about procedure before a court or of the execution of a judgement."[46]

The traditional view is that, in the Old Babylonian period, the State began assuming more control over judicial procedure, and cases were tried "under secular authority" rather than "in temple grounds."[47] Another theory suggests that, instead of a transition from religious to secular, there was instead "a separation of responsibility between the civil and religious authorities."[48] Veenker points out that prior to Hammurabi there were State judges — like the "royal judge" — who appear to have been more involved with adjudication than temple judges.[49] Thus, it is perhaps more likely that the State was involved in adjudication early on, but became more controlling during the Old Babylonian period. In fact, by the Old Babylonian period, Veenker concludes that "one might well question the very existence of a temple authority...."[50]

In his essay, "Legal and Social Institutions of Ancient Mesopotamia," Greengus formulates the following picture of Mesopotamian court jurisdiction:

> Local courts handled most claims dealing with movable property;
> this included conflicts over boundaries, sale, inheritance, and cases
> involving burglary or theft of property. Disputes between merchants
> were often handled by the *karum*, or "port authority." Situations in-
> volving loss of life or offenses meriting capital punishment would,

---

46. DRIVER & MILES, BABYLONIAN LAWS 220.

47. Yoffee, *Context and Authority* 104–105. *See* Ronald A. Veenker, The Old Babylonian Judiciary and Legal Procedure (1967) (unpublished Ph.D dissertation, Hebrew Union College-Jewish Institute of Religion (Cincinnati, OH 1967)) 10 [hereinafter, Veenker, Legal Procedure]("Most scholars have believed that the administration of justice was controlled by the temple, at least prior to the rule of Hammurabi. * * * [B]y the time of Hammurabi, the administration of justice was under state control." (footnote omitted)).

48. Veenker, Legal Procedure 11 (Citing the work of Cuq).

49. *Id.* at 19 ("Therefore, with regard to persons actively engaged in adjudication, if any trend is indicated, it would seem to be in favor of a state or secular jurisdiction.").

50. *Id.* at 29.

however, be handled by royal judges and officials. These situations included homicide, treason, and adultery when the parties were caught in the act. The royal judges did not function as a court of higher appeal except when the royal court—often the king himself—was called upon to hear complaints of malfeasance on the part of officials and to order redress or restitution.[51]

As a rule, local judges had authority to try cases involving kinship relations or cases in which the litigants were "not members of public organizations."[52] In cases involving more serious disputes, such as adultery, the State—or more specifically, the king—had jurisdiction. Yoffee summarizes Old Babylonian jurisdiction by stating: "[S]ome disputes, because of their very nature, were properly resolved under community auspices, but other disputes could not be resolved by such local authorities. In some cases the only legitimate triadic authority that overarched the disputants would, in fact, be the state."[53]

§ 2.02 LAWSUITS: TRIAL PROCEDURE

The Sumerian word for lawsuit is *dīnum*. We have a cuneiform record of a murder trial that took place around 1800 B.C. In it we get a vague sense of the procedure followed. The complaint was first made before the king of Isin. The king, in turn, ordered that the complaintants take up their case with the Assembly of Nippur. The Assembly then listened to the arguments, announced its verdict, and delivered the defendants over for execution. Hammurabi and subsequent rulers issued ordinances that established procedures for conducting lawsuits. Procedures varied, depending on the types of issues involved (*e.g.*, contracts, personal injury, homicide, etc.). Although following specific procedures was important to a degree, according to Driver and Miles, "there is no record of a case in which a man was deprived of justice by a technicality or by an error made by him in procedure."[54]

Some scholars have described the ancient Mesopotamian litigation procedure as a contract. According to this model, the litigants agree, as if by a contractual arrangement, to abide by the decision of the court. Thus, the "judges and court officers serv[e] as witnesses" and "[t]he decisions then

---

51. SAMUEL GREENGUS, *Legal and Social Institutions of Ancient Mesopotamia, in* 1 CIVILIZATIONS OF THE ANCIENT NEAR EAST at 469, 473.

52. Yoffee, *Context and Authority* 105.

53. *Id.* at 106.

54. DRIVER & MILES, BABYLONIAN LAWS 53.

function as contracts in succeeding stages of a complicated litigious process."[55]

In many cases parties were not permitted any opportunity to appeal decisions to a higher authority. The clay tablets that record legal decisions frequently state that the parties shall not be allowed to reopen a case. In fact, ordinarily at the conclusion of a lawsuit, the prevailing party received a document that recorded the judge's decision or verdict. This document stated that it was a " 'tablet of no complaining,' or less literally, 'document of no (further) contest.' "[56] The phrase used was *tuppi lā ragāmim*. Thus, the *tuppi tuppi lā ragāmim* served an evidentiary function, showing that the case was essentially *res judicata*—and the losing party could not initiate any further legal proceedings regarding the same matter. But several court documents indicate that, under certain conditions, a party could bring a second suit, even if he had lost in an initial trial. A second trial was possible if new evidence was discovered or if some material mistake had been made in the first trial. The texts of "second trials" show that the party who lost in the first litigation in most cases lost in the second as well, and that he usually had to pay an additional fine. Thus, Veenker summarizes the prospects for "appeal" in Old Babylonian law as follows:

> Although one cannot call the third stage [*i.e.,* the "second trial"] "appeal" in the manner of modern jurisprudence, it is, nevertheless, a legitimate and distinct litigation, i.e., the plaintiff at this stage can win his case. So we see that judicial decisions could be altered and that the directives "he shall not raise further claim" were not irrevocable or absolute. Rather, one can unde[r]stand these directives to have meant, "If he raises further claim, he does so at his own risk."[57]

§ 2.03 EVIDENCE

In ancient Mesopotamia, as in many modern trials, evidence could be a life and death matter. For example, in Hammurabi's Laws, a father-in-law received capital punishment (he was bound and cast into the water) if he had sexual relations with his-daughter-in-law *after his son had had sexual relations with her* (HAMMURABI ¶155). But he merely paid 30 shekels as punishment for nearly the same offense if his son had *not* yet had sex with

---

55. Yoffee, *Context and Authority* 98 (citation omitted).

56. Ronald A Veenker, *An Old Babylonian Procedure for Appeal: Evidence from the tuppi lā ragāmim,* HEBREW UNION COLLEGE ANNUAL 1–15 (1974).

57. *Id.* at 14 (footnote omitted).

her (HAMMURABI ¶156). Thus, in order to avoid capital punishment, a father-in-law who was accused of having had sex with his daughter-in-law would have to prove either that he had not had sex with her at all, or if he had, he would have to prove that he had done so *before* his son had had sex with her. One can imagine the tremendous obstacles to proving the chronological sequence of events in such a case!

The Mesopotamians understood the importance of tangible evidence. There is a law in Lipit-Ishtar's collection that states: "If a man rescues a child from a well, he shall [take his] feet [and seal a tablet with the size of his feet (for identification).]" (LIPIT-ISHTAR ¶20). Texts that record lawsuits often relate that the parties introduced a number of written documents (*e.g.*, contracts) and witnesses to provide evidence at trial. Some laws had the effect of discouraging lawsuits in cases where a plaintiff's evidence was weak. For example, in Lipit-Ishtar's collection one law states: "If a man, without grounds(?), accuses another man of a matter of which he has no knowledge, and that man does not prove it, he shall bear the penalty of the matter for which he made the accusation." (LIPIT-ISHTAR ¶17).

In the Old Babylonian period, "the admission of verbal evidence was accompanied by the oath."[58] There were a number of circumstances in which the taking of an oath regarding a matter was considered conclusive evidence of the oath-taker's truthfulness. In addition to the instances where the law collections required the use of oaths, it was also possible for the Assembly or the judges to require a party or a witness to take an oath, if the evidence was otherwise contradictory. And there were, in fact, cases where a party lost his case because he refused to take an oath. Through the Old Babylonian period, it was the temple that was responsible for administering oaths and conducting the Divine River Ordeal (see below) in conjunction with legal controversies. The temple had the sacred objects necessary for administering oaths. Veenker summarizes this process as follows:

> In cases where the court has convened in the temple, the witness appears to exonerate himself there, before (in most cases) a divine emblem; in the language of the documents he is "given for the divine oath." However, when the court has convened outside the temple, a point is made of "giving" the witness *to the temple* for the administering of the oath. It may be that the prime importance of the temple in the administration of justice was the fact that it contained the emblems whereby the witness might give deposition.[59]

---

58. Veenker, Legal Procedure 45.
59. *Id.* at 22.

Another type of evidence occasionally used in the Mesopotamian laws is the Divine River Ordeal. Saggs describes the Mesopotamian use of the Divine River Ordeal in litigation:

> When there was a clash of evidence, and neither side admitted guilt by refusing the oath by the life of the gods, the decision would then be handed over to the gods themselves. This was given, as in many other cultures, by the Ordeal. In Babylonia the Ordeal was by the river, and the rule—opposite to that found in mediaeval England—was that the guilty person sank and the innocent was saved."[60]

§ 2.04 WITNESSES & PERJURY

Strict penalties for perjury encouraged witnesses to tell the truth while testifying in lawsuits. As a rule, witnesses and litigants who were found guilty of perjury were punished by imposing the penalty that would have been given the accused if *he* had been found guilty of the transgression. In Hammurabi's Laws, if a witness was found guilty of perjury, he was required to pay the monetary penalty involved in the case (HAMMURABI ¶4). Similarly, both the first and third provisions in Hammurabi's Laws impose capital punishment for false statements in capital cases.[61] Capital punishment was also the penalty for perjury—or at least unsubstantiated claims—in cases involving lost property (HAMMURABI ¶¶11, 13). The Laws of Lipit-Ishtar appear to have employed the same general principle (LIPIT-ISHTAR ¶17).

§ 2.05 ENFORCEMENT OF JUDGMENTS

One recurring problem with many ancient judicial systems is that there was no means of enforcing judicial decisions. We are accustomed to expecting physical enforcement in modern law through government agencies like sheriffs, deputies, police, and marshals. Driver and Miles point out that a lack of "teeth" was certainly problematic during the Old Babylonian period:

---

60. SAGGS, BABYLON 219 (Quoting Hammurabi's provision concerning witchcraft—HAMMURABI ¶2). *See* Tikva Simone Frymer-Kensky, The Judicial Ordeal in the Ancient Near East (1977) (unpublished Ph.D. dissertation, Yale University (New Haven)) (this two-volume dissertation is a comprehensive analysis).

61. *See infra* §3.05[G].

> How far, if at all, the decisions of a court were enforced by public authority is not known; there was no police, no public prosecutor, and no public executioner. The duty of the judge was to find the facts of the case before him and to declare what was the law applicable, but he seems to have had no power to execute his judgement.[62]

Scholars suggest that in order to enforce judgments, the aggrieved party had to physically bring the perpetrator before the judges.[63] As a last resort, presumably, the winning party to a lawsuit would have been allowed to seize the loser's property or even the loser himself as a means of self-help "enforcement." But this brand of self-help enforcement would have produced essentially the same results as the physical (*i.e.* violent) solutions that must have been in place prior to orderly judicial settlements, and thus could not have been preferred. By the Old Babylonian period, it seems likely that the decisions of judges were binding on the parties; they were not merely proposals for settlement that the parties could accept or reject.

§2.06 CHAPTER SUMMARY

The prologue of Hammurabi's Laws specifically points to the existence of legal procedure as one of the hallmarks of justice. In ancient Sumer, the citizen Assembly probably handled most legal disputes within the community; functioning like a make-shift court of peers. By about 2000 B.C., small groups (perhaps 3–6 persons) of judges had begun taking responsibility for judicial decisionmaking instead of the Assembly. On occasion—and perhaps only in certain types of cases (*e.g.*, adultery and other capital cases)—the king served as a kind of supreme judge. By the Old Babylonian Period, the State (*i.e.*, secular) courts—not the temple—adjudicated most legal disputes.

We know that Hammurabi and other leaders established procedural rules, but we are aware of little that is definitive regarding actual trial procedure. Witnesses gave testimony under oath and under the fear of strict penalties for perjury, and parties could bring documents and material evidence to help them prove their cases. In a few circumstances, the River Ordeal functioned as a dispositive evidentiary tool. Appeal—in the modern sense—seems to have been out of the question. One of the major problems with the legal system was the difficulty in actually enforcing a decision once it was made.

---

62. DRIVER & MILES, BABYLONIAN LAWS 493.
63. *Id.* at 494 (Citing HAMMURABI ¶127 as an illustration).

CHAPTER 3

Substantive Law

§ 3.01 PERSONAL STATUS

[A] INTRODUCTION

The law collections of both Ur-Nammu and Lipit-Ishtar recognized fundamentally two social classes: freemen and slaves. Hammurabi's Laws indicate that the Old Babylonian society of his day had three distinct classes: 1) *awilu* ("the ordinary citizens of Mesopotamian towns"[64]); 2) *mushkenu* (a difficult term to translate that probably means "some kind of military or civilian 'state dependant' who submitted to certain obligations and restrictions in return for some kind of privileges"[65]); and 3) *wardu* (slaves).

For some reason, the native-born citizens of Nippur, Babylon, and Sippar in Babylonia and the citizens of Assur and Harran in Assyria enjoyed special privileges of free citizens. They were exempt from *corveé* work, military service, and had some degree of tax exemption as well. For the citizens of these cities, then, citizenship bestowed significant privileges. This unique, privileged legal status was called *kidinnutu*. In addition, the citizens of Nippur, Babylon, and Sippar also had a privilege relating to lawsuits: the

---

64. Roux, Ancient Iraq 204. *See also* Westbrook, Old Babylonian Marriage Law 67 ("The term *awīlum* is generally agreed to be used in three senses in CH: (i) a man (i.e. a person in general), (ii) a free man (as opposed to a slave), (iii) a nobleman.") (footnote omitted).

65. Roux, Ancient Iraq 191 (footnote omitted). *See* S.N. Kramer and A. Falkenstein, *Ur-Nammu Law Code*, 23 Orientalia 40, 42 (1954). (Kramer and Falkenstein note that neither Ur-Nammu's law collection nor the collection of Lipit-Ishtar had a "social grouping corresponding to the *muškēnum* of the Hammurabi Code. (footnote incorporated))." For more on the social status of the *mushkenum, see* Driver & Miles, Babylonian Laws 93–95. According to Driver & Miles, for example, some documents show *mushkenu* owning land and houses, and making valid marriage contracts. Driver & Miles, Babylonian Laws 95. *See also* Roth, Law Collections 14, 24, 36, 43, 46, 58, 72–73 (explaining the various social classes in the law collections).

king was not permitted to fine them or imprison them, furthermore, he could not dismiss their legal claims. They also were exempt from taxes on their flocks. In most ancient Mesopotamian towns, it is likely that all male citizens were members of the Assembly in its earliest stages, with the elders playing the most important roles.

According to Westbrook, "[f]oreigners in the ancient Near East were in a precarious position. They had no legal rights outside of their own country or ethnic group unless they fell under the local rulers' protection."[66] But apparently non-citizens were permitted to have limited access to most Mesopotamian cities. Merchants, diplomats, and foreigners seeking political asylum could enter a city if they had royal permission. There is also evidence that, to a limited degree, non-citizens could actually reside in harbor areas (technically outside of the city). A text from Ugarit mentions non-citizens in Carchemish who were allowed to live within the city gates. There was a certain area in the city called the *bit ub(a)ri* where foreign visitors and merchants could reside.

[B] WOMEN

Women seem to have enjoyed more liberty and social status when Sumerian city-states were in their earliest stages of development than in some subsequent periods. At the dawn of Sumerian civilization, women, for example, served temples in a variety of ways. They could receive grants of rations and allotments, and they could also serve as priestesses or, perhaps, temple prostitutes. The priestesses "were drawn from all classes, from the king's daughter to the daughter of the humblest free man."[67] Importantly, it appears that they also participated in the general Assembly of all citizens. Some Assyriologists even believe that early Sumerian women were permitted to have more than one husband at a time, but recent scholarship suggests that polyandry was unlikely.

Later, by the time of the society depicted in the *Epic of Gilgamesh* (*c.* 2600 B.C.), women were no longer entitled to take part in the deliberations of the Assembly. In Hammurabi's day (*c.* 1750 B.C.), a woman could enter into a binding agreement with her husband that his creditors would not be permitted to take her as a "debt-hostage." (HAMMURABI ¶151). Women could also own and sell property. And women could serve as scribes.

---

66. Raymond Westbrook, *Slave and Master in Ancient Near Eastern Law*, 70 CHICAGO-KENT L. REV. 1631, 1639 (1995).

67. DRIVER & MILES, BABYLONIAN LAWS 358.

[C] SLAVES[68]

There were basically three broad categories of slaves in ancient Mesopotamia: 1) debt-slaves (who owed their status to debt); 2) chattel-slaves (who
owed their status to birth, conquest, or purchase); and 3) famine-slaves
(who voluntarily entered servitude during periods of severe food shortage).
During the pinnacle of Sumerian culture, female slaves outnumbered male.
Their owners used them primarily for spinning and weaving.

In the Early Dynastic period (*c.* 2900–2350 B.C.), there were very few
slaves, and those who were in Mesopotamia were mostly prisoners of war.
Temples and the palace owned most of the slaves, and they lived in bar-
racks. It was later that private individuals began owning slaves. By the Third
Dynasty of Ur (*c.* 2112–2004 B.C.), it had become possible for free citizens
to be enslaved either by being seized by their creditors or by being sold by
their parents. In Hammurabi's day, the majority of slaves were purchased
abroad (*i.e.,* not captives of war). A number of people entered slavery as a
consequence of famine as well. We also know that some persons could become slaves as a result of breach of contract. If a slave owner accepted payment in an amount worth twice the value of his slave, that slave could
legally gain his freedom. (Lipit-Ishtar ¶14) ("If a man's slave contests his
slave status against his master, and it is proven that his master has been
compensated for his slavery two-fold, that slave shall be freed."). A certain
type of slave, called a *miqtu,* could not be sold if the *miqtu* had been given
as a gift by the king (Lipit-Ishtar ¶15) ("If a *miqtu*-person is a gift of the
king, he will not be appropriated.").

Slavery was a status subject to change. We know that a slave could marry
a free woman (Hammurabi ¶175), but we know very little about the legal
status of a free-woman and slave-male marriage. And we can only surmise
that the slave's master must have assented to a marriage of this type. A slave
could own property and, in some instances, buy his own freedom with
property that he had acquired. When a slave died, his master inherited the
slave's property.

It seems likely that certain formalities had to be observed when a chat-
tel-slave was manumitted in order for the transaction to be valid (SLHF (ii

---

68. Part of the discussion of slaves is included in the section on Status because
some laws relate to slaves in terms of status. But much of the discussion about slaves is
included in the section on Property law (*i.e., infra* §3.02[F]) because the majority of
laws regarding slaves relate to them as property rather than as persons with a distinct
status. *See* Good, 19 Stan. L. Rev. 947, 962 (1967) ("With legislation relating to slaves
we are perhaps closer to the law of property than to the law of persons. A slave was
property....").

4–6)). There is a reference in a document relating to manumission that the tablet itself was "kilnfired." There are also references to smashing a pot and "clearing a man's forehead," but many details are still uncertain. We do not know, for example, whether some type of court order was needed, or whether a simple declaration of freedom by the slave's master was all that was necessary to finalize manumission. It is likely that many slaves who were given their freedom were manumitted by a reciprocal agreement— the master agreeing to give the slave his freedom in return for the slave's promise to care for his master in old age. In Hammurabi's Laws, "a master's slave-concubine and his issue by her were to be freed automatically upon his death." (HAMMURABI ¶171). A master could also manumit his slave by a contract of adoption. For debt-slaves, manumission was possible through redemption—paying back the debt, or, according to Hammurabi's Laws, a court might order release after three years (HAMMURABI ¶117). Kings also could use their discretion and release debt-slaves either as a result of individual petitions or by *misharum*.[69] Famine-slaves could gain their freedom by redemption too (probably stipulated in their contract).

The Laws of Eshnunna contain a number of sections dealing with situations where a slave woman attempted—illegally—to find a way for her child to be raised as a free citizen. When a slave woman gave her child to an *awilu* woman to raise (apparently hoping to have her child grow up as a free person), if the slave-mother's owner later discovered the child, even after the child had grown into adulthood, the owner was entitled to take the slave back as his property (ESHNUNNA ¶33). Similarly, when a palace slave gave her child "to a commoner (*mushkenum*) for rearing," the palace was entitled to reclaim the child (ESHNUNNA ¶34). But if someone actually "adopted" a "child of a slave woman of the palace" (perhaps this means instead of merely taking informal custody), then the adopter was required to give a slave of equal value to the palace in return (ESHNUNNA ¶35).

Slaves were given a certain degree of freedom. For example, slaves were allowed to marry each other. There is a rather ambiguous law that addresses the status of a female slave when her husband later gains his freedom (UR-NAMMU ¶4). When a male slave married "a native woman [perhaps this means "free"]," the man was required to give his master one male child, but all other children were considered free (UR-NAMMU ¶5). When a male slave married an *awilu* woman, and she then bore children, the slave's owner was not entitled to take the children as slaves.[70] Children of concu-

---

69. *See supra* § 1.10.
70. According to Hammurabi's Laws, the owner in this circumstance: "will have no claims of slavery against the children...." HAMMURABI ¶175.

bines were considered slaves also unless the master acknowledged them as his legitimate offspring.

The Laws of Eshnunna prohibited slaves from buying anything from either merchants or woman inkeepers (ESHNUNNA ¶15) ("A merchant or a woman innkeeper will not accept silver, grain, wool, oil, or anything else from a male or female slave."). Under some circumstances, the Laws of Eshnunna required slaves "to bear fetters, shackles, or a slave hairlock" to identify them as slaves (ESHNUNNA ¶52). A slave who bore fetters, shackles, or a slave hairlock was not permitted to "exit through the main city-gate of Eshnunna without his owner." (ESHNUNNA ¶51). Hammurabi's Laws prohibited a barber from intentionally "shav[ing] off the slave-hairlock of a slave [*i.e.*, a slave not belonging to him] without the consent of the slave's owner." (HAMMURABI ¶226). The law punished the guilty barber by amputation of his hand (so that he could not repeat the offense) (HAMMURABI ¶226). If, however, someone deceived the barber, and induced him under false pretenses to shave off a slave's slave-hairlock, the barber was exonerated if he swore that he did not know that the person who deceived him was not the slave's owner (HAMMURABI ¶227). In this case, the person who deceived the barber was executed and hanged "in his own doorway." (HAMMURABI ¶227).[71]

§ 3.02 PROPERTY

[A] INTRODUCTION: PRIVATE PROPERTY, AGRICULTURE, AND IRRIGATION

In the most ancient times, the principal god of a community was probably considered the owner of all of the land. After the fall of the Ur III Dynasty (2112–2004 B.C.), however, it became common for private individuals to own land. By the Old Babylonian period (*c.* 2000–1600 B.C.), collegia of temple priests, administrators, and the like, jointly owned shares of fields, but each share was considered as held "in private ownership and [the owner] was entitled to sell it, to give it as a dowry, or to leave it to his heirs."[72] In short, as Ellickson and Thorland put it, "there is universal agree-

---

71. Compare HAMMURABI ¶21 (guilty defendant hanged in doorway) and HAMMURABI ¶153 (adultress who has her husband killed is impaled).

72. Holly Pittman, *Cylinder Seals and Scarabs in the Ancient Near East, in* 3 CIVILIZATIONS OF THE ANCIENT NEAR EAST 1589, 1589–98, 1592, 1595–96, 1599–1600 (Jack M. Sasson ed., 1995); OPPENHEIM, ANCIENT MESOPOTAMIA 190.

ment that outright private ownership of agricultural lands was widespread in northern Babylonia by the start of the second millennium (the Old Babylonian period)."[73] Frequently, people used cylinder seals to designate private property as their own. Certainly, by the Old Babylonian period, Mesopotamian law recognized the existence of several classes of property, such as land, the fruits of land, movables, and intangibles.

Agriculture was of primary importance to the economy and society in ancient Mesopotamia. The date palm was the most important crop — analogous in many respects to olives in the Mediterranean.[74] Irrigation canals were vital to both agriculture and urban life in Mesopotamia. Thus, central control and constant maintenance were essential. Because the right to use and the obligation to maintain irrigation canals were both so important, the Mesopotamians formulated laws governing the use and maintenance of the common irrigation system.

[B] SALE OF LAND, PRICES, DEEDS & RECORDATION OF REAL PROPERTY

Once private ownership of real property was recognized, it became possible to sell private property. According to Ellickson and Thorland, "The oldest legal documents ever unearthed involve land sales in Mesopotamia. These are pictographic and date from the beginning of the third millennium."[75] A buyer was free to buy any house not encumbered by a service obligation,[76] using as a means of payment "grain, silver, or any other commodity." (HAMMURABI gap ¶c). Some laws established fixed prices for the sale of real estate. For example, one law collection from about 2100 B.C. fixed the price for one *sar* of land (about 36 square meters) at about 1 shekel of silver (LAWS OF X ¶r). There were "[w]ide variations in real estate

---

73. Ellickson & Thorland, *Ancient Land Law*, 71 CHICAGO-KENT L. REV. 321, 340 (1995) (footnote omitted). *But see* Renger, *Ownership or Possession of Arable Land in Ancient Mesopotamia*, 71 CHICAGO-KENT L. REV. 269, 295–300 (1995) (Renger argues that most of the arable land during the Old Babylonian period was owned and operated by kings or large estates: "In the Old Babylonian period, private ownership of arable land plays no role, or at least not a measurable role, in the southern part of the alluvial plain of Mesopotamia...." (*Id.* at 295); "Not only was arable land cultivated directly by the palace or other institutional households, but also large portions of the arable land were farmed individually by holders of sustinence or tenancy fields. Privately owned fields, however, are only scarcely attested." (*Id.* at 300.)).

74. *See infra* §9.02[B].

75. Ellickson & Thorland, *Ancient Land Law*, 71 CHICAGO-KENT L. REV. 321, 376 (1995).

76. *See infra* §3.07[B][3].

prices per unit of area" in the third and second millennia, but in Nuzi during the Old Babylonian period, "fields sold for approximately the value of one year's grain harvest."[77]

There is evidence which suggests that real estate sales required some sort of written documents in order to be considered valid. We have a number of contracts that record the sale of land and houses. Such documents are common beginning in the Ur III period (2112–2004 B.C.). Saggs translates one Old Babylonian text as follows:

> 1 1/2 sar (of land) with a house built on it, next to the house of Kununu and next to the house of Irraya, Arad-Zugal has bought from Arad-Nanna. He has paid him 8 1/2 shekels of silver as its full price.
>
> Arad-Nanna has taken an oath by the king that he will not in the future say 'it is my house'.
>
> [The names of the witnesses, and the date, follow.][78]

Once a sale had taken place, it was common for "the clay tablets memorializing land sales… [to be] stored together in records offices…."[79]

Certain kinds of property, however, either had restrictions on alienability or were entirely inalienable. For example, because of the necessity of preserving the "patrimonial home base," during the first half of the third millennium, family members appear to have had some type of veto power over the "transfer of family land."[80] In addition, a "field, orchard, or house of a soldier, fisherman, or state tenant" (*i.e.*, the royal grant of land) could not be sold (HAMMURABI ¶36). If such property were sold, the sale was considered invalid, and the buyer forfeited the purchase price ("his silver") (HAMMURABI ¶37). Furthermore, this same kind of property—property that a soldier, fisherman, or state tenant acquired "attached to his service obligation" (*ilkum*)—could not be "assigned in writing to his wife or daughter," nor could it be given "to meet any outstanding obligation." (HAMMURABI

---

77. Ellickson & Thorland, *Ancient Land Law*, 71 CHICAGO-KENT L. REV. 321, 406–07 (1995).

78. SAGGS, BABYLON 293–94. *See* Ellickson & Thorland, *Ancient Land Law*, 71 CHICAGO-KENT L. REV. 321, 380 (1995) (Using the same example as Saggs, they relate: "A cuneiform land-sale text typically covered only the basics: identity of the parties; barebones land description; price paid; revendication clause; and witnesses." (footnote omitted)).

79. Ellickson & Thorland, *Ancient Land Law*, 71 CHICAGO-KENT L. REV. 321, 384 (1995) (Ellickson & Thorland say that this practice dates back to approximately 2500 B.C.).

80. *Id.* at 388.

¶38). But a soldier, fisherman, or state tenant *was* permitted to "assign in writing to his wife or daughter" or to pay debts with "a field, orchard, or house which he himself acquire[d] by purchase." (HAMMURABI ¶39).[81] Special rules also applied to protect the interests of soldiers and fishermen when they were away from home. When a soldier or fisherman was taken captive abroad, if his property (field and orchard) was transferred to another in his absence, upon his (the captive's) return, he was entitled to have his land returned to him (HAMMURABI ¶27). If the captive soldier or fisherman had a son who "is able to perform the service obligation," then the property was transferred to him (HAMMURABI ¶28). If the son was too young, one-third of the land was given to the mother, and the mother raised the son (HAMMURABI ¶29). If either a soldier or fisherman abandoned "his field, orchard, or house because of the service obligation" for three years, and someone else took possession and performed the obligation for those three years, the soldier/fisherman lost his rights to the person who took the property and performed the service obligation (HAMMURABI ¶30). This is something like the modern concept of adverse possession but not precisely. If the solder/fisherman was gone for only one year, he retained possession and ownership upon his return (HAMMURABI ¶31).

There is, in addition, a very interesting law in Hammurabi's Laws pertaining to situations where a soldier or fisherman was captured "while on a royal campaign." If a merchant bought back the prisoner from his captors, the law provided that the soldier/fisherman would repay the merchant from his own estate if he had sufficient funds. If he did not have sufficient funds, then his city's temple would repay the merchant, unless the temple's funds also were insufficient, in which case, the palace would repay the merchant. However, in no case were the soldier/fisherman's "field, orchard, or house" to "be given for his redemption." (HAMMURABI ¶32). This amounted to a kind of social insurance for prisoners of war.

One other law, from the Laws of Eshnunna, creates a rule that is somewhat unique regarding the sale of real property. When a man becomes so poor that he has to sell his house, if the new owner later decides to sell it, the former owner of the house has the legal right to redeem it (ESHNUNNA ¶39). This amounts to a right of first refusal for people who have to sell their houses after falling on hard times.

---

81. This provision is somewhat similar in principle to the story of the Egyptian Ḥapdjefai, who segregated the property that was his by virtue of being a nomarch from his other property. This ability to separate property is a rather sophisticated legal conception. *See infra* § 6.06[C].

[C] LEASE OF FIELDS

A number of laws in the law collections deal with the rights and obligations of lessors and lessees of fields for cultivation. One such law suggests that a lessee ordinarily paid about one-quarter of his annual crop as rent to the lessor (SLHF viii 20–21). One provision sets a specific rental price for real estate: one shekel of silver is the price to rent "one *sar* of a roofed-over area." (Laws of X ¶s). Driver and Miles use actual texts to show that "a contract under which the owner receives one-third is by far the most common type."[82] Hammurabi's Laws provide that when a renter fails to cultivate a field, he must pay the owner "grain in accordance with his neighbor's yield, and he shall plow and harrow the field which he left fallow and return it to the owner of the field." (Hammurabi ¶¶42–43). In essence, these laws require a renter who breaches his contract to pay what modern contract law calls expectation damages[83] (the amount of grain that he expects to receive based on the amount produced in his neighbor's field). These laws also impose an injunction on the breaching party — requiring him to plow the field before returning it to the owner.[84] In Ur-Nammu's Laws, when an owner "gives a field to another man to cultivate" and he fails to cultivate it, he must pay "720 silas of grain per 100 sars." (Ur-Nammu ¶32). In Lipit-Ishtar's Laws, when a man receives "fallow land for the purpose of planting an orchard," and fails to do so, "they shall give the fallow land which he neglected to one who is willing to plant the orchard as his share." (Lipit-Ishtar ¶8). When a renter negligently fails to cultivate a field for three years, in the fourth year he must plow it under, return possession to the owner, and pay "3,000 silas of grain per 18 ikus (of field)." (Hammurabi ¶44).

It is always interesting to see how legal systems deal with issues such as impossibility, impracticability, and "acts of god." In contract law, the ques-

---

82. Driver & Miles, Babylonian Laws 131.

83. *See infra* §3.07[B][7]. Driver & Miles make this point clear: "The damages are compensatory, not penal, as their object is to put the injured party in as good a position as that in which he would have been if the contract had been performed." Driver & Miles, Babylonian Laws 137 (footnote omitted).

84. Driver & Miles explain the logic of these provisions. According to them, in ¶42 the cultivator merely did a poor job, whereas in ¶43 he failed to perform at all — he planted nothing. "The offence, therefore, is more serious and the damages correspondingly more severe." Driver & Miles, Babylonian Laws 137. It is the additional task of ploughing — an injunction — that makes the damages more severe: "deep ploughing in order to restore it to good condition." "This is right and logical; for the owner cannot be expected to make good the farmer's deliberate neglect by his own labour or at his own charges." *Id.* Driver & Miles maintain that, according to actual documents of the time, the owner usually had the responsibility of ploughing when the farmer's contract was finished. *Id.* at 139.

tion often boils down to a question of who will absorb the loss when some unforeseen circumstance makes performance impossible or impracticable. In Hammurabi's Laws, there are several laws that contemplate such situations in relation to the rental of fields for cultivation. These laws tend to apportion loss based on whether the renter had paid his fee prior to the onset of the circumstance that created the impossibility or impracticability. If he had, then he bore the risk (HAMMURABI ¶45);[85] if he had not, then the renter and owner split the loss (HAMMURABI ¶46).[86] But as a practical matter, any payment made before the harvest was probably just a small sum or deposit. Thus, as a general rule, if the renter had paid, that meant that the harvest had already been gathered too; and consequently, in reality, there was very little "risk" that the renter would bear.

In the case where a tenant paid his annual rent in advance, and then the landlord evicted him "before the expiration of the full term of his lease," the landlord was required to return the tenant's entire rental payment ("forfeit the silver that the tenant gave him") (HAMMURABI gap ¶g). This remedy for breach of a landlord-tenant contract seems punitive. The landlord does not even get to keep a pro rata portion of the rent.

[D] GARDENERS

Somewhat similar to the laws relating to lessors and lessees are the provisions in Hammurabi's Laws concerning gardeners. One such law suggests that there was an established division of fruits when a gardener was responsible for pollinating an owner's date palms: the gardener kept one-third of the yield while the owner took two-thirds (HAMMURABI ¶64).[87] Another law provides that when a landowner entrusts a field to a gardener to plant a date orchard, he is responsible for cultivating it for four years. "[I]n the fifth year, the owner of the orchard and the gardener...divide the yield in equal shares," but the owner gets to choose his share first (HAMMURABI ¶60). If the gardener had left a portion of the field uncultivated, that uncul-

---

85. This law provides that when a field renter has already paid his rent, the renter bears the risk of loss ("the loss is the cultivator's alone") when "the storm god Adad devastates the field or a flood sweeps away the crops," not the owner.

86. This law provides that if the field renter has not yet paid rent "before the catastrophe destroys the field," then the owner and renter "shall divide whatever grain there is remaining in the agreed proportions."

87. Driver & Miles say that the most common types of contracts of this nature give the owner one-third of the crop, but that some also give the owner three-fourths and some give him one-half. DRIVER & MILES, BABYLONIAN LAWS 131–132. *See also* *Id.* at 158, 163–164.

tivated portion was included in *his* share of the yield (HAMMURABI ¶61). If, for some reason, a gardener completely failed to cultivate an orchard, he was required to pay an amount equal to "the estimated yield of the field for the years it is left fallow," using the neighbor's yield as a basis for estimation. In addition, the gardener was required to "perform the required work on the field and return it to the owner...." (HAMMURABI ¶62). When a gardener failed to pollinate the date palms in an orchard, causing a decrease in yield, he was required to pay the owner "in accordance with his neighbor's yield." (HAMMURABI ¶65).

[E] LIABILITY OF AN OWNER OF REAL PROPERTY & TRESPASS

There is one law in Hammurabi's Laws that imposes liability on an owner of real property for damage caused on his property. That law states that when a shepherd takes care of cattle, sheep, or goats for their owner, and keeps them in an enclosure owned by a third party, if either a lion kills an animal or "an epidemic" breaks out, the owner of the enclosure is liable for the loss (HAMMURABI ¶266).[88]

There are several laws that concern trespass on agricultural land. In Hammuarabi's Laws, for example, if a shepherd grazes his sheep on a landowner's property without permission, the shepherd is required to pay an amount of grain, based on the size of the field—"6,000 silas of grain per 18 ikus (of field) to the owner of the field." (HAMMURABI ¶57). Another provision states that if a shepherd allows his sheep to graze in a field "after the termination of pasturing," he must pay to the owner "18,000 silas of grain per 18 ikus (of field) (HAMMURABI ¶58). Presumably this injury was deemed far more severe than merely grazing one's sheep on another's property. This is because the phrase "after termination of pasturing" probably denotes a particular season; probably a time when crops were in a more advanced stage of development. Thus, damage at that time would be more difficult to rectify. According to Lipit-Ishtar's Laws, a man who cut down a tree in another's orchard had to pay "20 shekels of silver." (LIPIT-ISHTAR ¶10) (*See also* HAMMURABI ¶59 (30 shekels payment for cutting down another's date tree)). If someone cultivated another's field and sued claiming the right to harvest the crop (arguing that the owner neglected his field), the trespasser had to "forfeit his expenses." (UR-NAMMU ¶30).

---

88. The shepherd was required to take an oath claiming that he was not responsible for the damage ("clear himself before the god").

[F] SLAVES

We considered some laws concerning slaves in the context of "personal status" in § 3.01[C]. Nevertheless, many laws concerning slaves have more to do with the "property" aspects of slaves than with slaves as human beings *per se.* Thus, it is necessary here to turn our attention to slave laws that relate to slaves as property, not people. Ordinarily, private citizens acquired household slaves in one of four ways. A slave could be bought, born in the household to another slave, obtained through warfare, or acquired from debt.

According to Hammurabi's Laws, if someone discovered a fugitive slave, and the slave refused to identify his owner, the finder was required to take the slave to the palace; and the palace was then responsible for returning the slave to his owner (HAMMURABI ¶18). If the finder, instead, kept the slave in his own house, and the slave was later discovered there, the finder was put to death (HAMMURABI ¶19). If the slave escaped from the finder's custody, the finder was not held responsible if he swore "an oath by the god to the owner." (HAMMURABI ¶20). The Laws of Lipit-Ishtar provide that when someone harbored a fugitive slave of the same city for one month, the harborer had to "give slave for slave." (LIPIT-ISHTAR ¶12). But if he did not have a slave to give, he had to instead pay 15 shekels of silver (LIPIT-ISHTAR ¶13). Hammurabi's Laws levy stiffer penalties. A person received the death penalty for either assisting a slave in his escape "through the main city-gate" (HAMMURABI ¶15) or for harboring a slave in one's house (HAMMURABI ¶16). Westbrook notes, however, that Mesopotamian law also provided a carrot as well as a stick: "By the same token, one who brought back a fugitive slave was entitled to a reward from the slave's master, set by the law codes at between two and six shekels of silver."[89]

The civil penalty under the Laws of Eshnunna for "deflowering" someone else's female slave is 20 shekels of silver (ESHNUNNA ¶31). Under Ur-Nammu's Laws, the same offense carries a five-shekel payment (UR-NAMMU ¶8). In an ancient document from Nippur, we discover that the penalty for this offense could be quite steep: "The assembly of Nippur addressed (the litigants): 'Because he deflowered the slave girl without (her) owner('s knowledge), Lugal-melam is to pay 1/2 mina of silver [*i.e.,* 30

89. Raymond Westbrook, *Slave and Master in Ancient Near Eastern Law,* 70 CHICAGO-KENT L. REV. 1631, 1672 (1995) (Citing UR-NAMMU ¶14, LIPIT-ISHTAR ¶¶22–23, and HAMMURABI ¶17). In Hammurabi's Laws, when someone returned a fugitive slave, the reward was 2 shekels of silver. HAMMURABI ¶17. DRIVER & MILES, BABYLONIAN LAWS 107. One of Ur-Nammu's Laws also established a fixed reward for someone who returned a runaway slave to his master. UR-NAMMU ¶17.

shekels] to Kuguzana her owner'...."[90] The slave's owner retained the deflowered slave.

In Hammurabi's Laws, when an *awilu* strikes a female slave owned by another *awilu* and thereby causes her to miscarry, the striker must pay 2 shekels of silver (Hammurabi ¶213). If the female slave dies, he has to pay the owner 20 shekels (Hammurabi ¶214). This is somewhat analogous to the modern concept called trespass to chattels. Fundamentally, when someone damages another's property, the civil remedy is payment equal to the loss in value of the damaged property.

Hammurabi's Laws grant an implied warranty of title for a slave buyer: "If a man purchases a slave or slave woman and then claims arise, his seller shall satisfy the claims." (Hammurabi ¶279). Actual contracts from the Old Babylonian period show that this provision provided assurance to the buyer that the seller had good title to transfer to the buyer. Ancient slave-sale contracts contain "[a]s many as fifteen different warranties... although almost never in the same document."[91] Some of these express warranties state that the slave will not escape, that the slave will not be delinquent, that the slave is not actually free, and that the slave will not die during the first 100 days.

If a slave falsely alleged that his owner was not his owner, the owner was entitled to bring charges against the slave, with the penalty of having an ear cut off (Hammurabi ¶282). This law suggests that, absent such a denial, a master did not have carte blanche to maim a slave. Documents from Nuzi report that a slave could be punished for this same transgression by blinding.[92] In Ur-Nammu's Laws, a slave woman was punished by having her mouth washed out with a litre of salt if she cursed "someone acting with the authority of her mistress." (Ur-Nammu ¶25).

[G] MISCELLANEOUS

[1] ACQUISITION OF PROPERTY THROUGH PAYING TAXES

In Lipit-Ishtar's Laws, if a property owner defaults on his property taxes, and someone else begins paying the property taxes and continues to do so for three years, the person who assumed the tax burden becomes rightful owner instead of the defaulter (Lipit Ishtar ¶18).

---

90. J.J. Finkelstein, *Sex Offenses in Sumerian Laws*, 86 J. of the American Oriental Soc. 355, 359 (1966).

91. Raymond Westbrook, *Slave and Master In Ancient Near Eastern Law*, 70 Chicago-Kent L. Rev. 1631, 1663 (1995).

92. *See Id.* at 1667.

[2] ADJACENT PROPERTY OWNERS

There are a few provisions in the law collections that deal with the rights and obligations of adjacent property owners. One such law suggests that adjacent property owners shared responsibility for the maintenance of a common wall (SLHF (iii 18–19)). We have another law that concerns adjacent property owners who contract—one owner agreeing not to build a house and not to place beams on their common wall (SLHF (iii 32–38)). Another provision states that an adjacent property owner who rebuilt a common wall "by himself" was entitled to payment from the adjacent property owner "for the maintenance expenses for the common wall" (it does say how much—one and a half shekels—but we do not know what proportion that amount represents) (SLHF (iii 26–31)).

[3] "ANCIENT KUDURRUS" & KUDURRUS

As early as 3000 B.C., the Mesopotamians recorded the size of their fields on large stone documents (*e.g.*, tablets, plaques, and stelae). The practice of using large stones to memorialize information about tracts of land (including the acreage and various transactions involving the transfer of ownership) continued off and on throughout the second millennium until about 2250 B.C. Modern scholars refer to these monuments as "ancient *kudurrus*." About sixty such ancient *kudurrus* have been discovered and studied. They come from both northern and southern Mesopotamia and relate to tracts of land that are both large and small—some as large as 1,600 acres and as small as 15 acres. It is not until after the time of Hammurabi that we find the use of *kudurrus*, or boundary stones, to indicate the demarcation of agricultural lands. We have over eighty of these pillar-shaped stone boundary markers. Most date from roughly 1400–650 B.C., but only a fraction can be dated with any measure of certainty. As a rule, the *kudurrus* were set up in circumstances where the king granted land; thus, they serve to publicize the royal grant.

§ 3.03 FAMILY LAW

[A] INTRODUCTION

As a rule, the Mesopotamian family unit was relatively small. The father was the head of the family and exercised significant control over his wife and children. In the Old Babylonian period, it was possible for a man to have a primary wife and a secondary wife. Apparently, however, one wife was the norm and economic reality throughout most of Mesopotamian history. Both husband and wife were responsible for debts incurred after the wife "enters the man's house." (Hammurabi ¶152). The ancient Mesopotamians used contracts to regulate many aspects of family law. We have, for example, cuneiform marriage contracts, adoption contracts, and divorce settlements. From the Old Babylonian period, we even have contracts for the nursing and upbringing of children.

[B] MARRIAGE

[1] ENTERING AND MAINTAINING MARRIAGE

There is an obscure law from a Sumerian student text (c. 1800 B.C.) that seems to permit a man to marry a girl if: 1) he had sexual relations with her; and 2) he had not been identified by the girl's parents; and 3) he had declared that he would marry the girl. (SLEX ¶7') ("If he deflowers in the street the daughter of a man, her father and her mother do not identify(?) him, (but) he declares 'I will marry you'—her father and her mother shall give her to him in marriage.").[93] Otherwise, most evidence suggests that the ancient Mesopotamians observed formalities, customs, ceremonies, and various legal requirements as antecedents to a valid marriage. The Old Babylonian term for husband was *mutum* and the term for wife was *aššatum*. Contemporary documents, the Laws of Eshnunna, and Hammurabi's Laws used the verb *ahāzum* to express the concept "to take for marriage" or "to marry." A couple was not legally considered husband and wife if the man had failed to obtain the consent of the bride's parents and also had failed to observe the nuptial feast (Eshnunna ¶27). This was the case even if they had lived together for as much as an entire year (Eshnunna ¶27-33). Many scholars have argued that Hammurabi's Laws required a contract (*riksātum*) of marriage in order for a marriage to be considered valid (Hammurabi ¶128).[94] It seems quite clear, however, that *riksātum* in this context does not mean a *written* contract but rather an "agreement" of the parties (*i.e.*, ordinarily the parents) in a more abstract sense.

---

93. Roth admits that this is a very difficult provision and notes that her translation is considerably different from previous attempts. Roth, Law Collections 45, n.4.
94. Driver & Miles state that this contract is a "contract of marriage" (Citing the work of Koschaker). Driver & Miles, Babylonian Laws 245. They say that the main verb in this provision refers to consummation of marriage, but that it means cohabitation and more than merely a sexual relationship. Driver & Miles, Babylonian Laws 246. *But see* Westbrook, Old Babylonian Marriage Law 61.

The girl, typically in her teens, was ordinarily not a party to the marriage contract. Usually her father fashioned the agreement on her behalf. If a father died before his daughter married, the girl's brothers inherited the obligation to "give her in marriage." (LIPIT-ISHTAR ¶23).

[2] MARRIAGE GIFTS & DOWRY

The two most prominent marriage gifts were the *biblum* and the *terhatum*. The *biblum* probably was comprised of provisions for the marriage feast or "a gift made by the groom's party to the bride's party on the occasion of marriage."[95] The *terhatum* appears to have been a sum that the groom brought to the bride's father which gave the groom "the right to claim the bride in marriage."[96] Technically, once the *biblum* and *terhatum* had been brought to the girl's father, Old Babylonian law considered the marriage "inchoate," and it could then be "completed by the delivery of the bride to the bridegroom...."[97] But we are not certain of precisely what act or acts constituted the "completion" of marriage.

If the bride and groom were minors, the marriage contracted-for was considered "inchoate," and there were two possible scenarios: "standard inchoate marriage" and "*kallūtum* inchoate marriage." "Standard inchoate marriage" occurred when the groom brought the *terhatum* to the father-in-law's house but the girl remained in her own house; and then later, when she was older, she moved in with her new husband's family. The "*kallūtum* inchoate marriage" occurred when the groom brought the *terhatum* to the father-in-law's house and subsequently the girl went to live in her father-in-law's house, and lived there as a quasi daughter until she was older and able to formally become a wife. In the latter case, the young girl was referred to

---

95. WESTBROOK, OLD BABYLONIAN MARRIAGE LAW 65, 101–102.

96. *Id.* at 59 ("[T]he *terhatum* was a real price for a right over the bride, but one less than ownership."); *Id.* at 60 ("Where the parents demand it, the *terhatum* is nothing other than payment for the right to control over their daughter."). Westbrook explains that this is clearly not a sum used for a "purchase and sale" of the bride: "[T]he amount of the *terhatum* at its highest is too low to constitute a real purchase-price of a wife — it would not suffice to purchase a slave, and in particular is often lower than the dowry given by the father to the bride." *Id.* at 55 (footnotes omitted). *See also Id.* at 56, 66.

97. MARTEN STOL, *Private Life in Ancient Mesopotamia, in* 1 CIVILIZATIONS OF THE ANCIENT NEAR EAST at 485, 489; DRIVER & MILES, BABYLONIAN LAWS 249–250. Driver & Miles suggest that the *biblum* may have been "the provisions for the marriage-feast which presumably...were given while the marriage was still inchoate." *Id.* at 250. *See also* WESTBROOK, OLD BABYLONIAN MARRIAGE LAW 8 (characterizing Driver & Miles's term "inchoate marriage" as a "major contribution to the general understanding of OB [*i.e.*, Old Babylonian] marriage...."), and *Id.* at 29.

as a *kallatum* and the marriage was called "a *kallâtūtu* marriage." (HAM-
MURABI ¶¶155–156). Finally, when the bride left her home to enter the
groom's, the bride's father gave her (for the groom to keep in his possession) a dowry.[98]

In Hammurabi's Laws, the word used for dowry is *šeriktum* but in some
contemporary documents the word used for dowry was *nudunnûm*. The
precise meaning of *nudunnûm* is unclear. Some documents use it as a synonym for dowry but others indicate that the *nudunnûm* was some kind of
gift given by the husband to the wife at the beginning of marriage. In his
book, *Old Babylonian Marriage Law*, Westbrook hypothesizes:

> The term *nudunnûm* means a wife's marital property, comprising
> the dowry given to her by members of her own family and gifts
> from her husband. The term can refer to either of the individual
> components or both together. In [Hammurabi's Laws], one of these
> components, the dowry, is referred to by a special term: *šeriktum*. It
> is thus distinguished from the rest of the *nudunnûm*. . . .[99]

The *nudunnûm* was used to support the wife in the event that her husband
should predecease her, and then, upon her death, it devolved to her children. The most common form of dowry was movable goods. There were
instances where land was included as well, but not money.

During the marriage, the husband possessed and controlled the dowry
but, technically speaking, the wife had a life estate in it.[100] When the husband died, if they had had children, the widow retained the dowry (HAM-
MURABI ¶171). When she died, it passed to her sons (if any), or, if she had
no sons, it devolved to her father's house (ESHNUNNA ¶18). In addition, if
her husband divorced her because she had no sons (or in circumstances
where she was otherwise innocent), she was entitled to take her dowry with
her (HAMMURABI ¶¶138, 149, 163–164). If he divorced her in circumstances where she was the guilty party, the husband retained the dowry.

---

98. Contemporary documents show that the mother could also give the dowry.
WESTBROOK, OLD BABYLONIAN MARRIAGE LAW 89. In addition, if the father had died
before giving his daughter a dowry, it was the brothers of the bride who were responsible for providing her with the dowry (at least in the case of a *šugitum* priestess).
HAMMURABI ¶184.

99. WESTBROOK, OLD BABYLONIAN MARRIAGE LAW 25. *See also Id.* at 27 ("In
summary, we would argue that the difference in terminology between the law-codes
and the documents of practice does not reflect a contradiction but merely different
approaches to expressing the same concept, conditioned by the different nature of the
two sources.").

100. *See infra* §3.04[C][1].

In a situation where a man promised to marry a woman and brought marriage gifts (*biblum* and *terhatum*) to her father, he was required to forfeit the marriage gifts if he thereafter changed his mind and decided to marry another (HAMMURABI ¶159). But if, instead, the bride's father changed *his* mind and decided to reject the would-be the groom, then the bride's father had to pay the groom twice the value of the marriage gifts that he had brought ("twofold everything that had been brought to him") (HAMMURABI ¶160; UR-NAMMU ¶15; LIPIT-ISHTAR ¶29; ESHNUNNA ¶25). If the bride's father changed his mind due to a slanderous accusation by one of the groom's "comrades," then it was the comrade who committed the slander who was liable to the groom for twice the value of his marriage gifts (HAMMURABI ¶161; LIPIT-ISHTAR ¶29). The same law also provided that the slanderous comrade was not allowed to marry the bride who was involved. Presumably, the law was intended to prevent a man from slandering a groom in hopes of securing the bride for himself.

[3] PROTECTION OF MARRIAGE FOR SOLDIERS

Under Eshnunna's Laws, if a man was taken as a prisoner, no matter how long he was absent, and even if another man married his wife and fathered children by her during his absence, upon his return, he was entitled to "take back his wife." (ESHNUNNA ¶29). However, if instead a man intentionally repudiated his city and fled, he was not entitled to reclaim his wife upon his return (ESHNUNNA ¶30). Hammurabi's Laws take these basic principles and add more. If a man was taken prisoner, his wife was not permitted to move in with another man so long as she had "sufficient provisions" in her house (HAMMURABI ¶133a). But if provisions were insufficient, she could move in with another man with impunity (HAMMURABI ¶134). In such a case, even if the woman had children by the second man, if the original husband returned home, the woman was legally bound to return to him. Her children "inherit[ed] from their father." (HAMMURABI, ¶135). Thus, the second marriage was, in essence, valid. It was merely voidable in the event that the first husband returned. If, on the other hand, a man simply deserted his city—as opposed to having been taken prisoner—his wife was permitted to move in with another man, and was not required to go back to her original husband in the event that he later returned from his desertion (HAMMURABI ¶136; ESHNUNNA ¶30). In any event, it is likely that the "second husband" was indeed considered married to the woman. In other words, the woman who left her first husband on account of insufficient provisions or on account of his desertion was deemed married to the man with whom she lived. In fact, the second husband is referred to by a special term, *hāwirum*, to distinguish his role from that of the original husband.

[4] POLYGAMY & FIDELITY IN MARRIAGE

In ancient Mesopotamia men ordinarily were monogamous. A man usually married only one wife who shared his social status. There were some exceptions, however, that permitted polygamy. In particular, Hammurabi's Laws provide that a man could marry more than one woman under at least three circumstances: 1) when his wife was a priestess who, by virtue of her status as a priestess, was not allowed to bear children (HAMMURABI ¶¶144–145); 2) when his wife was extremely ill (HAMMURABI ¶148; LIPIT-ISHTAR ¶28); and, 3) when his wife was guilty of severe misconduct (but not adultery) (HAMMURABI ¶141). The two wives ordinarily had one of two legal relationships: mistress/slave or sisterhood (either by blood or adoption). In an ordinary, monogamous marriage, an ancient Mesopotamian husband was permitted to have sex with temple prostitutes. Adultery was "an offence against a husband but not against a wife."[101] As a rule, prostitution in the ancient Near East was legal.

[5] SPECIAL MARRIAGE RIGHTS OF CERTAIN WOMEN

There were certain classes of women who had special marriage rights. Two such groups of women were temple dedicatees named *šugitu* and *naditu*. When a *šugitu* or *naditu* married and had children, if her husband decided to divorce her, she was entitled: 1) to have her dowry returned; 2) to have one-half of her husband's "field, orchard, and property"; and, 3) later, after her children had grown, she was entitled to a share of property equal to that of her sons (HAMMURABI ¶137).

[C] DIVORCE

[1] GENERAL

When a marriage was in its "inchoate" stage,[102] a "mere declaration seems to have been sufficient for…dissolution…."[103] When a marriage had been completed (*i.e.*, it had gone beyond the inchoate stage), the most common means of effectuating a divorce was for the husband to declare a symbolic phrase to his wife: "You are not my wife."[104] It is likely that the

---

101. DRIVER & MILES, BABYLONIAN LAWS 286. *See infra* §3.05[D][2] concerning adultery as a crime.
102. *See supra* §3.03[B][2].
103. DRIVER & MILES, BABYLONIAN LAWS 290. HAMMURABI ¶159.
104. WESTBROOK, OLD BABYLONIAN MARRIAGE LAW 69; DRIVER & MILES, BABYLONIAN LAWS 292–292.

husband was required to make this declaration in the presence of his wife and witnesses, but apparently court proceedings were not mandatory. Some Old Babylonian documents mention this formal language, settlement money, and the symbolic act of "cutting the fringe of her garment" (*sissiktam batāqum*).

A man was required to leave his house if he divorced his wife after having had children by her, and then remarried (ESHNUNNA ¶59). It seems likely that children ordinarily stayed with their mother in cases where a husband divorced his wife without justification. The converse appears to have been true as well: when a man divorced his wife for a good reason, the children probably went with him. In Lipit-Ishtar's Laws, after a young married man visited a prostitute, the judges could forbid him to revisit the prostitute (LIPIT-ISHTAR ¶30). If he then divorced his wife and paid her a divorce settlement, he still was not allowed to marry the prostitute (LIPIT-ISHTAR ¶30). Scholars disagree as to whether a wife had the legal capacity to divorce her husband. If wives were legally permitted to do so, apparently it was a right that they had merely in the abstract; for as a matter of practice, they did not.

[2] GROUNDS FOR DIVORCE

It may have been a criminal offense for a wife to appropriate goods, squander household possessions, or disparage her husband, and then to leave him. In these circumstances, a husband could divorce his wife and did not have to pay her anything (HAMMURABI ¶141). Even if he decided not to divorce her, he was still permitted to marry another, and the first wife was allowed to "reside in her husband's house as a slave woman." (HAMMURABI ¶141). A wife was entitled to repudiate her husband if he was "wayward" and if she was "circumspect and without fault." In that case, she was allowed to take her dowry and return to her father's house (HAMMURABI ¶142). On the other hand, if an investigation revealed that she was not circumspect but instead it was *she* who was "wayward," she was "cast . . . into the water." (HAMMURABI ¶143). In Lipit-Ishtar's Laws, a man was allowed to marry a second wife if his first wife "lost her attractiveness" or became "paralytic." Under these circumstances, however, the first wife stayed in the home and the second wife helped care for her (LIPIT-ISHTAR ¶28). As a rule, a divorced woman was entitled to remarry.

According to the Laws of Hammurabi, although a man was not permitted to divorce his wife if she contracted *la'bum* (some kind of severe disease, perhaps malaria), he was, apparently, allowed to marry a second wife. But in these circumstances, he was required to care for his sick wife in special quarters built for her (HAMMURABI ¶148). This provision seems to apply whether the diseased wife had borne children. If the diseased wife refused to stay with her husband, he was required to return her dowry, and she could leave (HAMMURABI ¶149). A standard legal form book from about 1700 B.C. provides that a husband who "despised" his wife was permitted to divorce her so long as he paid "a divorce settlement in silver." (SLHF (iv 12–14)).

[3] DIVORCE PAYMENTS

Many Old Babylonian marriage contracts contain provisions that established a payment (usually a fixed sum between 10 shekels and one mina) that a husband had to make if he divorced his wife. Old Babylonian documents refer to the lump sum of money that a husband paid to his wife upon divorce as *uzubbûm*. A husband did not have to make that payment if he divorced his wife for sufficient cause. Under Ur-Nammu's Laws, a man could divorce "his first-ranking wife," but he had to pay her 60 shekels of silver as a divorce settlement (UR-NAMMU ¶9). If a man divorced a woman who had previously been a widow (so that this was her second marriage), he had to pay her 30 shekels of silver as a divorce settlement (UR-NAMMU ¶10). But a man who only had had "sexual relations with the widow without a formal written contract [of marriage]," did not have to pay anything to her if they separated (UR-NAMMU ¶11).

A man of the upper class in Hammurabi's day could divorce his "first-ranking wife who did not bear him children." (HAMMURABI ¶138). In order to do so, he had to give her a settlement payment consisting of her dowry plus silver equal to the money and property that he had given his wife's family as "bridewealth" (*terhatum*) prior to their marriage (HAMMURABI ¶138). If he had not given any *terhatum*, then he had to pay "60 shekels of silver as a divorce settlement." (HAMMURABI ¶139). A "commoner" could divorce his wife upon paying her 20 shekels of silver (HAMMURABI ¶140).

[D] PARENTS, CHILDREN, & CAREGIVERS

[1] CHILD CUSTODY & ADOPTION

Ancient Mesopotamians customarily adopted infant children, although occasionally adults were adopted as well. They adopted for a number of practical reasons. For example, a couple might adopt a child to procure a son for the following reasons: 1) so that the family itself could be perpetuated; 2) so that there would be someone to carry on a family business; 3) so that there would be someone to care for the parents when they were elderly; or 4) so that there would be someone to perform religious rites when the parents died. A well-to-do childless couple could adopt an orphan or child of a poor family.

Upon their adoption, children legally lost the right to inherit from their biological parents. Rather, adopted children had roughly the same legal rights as any natural children of their adoptive parents. If adoptive parents failed to treat them as equals, adopted children returned to their biological parents (HAMMURABI ¶190). Interestingly, in Hammurabi's Laws, parents who adopted a child could legally "disinherit" that child later if they had children of their own. But in that case, the disinheritance was not complete, for the adopted child was entitled to a one-third share of his adoptive parents' estate (HAMMURABI ¶191).

Hammurabi's Laws provided that if a child was adopted *at birth* and then raised by his adoptive parents, the biological parents were not later permitted to reclaim the child (HAMMURABI ¶185). However, if a child was adopted as "a young child" (*i.e.,* later than "at birth"), and the child engaged in "seeking his father and mother," then the adoptive parents were required to return the child to his biological parents (HAMMURABI ¶186).

Adoptive parents were required to sell their adopted son into slavery (and he thus lost all rights to their property) if he repudiated them and declared that they were not his father and mother (SLEX ¶4'). By the same token, if it was the adoptive parents who said to the adopted son "You are not our son," they forfeited their estate (to him?) (SLEX ¶¶5', 6').

Children reared by members of a group of temple dedicatees were not permitted to claim openly that those who raised them were not their parents. If such children denied that those who reared them were their parents, the penalty was to have their tongues cut out (HAMMURABI ¶192). If such a child left his home and returned to his biological father, the penalty was to have his eye plucked out (HAMMURABI ¶193). When a craftsman took on a young apprentice, once the boy learned his master's craft, his parents were no longer entitled to reclaim him (HAMMURABI ¶188). However, if the craftsman failed to teach the child his craft (or if the boy could not or would not learn it), then the child had to "return to his father's house." (HAMMURABI ¶189). Apparently, these laws envision that a craftsman would adopt a boy with the specific intent that he would learn his adoptive father's business and later inherit it. If a father failed to "give the food, oil, and clothing rations (to the caregiver)" to whom he had entrusted his child for three years, he was required to pay the caregiver 10 shekels of silver and was also required to take back his child (ESHNUNNA ¶32).

[2] CHILD CONDUCT & PROPERTY OF CHILDREN

The first time that a son committed "a grave offense deserving the penalty of disinheritance," he was pardoned; a father was allowed to disinherit his son the second time (HAMMURABI ¶169). A child was not permitted to strike his father. The penalty was to "cut off his hand." (HAMMURABI ¶195).

A widow with young children was allowed to move in with another man if the judges first approved the move. However, the widow and new husband were required to write down an inventory of the deceased husband's estate. They acted as trustees of that estate on behalf of the widow's children by her first marriage. If someone bought "household goods of the children of a widow," that transaction was considered void. The buyer had to return the property but was not allowed to recover his purchase price (HAMMURABI ¶177).

§ 3.04 INHERITANCE & SUCCESSION

[A] INTRODUCTION

In actual Old Babylonian practice, a person's estate was usually divided shortly after death, under the supervision of temple judges. A person's heirs even inherited the obligation to pay the deceased's debts. It is likely that at some early time in Sumer, only males—sons—inherited. But by the Old Babylonian period, "both the widow and the daughters had certain claims to inherit."[105] As a rule, Mesopotamian law provided that all heirs, no matter how many, equally shared an inherited estate (SLHF (iv 31–34)). But in southern Mesopotamia, the eldest son was entitled to a share of his father's estate superior to that of his siblings. In addition, inheritance laws provided resources for dowries for daughters and financing for weddings for younger brothers. It was usual for brothers to inherit real property as tenants in common so that it could not be broken into smaller parcels.

[B] ORDER OF SUCCESSON: SONS FIRST

Sons were first in line to inherit. But what happened to a son's inheritance if he predeceased his father? Suppose a son (A) was born to a father

---

105. DRIVER & MILES, BABYLONIAN LAWS 331.

(B), and suppose that A had two brothers, C and D. Suppose, in addition, that A himself had sons X and Y. If son A were to die before his father, B, then when B died, A's sons (X and Y) were entitled to split their father's (A's) share. A's sons stood in the shoes of their father. In this simple example, C would receive one-third share of B's estate, D would receive one-third share of B's estate, and X and Y each would receive one-sixth (*i.e.,* one-half of their father's (A's) one-third share) of B's estate.

If a man's sons were minors at his death, the widow administered the sons' estate. If she remarried, both she and her new husband jointly took the responsibility — as trustees — to administer the sons' estate. The sons took possession of their shares when they reached the age of majority. It was then, also, that their mother became entitled to her share (if she had one). Generally speaking, the mother was entitled to a share only if she had no *nudunnûm*.[106] In any event, her share was a life estate that passed to her sons upon her death or remarriage.

If a man had failed to provide a bridewealth (*terhatum*)[107] for his youngest son (assuming that his older sons had already married), upon his death, the older brothers were required to give to their youngest brother both the amount for his *terhatum* and also his share of the paternal estate (HAMMURABI ¶166).

In both Lipit-Ishtar's Laws and Hammurabi's, a father, "during his lifetime," was permitted to give a gift in "a sealed document" to "his favored son." (LIPIT-ISHTAR ¶31; HAMMURABI ¶165). If he did so, after his death, his other heirs were not permitted to contest the gift that he gave to his favored son. A father could only disinherit his son for cause. Apparently, this was true whether the son in question was biological or adopted. A father was entitled to disinherit a son only if "the judges" investigated and determined that the son was twice "guilty of a grave offense deserving the penalty of disinheritance."(HAMMURABI ¶¶168–69). For the first such offense, the judges merely gave the son a warning (HAMMURABI ¶169). In addition, a son could be disinherited by operation of law: if a man was caught having sexual relations with his father's "principal wife" after his father's death, that man was "disinherited from the paternal estate." (HAMMURABI ¶158).[108]

---

106. *See supra* § 3.03[B][2]. *See also* HAMMURABI ¶172.

107. *See supra* § 3.03[B][2].

108. *See* DRIVER & MILES, BABYLONIAN LAWS 321 (Driver & Miles maintain "that the woman was a wife or concubine of the father of the offender but not his mother, since §157 deals with that offence.").

[C] INHERITANCE BY A WIFE

[1] DEATH OF HUSBAND —
WIFE INHERITS LIFE ESTATE

After a woman's husband died, she was permitted to live in her husband's house (HAMMURABI ¶171). She was not, however, allowed to sell the house because she retained only a life estate (or an interest very similar to what we call a life estate). Upon the widow's death, only her own children inherited her estate (HAMMURABI ¶171). Even if she married again and had children by a second husband, only *her* children (including children of both marriages — but not her husband's children from a previous marriage [*i.e.*, not step-children]) were entitled to inherit her dowry (HAMMURABI ¶¶173–174). All of her own children inherited equally (HAMMURABI ¶¶173–174).

[2] "SEALED DOCUMENT"

Hammurabi's Laws permitted a husband to execute "a sealed document" in favor of his wife granting to her "a field, house, or movable property." (HAMMURABI ¶150). The effect of such a property transfer was to shield that property from the widow's children after her husband's death. The widow, however, was not allowed to give her estate "to an outsider." Rather, she was legally bound to give it only "to whichever of her children she love[d]."(HAMMURABI ¶150).

[3] A SPECIAL CIRCUMSTANCE

When an *awilu* man was engaged, and if he had already brought the bridewealth (*terhatum*) to his prospective father-in-law's house, if either he or his bride died, the *terhatum* was returned to "the widower or his heir."(ESHNUNNA ¶17). If, on the other hand, one of them died *after* the marriage and *after* the couple had begun living together, then the widow or his heir took back only a specified portion of the bridewealth, not all of it (ESHNUNNA ¶18).

[D] INHERITANCE BY FEMALE CHILD

The Laws of Lipit-Ishtar allowed that when a man died "without male offspring, an unmarried daughter...be[came] his heir."(LIPIT-ISHTAR ¶b). When a girl became a member of one of three special temple groups (*ugbabtu, naditu,* or *qadištu*) while her father was alive, she was considered "an equal heir" along with her brothers (LIPIT-ISHTAR ¶22). In Hammurabi's Laws, there were a number of special inheritance laws that granted preferred inheritance rights and privileges to daughters who became members of certain special temple or priestess groups(HAMMURABI ¶¶178–184). Old Babylonian documents imply that a daughter did not necessarily have to be a priestess in order to be able to inherit a share of her father's estate. It is likely, however, that only unmarried daughters had these inheritance rights. Thus, an unwed daughter probably was entitled to either a dowry or a share of her father's estate. But the ancient documents do not say whether the daughter's share was equal to that of her brothers. Nevertheless, these laws confirm that women could own property and that daughters could have a life estate in their inheritance share.[109]

[E] DEATH OF WIFE—
INHERITANCE BY HER CHILDREN

Once a wife bore children, when she died, her children—not her father—were entitled to her dowry (HAMMURABI ¶162). If, on the other hand, a wife died without having children, her dowry was returned to her father upon the condition that he, in turn, was to return to his son-in-law the bridewealth (*terhatum*) that he (*i.e.,* the son-in-law/husband) had brought to his father-in-law at the inception of the marriage (HAMMURABI ¶163). If a man married a second time, his children by his first wife were not entitled to any of the dowry of his second wife (it belonged "only to her children") (LIPIT-ISHTAR ¶24; HAMMURABI ¶167). In essence, a dowry was considered property that was owned as a life estate that passed to a woman's offspring. When a father died, children by both wives divided their father's property equally (LIPIT-ISHTAR ¶24; HAMMURABI ¶167).[110]

[F] CHILDREN OF FEMALE SLAVES & FREE MALES

It was possible for a free man to father children by both his wife and a slave woman. In Hammurabi's Laws, if the man acknowledged his children

---

109. Driver & Miles also raise the possibility that the words for "sons" (*mârū*) and "brothers" (*ahhū*) refer to daughters and sisters as well in the context of inheritance law. DRIVER & MILES, BABYLONIAN LAWS 338–341.

110. Driver & Miles summarize HAMMURABI ¶167 as follows:

This section aims at setting out the inheritance of the sons of two marriages and therefore takes no trouble about the life-interest of the widow in her *šeriktum* or in her *nudunnûm*; the former being derived from the wife's family, must go only to her own sons or revert to her father's house, but the latter, coming from the husband's house, descends to his sons by any wife.

DRIVER & MILES, BABYLONIAN LAWS 271 (footnote omitted).

by the slave by calling them "my children," and treated them as his children while he was alive, then, after his death, both the children by his wife and the children by the slave were entitled to equal shares of their father's estate (HAMMURABI ¶170). It was, nevertheless, a son by his wife who was considered "the preferred heir." (HAMMURABI ¶170). The preferred heir was permitted to "select and take a share first." (HAMMURABI ¶170). If, on the other hand, the father did not acknowledge the slave's children as his, then those children were not entitled to any of their father's estate upon his death (HAMMURABI ¶171). In that case, however, both the slave woman and her children were given their freedom upon his death (HAMMURABI ¶171).

Under the Laws of Lipit-Ishtar, when a married man had children by both his wife and also by a slave, he was required to free the slave woman and her children. The children of his legitimate wife, however, were not required to share their father's estate with the children of the slave woman (LIPIT-ISHTAR ¶25). Also, according to Lipit-Ishtar's Laws, when a man had no children by his wife but did father a child by a prostitute, the prostitute's child was considered his heir, and he was required to "provide grain, oil, and clothing rations for the prostitute." (LIPIT-ISHTAR ¶27). But in this situation, as long as the man's wife was alive, the prostitute was not allowed to live in the man's house (LIPIT-ISHTAR ¶27).

[G] WILLS

Marten Stol bluntly asserts: "Drawing up wills was not done in Babylonia...."[111] According to Driver and Miles, "Testate succession in the strict sense did not exist...; there was no such instrument as a will or testament by which a revocable disposition to take effect after the testator's death is made a part or the whole of his estate."[112] The ancient Mesopotamians used other forms of conveyance to accomplish many of the same objectives that modern legal systems achieve with wills. For example, a man could adopt another in order to transfer wealth. An adoptee then inherited as a son. During his life a man could also grant property to his wife. She then had a life estate in that property after his death. In addition, a man could grant property to his favorite son on the condition that the son would take possession upon his father's death.

---

111. MARTEN STOL, *Private Life in Ancient Mesopotamia, in* 1 CIVILIZATIONS OF THE ANCIENT NEAR EAST at 485, 494.
112. DRIVER & MILES, BABYLONIAN LAWS 343 (footnote omitted).

§ 3.05 CRIMINAL LAW

[A] INTRODUCTION

Perhaps the most curious and enigmatic criminal law in the ancient Mesopotamian law collections is the second of Ur-Nammu's Laws: "If a man acts lawlessly(?), they shall kill him." (UR-NAMMU ¶2). What makes this law so difficult to interpret, of course, is that we have not a clue as to what "lawlessly" means. Presumably, it must have encompassed serious misconduct, since other laws in Ur-Nammu's collection make it clear that minor transgressions were not considered capital offenses (*e.g.,* UR-NAMMU ¶¶13, 14, 18, 19, *etc.*).

There are, indeed, very few texts that record the results or proceedings of ancient Mesopotamian criminal trials. The paucity of contemporary documents forces us to rely on the law collections for most of our information regarding criminal law. The collections contain laws that deal with many specific types of crimes, such as homicide, rape, military offenses, robbery, forgery, and embezzlement.

[B] HOMICIDE

One of Ur-Nammu's laws tersely states: "If a man commits a homicide, they shall kill that man." (UR-NAMMU ¶1). In the Laws of Lipit-Ishtar, a person found guilty of striking a woman in such a way that the blow caused her both to miscarry and to die, herself, received a death penalty (LIPIT-ISHTAR ¶¶d–e). Hammurabi's Laws do not overtly state that homicide was a crime punishable by death, but the very first law in the great collection directs that when a man accused another of homicide and failed to "bring proof," the accuser was put to death (HAMMURABI ¶1). By implication it is, therefore, logical to assume that homicide itself was also punished with execution. Scholars have remarked that it seems odd that Hammurabi's Laws do not directly address murder as a crime *per se*.[113] But they also note that "it seems clear from other sections of the Laws that a distinction between

---

113. DRIVER & MILES, BABYLONIAN LAWS 59 ("It is strange that Hammurabi gives no description of the crime of murder...."). Also, regarding the absence of any laws relating directly to homicide, Driver & Miles state: "it is remarkable that there is no direct prohibition of homicide and no discussion of that crime in these Laws." "[I]t may be...that homicide in Babylonia still gave rise to a blood feud...." Id. at 314.

'murder' and 'manslaughter' was to some extent recognized by him [*i.e.*, Hammurabi]...."[114]

In Hammurabi's Laws, it was a capital crime for a woman to arrange to have her husband killed. The law contemplates a circumstance where a wife has her husband murdered "on account of (her relationship with) another male...." (HAMMURABI ¶153). The method of execution for this crime was impalement. Indeed, we possess an account of a trial, the famous Nippur Homicide Trial, in which a widow was accused of conspiring in her husband's murder. The widow was convicted and sentenced to death for her conspiracy along with the three men who actually murdered the husband.

It was not uncommon for a creditor to take a family member of a debtor as a "debt-hostage" (*nepûtum*).[115] It was, however, also possible for someone to be "pseudo-creditor" who did not actually have a claim against another. If such a pseudo-creditor took a family member as a "debt-hostage" and caused that family member's death, he was punished by death (ESHNUNNA ¶24).

[C] THEFT CRIMES

[1] INTRODUCTION & GENERAL PROVISIONS

The Reforms of Urukagina (Uru-inimgina) contained some provisions that related to theft. For example, priests were prohibited from entering a commoner's garden and chopping down a tree or removing produce. There was also a provision in Urukagina's (Uru-inimgina's) Reforms that forbade a person of the upper class from taking fish from a commoner's fish pond.

In the Sumerian Law Handbook of Forms, many thefts resulted in penalties based on the value of the property stolen. Ordinarily, a thief was ordered to pay a factor of the value of the object(s) taken as compensation to the property owner. For example, a thief had to pay double the value of a boat or pig (SLHF (iii 10–12), (iii 13–15)). In Hammurabi's Laws, some sections establish a fixed amount of compensation for theft; such as the theft of agricultural implements (*e.g.*, 5 shekels for theft of a plow) (HAMMURABI ¶¶259–260 (5 shekels for a plow stolen "from the common irrigated area"; 3 shekels for theft of "a clod-breaking plow or harrow")). Driver and Miles suggest that the reason why this penalty for theft is relatively lenient is because such implements might have been either left out in a field and then taken (*i.e.*, the finder may have presumed

---

114. *Id.* at 59 (citing to HAMMURABI ¶¶116, 207–210, and 229–230). *See generally Id.* at 314–317.

115. *See infra* §3.07[C][3].

them abandoned) or the "thief" may have borrowed them to begin with (a bailment).[116] A shepherd, who was found guilty of altering the brand on sheep or cattle and selling them, paid ten-times their value as recompense (HAMMURABI ¶265). Even though this offense is described as a theft, this law treats the shepherd's crime more like that of the bailee in HAMMURABI ¶¶253–255[117] where compensatory payment is made—not the death penalty. If a consignee failed to deliver goods as promised for his consignor, the consignee was liable to his consignor for five-times the amount of property that had been consigned to him (HAMMURABI ¶112). In most instances of theft, it was the victim who initiated legal proceedings, not the government. This may be a reason why monetary compensation was the ordinary punishment for theft instead of incarceration or corporal punishment.

In Hammurabi's Laws, one provision punishes theft of "valuables" from a temple or a palace, or receiving "valuables" stolen from a temple or palace, by death (HAMMURABI ¶6). On the other hand, another provision provides that when someone steals "an ox, a sheep, a donkey, a pig, or a boat" from a temple or palace, his penalty is not death, but to pay back thirty-times that which he stole (HAMMURABI ¶8). Obviously there is an apparent inconsistency between ¶6 and ¶8. It is possible that the livestock enumerated in ¶8 were considered less dear than the valuables in ¶6. But probably these two provisions evolved from two separate legal traditions: one based on capital punishment and one based on monetary damages. If the theft-victim was a commoner instead of a temple or palace, the thief was required to pay back only ten-times what he stole (HAMMURABI ¶8). But if the thief in either case did not have sufficient resources to pay back the livestock or boat, the penalty was death (HAMMURABI ¶8).[118]

There is a unique provision in Hammurabi's Laws dealing with firefighters who steal goods from a burning house. If a volunteer firefighter stole belongings from a house where he was fighting a fire, his punishment was to be put to death by throwing him into the very fire that he was helping to extinguish (HAMMURABI ¶25).

Two striking provisions in Hammurabi's Laws furnish a kind of social theft insurance and life insurance for victims of robbery (HAMMURABI

---

116. DRIVER & MILES, BABYLONIAN LAWS 80–81, 450.

117. *See infra* §3.07[B][4].

118. For a discussion of the apparent contradiction between this provision and HAMMURABI ¶¶9–11, *see* Westbrook and Wilcke, *The Liability of an Innocent Purchaser of Stolen Goods*, 25 ARCHIV FÜR ORIENTFORSCHUNG 111–120 (1974–1977). *See also* DRIVER & MILES, BABYLONIAN LAWS 81, 95–105.

¶¶23–24). One law established that if the robber was not apprehended, "the city and governor in whose territory and district the robbery was committed" will replace the stolen property to the victim, provided that he was able to "establish the extent of his lost property before the god...." (HAMMURABI ¶23). The other law mandated that the city and the governor had to pay 60 shekels of silver to the victim's family in the event that someone was killed in the course of a robbery (HAMMURABI ¶24).

[2] SELLING GOODS UNDER FALSE PRETENSES & THEFT BY FRAUD

Hammurabi's Laws recognized that sales transactions were suspicious when the seller was either a minor ("a son of a man") or a slave. It was, of course, possible that the youth or the slave did not have authority to sell the man's goods (*i.e.* he had essentially stolen them to sell). Therefore, when either a minor or a slave tried to sell goods, the Laws of Hammurabi required that there be either witnesses to the sale or a written contract as evidence of the sale (HAMMURABI ¶7). If the buyer had neither witnesses nor a written contract to such a sale, the law considered *him* a thief and imposed a death penalty (HAMMURABI ¶7). Here we see the importance that the ancients placed on evidence to corroborate the truth: either something in writing or the testimony of witnesses.[119]

The ancient Mesopotamians also appreciated that taking possession of another's property by fraudulent means was a kind of theft. One of the Laws of Eshnunna provides that for theft of a boat "under fraudulent circumstances" the guilty party was required to pay 10 shekels (and presumably he also had to return the boat) (ESHNUNNA ¶6).

[3] BLACK MARKET RESALE

In the ancient world, like the modern, some unscrupulous characters made a living by stealing goods and then reselling them on the black market. Legal systems throughout the ages have experimented with different solutions to the problems that arise when an innocent purchaser buys stolen goods. On the one hand, the good faith purchaser believes that he has a right to the goods that he has bought. On the other hand, the original owner whose goods were stolen and resold feels that he has a superior claim to his property since his property was taken illegally. One of the longest provisions in Hammurabi's Laws, ¶9, addresses this situation. This

---

119. *See also* HAMMURABI ¶105 (Law requiring trading agents to obtain written receipts of transactions in order to be eligible for reimbursement).

law requires both the original owner and the good faith purchaser to provide witnesses. The owner's witnesses must identify the goods as his. The purchaser's witnesses, on the other hand, must declare that they were witnesses to the purchaser's sale. The parties are given up to six months to bring their witnesses. The one who fails to bring his witnesses within six months is "assessed the penalty for that case." (HAMMURABI ¶13). Furthermore, the purchaser must "produce the seller." If the judges believe all of the witnesses of both parties, Hammurabi's law dispenses justice as follows: 1) the stolen goods are returned to their original owner; 2) the aggrieved purchaser recoups his purchase price "from the seller's estate"; and, 3) the criminal seller is given a death sentence (HAMMURABI ¶9).[120] It is, however, essential that the purchaser either produce the seller or the witnesses who observed the sale. Otherwise *he* is treated as the thief and given the death penalty ("then it is the buyer who is the thief, he shall be killed") (HAMMURABI ¶10; ESHNUNNA ¶40 (the buyer must "establish the identity of the seller.")). Similarly, if the man claiming to be the original owner is unable to produce witnesses authenticating his prior ownership, then it is he who is executed (HAMMURABI ¶11).

[4] EMBEZZLEMENT

Embezzlement is a kind of theft. Embezzlement occurs when someone who is entitled to possession of another's property appropriates the property in a manner that manifests an intent to take title to it (not mere possession). For example, a bank teller is legally entitled to possess your cash deposit. If, however, the teller pockets your money, that is embezzlement. Hammurabi's Laws criminalized embezzlement in the context of a cultivator (HAMMURABI ¶253). The particular provision deals with a situation where a property owner contracts with a cultivator to care for his property (*i.e.*, cultivating fields, caring for cattle, storing grain, etc.). In other words, the cultivator has legal *possession* of the owner's property. If, however, the cultivator embezzled "seed or fodder," he was punished by amputation of a hand. In one actual case of a man who embezzled grain, the perpetrator

---

120. W.F. Leemans has shown, however, that in one actual court case of this kind "the theft was settled by means of an indemnification, with, perhaps, an additional fine." W.F. Leemans, *Some Aspects of Theft and Robbery in Old Babylonian Documents, in* SCRITTI IN ONORE DI GIUSEPPE FURLANI 661, 665 (1957) (footnote omitted). The modern law of the Uniform Commercial Code reaches a result different from Hammuarabi's Laws; giving possession to the good faith purchaser for value. The original owner must seek damages from the thief-seller. In terms of policy, the UCC tries to encourage commercial transactions. Thus the UCC opts not to punish the good faith purchaser for value. *See* UNIFORM COMMERCIAL CODE §2-403.

was punished by: 1) being forced to repay the sum plus interest; and 2) having to pay the profit he had made when he sold the grain.[121]

[D] SEXUAL CONDUCT

[1] RAPE & INCEST

As a rule, a man received capital punishment for rape when the victim was either married or contracted-for-marriage at the time of the rape. After a man had delivered marriage gifts to his fiance's father, it was a capital offense for another man to abduct and rape her (ESHNUNNA ¶26; HAMMURABI ¶130; UR-NAMMU ¶6).[122] The woman who was the victim of rape was released (HAMMURABI ¶130). Hammurabi's Laws made incest with one's daughter a criminal offense. A man found guilty of incest with his daughter was banished from his city (HAMMURABI ¶154). The daughter was not punished. If a man was found guilty of having sexual relations with his mother (after his father's death), both he and his mother received capital punishment by burning (HAMMURABI ¶157). A father-in-law who was caught having sexual relations with his daughter-in-law suffered the death penalty ("they shall bind that man and cast him into the water") (HAMMURABI ¶155).

[2] ADULTERY

In his essay "Private Life in Ancient Mesopotamia," Stol notes that adultery was an offense that could only be committed by a woman, not a man: "A husband's extramarital liasons were not punishable as adultery. Adultery could be committed only by a married woman: it was an offense by the wife against her husband."[123] The Laws of Eshnunna provided that a married woman found guilty of adultery ("seized in the lap of another man") received capital punishment (ESHNUNNA ¶28). Ur Nammu's Laws were more specific, imposing the death penalty where the married woman herself "initiate[d] sexual relations." (UR-NAMMU ¶7). One of Hammurabi's Laws stipulated that a woman caught in adultery was to be bound and "cast... into the water" along with her lover (HAMMURABI ¶129). If the woman's husband wished to spare her, however, he could. In that case, the king also

---

121. SAGGS, BABYLON 193.
122. *See* WESTBROOK, OLD BABYLONIAN MARRIAGE LAW 29, 35, 48; DRIVER & MILES, BABYLONIAN LAWS 277, 282 (Driver & Miles explain that the girl in this provision "is still living in her father's house and is inchoately married and a mere child." (footnote omitted)).
123. MARTEN STOL, *Private Life in Ancient Mesopotamia, in* 1 CIVILIZATIONS OF THE ANCIENT NEAR EAST at 485, 494.

spared her lover (HAMMURABI ¶129). An adultress whose husband had
been taken as a prisoner of war may have received a lesser penalty. Hammurabi's Laws state that if a woman whose husband was taken prisoner did
"not keep herself chaste," she would be "cast…into the water." (HAM-
MURABI ¶133b).[124] It is unclear whether this provision is tantamount to a
death penalty or whether it is the equivalent, instead, of submitting to the
Divine River Ordeal.[125] It may be that the law viewed her husband's having
been taken prisoner as a mitigating circumstance.

In Hammurabi's Laws, we learn that if a husband accused his wife of
adultery (but she has not been caught in the act), the wife may swear an
oath to her innocence. Then, she may "return to her house." (HAMMURABI
¶131). If a third party accused a woman of adultery (but she has not been
caught in the act), "she shall submit to the divine River Ordeal for her husband." (HAMMURABI ¶132). These two laws are very interesting. The first
leads us to believe that, when a husband accused his wife of adultery, so long
as she swore an oath of innocence, she could not be convicted in the absence
of eyewitness testimony. The second, however, says that she will have to submit to the divine River Ordeal if the accuser is someone other than her husband. The presumption operating here seems to be that a husband is more
likely to fabricate an accusation of his own wife's adultery than a third party.

[E] MILITARY CRIMES

Under Hammurabi's Laws, it was a capital offense for either a soldier or
a fisherman to hire a substitute to go on a royal campaign on his behalf
(HAMMURABI ¶26).[126] An individual who informed the authorities of a soldier's or fisherman's deception was granted "full legal possession of his [the
soldier's or fisherman's] estate." (HAMMURABI ¶26). It was also a capital offense for "either a captain or a sergeant" to accept and employ either substi-
tutes or deserters (HAMMURABI ¶33).

There are provisions in Hammurabi's Laws prohibiting officers from
abusing their power by taking things that rightfully belonged to their sol-

---

124. This provision should be read in conjunction with ¶133a and ¶¶134–135
which permit a woman to seek the protection of another man in certain circumstances. See supra §3.03[B][3].

125. See supra §2.03.

126. Driver & Miles describe the "soldier" in Hammurabi's Laws as "a member of
the military force but whose main duty is to preserve public order and generally act as
a policeman." DRIVER & MILES, BABYLONIAN LAWS 114 (footnote omitted). They say
that the "fishermen" were employees of the crown. Id. at 115.

diers, oppressing soldiers, or hiring out their soldiers to influential persons (HAMMURABI ¶34). The penalty for such an abuse of power is death (HAMMURABI ¶34). In the Laws of Eshnunna, military officials along with "any person in a position of authority" can be charged with theft for taking possession of a fugitive slave or stray ox or donkey without bringing it to the capital city within the period of one month (ESHNUNNA ¶50).

[F] "CRIMINAL" TRESPASS & "CRIMINAL" NEGLIGENCE

Trespass and negligence are ordinarily dealt with in tort law. Nevertheless, in certain situations, the culpability involved is so egregious or severe, that the law treats the offense with heightened severity. Such is the case in ancient Mesopotamia with trespass and negligence. The Laws of Eshnunna made it illegal for someone to trespass in another's field or house (ESHNUNNA ¶¶12–13). One can only assume that these laws were—at least in part—intended to curb theft (*See* LIPIT-ISHTAR ¶9) (combining the concepts of trespass and theft in one provision). The penalty for trespass during the daytime was 10 shekels (ESHNUNNA ¶¶12–13; LIPIT-ISHTAR ¶9). Trespass at night, however, was considered a capital offense (ESHNUNNA ¶¶12–13). It is likely that nocturnal trespass was considered a more serious offense because of the perceived higher risk of injury to a property owner under cover of darkness. This is analogous to the distinction recognized in many legal systems between theft (stealing in the daytime) *versus* burglary (stealing at night). Hammurabi's Laws dealt with breaking and entering very strictly: "If a man breaks into a house, they shall kill him and hang(?) him in front of that very breach." (HAMMURABI ¶21).[127]

Hammurabi's Laws contain two laws that are arguably criminal negligence. These provisions impose severe penalties on a contractor who constructs a house so poorly that it collapses and kills someone (HAMMURABI ¶¶229–230). If the collapse kills the owner, the contractor himself receives the death penalty (HAMMURABI ¶229). If the collapse kills the owner's son, it is the contractor's son who is put to death (HAMMURABI ¶230). In addi-

---

127. *See* Ellickson & Thorland, *Ancient Land Law*, 71 CHICAGO-KENT L. REV. 321, 343 (1995). This is a unique punishment in Hammurabi's Laws and in Mesopotamian law in general. Driver & Miles observe: "The punishment then reflects the crime: as he has made a hole in the wall of the house, so a hole is made in his body." DRIVER & MILES, BABYLONIAN LAWS 108. Compare HAMMURABI ¶227 (Guilty defendant is hanged in the doorway).

tion, two of the Laws of Eshnunna treat negligence as so severe that it is considered a capital offense (ESHNUNNA ¶58, ¶60). In each case, the negligence involves a person's failure to prevent injury. One law deals with the situation where the owner of a wall ignores the warning of municipal officials that his wall is buckling and in need of repair (ESHNUNNA ¶58). When the wall collapses and kills "a member of the *awilu*-class," the law states that it is "a capital case" that must be "decided by a royal decree." (ESHNUNNA ¶58). A related law mandates a death penalty for a guard whose negligence allows a burglar to break into a house (ESHNUNNA ¶60).

[G] FALSE WITNESS/PERJURY

Ur-Nammu's Laws impose a fine of 15 shekels on a witness who committed perjury (UR-NAMMU ¶28). If a witness refused "to take the oath," his penalty was to "make compensation of whatever was the object of the case." (UR-NAMMU ¶29). The very first law in Hammurabi's Laws makes it a capital offense to accuse another of homicide falsely: "If a man accuses another man and charges him with homicide but cannot bring proof against him, his accuser shall be killed." (HAMMURABI ¶1). The third of Hammurabi's Laws provides that when someone "cannot bring evidence for his accusation" in a capital case, his punishment is death (HAMMURABI ¶3). Hammurabi's Laws also penalize someone who accuses either a certain kind of priestess called an *ugbabtu* or a married woman and fails "to bring proof." (HAMMURABI ¶127). This law does not specify just what the accusation had to concern. The penalty for an unsubstantiated claim under this provision is flogging and having half his hair shaved off (HAMMURABI ¶127).[128]

[H] MISCELLANEOUS CRIMES

[1] RELIGIOUS OFFENSES

Certain classes of priestesses were prohibited from either opening a tavern or entering one "for some beer." (HAMMURABI ¶110). The penalty was death by burning.[129] This law was probably intended to keep the priestesses from associating with prostitutes, since the tavern was either a place where prostitutes gathered or it may have been a brothel itself.

---

128. DRIVER & MILES, BABYLONIAN LAWS 279 (Driver & Miles assert that shaving half of a person's head was a form of public ridicule, causing shame and embarrassment.).

129. *Id.* at 206 (Driver & Miles suggest that burning as a punishment is based on religious sacrifice).

[2] WITCHCRAFT

There are laws prohibiting some brand of witchcraft, but "we have no evidence for witches being actually criminally prosecuted...."[130] Hammurabi's Laws use the divine River Ordeal as a means to determine whether someone is guilty of witchcraft (HAMMURABI ¶2). If the accused is overwhelmed by the water (and therefore adjudged guilty), his accuser is granted "full legal possession of his estate." (HAMMURABI ¶2). On the other hand, if the accused survives the divine River Ordeal, the accuser is put to death and the accused is granted "full legal possession of his accuser's estate." (HAMMURABI ¶2).

[3] FALSE IMPRISONMENT/KIDNAPPING

One of Ur-Nammu's Laws prohibits an individual from restricting another's freedom of movement. Perhaps this is a law prohibiting false imprisonment: "If a man detains(?) (another), that man shall be imprisoned and he shall weigh and deliver 15 shekels of silver." (UR-NAMMU ¶3). In Hammurabi's Laws, kidnapping is a capital offense (HAMMURABI ¶14).

[4] HARBORING CRIMINALS

A woman innkeeper was required to turn in criminals who congregated in her house. If she failed to do so, she received the death penalty (HAMMURABI ¶109).

[I] PUNISHMENTS

The most common penalties for conduct that we would characterize as criminal are: 1) death (by drowning, burning,[131] or impalement[132]); 2) mu-

---

130. Walter Farber, *Witchcraft, Magic, and Divination in Ancient Mesopotamia, in* 3 CIVILIZATIONS OF THE ANCIENT NEAR EAST 1895, 1898 (Jack M. Sasson ed., 1995). *See also* SAGGS, BABYLON 317.

131. Burning as a penalty was probably based on the concept of religious sacrifice. DRIVER & MILES, BABYLONIAN LAWS 206. *See also Id.* at 495–496 (Identifying specific provisions in Hammurabi's Laws in which death by burning is the punishment: ¶25 (For looting during a fire); ¶110 (For a priestess who operates or frequents an inn); and ¶157 (For a man and his mother who commit incest with one another after the father/husband's death)).

132. *See* DRIVER & MILES, BABYLONIAN LAWS 496 (Identifying specific provisions in Hammurabi's Laws where impalement is the punishment: ¶153 (For a woman who kills her husband on account of her lover); ¶21 (For a burglar who breaks into a house) (This reference appears to be erroneous since ¶21 clearly refers to "hanging" as the punishment); ¶227 for an "*awīlum*" who has wrongfully procured the removal of the owner's mark from a slave....")).

tilation (such as amputation of a limb or appendage);[133] 3) payment of compensation, multiple damages, or fines; 4) banishment (HAMMURABI ¶154) ("If a man should carnally know his daughter, they shall banish that man from the city."); and, 5) public flogging (*see e.g.,* HAMMURABI ¶202) ("If an *awīlu* should strike the cheek of an *awīlu* who is of status higher than his own, he shall be flogged in the public assembly with 60 stripes of an ox whip."). The punishment of being "cast into the water" poses some problems of interpretation. If the criminal was bound (as was the case for all men cast into the water in Hammurabi's Laws), it is unlikely that he would have had any chance for escape. If, on the other hand, the criminal was not bound, apparently escape and exoneration were possible. In Hammurabi's Laws, women are cast into the water as a penalty in four laws (HAMMURABI ¶¶108, 129, 133, 143) but are only described as "bound" in one (HAMMURABI ¶129) — where an adultress has been caught *in flagrante delicto* with her lover. Driver and Miles conclude that drowning is actually employed as a punishment five times[134] for three kinds of offenses in Hammurabi's Laws: 1) for adultery (HAMMURABI ¶¶129, 133, 143); 2) for incest with a daughter-in-law (HAMMURABI ¶155); and, 3) for a woman inkeeper (ale-wife) cheating her customers (HAMMURABI ¶108).

§ 3.06 TORTS

[A] THE PROBLEM OF CATEGORIZATION (BATTERY, NEGLIGENCE, STRICT LIABILITY)

In Hammurabi's Laws, there are a number of provisions that cover situations that we today might be tempted to classify as battery, but it is not always entirely clear (HAMMURABI ¶¶195–208). This ambiguity arises because many of the provisions which at first appear to be simple instances of battery are unclear as to whether the conduct described in them is intentional, negligent, or neither. For example, one famous law states: "If an *awīlum* should blind the eye of another *awīlum*, they shall blind his eye." (HAMMURABI ¶196). The law that immediately follows is of the same general nature: "If he should break the bone of another *awīlum*, they shall break his bone." (HAMMURABI ¶197; *See also* HAMMURABI ¶200 (knocking

---

133. *See Id.* at 499 (Driver & Miles identify specific provisions in Hammurabi's Laws where particular parts of the body are mutilated or amputated: hand (¶¶195, 218, 226, 253); ear (¶¶205, 282); tongue (¶192); breast (¶194); eye (¶193)).
134. *Id.* at 495.

out a tooth)). Under modern tort law, the acts described in these provisions would be classified as batteries only if the tortfeasor *intentionally* caused the harmful or offensive contact (*i.e.*, the physical contact that caused the blindness or the broken bone) with the victim. Modern tort law would characterize these acts as negligent only if the tortfeasor's conduct that caused the blindness or broken bone failed to conform to the standard of what a reasonable person would have done under similar circumstances. For example, arguably it would not be negligent for an individual to strike another acidentally with a stick (causing blindness or a fracture) if he was in the process of defending himself from an attacking dog; especially if a reasonable person in the position of the person being attacked by the dog would have been unaware of the victim's presence (for example, if the victim had walked up from behind just as the dog began its attack).

As these two laws are written, they seem to describe situations where liability would be imposed in a *strict liability sense* (*i.e.*, merely because an actor *caused* personal injury). These laws do not say that the blinding or fracture need have been intentional. Nor do they require that the conduct involved was negligent (*i.e.*, failing to act like a reasonable person would have under the circumstances). Rather, these laws appear to impose liability regardless of whether the tortfeasor intended the injury, caused the injury negligently, or did so accidentally—like the example of the person defending himself with a stick. We would call this liability—liability based on causation alone—*strict liability*.

A number of Hammurabi's laws appear to recognize the notion that modern legal systems characterize as "negligence." For example, when boats collided on a river, Mesopotamian law imposed liability on the upstream boat (HAMMURABI ¶240; SLHF (v 27–31), (v 32–36)). The legal presumption operating is that an upstream captain has a greater opportunity to avoid a collision than a downstream captain because he has more control, since he travels at a slower speed. Another law that appears to rely on the concept of negligence is HAMMURABI ¶267. According to this law, if a shepherd negligently allowed mange to spread within an enclosure, he had to replace the sheep, goats, or cattle that were damaged by the mange. Presumably, this situation involves negligence on the part of the shepherd, unlike the situation in HAMMUARABI ¶266 where the shepherd takes an oath claiming no responsibility, and the property owner (*i.e.*, the owner of the enclosure) is adjudged liable for the injury to the animal.

Still, since it is often unclear whether many of the provisions in the ancient Mesopotamian law collections address situations that involve what we would characterize as "fault" (*i.e.*, either intentional or negligent conduct), absent evidence to the contrary, it may simply be best to admit that many of these laws *could* refer to situations involving any of the three: 1) intent (liability based on the tortfeasor's deliberate attempt to strike or harm the victim); 2) negligence (liability based on the tortfeasor's failure to act like a reasonable person under the circumstances); or 3) strict liability (liability based on mere causation).

[B] THE INFLUENCE OF "STATUS" ON TORT DAMAGES

Class—or personal status—made a significant difference in how Hammurabi's Laws assessed damages for torts.[135] When a member of the *awilu* class injured a commoner or a slave (*i.e.,* not another *awilu*), damages were ordinarily monetary compensation rather than *lex talionis* (retribution). For example, when an *awilu* either blinded a commoner's eye or broke a commoner's bone, he paid 60 shekels of silver as compensation (HAMMURABI ¶198) (*See also* HAMMURABI ¶201) ("If he should knock out the tooth of a commoner, he shall weigh and deliver 20 shekels of silver."). If it was a slave whose eye had been blinded or bone broken by an *awilu*, then the compensation was one-half of the slave's value (no doubt paid to the owner) (HAMMURABI ¶199). But the payments for compensation are not mathematically consistent across the board. There are some puzzling inconsistencies.

One act that seems to have special significance is a "strike" on the cheek.[136] When an *awilu* strikes the cheek of another *awilu* who is "of status higher than his own," Hammurabi's Laws treat the offense more like a criminal matter than a tort: the perpetrator is "flogged in the public assembly with 60 stripes of an ox whip." (HAMMURABI ¶202). If, instead, the victim is "his equal," then compensation is 60 shekels (HAMMURABI ¶203). The pattern with respect to status that prevails for other torts holds true in the case of a slap to the cheek: the penalty is milder when a commoner is the victim and it is more severe if the perpetrator is from a class lower than his victim. For example, a commoner who strikes another commoner's cheek pays only 10 shekels as compensation (HAMMURABI ¶204). If a slave strikes an *awilu*'s cheek, Hammurabi's Laws provide mutilation as a penalty: "they shall cut off his ear." (HAMMURABI ¶205).

---

135. *See supra* §3.01 regarding legal status.
136. For a perceptive analysis of the cheek-slapping provisions in the Laws of Hammurabi and other documents related to this offense, *see* Martha T. Roth, *Mesopotamian Legal Traditions and the Laws of Hammurabi*, 71 CHICAGO-KENT L. REV. 13, 26–37 (1995).

[C] CATALOGUE OF TORTS & COMPENSATION

There are a number of laws that establish compensation for causing a woman to miscarry.[137] The compensation varies depending on the status of the woman and on the degree of fault involved (*i.e.,* an intentional act carries a stiffer penalty than one simply involving negligence). The student exercise tablet of Bēlshunu (*c.* 1800 B.C.) provides that compensation for causing a miscarriage is 20 shekels if the tortfeasor's act was intentional ("strikes") (SLEX ¶2') and only 10 shekels if the act was negligent ("jostles") (SLEX ¶1'). These two provisions reveal a sharp distinction between injuries caused intentionally versus injuries caused negligently. In Lipit-Ishtar's Laws, striking "the daughter of a man" and causing a miscarriage cost the tortfeasor 30 shekels (LIPIT-ISHTAR ¶d). If it was "the slave woman of a man" instead of a daughter who miscarried because of a blow, the damages were set at 5 shekels. Curiously, by the time of Hammurabi's Laws, damages for this type of intentional tort decreased. If a member of the *awilu* class caused an *awilu* woman to miscarry, he was required to pay 10 shekels (HAMMURABI ¶209). If the woman was a commoner, the penalty was only 5 shekels (HAMMURABI ¶211). If the woman was a slave, he paid only 2 shekels. But the stakes were proportionately higher in the event that the woman, herself, in addition to losing her fetus, also died. If the woman was of the *awilu* class, the law imposed a death sentence on the tortfeasor's daughter (HAMMURABI ¶210). If the woman involved was a commoner, the guilty party had to pay 30 shekels (HAMMURABI ¶212). If the woman was an *awilu*'s slave, the tortfeasor paid 20 shekels (HAMMURABI ¶214).

In Ur-Nammu's Laws, many acts involving personal injury that we would probably classify either as types of battery or negligence[138] had fixed amounts of compensation. The general rule was for the tortfeasor to pay money damages to the victim. For example, when someone cut off another's foot, he had to pay 10 shekels of silver as compensation to the victim (UR-NAMMU ¶18). When someone broke another's bone with a club, he paid 60 shekels (UR-NAMMU ¶19). It cost the tortfeasor 40 shekels for cutting off someone's nose (UR-NAMMU ¶20) and 2 shekels for knocking out someone's tooth (UR-NAMMU ¶22).

---

137. *See* DRIVER & MILES, BABYLONIAN LAWS 413–416. *See also* Lafont, *Continuity and Pluralism* 108; Good, *Capital Punishment* 19 STAN. L. REV. 947, 953 (1967) ("Five separate codes envision the situation of a blow to a pregnant woman resulting in a miscarriage. Code of Hammurabi sections 209–14 deal with six separate possibilities.").

138. The classification would depend primarily upon whether the tortfeasor acted intentionally or negligently. *See supra* §3.06[A].

The Laws of Eshnunna regarding personal injury were similar: the tort-feasor paid money damages to the victim. The amount was established by the Laws and varied depending upon which body part had been injured and how severe the injury was. The following are the injuries covered by these Laws:

* biting off a nose................60 shekels (Eshnunna ¶42)
* an eye...........................60 shekels (Eshnunna ¶42)
* a tooth.........................30 shekels (Eshnunna ¶42)
* an ear..........................30 shekels (Eshnunna ¶42)
* a slap to the cheek.............10 shekels (Eshnunna ¶42)
* cutting off a finger.............20 shekels (Eshnunna ¶43)
* knocking someone down
  in the street and thereby
  breaking his hand..............30 shekels (Eshnunna ¶44)
* knocking someone down
  in the street and thereby
  breaking his foot...............30 shekels (Eshnunna ¶45)
* injuries inflicted "in the
  course of a fray"...............10 shekels (Eshnunna ¶47)
* breaking a collarbone.........20 shekels (Eshnunna ¶46)

[D] ACTUAL WARNINGS OF FORESEEN DANGERS

A number of laws from ancient Mesopotamia impose liability in instances where a tortfeasor receives a warning, putting him on notice that his property poses a danger to others. In modern tort terminology, we refer to this as not just *foreseeable* but actually a *foreseen* danger. Presumably, when one has been warned of a foreseen, dangerous situation, a reasonable person should take reasonable steps to reduce the likelihood of injury. Thus, Mesopotamian law held warned persons responsible for the resulting injuries when they failed to take remedial measures. For example, suppose that a property owner warned his neighbor that he (the neighbor) was neglecting his property in such a manner that a robber could gain access to his (the complaining property owner's) house: "Your fallow land has been neglected; someone could break into my house. Fortify your property!" (Lipit-Ishtar ¶11). If a robber did thereafter break into the house via the negligently maintained property, the negligent neighbor was liable for the loss incurred (*i.e.,* he had to "restore to the owner of the house any of his property that he lost") (Lipit-Ishtar ¶11) (*See also* Hammurabi gap ¶e) (same principle).

[E] FAILURE TO MAINTAIN PROPERTY THAT DAMAGES ANOTHER & DAMAGE TO PROPERTY

[1] PROPERTY THAT DAMAGES ANOTHER

Due to the importance of irrigation canals for agriculture, Hammurabi's Laws imposed liability on persons whose failure to adequately maintain the embankments of the canals caused flood damage to others (HAMMURABI ¶53). As a rule, a property owner whose lack of maintenance caused damage was required to pay compensatory damages (*i.e.,* "replace the grain whose loss he caused") (HAMMURABI ¶53) (*See also* HAMMURABI ¶55 — similar provisions). This general rule does not punish the negligent owner; rather, it merely restores the *status quo ante.* It tries to put the victim back in the position that he would have been in if the negligent conduct had not occurred. The law also exacted a severe penalty if the owner who caused the damage was unable to supply replacement grain. In that case, the neighbors were permitted to sell him into slavery and to sell his property in order to satisfy the judgment (HAMMURABI ¶54).

[2] DAMAGE TO PROPERTY

One of Ur-Nammu's Laws states: "If a man floods(?) another man's field, he shall measure and deliver 720 silas of grain per 100 sars of field." (UR-NAMMU ¶31). Another text provides that when one person flooded another's field, he had to "replace the grain [*i.e.,* the grain that the water destroyed] according to (the yields of the fields of) his neighbors." (SLHF (iv 35–41)). This law uses the neighbor's field as a basis for estimating the amount of grain that might have been produced in the field that was destroyed.[139] In this way, the law prohibits a windfall in the event that the area suffered from bad storms or drought.

[F] LIABILITY FOR DAMAGE CAUSED BY OXEN

It is clear that oxen were important to the well-being of the economy in ancient Mesopotamia. They were the principal beasts of burden. When an ox caused damage, its owner was not necessarily responsible for compensating the injured party. For example, in Hammurabi's Laws, one law states: "If an ox gores to death a man while it is passing through the streets, that case

---

139. *See infra* §3.07[B][7].

has no basis for a claim." (Hammurabi ¶250). According to Finkelstein, this law reflects the concept of contributory negligence in Mesopotamian law: "It was the victim, by his own carelessness, who got in the animal's way, and was gored to death as a result. It is the fact of contributory negligence, then, that frees the owner of the ox of any possible liability, which would otherwise be inexplicable."[140] Similarly, in the Laws of Eshnunna, when an ox gores another ox to death, the owner of the goring ox is required to pay the dead ox's owner one-half of the value of "the living ox" but he also receives one-half of the "carcass of the dead ox." (Eshnunna ¶53).

The ancient Mesopotamians recognized that oxen were, to a certain degree, uncontrollable, and that when one ox gored another ox to death the two owners needed to share the loss almost equally. But if the goring ox was "a gorer" (*i.e.*, if the ox had a history of goring—so that the owner had actual notice of the ox's dangerous propensity), then the owner had to pay higher damages.[141] This makes sense. If an animal owner knows that his animal has caused injuries in the past, the owner has a heightened responsibility to take precautions to reduce the risk that the animal will cause similar injuries in the future. Thus, when the town authorities had notified an ox's owner that his ox was a gorer, and told him to restrain the animal, if the ox subsequently gored a man to death, the owner had to pay 30–40 shekels of silver (the amount varied depending on which collection of laws applied) (*e.g.*, Eshnunna ¶54) (setting damages at 40 shekels). The same rule applied to a vicious dog when authorities had warned the dog owner and the dog subsequently bit and killed a man (Eshnunna ¶56) (Hammurabi ¶251) (setting damages at 30 shekels).

The provisions that follow in the text of both the Laws of Eshnunna and Hammurabi's Laws illustrate again the significance of status:[142] they maintain that, if the victim of the ox's goring is a slave, the compensation is markedly less (15 shekels instead of 40 in the Laws of Eshnunna and 20 shekels instead of 30 in Hammurabi) (Eshnunna ¶55) (Eshnunna ¶57) (analogous provision regarding a vicious dog) (Hammurabi ¶¶229–231) (penalties vary for a house builder depending upon whether the victim of a collapsed house is a free man or a slave).

---

140. J.J. Finkelstein, *Sex Offenses in Sumerian Laws*, 86 J. of the American Oriental Soc. 355, 364, n. 30 (1966).

141. *See supra* §3.06[D].

142. *See supra* §§3.01, 3.06[B].

[G] PHYSICIAN'S LIABILITY

A number of provisions in Hammurabi's Laws deal specifically with the liability of doctors who cause injury or death while performing surgical procedures. As is the case with other personal injuries, the laws concerning a physician's liability impose higher damages when the victim is an *awilu* and lower damages when the victim is either a *mushkenu* or slave (HAMMURABI ¶¶221–223). One law states that when a doctor's surgery causes blindness or death, his penalty is amputation of a hand (HAMMURABI ¶218). If a slave dies as a result of surgery, the doctor has to replace the slave with another "of comparable value." (HAMMURABI ¶219). For blinding a slave in surgery, a doctor pays one-half of the slave's value as compensation (HAMMURABI ¶220). If a veterinarian's surgery causes the death of an ox or donkey, the veterinarian is required to compensate the animal's owner with one-quarter of the animal's value (HAMMURABI ¶225).

[H] DEFAMATION RELATING TO SEXUAL MISCONDUCT

In modern tort law, defamatory statements that falsely accuse persons of sexual misconduct are treated as more serious than most other types of ordinary defamation. This may have been the case in ancient Mesopotamia as well. In Ur-Nammu's Laws, when someone accuses "the wife of a young man of promiscuity," if the River Ordeal indicates that the accusation is false, the accuser is required to pay 20 shekels of silver (UR-NAMMU ¶14). In the Laws of Lipit-Ishtar, when someone falsely accuses "another man's virgin daughter" of having "had sexual relations," the compensation paid is 10 shekels (LIPIT-ISHTAR ¶33).

[I] AFFIRMATIVE DEFENSES TO TORT: ASSUMPTION OF RISK & CONTRIBUTORY NEGLIGENCE

There are a few laws from the Old Babylonian period that suggest that the ancient Mesopotamians of the eighteenth century B.C. appreciated a legal concept that modern tort law classifies as either assumption of risk or contributory negligence.[143] One particular provision comes from the Laws

---

143. *See supra* § 1.07[B][6].

of Eshnunna (ESHNUNNA ¶47A)[144] and three are in Hammurabi's Laws (HAMMURABI ¶¶206–208)). The Eshnunna law states that when one man causes "the death of another member of the *awīlum*-class" "in the course of a brawl," the penalty is to pay 40 shekels of silver (ESHNUNNA ¶47A). The fact that the death occurs during the course of a brawl is essential. This death is not treated like an intentional homicide. Even as early as the Laws of Ur-Nammu (*c.* 2100 B.C.), the penalty for homicide was death (UR-NAMMU ¶1). In the case of a death that occurs in the midst of a brawl, however, some of the fault for the death lies with the deceased himself. The word "brawl" implies that both men are to blame for the violence. In modern tort terminology we would say that the dead man either *assumed the risk* of death by taking part in a brawl or that *his fault contributed* to his own injury.

Similarly, in Hammurabi's Laws, a person who inflicts injuries on another in the course of a brawl is punished less severely than otherwise. For example, when an *awilu* injures another *awilu* in a brawl, the person causing the damage is required to swear an oath stating that he did not strike the other man "intentionally," and he only has to pay the victim's medical expenses (but no punitive damages) (HAMMURABI ¶206). Like the provision in the Laws of Eshnunna, Hammurabi's Laws also contain a law that mitigates damages to a payment of 30 shekels when a death occurs in the midst of a brawl between two *awilu* (HAMMURABI ¶207). If the victim is a commoner, the tortfeasor only has to pay 20 shekels (HAMMURABI ¶208) ("If he (the victim) is a member of the commoner-class, he shall weigh and deliver 20 shekels of silver.").

§ 3.07 TRADE, CONTRACTS, & COMMERCIAL LAW

[A] TRADE

[1] EARLY FOREIGN TRADE

The earliest foreign trade—at least on a modest scale—had certainly begun by the Neolithic period (*c.* 7000 B.C.) at Jarmo in Northern Iraq. Probably the earliest trading was conducted by simple barter. In the Ubaid period (*c.* 4500–4000 B.C.), the Mesopotamians imported lumber for temples. The presence of cylinder seals in Egypt (dating from the last centuries

---

144. Possibly ¶47 is a similar provision but it is a little less certain than ¶47A.

of the fourth millennium B.C., the Uruk period (*c.* 3500–3100 B.C.) and the Jemdat Nasr period (*c.* 3100–3000 B.C.)) suggests cultural exchange between the peoples of Mesopotamia and Egypt. In addition, evidence from pottery and cylinder seals implies that some degree of trade between Mesopotamia and the Aegean islands existed in the fourth millennium. In the Early Dynastic period (*c.* 2900–2350 B.C.), they traded domestic grain for precious stones and timber from foreigners. Because Mesopotamia had virtually no timber, stones, or metal, the Sumerians were forced to establish foreign trade routes early in their history. Perhaps as early as 2700 B.C., caravans traveled to the mountains of Iran carrying grain (barley) which they exchanged for lapis lazuli and other stones. Both art and artifacts show that the Mesopotamians traded with the Indus Valley in the third millennium B.C. Because they carried on extensive trading from a very early period in their history, the ancient Mesopotamians needed contract rules and a Law Merchant.

[2] TRADE, MARKETS & MERCHANTS DURING THE TIME OF THE GREAT LAW COLLECTIONS

A significant amount of foreign trade during the period of the great law collections (*i.e.,* 2300–1600 B.C.) consisted of trading textiles for metal, stone, timber, spice, and perfume. Mesopotamian traders ventured to places such as Kanesh (a city just under 200 miles south of the Black Sea; approximately 500 miles from Assur), India, Cyprus, Northern Syria, Magan, Gubi, Tilmun, Lebanon, Kimash (a city in the mountains of western Iran), Hahu (in Asia Minor), the Persian Gulf, Aleppo, and the Orontes Valley. Among the varied products imported were metals, timber, precious stones, spices, perfumes, wine, beads, ivory, onions, and rare animals. The Mesopotamians also imported wool, hair, and leather in exchange for textiles produced by workshops in the great temple and palace organizations.

The seas and rivers provided the primary media of transport for foreign trade. Ur served as the principal seaport for all of Mesopotamia. In addition to maritime trade, the Mesopotamians developed "several well-traveled roads [that] supported a process of continuous give and take...."[145] Most domestic trade within Mesopotamia proper was conducted by boats on the Tigris and Euphrates.

The harbor area—which was called the *kar* in Sumerian and *karu* or *kārum* in Akkadian—was the hub for commercial activity in most Mesopotamian towns. The merchants of the Old Babylonian period were called

---

145. OPPENHEIM, ANCIENT MESOPOTAMIA 37.

tamkarūm. The word *tamkarūm* also refers to several different types of commercial professions. For example, slave traders, sea merchants, overland traders, brokers, merchant bankers, money lenders, and even some government agents were all referred to as *tamkarūm*.

[B] CONTRACTS

[1] INTRODUCTION

The Akkadian term for "contract" in a general sense is *riksātum*. The word *riksātum* was used to denote transactions involving the sale of goods, deposit, hiring for services, agency, trust, and marriage. Various laws in the law collections required a seal or imposed a penalty if a merchant failed to use a sealed document (*See e.g.,* HAMMURABI gap ¶m; SLHF (ii 34–36)). Many contracts were considered invalid unless there were witnesses present and their names were inscribed at the end of the text. Occasionally, parties took oaths when making a contract. Thus, the two most common legal requirements for valid contracts in ancient Mesopotamia appear to have been: 1) the presence of witnesses; and, 2) a written document recording the obligations of the parties.

Mesopotamian contract law did not require any one specific formula necessary for validity. Instead, contracts—sales contracts in particular—appear in a wide variety of forms. Nevertheless, during certain periods, many contracts contained common elements and patterns. Instead of a signature, Mesopotamian contracts required the parties who undertook contractual obligations to make a mark in the soft clay of the document. The most common methods of making such a mark to indicate that the party was present and therefore consented to the obligation were: 1) with a cylinder seal; 2) with a seal ring; and, 3) with the hem of a garment.

One unique practice—especially prevalent during and after the Ur III period (*c.* 2112–2004 B.C.)—was to encase the original cuneiform tablet in a clay envelope. A duplicate copy of the contract was written on the outside of the clay envelope itself. In the event of a subsequent dispute about the agreement, the tablet on the inside was consulted and treated as the controlling document. This duplicate text was intended to deter any attempts to alter the wording of the contract in the envelope's text.

[2] CAPACITY TO CONTRACT

We know very little about the laws concerning an individual's capacity to enter into contracts. A woman could enter into a binding agreement with her husband promising that his creditors would not be permitted to take her as a "debt-hostage." (HAMMURABI ¶151). Women could also own and sell property (HAMMURABI ¶¶39–40). Before a man could legally be given credit, he had to have either "received his inheritance share [from his father] or a slave." (ESHNUNNA ¶16).

[3]   CONTRACTS VOID DUE TO PUBLIC POLICY

A community generally considers certain types of transactions void when the community, as a whole, believes that such transactions violate public policy. For example, in modern America, a contract to build a counterfeiting machine is void because it violates public policy. In ancient Mesopotamia, there were a few laws that prohibited specific kinds of contracts in this manner. For example, a contract to purchase "a field, orchard, or house" from a "soldier, fisherman, or state tenant" was void. The seller was entitled to reclaim his real property and the buyer forfeited his payment (HAMMURABI ¶41). A contract to purchase from a soldier livestock that the king had given him was also void (HAMMURABI ¶35). Thus, as a rule, property given by the king to servicemen was deemed inalienable. One of the Laws of Eshnunna prohibited merchants and women innkeepers from accepting "silver, grain, wool, oil, or anything else from a male or female slave."(ESHNUNNA ¶15). Hence, these contracts with slaves were also void due to public policy.

[4]   BAILMENT CONTRACTS

We have a fair amount of information about bailment contracts in ancient Mesopotamia.[146] A bailment usually occurs when an owner of personal property (the bailor) temporarily transfers possession of his property to another person (bailee). For example, if I loan my hoe to my neighbor, I am the bailor and he is the bailee. It is considered a bailment whether or not I charge a fee for the loan of the implement. According to Hammurabi's Laws, in order to have a valid bailment contract (at least a bailment for the benefit of the bailor), the agreement had to be in writing, and the objects that were to be bailed had to be shown to witnesses (HAMMURABI ¶¶121–123).

Both the Laws of Lipit-Ishtar and Hammurabi's Laws provide that when a renter broke a rented ox's horn or tail, the renter had to pay one-quarter

---

146. One must be cautious about applying the modern concept of bailment to ancient law collections. Jackson has pointed out this problem clearly. BERNARD S. JACKSON, ESSAYS IN JEWISH AND COMPARATIVE LEGAL HISTORY (ch. 3 "Principles and Cases: The Theft Laws of Hammurabi") 70 (1975) ("It is the anachronistic search for principles which insists on finding common ground between these cases, by subsuming them all beneath the common concept of 'bailee'. But the Laws of Hammurabi have no word for 'bailee'. Such a general conception is entirely absent.").

of the ox's value (in silver) as compensation to the ox's owner (Lipit-Ishtar ¶¶36–37; Hammurabi ¶248).[147] Both Hammurabi's Laws and a student tablet of laws from about 1800 B.C. fixed an oxen renter's damages at one-quarter of the animal's value when he (the renter) severed the ox's hoof tendon (Hammurabi ¶248; Rented Oxen ¶3). Lipit-Ishtar's Laws established damages for the same offense at one-third of the ox's value (Lipit-Ishtar ¶34), and also state that if the renter were to destroy the animal's eye, he had to pay in silver one-half of its value (Lipit-Ishtar ¶35; Rented Oxen ¶1 (same); Hammurabi ¶247 (same)).

Hammurabi's Laws recognize the need to consider fault and negligence when deciding whether a bailee should be liable for the loss of a bailed draft or other domestic animal.[148] For example, ordinarily a bailee of an ox or donkey was not liable to the owner/bailor for loss in the event that a lion killed the animal either "in the open country" or while it was yoked (Hammurabi ¶244; SLHF (vi 32–36)). Presumably, the bailee in this situation could not be responsible for a loss caused by the attack of a wild animal.[149] By the same token, if any other "act of god" caused the ox's death, the bailee was not held responsible (Hammurabi ¶249). On the other hand, if a bailee caused the death of a rented animal "either by negligence or by physical abuse," he was legally bound to replace the animal with another of comparable value (Hammurabi ¶245; see also Hammurabi ¶263).[150] Such negligence apparently included situations where a rented ox was just plain lost (SLEX ¶10').

These rules could create interesting problems of proof. For example, if a renter lost his rented ox, it would be to his advantage to try to prove that a lion had attacked and killed the ox. Also, when a rented ox died "while crossing a river," the general rule was that the renter was liable to the owner for the full value of the ox (Rented Oxen ¶6; SLHF (vi 23–31)). Arguably, the renter should be responsible for deciding when and where to cross a river. That is, perhaps, why Mesopotamian law considered the renter at

---

147. Another set of student-copied laws provided that when a renter cut off an ox's horn, he had to pay one-third of its value. Rented Oxen ¶2. The same student tablet contains a provision specifying damages when the renter cuts off the ox's tail, but the text is too damaged for us to determine what the payment was for such an injury. Rented Oxen ¶4.

148. See supra §3.06[A].

149. For other similar provisions in ancient Mesopotamian collections, see Rented Oxen ¶¶7–8; SLEX ¶9'; SLHF (vi 16–22).

150. Compensation of this sort seems comparable to tort compensation in contemporary America where returning the plaintiff to the status quo ante is the general goal. See also Driver & Miles, Babylonian Laws 438, 455–456, 461, 464.

fault in this situation. Similarly, a bailee, under Hammurabi's Laws, had to replace the animal if he caused damage so severe that it was rendered virtually useless (*i.e.,* broke its leg or cut its neck tendon) (HAMMURABI ¶246).

When the renter of a boat agreed to follow a certain route, if he breached his contract and failed to follow that route, and if the boat sank, he had to both replace the boat and pay the cost ("in grain") of the rental (LIPIT ISHTAR ¶5; SLHF (iv 42–v 11)).[151] A boat renter had to pay as much as one-half the boat's value if he caused certain kinds of damage to it (SLHF (v 12–20)). Hammurabi's Laws provide that a boatman who rented a boat and negligently caused it "to sink or to become lost," had to "replace the boat for the owner of the boat." (HAMMURABI ¶236–237; *see also* LIPIT-ISHTAR ¶4, ESHNUNNA ¶5). If the boatman was able to raise the boat, he only had to pay the owner one-half of its value (HAMMURABI ¶238).

In Hammurabi's Laws, a bailee of grain was strictly liable to his bailor and, in the event of any loss, was required to pay double the amount of grain that was stored (HAMMURABI ¶120).[152] This was the law even in situations where "[t]he contract was merely a gratuitous deposit with a friend for safe custody."[153] Under the Laws of Eshnunna, when a bailee lost bailed goods "without evidence that the house ha[d] been broken into," the bailee had to replace the bailor's goods (ESHNUNNA ¶36). But he did not have to replace bailed goods if they were stolen, so long as some of his property also had been stolen along with the bailed goods (ESHNUNNA ¶37). Hammurabi's Laws changed this rule. According to Hammurabi, even if some of the bailee's goods had been stolen along with the bailor's, the bailee was still liable to the bailor for the loss of the bailed goods: "the householder who was careless shall make restitution and shall restore to the owner of the property that which was given to him for safekeeping and which he allowed to be lost…." (HAMMURABI ¶125).

[5] CONTRACTS ON AN INTERNATIONAL SCALE: TREATIES

It would be difficult to say that the ancient Mesopotamians developed "international law" on any kind of broad scale or in a complex manner. In-

---

151. A student exercise tablet of laws provides that "until he restores the boat" the renter in this situation "shall measure and deliver one-half of its hire in grain to its owner." SLEX ¶3'.

152. *See also* HAMMURABI ¶124 ("If a man gives silver, gold, or anything else before witnesses to another man for safekeeping and he [*i.e.,* the bailee] denies it, they shall charge and convict that man, and he shall give twofold that which he denied.").

153. DRIVER & MILES, BABYLONIAN LAWS 236.

stead, most international law in ancient Mesopotamia was limited to treaties and alliances between or among states. Thus, in many respects, it is suitable to consider these international agreements in the context of general contract law. The Mesopotamians believed that the gods gave mankind international law: a concept of treaties and alliances and the treatment of nations defeated in war. In order to make treaties and alliances binding, leaders had to swear oaths in the presence of the gods. According to Greengus, "the earliest [treaty] example comes from Ebla during the third millennium."[154] Beginning with the Sumerians and then intermittently throughout Mesopotamian history, warring states terminated hostilities by means of formal peace treaties.

A significant portion of what we know about international agreements comes from letters written at Mari at the beginning of the second millennium B.C. (*i.e.*, before the reign of Hammurabi). In order to formalize their alliances, heads of individual states took oaths and performed other rituals or symbolic acts, such as "the touching the throat."[155] Leaders often cemented alliances by arranging a marriage between members of the royal families. Furthermore, when states were about to negotiate regarding the potentiality of becoming allies, they occasionally exchanged hostages to ensure that the discussions would be conducted in good faith. We know of one instance when negotiations failed and the hostages were executed. Ordinarily, when states negotiated a treaty, they agreed not only to a military alliance, but also to extradite criminals and permit free trade and transportation.

[6] MISCELLANEOUS CONTRACT RULES

[A] IMPLIED WARRANTIES

Hammurabi's Laws contain two implied warranties that establish fixed lengths of time for the performance of a product or service. One such law imposes an implied one-year warranty on a boatman's caulking services. Under the terms of the implied warranty, a boatman whose caulking proves to be defective within one year's time must do the work over again at his own expense (HAMMURABI ¶235). The other implied warranty relates to the sale of slaves. If a slave exhibits signs of epilepsy within one month after being sold, the buyer is entitled to revoke acceptance of the slave and the seller is required to return the purchase price to the buyer (HAMMURABI

---

154. SAMUEL GREENGUS, *Legal and Social Institutions of Ancient Mesopotamia, in* 1 CIVILIZATIONS OF THE ANCIENT NEAR EAST at 469, 482.
155. *Id.*; SAGGS, BABYLON 224.

¶278).[156] This is one area where Hammurabi's Laws may have had a normative effect on subsequent legal practice. In the period after the promulgation of Hammurabi's Laws, many slave contracts began including an express warranty of this kind.

[B] ORDER OF PERFORMANCE & TIME FOR PAYMENT

In many contracts the general presumption is that the buyer or bailee will pay the seller or bailor at the time that the seller or bailor transfers possession of the subject property. However, there are certain types of contracts where a buyer's or bailee's performance (i.e., payment) is delayed. For example, when a boatman rented a boat for a period of one year, the presumption was that the boatman would pay the owner/bailor his fee "in grain" at the end of the year (SLHF (v 37–44)). This practical rule permitted a boatman to acquire sufficient grain during the course of the rental period. It would have been impractical to require a boat bailee to pay rental in advance (since it was by using the boat that the renter would acquire enough money to pay the rent).

[C] CONSIGNMENT

There was a special law in Hammurabi's Laws that dealt with consignment contracts. If a consignee failed to deliver goods for his consignor as promised, the consignee was liable to his consignor for five times the amount of property that had been consigned to him (HAMMURABI ¶112).

[D] EXCUSES FOR NON-PERFORMANCE OF A CONTRACT: CONTRACTS VOIDABLE DUE TO IMPOSSIBILITY OR IMPRACTICABILITY

Ordinarily a person who rented a field for cultivation owed the owner a percentage of his yield. If, however, the renter was unable to pay because storms, flooding, or drought had ruined his crops, he was excused from payment for that year ("in that year he will not repay grain to his creditor")

---

156. See DRIVER & MILES, BABYLONIAN LAWS 429 (Also pointing out that a slave was guaranteed not to flee for three days). See also Id. at 479.

(HAMMURABI ¶48).[157] This law recognizes a principle that modern contract law considers an excuse. In modern law we would say that the renter did not have to pay because his performance is either "impossible" or "impractical" due to an unforseen change in circumstances.

[7] REMEDIES FOR BREACH OF CONTRACT

The ancient Mesopotamian law collections contain several provisions that establish damages for breach of contract. Taken as a whole, these provisions tend to give either: 1) expectation damages (*i.e.,* damages intended to put the non-breaching party into the economic position that he would have been in if the breaching party had performed instead of breaching) plus consequential damages (damages that result from the breach and that were reasonably foreseeable at the time of making the contract); or 2) damages that impose penalties for breach of contract and which can have the *in terrorem* effect of deterring breach and coercing performance thereby. A few laws concerning breach of a marriage contract may have been attempts to liquidate damages.

One example of expectation damages can be found in a law of Hammurabi's relating to a gardener who fails to pollinate the date palms in an orchard, causing a decrease in yield. In this provision, the gardener who breached his contract to pollinate the orchard was required to pay the owner "in accordance with his neighbor's yield." (HAMMURABI ¶65). The gardener who breached his contract by failing to pollinate the date palms was required to pay the difference between that which he promised (*i.e.,* pollinated crops that bear fruit) *versus* that which he delivered (*i.e.,* unpollinated, failing crops). The neighbor's yield is used simply as a tool for establishing a reasonable expectation for the yield that the gardener could have achieved if he had kept his bargain (*i.e.,* an analogue for compar-ison).[158]

Several provisions in the Mesopotamian law collections establish penalties for breach of contract. One of Hammurabi's Laws provides for a harsh penalty in the event that a tenant-farmer was unable to "satisfy his obligation" to the field's owner: the insolvent contract breacher was "dragged around through that field by the cattle." (HAMMURABI ¶256). Jurispruden-

---

157. *See Id.* at 141–145. According to Driver & Miles, "The debtor remains liable to repay the capital sum lent but is excused payment of the interest of that year and no more; the other terms of the contract remain in force." *Id.* at 145. *See also* HAMMURABI ¶¶55–56 (cases where floods destroy crops).

158. Driver & Miles note that a number of provisions (*e.g.,* HAMMURABI ¶¶42, 43, 55, 62, 65) use the neighbor's yield as a measure of damages. DRIVER & MILES, BABYLONIAN LAWS 135–136. *See also* HAMMUURABI ¶¶ 233, 232, and SLHF (iv 42–v 11).

tially speaking, it is interesting to see a legal system employing physical punishment as a substitute for money damages when a person was unable to pay the compensation required. One of the Laws of Eshnunna imposes damages for breach of contract that amount to ten times the contract sum (ESHNUNNA ¶9). That law provides that when a workman received one shekel as payment in advance to work as a harvester, if he breached his contract by failing to harvest, then he was required to pay 10 shekels to the man for whom he was supposed to have performed the work. This measure of damages appears punitive and designed to try to coerce the laborer into performing (to avoid having to pay damages by a factor of ten). Presumably, it would cost the landowner less than 10 shekels for every one (*i.e.,* every one shekel that he was paying the original worker) to replace the workman with a substitute laborer.[159]

The laws dealing with breach of promise to marry may have been designed to liquidate damages in an amount which estimates the actual loss that might reasonably occur. Once a man promised to marry a particular woman and brought marriage gifts to her father, if he then changed his mind in favor of another woman, he forfeited the marriage gifts to the woman's father (HAMMURABI ¶159).[160] If, on the other hand, it was the bride's father who changed his mind (not the groom), then the bride's father had to pay the groom twice the value of the marriage gifts that he had brought ("twofold everything that had been brought to him") (HAMMURABI ¶160; UR-NAMMU ¶15; LIPIT-ISHTAR ¶29; ESHNUNNA ¶25).[161]

[C] GENERAL COMMERCIAL LAW

[1] AGENCY

Hammurabi's Laws contain a number of provisions dealing with agency. The Laws contemplate that a principal might give an agent either money (so that he could travel and make investments or purchases) or goods (so

---

159. There is, in addition, a curious law in Hammurabi's Laws that also appears to impose a penalty of sorts—but not really for breach *per se.* That law applies to situations where a seller dies: "If the seller should die, the buyer shall take fivefold the claim for that case from the estate of the seller." HAMMURABI ¶12. For more on this provision *see* Westbrook and Wilcke, *The Liability of an Innocent Purchaser of Stolen Goods,* 25 ARCHIV FÜR ORIENTFORSCHUNG 111, 112–113 (1974–1977). *See also* DRIVER & MILES, BABYLONIAN LAWS 81, 95–105.

160. *See supra* §3.03[B][2].

161. *See* DRIVER & MILES, BABYLONIAN LAWS 252.

that he might trade or sell them). As a rule, the Laws of Hammurabi require an agent to keep a written receipt for his transactions (HAMMURABI ¶¶104–05). In practice, "[n]ormally, loans lent by investing capitalists are due at the safe return of the expedition."[162]

Hammurabi's Laws also impose a duty on the agent to account to his principal for interest over the course of his agency (HAMMURABI ¶100). Hammurabi's Laws regarding agency appear to be, nevertheless, somewhat inconsistent on this issue. One law virtually demands that an agent make a profit for his principal. If an agent failed to make a profit, he was required to pay his principal double the amount that the principal initially gave to him (HAMMURABI ¶101). The next provision in the Laws, however, seems inconsistent. It states that, if an agent incurred a loss, he merely had to return "the amount of the capital sum." (HAMMURABI ¶102). Hammurabi's Laws also excuse an agent if "enemy forces" compelled him to abandon his goods on his journey (HAMMURABI ¶103).[163] An agent who fraudulently denied that his principal had given him money was required to pay his principal treble the amount that he had taken in the first place (HAMMURABI ¶106). A principal who fraudulently denied that his agent had repaid him what was due was required to pay six-times the amount that he (the principal) had given to him (the agent) (HAMMURABI ¶107).

As a rule, a principal who financed a land merchant was entitled to a profit of at least 50% and perhaps as much as two-thirds of the total profit. For a sea merchant, however, the principal ordinarily received a fixed sum rather than a percentage of the profit. Presumably, this was because the risk of total loss was much greater on sea voyages.

[2] BUSINESS ORGANIZATIONS

The two major business organizations in ancient Mesopotamia—the palace and temple—received the lion's share of their income from rents and taxes on agricultural estates. The palace received tribute from abroad, produce, rents, and taxes from its land, and goods produced in the royal workshops. In some respects, the temple also was like a corporation. In addition, professional associations developed and specialized crafts grew from a tradition of both families and clans. During the Old Babylonian period, brewers, smiths, carpenters, and similar artisans and craftsmen organized

---

162. A.L. Oppenheim, *The Seafaring Merchants of Ur*, 74 J. OF THE AMERICAN ORIENTAL SOC. 6, 10 (1954).

163. *See also supra* §3.07[B][6][D] regarding impossibility and impracticability as excuses for non-performance of contractual obligations.

into guilds. These were called *ugula* (Sumerian) or *aklum* (Akkadian). These guilds, however, were not independent like their progeny later in Medieval Europe, but rather operated under the auspices of either a temple or palace. Certain learned professions, however, were organized independently (*i.e.*, not as part of the temple or palace). These were the *mašmaššum* (experts in exorcism and apotropaic rituals), *bârūm* (divination experts), doctors, and scribes. In the Old Babylonian period (*c.* 2000–1600 B.C.), a group of copper importers pooled their capital and shared the risks and profits of their enterprise. There is also some evidence for commercial banking on a limited scale.

A partnership in ancient Mesopotamia, *tappûtum*, was not really analogous to a partnership in modern American law. Instead, their partnerships were more like what we call joint ventures where both the purpose and relationship are relatively temporary. According to Hammurabi's Laws, partners were required to "equally divide the profit or loss." (HAMMURABI gap ¶cc). Based on actual partnership documents, some scholars have interpreted this to mean that partners shared the profit pro rata—"according to the contribution that each has made to the partnership," not that they divided profit and loss "in equal shares."[164] Apparently, when one partner decided to sell his share of the partnership, he was legally required to offer his share for sale first to his fellow partners (*i.e.*, before offering it to any outsider) (ESHNUNNA ¶38).

[3] DEBTOR-CREDITOR LAW

The law collections contain many provisions that relate to debtor-creditor law. Before a man could legally be given credit, he had to have either "received his inheritance share [from his father] or a slave." (ESHNUNNA ¶16).[165] Hammurabi's Laws expressly prohibited a creditor from using self-help to obtain repayment of a loan from his debtor. According to the pertinent provision, a creditor who "has a claim of grain or silver against another man" was not permitted to take grain in repayment himself without the debtor's permission. If he did, he was required to return what he had taken, and, in addition, he forfeited "whatever he originally gave as the loan." (HAMMURABI ¶113). This law must have encouraged the use of the legal system and, at the same time, discouraged self-help (which could easily lead to violence).

Hammurabi's Laws also allowed debtors to repay loans with goods and commodities of equivalent value rather than requiring repayment of loans "in-kind." (HAMMURABI gap ¶¶l,u,v,z; HAMMURABI ¶51). One provision

---

164. DRIVER & MILES, BABYLONIAN LAWS 187 (Citing the work of Eilers).
165. *See supra* §3.07[B][2].

that articulates this rule states that a creditor "will not object; he shall accept it." (HAMMURABI gap ¶z). More than one law, however, synthesizes and balances the last two principles; namely, that a creditor cannot use self-help and that a debtor may satisfy a debt with a payment that is not in-kind. For example, one provision contemplates a situation where a debtor has "nothing to give in repayment" though he does have a pollinated date orchard. This law provides that the debtor in this circumstance may not simply tell his creditor to "Take away as many dates as will be grown in the orchard as payment for your silver." Instead, it requires that the debtor sell the dates himself and then pay back the creditor both the principal and interest on the loan "in accordance with the terms of his contract." (HAMMURABI gap ¶a) (*See also* HAMMURABI ¶¶49–50) (same general principle).

One of Hammurabi's Laws expressly prohibits a creditor from defrauding a debtor by attempting to make a loan "according to the small weight" but taking payment "according to the large weight." (HAMMURABI gap ¶x).[166] The penalty for defrauding a debtor in this way is forfeiture of the entire loan. Another law prohibits a different kind of fraud: mathematical manipulation. If a creditor failed to deduct loan payments or if he added interest payments to the capital sum, the creditor was required to pay back double what the debtor had paid on the loan (HAMMURABI gap ¶w). This law seems punitive since it required the breaching party to repay more than expectation damages.[167]

If a creditor had a valid claim against a debtor, the creditor was legally permitted to "distrain" a member of the debtor's family; essentially holding the person as a "debt-hostage" (*neputum*) until the debt was paid (HAMMURABI ¶¶114–16). But if a man falsely claimed that another owed him a debt and thus held a family member of the falsely accused debtor, Hammurabi's Laws imposed a payment of 20 shekels per family member detained (HAMMURABI ¶114). The Laws of Eshnunna provide that, if the "debt-hostage" is a slave woman and the claim has no merit, the false creditor is required to pay the value of the slave (ESHNUNNA ¶22). If a "debt-hostage" dies a natural death while being held, the debtor has "no basis for a claim." (HAMMURABI ¶115). Presumably the fact that the claim is valid and the fact that the death is natural are essential in absolving the creditor

---

166. The precise interpretation of the language of "small weight" and "large weight" is uncertain, but the general notion of fraud is easy enough to understand. *See* DRIVER & MILES, BABYLONIAN LAWS 181.

167. *See also supra* §3.07[B][7] regarding contract damages.

in this situation. On the other hand, Hammurabi's Laws treat it as a criminal offense if the death of a "debt-hostage" is caused "from the effects of a beating or other physical abuse while in the house of her or his distrainer...." (HAMMURABI ¶116). If the debt-hostage who suffers such violence is the debtor's son, the penalty is capital punishment for the creditor's son (and the debt is absolved) (HAMMURABI ¶116). If the debt-hostage is the debtor's slave, the creditor has to pay 20 shekels of silver (and the debt is absolved) (HAMMURABI ¶116). The Laws of Eshnunna provide yet another variation on this theme (imposing a twofold penalty). If the debt-claim is baseless and the false creditor causes the death of a slave woman held as a debt-hostage, the false creditor has to replace her with two slave women as compensation (ESHNUNNA ¶23).

Also, a debtor voluntarily could sell or give his wife, son, or daughter to a creditor "in debt service" (*kiššātum*) for a maximum of up to three years (HAMMURABI ¶117). If a debtor gave a slave instead of a family member, there was no three-year legal limit on the length of debt service (HAMMURABI ¶118). As a last resort, it is also likely that a court could order a debtor to become a slave to his creditor.

[4] INTEREST RATES

The legal interest rate on a loan of silver in the Laws of Eshnunna is 20% (ESHNUNNA ¶21). Hammurabi's Laws fix the rate of interest for loans ranging from 20% (usually for a loan of money) to 33% (usually for a loan of grain) (HAMMURABI gap ¶t). But if a creditor attempted to charge a rate of interest higher than that permitted by law (*e.g.*, if he tried to charge the 33% grain interest on a 20% interest-bearing loan of silver), his penalty was to "forfeit whatever he had given." (HAMMURABI gap ¶u). Another law collection establishes similar rates. In the anonymous "Laws of X," the interest rate on a loan of 300 silas of grain (*i.e.*, about 300 litres of grain) is 33% (LAWS OF X ¶m). The interest rate on 10 shekels of silver is 20% per year (LAWS OF X ¶n).

[5] WAGES, PRICES, & FIXED-PRICE RENTALS

Mesopotamian laws dictated fixed prices for certain contracts. For example, a bailor of grain paid his bailee one-sixtieth of the amount stored as payment for storage (HAMMURABI ¶121) ("If a man stores grain in another man's house, he shall give 5 silas of grain per kur (i.e., per 300 silas) of grain as annual rent of the granary."). A woman inkeeper was entitled to fifty silas of grain at harvest to repay her for loaning one vat of beer (HAMMURABI ¶111). The Laws of Hammurabi specify a fixed price for the rental of an ox for a year (HAMMURABI ¶242/243). The rental price varies depending upon whether the ox is intended to be used for the rear of the team (1,200 silas of grain) or for the middle of the team (900 silas) (HAMMURABI ¶242/243).[168]

In most of the law collections, there are a number of provisions that specify sale prices, rental prices, and wages for certain types of labor.[169] For example, there are specific laws regulating the following:

* the rental price of oxen (LIPIT-ISHTAR ¶a; HAMMURABI ¶268).
* the rental price of a goat (HAMMURABI ¶270).
* the rental price of a donkey along with its driver (ESHNUNNA ¶10; HAMMURABI ¶269 (for threshing—without the driver)).
* the rental price of a wagon along with oxen and a driver (ESHNUNNA ¶3; HAMMURABI ¶271).
* the rental price of just a wagon (HAMMURABI ¶272).
* the rental price of a boat along with a boatman (ESHNUNNA ¶4).
* the rental price of just a boat (HAMMURABI ¶¶275–277).
* the sale price of various commodities such as: barley (ESHNUNNA ¶1); oil (ESHNUNNA ¶¶1–2); lard (ESHNUNNA ¶¶1–2); bitumen (ESHNUNNA ¶¶1–2); wool (ESHNUNNA ¶1); salt (ESHNUNNA ¶1); beer (LAWS OF X ¶l).
* the wages for various workers[170] such as: a harvester (ESHNUNNA ¶7); winnower (ESHNUNNA ¶8); sickle (ESHNUNNA ¶9A); common laborer (ESHNUNNA ¶11; HAMMURABI ¶257 (agricultural laborer), HAMMURABI ¶273); fuller (ESHNUNNA ¶14); boatman (HAMMURABI ¶¶234, 239); ox driver (HAMMURABI ¶258); herdsman (HAMMURABI ¶261); craftsman (HAMMURABI ¶274); woven-textile worker (HAMMURABI ¶274); linen-worker (HAMMURABI ¶274); stone-cutter (HAMMURABI ¶274); bow-maker (HAMMURABI ¶274); smith (HAMMURABI ¶274); carpenter (HAMMURABI ¶274); leatherworker (HAMMURABI ¶274); reedworker (HAMMURABI ¶274); builder (HAMMURABI ¶274); weaver (LAWS OF X ¶j).

---

168. As a rule, the heavier ox works nearer to the plough and the lighter ox is nearer to the front. DRIVER & MILES, BABYLONIAN LAWS 436. The price stated in these provisions is generally less than that found stated in contemporary documents. In one case as much as one-third less. *Id.*

169. Driver & Miles surmise that the rental rates enumerated in Hammurabi's Laws are for rental by-the-day, although this is not spelled out in the provisions. DRIVER & MILES, BABYLONIAN LAWS 469.

170. Contemporary documents indicate that the actual payments for workers such as these was about double the amount stated in the Laws. BOTTÉRO, WRITING, REASONING, AND THE GODS 164. *See also* DRIVER & MILES, BABYLONIAN LAWS 472 (Stating that the prices in Hammurabi's Laws are generally lower than those found recorded in contemporary contracts).

(One provision from Hammurabi's Laws that contains several of these wages amounts, ¶274, states that a craftsman and a textile worker received five barleycorns of silver per day. At this rate, a worker would have received one shekel of silver for every thirty-six days of work in Hammurabi's era.).

* the fees for a doctor performing various procedures (HAMMURABI ¶¶215–217, 221–223; LAWS OF X ¶¶f–i).
* the fees for a veterinarian (HAMMURABI ¶224).
* the fees for a building contractor (HAMMURABI ¶228).

[6] TAXES

The ancient Mesopotamians were obligated to pay certain taxes at various times throughout antiquity. Citizens were expected to pay taxes and to perform service obligations by maintaining and constructing roads and canals (corveé work), and by serving in the military. Citizens routinely paid direct taxes by making "periodic payments of fixed quantities of grain or metal...or delivery of a specified fraction of the crop harvested on the land...."[171] Unfortunately, we know very little about the specifics of these taxes. In the Ur-Nanshe Dynasty (c. 2500 B.C.), the Ensi (i.e., governor/mayor) and temple exacted taxes from the citizenry. Citizens paid taxes on cattle, fisheries, sheep, marriage, divorce, and even burial. Some taxes could be *paid* in sheep. Urukagina's (Uru-inimgina's) Reforms (c. 2350 B.C.) were designed especially to reduce heavy tax burdens.

In the Early Dynastic period (c. 2400 B.C.), inspectors who were responsible to the Ensi collected taxes. We have evidence from around 2000 B.C. that the Sumerian government "acting through temples, levied heavy customs on imported goods."[172] For the most part, a centralized palace bureaucracy levied and collected taxes, and officials in the palaces and temples recorded incoming taxes. We also know that there were certain import duties levied on specific goods, such as copper. One of Lipit-Ishtar's Laws created a special rule regarding property taxes. If a property owner defaulted on his property taxes, and someone else began paying the property taxes and continued to do so for three years, the person who assumed the tax burden became rightful owner instead of the defaulter (LIPIT ISHTAR ¶18).

The citizens of certain cities enjoyed some degree of exemption from taxes simply by virtue of their citizenship in those cities. For example, the inhabitants of Nippur, Babylon, and Sippar enjoyed special privileges. This

---

171. Ellickson & Thorland, *Ancient Land Law*, 71 CHICAGO-KENT L. REV. 321, 374 (1995).
172. SAGGS, BABYLON 275.

tax-exempt status was called *kidinnūtum*. During the Kassite rule (beginning about 1600 B.C.), the Kassite king frequently exempted Mesopotamian citizens from taxation.

§ 3.08 CHAPTER SUMMARY

[A] PERSONAL STATUS

The earliest law collections reveal a distinction (*i.e.,* a distinction regarding personal freedom and individual rights) between free persons and slaves. The laws of Hammurabi distinguish among the upper class *awilu*, the commoner *mushkenu*, and slaves. Citizens in certain towns enjoyed special privileges that exempted them from military service, public works, and taxation. Although foreigners had few rights outside of their homeland, most Mesopotamian cities permitted foreigners as residents with limited privileges. Sumerian women participated in the citizen Assembly and had greater rights than the women who lived later in the Old Babylonian Period. But the women in Hammurabi's day could own, buy, and sell property.

Most slavery in ancient Mesopotamia resulted from debt, birth, sale, warfare, or famine. The palace and temples owned most slaves at first, then about 2000 B.C. private individuals also acquired the right to own slaves. Slaves could own some property and had certain, limited, marriage rights. There were formalities that had to be observed in order to set a slave free. In some instances, slaves were required to have a particular haircut and on occasion they were bound in chains and shackles.

[B] PROPERTY

Both cylinder seals and ancient kudurrus (*c.* 2000–1600 B.C.) attest that private property was legally recognized. But the interdependence of the people on irrigation for agriculture encouraged cooperation as well as a recognition of individual property rights. Further evidence of the need to respect the property rights of others in the community can be seen in the laws that relate to adjacent property owners. Among the earliest records that we have are contracts from Mesopotamia memorializing the sale of land. Land sale contracts on clay tablets ordinarily describe the property boundaries, state the names of the buyer and seller, price, names of witnesses, and the date. Certain kinds of property, however, such as "a field, orchard, or house of a soldier, fisherman, or state tenant" (*i.e.,* land granted by the Crown), had restricted alienability. Several law collections address issues involved with the leasing of fields. It was common for a leasee to pay about one-third of his yield as a lease payment to his lessor. But if unforseen circumstances (such as a drought or severe storms) caused a lessee's crops to fail, Mesopotamian law ordinarily excused the lessee's payment. Similar principles governed the relationship between a gardener who agreed to cultivate a field and a field owner. Several laws were intended to compensate a property owner for damage done by trespassers. Slaves were considered valuable property. A number of laws were designed to protect the interests of slave owners. For example, there were strict penalties for failure to return a fugitive slave. And several laws provided compensation to a slave owner for damage done by others to his slave.

[C] THE FAMILY

As head of the family, a Mesopotamian father usually had one wife, and he used contracts to govern many family matters (*e.g.,* marriage, divorce, and adoption). Ordinarily, a bride's father reached an agreement for marriage with the groom and the couple observed formalities, customs, and ceremonies in order to effectuate a valid marriage. The groom typically gave two special gifts—the *biblum* and *terhatum*—to the bride's father and/or family. After the gifts were given, the marriage was considered "inchoate" and the bride, depending on her age, might move into the groom's household. Old Babylonian documents use two terms that refer to a dowry (or at least property that has many dowry-like characteristics)—*seriktum* and *nudunnûm*. Although the husband possessed and controlled it during their marriage, Babylonian law treated the dowry as property owned by the wife during her lifetime (and *her* children inherited it). Special laws established liquidated damages in the event that either the bride's father or the groom breached their marriage contract. Both the Laws of Eshnunna and the Laws of Hammurabi provide significant protection to ensure, if a soldier is taken prisoner of war, that his marriage will remain intact in his absence. Ordinarily, men had only one wife at a time, but there were a few exceptions in instances involving priestesses, severe illness, or a wife's misconduct. Some priestesses were entitled to unusual rights in the event of divorce.

Husbands—but not wives—could initiate divorce with merely a declaration of intent to do so. Certain misconduct was deemed justifiable grounds for divorce. Children usually stayed with their father if his divorce was justified. Both the law collections and contemporary marriage contracts indicate that a husband usually was required to pay a settlement to his wife upon diovorce when the divorce was without appropriate cause.

Adopted children acquired rights equal to biological children, and there were harsh penalties for adopted children and their adoptive parents if either denied the existence of the adoption. Apprenticeship was treated in many regards as equivalent to adoption, and both the craftsman and biological parents had specific, reciprocal obligations. Children who disrespected or disobeyed their parents could be either disinherited or punished severely. Old Babylonian law safeguarded the property of a deceased father (*i.e.*, in trust) for the benefit of his children.

[D] INHERITANCE & SUCCESSION

The ancient Mesopotamians used *inter vivos* (*i.e.*, among the living) transfers and adoptions to accomplish the kinds of property transfers that we today accomplish with wills. Otherwise, laws of succession dictated inheritance. As a rule, heirs inherited equal portions of a deceased's estate. Sons had superior inheritance rights. Special rules provided additional funds for a son who needed gifts for marriage. And special rules also permitted a father to bequeath extra inheritance for a "favored son". Particular laws also allowed a father to disinherit a son for cause. A widow inherited a life estate in her deceased husband's house. Her children inherited her dowry equally.

A daughter could inherit either a dowry or a share of her father's estate, especially if she was unmarried, a member of a certain temple group, of if she had no brothers. If acknowledged during the father's life, children born to slaves inherited on an equal basis with other children.

[E] CRIMINAL LAW

Most of our evidence for crime in ancient Mesopotamia is derived from the law collections. Intentional homicide (*i.e.*, murder) and conspiracy to commit intentional homicide were punished by death. Unintentional homicide (*i.e.*, manslaughter) was treated less severely. Typically, theft laws punished a thief by requiring him to pay anywhere from double the stolen object's value to thirty-times its value. One of Hammurabi's theft laws exacted death as a punishment for theft of valuables from a temple or palace, while others provided for fixed payments, and on occasion payments that depended upon the status of the victim. Hammurabi's laws also provided that special compensation would be paid by a municipality when a thief could not be found and also when a victim died in the course of a robbery.

The Laws of Hammurabi had provisions to prevent a minor or a slave from selling goods that he did not actually own. Similarly, Hammurabi's

Laws also contain rules designed to discourage sales on the black market and theft by embezzlement.

A man received the death penalty for rape of a woman who was either married or contracted-for-marriage. Various forms of incest were punished by death or banishment. Mesopotamian law only considered a wife's infidelity as adultery, not a husband's. Ordinarily, adultery was punished by death.

Hammurabi's Laws treated evasion of military service as a capital crime. Hammurabi's Laws also considered abuse of authority by military officers as a capital offense.

The death penalty was imposed for trespass at night and for breaking and entering a house. Hammurabi's Laws imposed the death penalty when a builder's negligence caused a collapse that resulted in another's death (*i.e.,* reflecting a concept of criminal negligence). Penalties for perjury and false accusation varied from flogging and shaving one-half of the perjurer's hair to payment of fines and even death. The law collections also contain criminal sanctions for a variety of conduct, such as priestesses associating with a tavern, witchcraft, false imprisonment and kidnapping, and concealing a criminal. Execution, mutilation, payment of compensation or fines, and banishment were the most common criminal punishments.

[F] TORTS

Mesopotamaian torts rarely fit easily or neatly into our modern legal categories of battery, negligence, and strict liability. We do know, however, that damages were usually higher when an upper class individual was injured and the damages were correspondingly lower when it was a commoner or a slave who was injured. The law collections ordinarily require a tortfeasor to pay a fixed amount of compensation to his victim. Typically, damages are based on several factors such as the relative status of the tortfeasor and his victim, the severity of the injury, the part of the body injured, and the intent (or lack thereof) on the part of the tortfeasor. When a person had been warned of a potential danger under his control and he failed to take remedial measures, if an injury resulted, he was liable. Ordinarily a property owner was responsible for damage caused by his property. Damage caused by oxen, however, is treated less severely than damage caused by other types of property (*e.g.,* flooding streams or canals that were inadequately maintained).

Hammurabi's Laws require that a doctor pay compensation or replace a slave for causing a slave's blindness or death during surgery. If the victim is an upper class citizen instead of a slave, the doctor's punishment is amputation of his hand. Similar provisions govern injuries caused by veterinarians.

Ur-Nammu's Laws and the Laws of Lipit-Ishtar require persons who falsely accuse either a married woman or an unmarried daughter of having had inappropriate sexual relations to pay money damages. Some laws recognize, when a victim either assumes the risk of injury or when a victim's own negligence contributes to his injury (*e.g.*, participation in a "brawl"), that such sonduct on the part of the victim should either reduce or erase the tortfeasor's responsibility.

[G] TRADE, CONTRACTS, & COMMERCIAL LAW

The earliest trading was probably accomplished by barter. The Babylonian merchants (*tamkarum*) traveled extensively to secure goods, such as timber, metals, stone, spices, and perfumes. Seals, witnesses, and writing were standard elements needed for valid contracts. Obligors typically "signed" contracts written in clay by affixing a mark intended for authentication using a cylinder seal, seal ring, or the edge of a garment. Merchants in the Ur III period often used a clay envelope that bore a duplicate copy of the contract that was enclosed. Women had the capacity to contract. Public policy prohibited persons from selling property that had been given to them by the king. Several law collections contain provisions that governed responsibilities between bailors and bailees. Such contracts (*i.e.*, bailment contracts) were deemed valid when in writing and when witnesses were shown the bailed property. Ordinarily, if a bailee's negligence caused damage to the bailed property, the bailee was required to compensate the bailor for his loss (in the case of animals and boats, for example, usually a proportionate percentage of the value of the loss). Hammurabi's Laws imposed strict liability on a grain bailee, and exacted double damages. Individual states used written agreements to formalize treaties and alliances. These international contracts were typically concluded by heads of state observing a number of formailities and rituals to punctuate various terms and conditions. We know of several specific miscellaneous "rules" of contract law: 1) implied warranties of quality (*e.g.*, boat repair, a slave's health/fitness); 2) payment was usually due upon the transfer of the subject property, but could be later depending on the nature of the transaction; 3) a consignee had to pay five-times the value of consigned property for failure to return it to the consignor; and, 4) agricultural renters were excused from payment of rent when drought or flood ruined their crops. The law collections provide several different remedies for breach of contract, depending on the circumstances. Some provisions require a breacher to pay expectation damages, while others impose rather severe penalties.

Beyond laws directly related to contract, a number of laws regulated the operation of business and commerce. For example, agency laws required agents to keep careful records and to account to their principals (often paying them one-half to two-thirds of their profits) both for profits and interest. Although the laws punished agents who fraudulently deprived principals of their share, the laws did, however, excuse agents of liability when highwaymen or enemies robbed them. Mesopotamian law recognized a varitey of business entities such as the palace, temples, craft guilds (*ugula* or *aklum*), and partnerships. Debtor-creditor laws forbade self-help without the debtor's permission, allowed debtors to repay loans using commodities rather than silver, and punished creditors who defrauded (or attempted to defraud) their debtors. But creditors were permitted to take either a slave or family member of a debtor as a debt-hostage (*nepûtum*) as a kind of security until the debt was paid. When a person claiming to be a creditor took a debt-hostage on invalid grounds, the laws treated such a pseudo/false-creditor severely. The laws allowed creditors to charge interst rates from 20% to 33% but punished creditors who over-charged. Certain provisions in the law collections established standard prices for specific types of sales of goods, leases, rentals, and wages for services and labor. Mesopotamian laws mandated that citizens: 1) pay direct property taxes (often in kind); 2) pay some taxes on marriage, divorce, and burial; and, 3) perform service obligations for the good of the community. The government, as a central authority, collected these taxes as well as customs duties on imports. The payment of taxes operated as evidence of ownership. The citizens of certain municipalities enjoyed a degree (at least) of tax exemption.

Unit II

Law in
Ancient Egypt

CHAPTER 4

Background and Beginnings of Egyptian Law

§4.01 INTRODUCTION

The ancient Egyptians knew that law was essential. Egyptian literature routinely contrasts the prosperous life that flourishes when people respect law, with the dismal state of affairs that exists when law has been suspended. The ancient Greeks credited the Egyptians with having a working legal system and laws. Diodorus Siculus went to Egypt in 59 B.C., and in Book I of his *General History*, discussed justice and Egyptian laws. Among other things, Diodorus claimed that five ancient Egyptian kings were known as "lawgivers." To be sure, "[t]he social, agricultural and industrial world of the Nile-Dwellers was not at the mercy of an arbitrary whim on the part of either King or Court, but was governed by a large body of long respected law embodying principles of justice and humanity."[1]

The Egyptians generally used ordinary, everyday words and phrases to record, describe, and explain legal matters. "The Egyptian word that corresponds most closely to our word *law*... is *hp*. This word can also connote custom, order, justice, or right, according to its usage."[2]

---

1. JAMES H. BREASTED, A HISTORY OF EGYPT 242 (1905) [hereinafter "BREASTED, HISTORY OF EGYPT"]. *See also* GIRGIS MATTHA, THE DEMOTIC LEGAL CODE OF HERMOPOLIS WEST XII (1975, preface additional notes, and glossary by George R. Hughes) [hereinafter "MATTHA, THE DEMOTIC LEGAL CODE OF HERMOPOLIS WEST"].

2. Janet H. Johnson, *The Legal Status of Women in Ancient Egypt, in* MISTRESS OF THE HOUSE MISTRESS OF HEAVEN: WOMEN IN ANCIENT EGYPT 175, 176 (Anne K. Chapel and Glenn E. Markoe eds., 1996). *See* R.O. FAULKNER, A CONCISE DICTIONARY OF MIDDLE EGYPTIAN 158 (1981) (Faulkner defines *hp* as "law, ordinance."). *See also* ELLEN BEDELL, CRIMINAL LAW IN THE EGYPTIAN RAMESSIDE PERIOD (Brandeis University, Ph.D. Dissertation) 11 (1973) [hereinafter "BEDELL, CRIMINAL LAW"]("In the Egyptian language the word *hp*, which appeared in the Middle Kingdom, signified 'law,' or 'regulation.'").

As early as the Old Kingdom (c. 2700–2200 B.C.), the Egyptians envisioned the god Osiris as a judge. And, apparently, there was already a legal system in place before then; perhaps by the 1st and 2nd Dynasties (c. 3150–2700 B.C.). The kings of this period received kingship from the gods with the understanding that they were to rule in accordance with the laws of the land. To this end, the early kings issued decrees. Because the Egyptians considered the king a god, he represented an unquestioned source of law. In short, the king's word had the force of law.

In this formative period, although the new State needed rules and regulations for administrative procedure and precedent, it seems unlikely that there were any written laws. The king and/or *ma'at* (roughly translated "justice"[3]) were responsible for laws. There was no legislative body and no legislation as such. Indeed, the earliest Egyptians must have thought that written laws were unnecessary in a world where the king was conceived of as a god incarnate. Thus, the king's word expressed divine law that was in harmony with the concept of *ma'at*. Presumably, the vizier[4] and local judges based their decisions on custom. And, theoretically, custom derived from the word of the god-king and his three divine qualities of *Hu, Sia,* and *Ma'at* (Authority, Perception, and Justice). In turn, the vizier and local judges must have rationalized that the omniscient will of the king dictated local custom. *Ma'at* was the one unifying, impersonal factor that influenced the judges' decisions. The god-king was both subject to and the earthly interpreter of *Ma'at*.

Thus, the situation in the 1st and 2nd Dynasties (c. 3150–2700 B.C.) was very different from the condition in Mesopotamia at the same time, where a tradition of written laws on public display was already evolving.[5] Since there were no written laws available for the early viziers to consult and follow, the kings simply instructed them to judge impartially and to avoid allowing favoritism to influence their decisions. To be sure, each vizier must have relied on his own subjective sense of fairness.

The Middle Kingdom (c. 2040–1674 B.C.) scribes recorded a large number of judicial documents. During the New Kingdom (c. 1552–1069 B.C.), a community of workers, who were employed to build tombs for the pharaohs, lived at Deir el-Medina. We have numerous contracts and records of lawsuits that they recorded on ostraca (pieces of broken pottery).[6] After the

---

3. *See infra* § 4.03.
4. *See infra* § 5.04.
5. *See supra* § 1.02.
6. *See infra* § 5.03[C].

political upheaval of the Amarna period (*c.* 1350 B.C.), the pharaoh no longer could claim his word as law. Instead, he came to be subject to impersonal law. Also priests began asserting their control over the civil courts. At the end of the 18th Dynasty, the pharaoh Horemhab (*c.* 1323–1294 B.C.) promulgated a well-known edict that contains a great deal of information about law. But his edict was not a law code per se. Instead, it was "a series of police regulations directed against specific malpractices and also a reorganization of the administrative machinery in the land, in order to control future abuses."[7] Shortly after Horemhab's Edict, Seti I (*c.* 1294–1279 B.C.) issued his Nauri Decree. Written in stone (literally) the Nauri Decree was eventually discovered in Nubia. According to Bedell, Seti I's Nauri Decree "gave privileges and exemptions to the temple of Osiris at Abydos, but it outlined a series of possible crimes against persons and property belonging to the Estate, and very specific punishments for the perpetrators of these offenses."[8] A decree that bears similarities to the Nauri Decree has been found at Elephantine. It is likely that Ramses III (*c.* 1186–1154 B.C.) promulgated that decree. It contains protections for the temple there dedicated to Khnum.

Scholars have debated whether the ancient Egyptians used a written code or collection of laws. We have not yet discovered, as we have from the same period in Mesopotamia,[9] any written law collections from ancient Egypt. Some Egyptologists have maintained, nevertheless, that they did have written laws. For example, Breasted, in his book *A History of Egypt* remarks: "There was a body of highly elaborated law, which has unfortunately perished entirely."[10] Erman comments: "The laws which guided the king and courts in their decisions are unfortunately unknown to us."[11]

7. See JOHN WILSON, THE CULTURE OF ANCIENT EGYPT 237 (1951) [hereinafter "WILSON, CULTURE OF ANCIENT EGYPT"]; *See also* NICOLAS GRIMAL, A HISTORY OF ANCIENT EGYPT 243 (Ian Shaw trans. 1992) [hereinafter "GRIMAL, ANCIENT EGYPT"] ("He set out in this edict the measures with which he was addresssing the abuses that had taken place due to over-centralization in Amenophis IV's reign. *** To this end Horemhab appointed judges and regional tribunes.... Legal power was split between Upper and Lower Egypt, shared between Thebes and Memphis respectively."); *Id.* at 74–75 (Noting that the 4th Dynasty King Shepsekaf also issued "a decree—the earliest known edict—which safeguarded the funerary estates of the earlier kings...."); BEDELL, CRIMINAL LAW 2; *Id.* at 151–152; BREASTED, HISTORY OF EGYPT 406.
8. BEDELL, CRIMINAL LAW 18. *See also Id.* at 151 (Referring to the Nauri Decree.).
9. *See supra* § 1.02.
10. BREASTED, HISTORY OF EGYPT 81. *See also Id.* at 165 ("The law ... has not survived...."); *Id.* at 242 ("Unfortunately the code ... has perished.").
11. ADOLF ERMAN, LIFE IN ANCIENT EGYPT 141 (original English trans. 1894 by H.M. Tirard, 1971) (footnotes omitted) [hereinafter "ERMAN, LIFE IN ANCIENT

Some of the early scholars who assumed that the Egyptians did have written laws once based that assumption, at least in part, on the belief that the forty objects depicted in artistic representations of the vizier were scrolls containing written laws to which the vizier could refer for help in his decision making. More recent study suggests that these objects were not scrolls of written laws but rather "were forty leather thongs which were the symbols of his disciplinary authority."[12] Indeed, other Egyptologists have argued that the earliest Egyptians did not have written laws. Théodorides, for example, expresses his skepticism, stating: "We have, after all, collections of Sumerian, Akkadian, Hittite, and Neo-Babylonian laws—but nothing of the kind from Egypt." "The Nile valley has given us no code, nor any copious theoretical treatises, but the application of law is coherent, despite peculiar features of procedure—the important point being that there was a procedure, with laws to organize it."[13] Recently, however, Lorton has positively maintained that "we now know for a certainty that law codes did exist in Pharaonic times, thanks to the fact that a recently published papyrus of 12th Dynasty date cites by subject matter five laws dealing with fugitives."[14] It is significant also that there exists a collection of laws from Hermopolis (the so-called "Hermopolis Legal Code") that may date from the first millennium B.C. Indeed it represents the first concrete evidence for written laws in ancient Egypt and appears to date from the 24th Dynasty (c. 700 B.C.). Our copy is probably from the third century B.C. It is the only extant Egyptian analogue to the great law collections from Mesopotamia. And, like its Mesopotamian cousins, it may be a collection of case decisions (or summaries) rather than a law "code" per se. Therefore, this Unit refers to the Hermopolis document not as a "code" but rather as "the Law Collection of Hermopolis." It contains sections concerning matters such as leasing real estate, contracts relating to a husband's marital obligations, family law, and inheritance. Nevertheless, whether the Egyptians had written laws or not, it seems certain that law played a significant role in their daily lives.

Egypt"]. *See also* David Taylor, *Law under the Pharaohs* 6 Pol'y Rev. 66 (1980); Lexikon der Ägyptolgie, Vol. 5 (1984), "Recht" 185.

12. Wilson, Culture of Ancient Egypt 172 (footnote omitted).

13. Aristide Théodorides, *The Concept of Law in Ancient Egypt, in* The Legacy of Egypt 291 (J.R. Harris ed. 1971) [hereinafter "Théodorides, *Concept*"]; *Id.* at 320 (footnote omitted). Théodorides also states: "Even documents relating to the legal practice are rare...." *Id.* at 291. *See also* Rudolf Anthes, *The Legal Aspect of the Instruction of Amenemhet,* 16 J. Near Eastern Stud. 176, 180 (1957) ("No codification of laws existed in Egypt, to our knowledge.").

14. David Lorton, *The Treatment of Criminals in Ancient Egypt,* 20 J. Economic & Social Hist. of the Orient 2, 5 (1977) (footnote omitted).

Since no written laws (*i.e.*, statutes) survive (at least from before the 24th Dynasty), scholars traditionally have turned to contracts, wills, deeds, family archives, and accounts of criminal trials as sources for ancient Egyptian law. "The legal documents which have been preserved are less numerous than one might have expected. Some wills were discovered . . ., as well as deeds of sale, census-lists, &c."[15] Such sources enable us to reconstruct a sketch of ancient Egyptian law. This sketch reveals both complexity and evolution. We see rules relating to such diverse topics as criminal law, sucession, wills, marriage and family law, property, contracts, and taxes. On balance, the substantive laws appear to have been designed to empower individuals and, to some degree, to promote fairness and equality. We even have evidence regarding international law. As Théodorides remarks: "[W]hat is striking is the modernity of this law. It gives Egyptian civilization, though remote in time, a structure close to that with which we are familiar."[16]

In addition to the legal documents available, literary evidence is also helpful. For example, in one Middle Kingdom text, *The Admonitions of an Egyptian Sage*, the protagonist describes the disorderly nature of Egypt during the First Intermediate Period (*c.* 2200–2040 B.C.) when chaos reigned and the judicial system was not functioning as it should:

> Indeed, the laws / of the council chamber are thrown out; indeed, men walk on them in public places, and poor men break them up in the streets.
> Indeed, the poor man has attained to the state of the Nine Gods, and the erstwhile procedure of the House of the Thirty is divulged.
> Indeed, the great council-chamber is a popular resort, and poor men come and go in the Great Mansions.[17]

Many other works of ancient Egyptian literature, specifically Middle Egyptian fiction, also provide valuable insight into law. Consequently, this Unit incorporates some literary evidence to supplement the detatched legal documents.[18] Indeed, in discussing the reliability of historical sources for the Middle Kingdom, Gardiner states:

---

15. Sir Alan Gardiner, Egyptian Grammar 23 (3d ed. 1978) (footnote omitted) [hereinafter "Gardiner, Egyptian Grammar"].

16. Théodorides, *Concept* at 320.

17. The Literature of Ancient Egypt 218 (William Kelly Simpson ed. 1972) (footnotes omitted) [hereinafter "Simpson, The Literature of Ancient Egypt"].

18. Despite certain weaknesses inherent in using literature as a source for legal study (*See* Edmund S. Meltzer, Book Review, 104.2 J. Am. Oriental Soc'y 363 (reviewing Robert Parant, L'affaire Sinouhe. Tentative d'approache de la justice repressive égyptienne au debut du II millenaire av. J.C. (1982)), many scholars have argued rather convincingly that such a law and literature approach is

If it be asked where our best historical material is to be found, our answer may seem to be almost a contradiction in terms; it is to be found in Egyptian fiction, where the authors were able to depict existing conditions and to vent their feelings with a freedom impossible when the predominant intention was that of boasting.[19]

§ 4.02 BASIC NOTIONS OF JUSTICE

In the Egyptian "judgment of the dead," the god Horus (the falcon-headed god) weighs the heart of the deceased (the heart symbolically represents the "soul") in scales against an ostrich feather. The woman who accompanies Horus is the goddess Ma'at, who symbolizes justice. The ostrich feather is Ma'at's symbol. She is often depicted wearing this "feather of truth" on her head, as something like a hat. As far as the ancient Egyptians were concerned, the judgment scene of Horus and Ma'at weighing the heart of the departed in the underworld was *the judgment*. If the heart is heavier than the feather, that means that it is heavy with evil deeds (*i.e.,* not full of truth and justice). When that happens, a special beast (the "devourer") summarily eats the departed. On the other hand, if the heart bal-

---

sound. *See e.g.,* T.G.H. JAMES, PHARAOH'S PEOPLE: SCENES FROM LIFE IN IMPERIAL EGYPT 74 (1984) ("Indeed, the evidence provided by literature is often of a particularly significant kind; for it may incorporate attitudes of mind and descriptions of procedures which are quite specific and very informative"); RICHARD POSNER, LAW AND LITERATURE: A MISUNDERSTOOD RELATION 1–17 (1988); JAMES B. WHITE, THE LEGAL IMAGINATION: STUDIES IN THE NATURE OF LEGAL THOUGHT AND EXPRESSION (1973); Sanford Levinson, *Law as Literature,* 60 TEX. L. REV. 373 (1982); Richard Weisberg, *Coming of Age Some More: "Law and Literature" Beyond the Cradle,* 13 NOVA L. REV. 107 (1988); Robert H. Weisberg, *The Law-Literature Enterprise,* 1 YALE J.L. & HUMAN. 1 (1988); Richard Weisberg, *Family Feud: A Response to Robert Weisberg on Law and Literature* 1 YALE J.L. & HUMAN. 69 (1988); Marijane Camilleri, Comment, *Lessons in Law From Literature: A Look at the Movement and a Peer at Her Jury,* 39 CATH. U. L. REV. 557 (1990).

19. SIR ALAN GARDINER, EGYPT OF THE PHARAOHS 61 (1961) [hereinafter "GARDINER, EGYPT OF THE PHARAOHS"]; Georges Posener, *Literature,* in THE LEGACY OF EGYPT 220, 251 (J.R. Harris ed., 2d ed. 1971) ("Egyptian literature was . . . essentially secular in its *raison d' être.* It had an independent existence and was cultivated for its own sake, for the mere pleasure it gave, and for the benefit of society and mankind."). *See also Id.* at 252.

Nevertheless, any reconstruction of this type is tentative. Gardiner reminds us that even with respect to what we might call Egyptian History: "It must never be forgotten that we are dealing with a civilization thousands of years old and one of which only tiny remnants have survived. What is proudly advertized as Egyptian history is merely a collection of rags and tatters." GARDINER, EGYPT OF THE PHARAOHS 53.

ances with the feather (*i.e.,* if it is in balance with justice), that means that the soul is full of righteousness, goodness, truth, and justice, and ought not be terminated. Thoth, the sacred god of scribes, also attends this weighing-in ceremony as evaluator (a court reporter, perhaps) and records the results. This visual representation provides an introduction to at least some aspects of how ancient Egyptians might have perceived justice. It seems simplistic. But it was so important to the ancient Egyptians that they made it a central part of their theology. As a rule, it is often impossible to separate the secular from the religious in analyzing ancient Egypt. There are strong religious overtones in nearly everything that the Egyptians did. Therefore, although this judgment scene is, strictly speaking, a religious representation, it still serves as a useful starting point for reflecting on and appraising the ancient Egyptians' sense of law and justice.

§4.03 MAʿAT

As a goddess, *Maʿat* held an important place in the Egyptian pantheon. As an abstract concept, *maʿat* significantly influenced individual and collective conduct in the daily life of the Egyptians. In mythology, *Maʿat* was the daughter of the sun god, Re. As mentioned before, when a person was judged after death, *Maʿat's* symbol, the ostrich feather of truth, was weighed against the deceased's heart. The goddess *Maʿat* was also important to judges and to their sense of duty. Judges were considered "priests of *Maʿat*," and many wore a small figure of the goddess as a pendant around their necks to symbolize their judicial office. To the ancient Egyptians, the concept *maʿat* was a central overriding principle in law. *Maʿat* represented a universal harmony and order—the way that things are supposed to be. *Maʿat* became the focal point of the legal system. *Maʿat* represented the natural order and balance of life in ancient Egypt. It had a religious, ethical, and moral connotation. It was the guiding principle for all aspects of life and represented the values that all people sought. "On a cosmic scale it represented order as opposed to primeval chaos; an order maintained through truth, justice, balance, tradition, and the virtually whole inventory of Egyptian principles."[20]

Grimal observes: "*Maʿat* occupies a unique place in the Egyptian pantheon: she is not so much a goddess as an abstract entity. She represents the equilibrium which the universe has reached through the process of cre-

---

20. McDowell, Jurisdiction 23 (footnote omitted).

ation, enabling it to conform to its true nature. As such, she is moderator of all things, from justice to the integration of a dead man's soul into the universal order at the time of the final judgment."[21]

Perhaps the most lucid and insightful explanation of *ma'at* as an abstract principle is Wilson's discussion in his book *The Culture of Ancient Egypt*. Wilson describes *ma'at* as a concept that is:

> variously translated as "truth," "justice," "righteousness," "order," and so on. Each of those translations may be apt in a certain context, but no one English word is always applicable. *Ma'at* was a quality which belonged to good rule or administration, but it cannot be translated as "rule," "government," "administration," or "law." *Ma'at* was the proper quality of such applied functions. Basically, *ma'at* had some of the same flexibility as our English terms "right," "just," "true," and "in order." It was the cosmic force of harmony, order, stability, and security, coming down from the first creation as the organizing quality of created phenomena and reaffirmed at the accession of each god-king of Egypt.**** The opposites of *ma'at* were words which we translate as "lying," "falsehood," and "deceit." That which was not consonant with the established and accepted order could be denied as being false. *Ma'at* comes closest to the moral connotation of our word "good."[22]

Tobin sums it up well when he states: "To the Egyptian mind, *ma'at* bound all things together in an indestructible unity: the universe, the natural world, the state, and the individual were all seen as parts of the wider order generated by *ma'at*."[23]

§ 4.04 JUSTICE & JURISPRUDENCE: THE ROLE OF LAW

[A] OVERVIEW

In addition to the universal concept of *ma'at*, several other important precepts and values helped to shape the character of justice and legal philosophy. In his tomb inscription, the vizier Rekhmire (*c.* 1479–1425 B.C.)

---

21. GRIMAL, ANCIENT EGYPT 47.
22. WILSON, CULTURE OF ANCIENT EGYPT 48.
23. Vincent Tobin, *Ma'at and Dike: Some Comparative Considerations of Egyptian and Greek Thought*, 24 J. AM. RESEARCH CENTER IN EGYPT 113 (1987).

articulated his approach to the administration of justice. Here we see aspects of his legal philosophy manifest in his recorded deeds:

> I judged both [the insignificant] and the influential; I rescued the weak man from the strong man; I deflected the fury of the evil man and subdued the greedy man in his hour...I succoured the widow who has no husband; I established the son and heir on the seat of his father. I gave [bread to the hungry], water to the thirsty, and meat, oil and clothes to him who had nothing...I was not at all deaf to the indigent. Indeed I never took a bribe from anyone...[24]

Prominent among the influential precepts and values in Egyptian jurisprudence are the following: 1) a strong preference for tradition as opposed to change (and a belief closely linked to tradition—the conviction that the world was basically secure and operating in a fixed, regular, and natural order—ma'at); 2) a view that rhetorical skill should be esteemed; and, 3) as Rekhmire's inscription illustrates, a desire to achieve impartiality and social equality.

[B] TRADITION & SECURITY

Perhaps no civilization has ever been so attached to tradition as the ancient Nile dwellers. They were conservative in the extreme. One explanation of why traditional things were settled and immutable is that nature supplied the Egyptians a secure world with fixed, harmonic routines. First, the topography of the Nile valley provided inherent protection from foreign invasion. Second, the consistent annual inundation of the river fostered a confidence in the orderliness of life and dictated recurring rituals, farming practices, and legal proceedings (e.g., redrawing property boundaries). This reverence for the past influenced the development of law in at least two ways that are actually interconnected. First, the judges kept records of their legal decisions in the vizier's archives so that they could consult them later as precedent. Consequently, and this is the second result of the Egyptian veneration for tradition, Egyptian law was very slow to evolve. The convention of vigorously following precedent meant that laws tended to remain in force without modification for extremely long periods of time.

---

24. T.G.H. JAMES, PHARAOH'S PEOPLE: SCENES FROM LIFE IN IMPERIAL EGYPT 57 (1984). See also BEDELL, CRIMINAL LAW 20 (Referring to the instructions for Rekhmire when he was installed as vizier. According to Bedell, "the vizier, as supreme judge, and the judges of local courts throughout Egypt were equipped with laws and instructions given directly by Pharaoh.").

[C] IMPARTIALITY & SOCIAL EQUALITY

Impartiality and equality are core concepts and essential components of basic fairness. These notions dictate that persons who are situated similarly ought to be treated similarly before the law. In the history of Egypt, the pinnacle of concern for legal neutrality and equality occurred during the late First Intermediate Period and Middle Kingdom (*c.* 2200–1785 B.C.). The instructions for the vizier Merikare emphasize the importance of judging objectively:

> The abomination of the god is a show of partiality. So this is the instruction; thou shalt act accordingly: thou shalt look upon him whom thou knowest like him whom thou dost not know, upon him who is close to thy person like him who is distant from thy house. As for the official who acts thus, he will flourish here in this office.[25]

In the same instruction, "the creator-god states that he has made all men equal in opportunity and that, if there be any violation of this equality, the fault is man's."[26] The early Middle Kingdom was a time when the Egyptians developed in their legal perspective a:

> disregard of political or economic barriers in the belief that all men have equal rights and opportunities — or should have such. It seems clear... that there was a belief in social justice for everybody at this time and that even the poorest man had rights to the gifts of the gods because the creator-god "made every man like his fellow."[27]

Wilson interprets this outlook as unique in human history, commenting: "When we consider that they stood more than a thousand years ahead of similar thinking by the Hebrews and the Greeks, we must give them all credit for a sublime vision."[28]

---

25. WILSON, CULTURE OF ANCIENT EGYPT 173 (footnote omitted).

26. *Id.* at 117. *See also* Théodorides, *Concept* at 307–308 (The Instructions for the Vizier, whose "composition must go back to the Thirteenth Dynasty," say that "justice is to be rendered in public and in such a way that every individual shall always secure his rights. To this end, appeal is made to a sense of equity and also, by implication, to jurisprudence....") (footnote omitted).

27. WILSON, CULTURE OF ANCIENT EGYPT 123. *See also Id.* at 314 ("[T]he Egyptians discovered the worth of the common man and insisted upon his sacred right to justice.").

28. *Id.* at 124.

[D] MA'AT, JUSTICE, & JURISPRUDENCE IN
THE TALE OF THE ELOQUENT PEASANT

The Tale of the Eloquent Peasant is a work of Middle Egyptian fiction that offers a wealth of material relating to ancient Egyptian notions of justice and jurisprudence. Khunanup is a peasant who is on his way to market when a noble named Nemtynakhte seizes his possessions and beats him. For most of the story Khunanup pleads his case against Nemtynakhte to the judge, Rensi. The peasant makes nine speeches before the judge. Three jurisprudential principles in the story stand out from the rest. First, justice is something that should be available to the poor and disadvantaged on an equal basis with the rich. Second, the story suggests that law is fundamentally a natural force, like the sun, wind, wild animals, or the current in the Nile. Third, it implies that a judge's duty is to control the natural force of law. Although there are many examples that illustrate these precepts, it will suffice here to mention only a few.

Khunanup, the peasant, frequently implores the judge, Rensi, not to be tempted by bribes and not to be influenced by the fact that he (*i.e.,* Khunanup) is a poor man. Thus, macroscopically, this tale is an exhortation to the judiciary to ignore class distinctions in decisionmaking and to concentrate, rather, on what is right.[29] Indeed, in the Middle Kingdom (*c.* 2040–1785 B.C.) "[i]t was ... not only religious belief and social axiom, but also formally announced royal policy, that before the bar of justice the great and the powerful must expect the same treatment and the same verdict accorded to the poor and the friendless."[30] In his second speech, Khunanup

---

29. *See* WILSON, CULTURE OF ANCIENT EGYPT 120 (Wilson observes that *The Tale of the Eloquent Peasant* "gives us the clear argument that *ma'at*-justice was not a neutral maintenance of past order or a negative repair of breaches of order but a positive search for new good."); *Id.* at 120–122 (Wilson interprets *The Tale of the Eloquent Peasant* and other Middle Kingdom texts as important for our understanding of *ma'at* and the broadened scope of that concept in the Middle Kingdom.); *Id.* at 122 ("*Ma'at* in the texts of this age did not carry its customary connotation of static order; it was not a matter of the pharaoh offering *ma'at* to the gods in token of the fact that the god-given order was stable and unchanging. *Ma'at* here was the positive force of social justice, of man's humanity to man. It was a magistrate who could be likened to the ferryman who carried over the poor widow without exacting a fare. It was a king who could be likened to a herdsman who wearied himself on behalf of his flock. In this near-democratic age, the emphasis was not upon the rights of the ruler but upon the rights of the ruled.").

30. JAMES HENRY BREASTED, THE DEVELOPMENT OF RELIGION AND THOUGHT IN ANCIENT EGYPT 252 (1912) [hereinafter "BREASTED, DEVELOPMENT OF RELIGION AND THOUGHT"]. *Cf.* JON MANCHIP WHITE, EVERYDAY LIFE IN ANCIENT EGYPT 131 (1963) (White makes the dubious claim that "questions of right and wrong were civil

addresses the judge, Rensi. He calls him the "Steering Oar of heaven, beam of earth, plumbline which carries the weight! O Steering oar, do not diverge; O Beam, do not tilt; O Plumbline, do not swing awry."[31] These metaphors are illuminating. Each—an oar, a beam, and a plumbline—is a man-made, physical device used by humans to control or measure natural forces. An oar makes it possible for people to direct their path in the water and temporarily to subvert the current and the wind. A wooden architectural beam contains the force of gravity. A plumbline uses gravity as a means to achieve or test verticality. Similarly, a judge is one who controls the law. Thus, these metaphors suggest that Rensi, like the oar, beam, and plumbline, is in a position to control a natural force too: namely, law. Thus, the ancient Egyptians viewed justice as being something like the forces of nature; a river's current, wind, or gravity. These images imply that Khunanup viewed law as a universal constant, a natural law.[32] It would be understandable if the ancient Egyptians perceived law as a natural phenomenon. As has been noted earlier,[33] the regularity of the Nile's annual inundation must have instilled in the minds of the ancient Egyptians a confidence in the natural order of the universe.[34]

Again in his third petition, Khunanup portrays justice as a physical device used to control or measure the natural order, like scales which are controlled by the force of gravity: "Will the balance deflect? Will the stand-balance incline to one side?"[35] Khunanup persists in using scale imagery to

---

questions, not religious ones. Morality was a social and legal matter, whereas religion was mainly concerned with magic.").

31. SIMPSON, THE LITERATURE OF ANCIENT EGYPT 36.

32. *See generally* JEROME HALL, FOUNDATIONS OF JURISPRUDENCE 21–53 (1973).

33. *See supra* § 4.04[B].

34. *See generally* GARDINER, EGYPT OF THE PHARAOHS 27–44.

35. SIMPSON, THE LITERATURE OF ANCIENT EGYPT 39. Scales are a symbol of impartiality. *See* Nili Shupak, *A New Source For the Study of the Judiciary and Law of Ancient Egypt: "The Tale of the Eloquent Peasant"*, 51 J. NEAR E. STUD. 1, at 16, n. 57 (1992) ("As in the case of the scales, which record an incorrect weight as a result of being unbalanced, so does the liar harm the norm of justice. For this reason, the judge overseeing justice is compared to a pair of scales and to a plummet and parts of his body to parts of the scales."). In his discussion of *The Eloquent Peasant*, Breasted notes that the scales "form a symbol which became widely current in Egyptian life, till the scales appear as the graphic means of depicting the judgment of each soul in the hereafter." BREASTED, DEVELOPMENT OF RELIGION AND THOUGHT 221–222. Breasted also relates a story of a vizier who perhaps went too far in his attempt to appear impartial:

In the Feudal Age [*i.e.*, the Middle Kingdom], a thousand years after the rise of the Old Kingdom, at the installation of the vizier, that official used to be referred to the example of an ancient vizier who had already become proverbial in the Pyramid Age. The cause of his enduring reputation was that he had decided a case, in which his relatives were involved, against his

describe the judiciary: "Is he a balance? It does not tilt. Is he a stand-balance? It does not incline to one side." "Does a balance tilt? It is its scalepans which weigh things . . ."[36] The prevalence of imagery representing man-made objects that are used to control and harness nature is striking. Such images imply that the ancient Egyptians considered law a natural force and considered that a judge's task was to manage and direct that natural force.

Khunanup perceives justice as a natural function, like breathing, shade, shelter, food, warmth, water, and a flooding river. He says: " 'The doing of justice is breath to the nose.' "[37] "Shade, do not act as the sun-heat; Shelter, do not let the crocodile take." The statement, "his possessions are (the very) breath to a poor man, and to take them away is to stop up his nose,"[38] echoes the peasant's earlier references to those who provide support for children, wives, and other dependents. A good judge is satiety for hunger, the sky's warmth for the cold, and water for thirst.[39] In the eighth petition, Khunanup characterizes good judges as "shelter from the aggressive."[40] The petitions also, not surprisingly, contain references to the inundation of the Nile. In the third petition, Khunanup argues that Rensi must "[r]estrain the robber, take counsel for the poor man . . . [and that he must] . . . not become an inundation against the petitioner."[41]

§ 4.05 CHAPTER SUMMARY

Although the ancient Egyptians had a functional legal system, it appears that they had little in the way of written law until about the eighth century B.C. Even then, the written law may not have been statutory, in the modern sense. We have abundant evidence for law in Egypt. Contracts, wills, accounts of trials, and records of taxation provide useful information. Evidence from literature supplements these traditional sources too. Still, the Egyptians did not develop a technical legal vocabulary, but instead used ordinary language to express law and legal concepts.

---

own kin, no matter what the merits of the case might be, lest he should be accused of partial judgment in favor of his own family.
Id. at 167 (footnote omitted). *See also Id.* at 243–244.
36. SIMPSON, THE LITERATURE OF ANCIENT EGYPT 47.
37. *Id.* at 39.
38. *Id.* at 43.
39. *Id.* at 43–44.
40. *Id.* at 46.
41. *Id.* at 39. Apparently, the judge and not the flood itself should be the one who controls the flooding.

In the Old Kingdom (*c.* 2700–2200 B.C.), the god-king established law simply through his presence on earth and his own volition. Custom and *Ma'at*, the Egyptian abstract sense of justice, guided the king's command. By the time of the New Kingdom (*c.* 1552–1069 B.C.), courts such as the local court at Deir el-Medina served communities to provide objective arbitration for citizens. Also in the New Kingdom, pharaohs such as Horemhab (*c.* 1323–1295 B.C.) and Seti I (*c.* 1294–1279 B.C.) issued edicts and decrees to address specific problems and to institute sweeping changes throughout Egypt.

The scene of the Judgment of the Dead symbolically illustrates some of the fundamental aspects of law in the abstract for the ancient Egyptians. A man's heart—representing his life deeds—must balance with *Ma'at's* feather. *Ma'at's* feather represented the totality of justice and truth. The goddess *Ma'at* symbolized the abstract principles of universal harmony and the natural order of the cosmos. *Ma'at* was ethical, moral, religious, and legal truth rolled into one. *Ma'at* represented equilibrium.

To implement *Ma'at*, the ancient Nile dwellers promoted certain values and protected individual interests in their quest to achieve justice. For example, the vizier, the most important judicial official, recognized the need to protect the weak and disadvantaged. He knew also how important it was not only to *be* impartial but also to *appear* impartial as well. The Egyptian sense of jurisprudence prized precedent and tradition. *The Tale of the Eloquent Peasant* illustrates that they considered: 1) that justice should be available for the poor as well as the rich; 2) that justice was a natural force; and 3) that judges were persons empowered to interpret and channel the tremendous force of the law to benefit humankind.

CHAPTER 5

Legal Procedure, Institutions, & Organization

§ 5.01 INTRODUCTION

Lorton asserts that "there were no professional judges or courts in our sense of the term."[42] Thus, it may be best to be skeptical about historical traditions relating to court structures and systems during pharaonic Egypt. Indeed, little is known about the courts during the Old Kingdom (c. 2700–2200 B.C.). During the New Kingdom (c. 1552–1069 B.C.), the vizier presided over the so-called "Great Court." In addition, ad hoc panels of judges could be commissioned to deal with individual cases such as the harem conspiracy trials or prosecutions of royal tomb robbers.[43] In short, for major crimes like theft of State property, tomb violation, or treason, the pharaoh often employed special investigative comissions. Other local courts handeled matters in individual communities. We know a fair amount about one such local court that operated at Deir el-Medina (mostly during the 19th and 20th Dynasties (c. 1295–1069 B.C.)) where those who were constructing and furnishing the New Kingdom royal tombs resolved their legal disputes. Typically, senior government officials were in charge of the Great Court and the special courts that were convened in the conspiracy and royal tomb robbery trials. For community courts like the one at Deir el-Medina, significant persons such as scribes and crew chiefs usually presided as arbiters (although occasionally laborers and even women took part in the decision making process). Occasionally, to add an extra measure of objectivity, judges from outside the community heard cases along with the local judges.

---

42. David Lorton, *Legal and Social Institutons of Pharonic Egypt, in* 1 CIVILIZATIONS OF THE ANCIENT NEAR EAST 345, 355 (Jack M. Sasson ed., 1995).
43. *See infra* § 5.13.

But these local courts ordinarily did not hear cases involving serious crimes such as homicide and rape. Crimes of that nature probably were under the jurisdiction of a court of higher authority.

§ 5.02 COURT STRUCTURE IN THE OLD & MIDDLE KINGDOMS

[A] OLD KINGDOM (*c.* 2700–2200 B.C.)

The Egyptians established a system for dispute resolution even as early as the Old Kingdom. By the 4th Dynasty (*c.* 2625–2510 B.C.), kings were extraordinarily powerful, and a high degree of centralization had developed. Even in this early era, the Old Kingdom government established a royal archive where deeds for land, contracts, wills, and royal decrees were kept. According to tradition, there were six courts of justice, also called the *Great Houses*. Each of the Six Great Courts had a chief justice. There was also a group called the "thirty great men of the south," each of whom served as a judge and district chief. Apparently, each of these "thirty great men of the south" also served as a judge on one of the Six Great Courts. A body known as The Southern Tens played some unspecified role in ajudication.

The Greeks called the local administrative districts in Egypt "nomes." There were twenty-two nomes in Upper Egypt and twenty in Lower Egypt. The kings of the 4th and 5th Dynasties probably appointed a chief administrator/local governor for each nome (nomarch), and that administrator, who had the title "judge," probably conducted trials in the nome's own law court. The local governors were not primarily judges, but they heard cases as part of their administrative duties.

The vizier was the most important government official and foremost judicial administrator in Egypt. Originally the vizier was chosen from the king's family. By the 5th Dynasty (*c.* 2510–2460 B.C.), however, royal relationship was no longer absolutely necessary. He supervised the Six Great Courts on which the local judges served. As was mentioned, in addition to the court of the vizier, there were local courts throughout Egypt. These were not standing tribunals but rather they were comprised of local administrative officials in each district who convenied to hear cases on an as-needed basis. Commissioners from the court of the vizier occasionally traveled to a distant town in order to collaborate with these local courts in rendering decisions. We are not sure how many local courts there were, but the local courts operating in Thebes (where the judges varied daily) and in Memphis were surely the most important.

[B] MIDDLE KINGDOM (*c.* 2040–1674 B.C.)

By the Middle Kingdom, most of the Old Kingdom court structure had become defunct. Some of the titles of officials continued to be used, but that is all that they were—titles. The court in the Middle Kingdom was different. The judges who served varied from day to day. Nevertheless, the judges were priests and elder officials who presumably possessed the wisdom and judgment necessary for sound decision making. During the late Middle Kingdom, individual nomarchs established their own law courts that functioned independently of the courts of the king.

§ 5.03 COURT STRUCTURE IN THE NEW KINGDOM (*c.* 1552–1069 B.C.)

[A] INTRODUCTION

In the New Kingdom, two bodies which once exercised significant adjudicatory roles during the Old and Middle Kingdoms—the Southern Tens and the Six Great Houses (courts)—no longer appear in any court documents and, apparently, were gradually phased out of existence. Because Egypt was such a vast kingdom—600 miles long—it was necessary for the king and the vizier to delegate some judicial responsibility to local bureaucratic officials. Local officials continued to function as judges although, as had been the custom before, they did not serve as judges exclusively. Judging was merely one of a local administrator's duties. Later, when the king appointed an additional vizier (*i.e.,* a Northern vizier in Heliopolis—probably by the early 18th Dynasty (*c.* 1500 B.C.)), he (*i.e.,* the Northern vizier) also heard petitions on a daily basis, as did his Southern counterpart.

[B] PHARAOH & THE COURTS

According to Breasted, in the New Kingdom (*c.* 1552–1069 B.C.), the king had a recognized judicial function. He determined the punishments for condemned criminals. The vizier prepared a written report and the king, upon reviewing it, sentenced the convicted criminal. But we know of other instances where the pharaoh was careful to exclude himslf from the sentencing decision. It is probably a positive sign, for example, that Ramses III (*c.* 1186–1154 B.C.) did not, on simply his own authority, summarily execute the conspirators involved in a plot on his life.[44] The fact that he appointed a special court, and instructed the judges to beware lest they conduct themselves unjustly, indicates that the New Kingdom Egyptians had repect for due process and the rights of the accused.

Some laws are attributed to the pharaoh. For example, tradition reports that the king promulgated laws concerning: 1) inheritance ("It is to the one who buries that property is given, says the law of Pharaoh."); 2) property ("Pharaoh has said, may every man do as he wishes with his belongings."); and, 3) a woman's dowry ("Pharaoh has said give the *sfr* (dowry?) of every woman to her.").[45] Occasionally, the pharaoh acted as the ultimate judge. But in many instances where the pharaoh is credited with having functioned as a judge, scholars suspect that it was actually a palace official who heard the case as the king's designate. In addition to acting as a judge, he selected court personnel (including the viziers), determined the scope of their authority, and maintained the power to legislate on his own. The pharaoh had the authority to discharge a judge and even the vizier himself.

Horemhab (c. 1323–1295 B.C.) is one New Kingdom pharaoh who deserves special mention for his contributions to court structure and the judiciary. In particular, he is known for his famous Edict. Upon taking the throne, Horemhab reorganized the courts first by establishing two permanent "Great Courts." The court in Heliopolis had jurisdiction in Lower Egypt (*i.e.,* the Delta region) and the court in Thebes was responsible for Upper Egypt (*i.e.,* Egypt south of the Delta). The vizier of lower Egypt presided over the court in Heliopolis and his counterpart in the south directed the Theban Great Court. The Great Courts only decided important cases or those with potentially grave consequences. In addition, Horemhab founded smaller, local courts to serve the needs of towns and villages. In addition to these standing local courts, some evidence suggests that traveling judges (circuit courts) may have provided adjudication for villages that were too small to have their own courts. In sum, then, Horemhab split legal authority between Upper and Lower Egypt, and he appointed new judges, gave them salaries, provided them with laws to use as precedents, and advised them not to associate with others and not to accept bribes. His new judges were mostly priests and officials. Horemhab's plan also exempted the courts from paying taxes of silver and gold. At the beginning of the 19th Dynasty (c. 1295 B.C.—in the period immediately following Horemhab), written laws may have begun to supplant the personal authority of the pha-

---

44. *See infra* §§ 5.13, 6.05[E].
45. *See* McDOWELL, JURISDICTION 235 (footnote omitted).

raoh. And, it is clear that the priests gained greater control of the civil courts.

[C] DEIR EL-MEDINA

By the 19th Dynasty (*c.* 1295–1188 B.C.), the court system had become a fixed institution. Because of the volume of documents uncovered by archaeologists, modern scholars simply know more about the court (* knbt*) at Deir el-Medina than any other. Deir el-Medina was a relatively small community.[46] The *knbt* at Deir el-Medina was usually composed of persons from the village "and outside authorities connected with Deir el-Medina."[47] The court met "in the open air...."[48] Even the pharaoh himself occasionally acted as a judge in cases involving individuals from Deir el-Medina. Although we tend to assume that the legal information that we draw from Deir el-Medina is representative of law in other ancient Egyptian communities, we cannot be sure. The place called the *htm*, the "enclosure", is the location where the *knbt* probably held its sessions. "Presumably there was also an open space either within the *htm* or near it where even a large group of people involved in the proceedings and curious onlookers could assemble."[49] According to McDowell, "most of the cases which came before the *knbt* concerned economic transactions."[50] As a rule, these cases involved allegations of breach of contract. Occasionally, the *knbt* performed the role of a notary; merely witnessing a transaction or a will.

[D] SPECIAL COURTS

In certain extraordinary circumstances, the king took it upon himself to appoint a special court to deal with unusually sensitive cases. When special courts were convened to handle extraordinary matters, the king usually appointed the highest officials available as judges. There are three kings who appointed famous special courts: 1) Pepi I (*c.* 2325 B.C.); 2) Ramses III (*c.*

---

46. McDowell, Jurisdiction 2 ("The only inhabitants were the workmen themselves and their families, at most periods from 40–60 households in all."). *See also* Grimal, Ancient Egypt 278 ("The total number of workmen...reached 120, meaning that the community as a whole must have numbered about 1200.").

47. McDowell, Jurisdiction 2. *See also* Bedell, Criminal Law 7–8 (Bedell says that the court at Deir el-Medina "can also be classified as a district or local court.").

48. McDowell, Jurisdiction 2.

49. *Id.* at 100.

50. *Id.* at 155.

1186–1154 B.C.); and, 3) Ramses IX (c. 1125–1107 B.C.). King Pepi I appointed a man named Weni to serve as judge for an extraordinary criminal trial because the king held Weni in such high regard. Among Weni's responsibilities was to write an opinion for his decision.[51] The chief justice and one of the judges "attached to Nekhen" occasionally heard special private cases; and, in one particular case involving treason in the royal harem, the king appointed two judges "attached to Nekhen" to hear the case (without the chief justice).[52]

§ 5.04 THE OFFICE OF VIZIER

The vizier headed the entire organization of the government. His office maintained all of the State archives and other important documents such as land records, wills, census administration, and tax registration. The vizier was often called the prophet of Ma'at. He was the supreme judge, the chief justice. The vizier ordinarily led the discussion in court and asked the litigants more questions than any other judges in the Great Courts of Thebes and Heliopolis. In minor disputes, the vizier often heard matters on his own without the assistance of other judges.

The vizier in the Middle Kingdom (c. 2040–1674 B.C.) refers to himself as the person "confirming the boundary records [and] separating a landowner from his neighbor."[53] As had been the case during the Old Kingdom (c. 2700–2200 B.C.), the vizier continued to function as the premier court administrator, overseeing the Six Great Houses (i.e., courts of law) and the "House of the Thirty."

When the king began appointing a second vizier (in the North), the two viziers split their jurisdiction on a geographic basis. In the New Kingdom (c. 1552–1069 B.C.), the southern vizier became the most powerful judicial official. When possible, the vizier met with the pharaoh every morning and he prepared criminal trial reports which the king used as a basis for sentencing.

---

51. See GARDINER, EGYPT OF THE PHARAOHS 95. Regarding Weni's appointment as judge, see BREASTED, HISTORY OF EGYPT 134; GRIMAL, ANCIENT EGYPT 82–83. See also infra § 6.05[E].

52. See BREASTED, HISTORY OF EGYPT 81 ("Special cases of private nature were 'heard' by the chief justice and a judge 'attached to Nekhen,' while in a case of treason in the harem, the accused queen was tried before a court of two judges 'attached to Nekhen,'especially appointed by the crown for that purpose, the chief justice not being one of them.") (footnotes omitted). For more about the phrase "attached to Nekhen," see infra § 5.05.

53. Id. at 166 (footnote omitted).

In the guidelines established for the vizier, Rekhmire, the pharaoh directs him to be impartial and advises him to admit his mistakes. And when he recognizes that he has made a mistake, the pharaoh advises him to steer the injured party to another judge for assistance. The vizier is told: "A magistrate's refuge lies in acting according to the regulations in doing what is specified. A petitioner who has been judged should not be able to say: 'I have not been allowed to plead my innocence.'" "Do not dismiss a petitioner before you have considered his words." "You should dismiss him only after you have let him hear the reasons why you dismiss him. See! The saying is: 'The petitioner prefers the consideration of his utterance to the judgement on the matter about which he has come.'"[54]

§ 5.05 JUDGES

Many of the Old Kingdom judges retained the phrase "attached to Nekhen," as part of their official title. This phrase was a vestige of an earlier time when "Nekhen (Hieraconpolis) was the royal residence of the Southern Kingdom."[55] Judges ordinarily heard cases as a group, rarely alone. Ancient sources tell us that, occasionally, Egyptian judges endeavored to instill fear in the litigants in an attempt to command respect from them. In an effort to curb bribery among judges, the pharaoh Horemhab (c. 1323–1295 B.C.), whom we have previously singled out as an innovator in judicial affairs,[56] exempted judges from taxation for their earnings (as judges). Presumably, the amount saved through tax exemption was sufficient to make taking bribes unnecessary. In concert with providing this tax exemption for the judiciary, Horemhab strengthened the penalty for accepting bribes, making it a capital offense. This same pharaoh, as today's American President often does, tried to influence the tide of jurisprudence with his judicial appointments: "Horemhab put into the courts of law individuals of a reactionary type. He tells us that he was at pains to seek out men 'of perfected speech and good character, able to distinguish the innermost thoughts.'"[57]

Scribes were especially important in legal endeavors. Some scribes mentioned in the Deir el-Medina legal documents were from Deir el-Medina it-

---

54. T.G.H. JAMES, PHARAOH'S PEOPLE: SCENES FROM LIFE IN IMPERIAL EGYPT 60–61 (1984).
55. BREASTED, HISTORY OF EGYPT 81.
56. See supra § 5.03[B].
57. WILSON, CULTURE OF ANCIENT EGYPT 237.

self but many came from the outside; like the scribes of the vizier. Indeed, the scribe of the vizier often served as a judge in significant litigation.

In the juridical texts from Deir el-Medina, many persons were referred to as *srw* ("magistrates") only when they were engaged in performing legal duties. For example, when townspeople served as judges, they were called *srw*. In some regards, the term was used in the way that we refer to modern jurors as "ladies and gentlemen of the jury." The title only applies while the jurors are serving. It is not a title that they otherwise retain. We do not know how the Deir el-Medina community selected judges for the court. As McDowell writes: "The members of the court varied from one session to the next according to no discernible pattern…, though they generally included the captains of the [workers] gang. These could be joined by lower ranking members of the gang, including simple workmen; also outside authorities such as the scribes of the vizier and the chiefs of police."[58] As was mentioned, in the Great Court in Thebes, the vizier acted as the chief judge. Similarly, in the court at Deir el-Medina, ordinarily there also appears to have been some individual who served as a chairman of the court. Often a scribe acted as something like a chief judge or foreman who presided over the court. Usually—though not always—at least one captain of the workmen served as a judge on the ḳnbt. It is particularly interesting that in nearly two-thirds of the cases in Deir el-Medina, either one of the scribes of the vizier or one of the chiefs of police (*3ṯw*) (*i.e.,* officials from *outside* of Deir el-Medina) served as judges on the ḳnbt. A scribe of the vizier, in particular, often assisted as a judge for especially important trials. Outsiders frequently served as judges in especially difficult cases. But occasionally, outsiders are on the court even in mundane, unexceptional trials. It is difficult to state with certainty how many judges served on a typical court at Deir el-Medina. For instance, the cases show three, four, five, seven, and twelve judges serving in different circumstances.

The composition of the Great Courts appears to have been somewhat more consistent but it too changed. The judges on the Great Courts—unlike the ḳnbt at Deir el-Medina—tended to be members of the upper class elite (*e.g.,* the chief priest of Amon, a royal butler, a scribe of the pharaoh, the mayor of Thebes, a military officer) rather than ordinary workers. In the Great Court at Thebes, the vizier and two royal butlers were consistenly

---

58. McDOWELL, JURISDICTION 144; *Id.* at 148, 159 ("The composition of the court varied from one session to the next."). *See also* BEDELL, CRIMINAL LAW 6–7 (Referring to the fact that "prominent citizens" ordinarily served on the local courts.); *Id.* at 52 ("[T]he members of the court changed regularly.").

on the panel. For several years during the reign of Ramses XI (c. 1098–1069 B.C.), three individual jurists appear in every case heard by the Great Court. They simply may have been quasi-permanent judges.

§ 5.06 OTHER COURT PERSONNEL & LAW ENFORCEMENT OFFICIALS

There were persons who worked in the courts or assisted in law enforcement other than the judges but we know very few details about them. For example, there were officials who administered beatings and other torture to witnesses. One court officer, called merely a "servant of the court" (*šms n ḫnbt*), may have inflicted these beatings, or, he may have simply been a part-time employee who carried messages, ran errands, or confiscated items in the name of the court. This last duty appears to have been his most important. Apparently, the persons known as "doorkeepers" also served as bailiffs for the court.

Although the term *m'ḏ3yw* originally denoted someone from Nubia, by the New Kingdom (c. 1552–1069 B.C.), *m'ḏ3yw* was the word for "police" or "desert rangers." "They were employed as policemen, guards, and patrols throughout Egypt, but perhaps particularly in desert and frontier regions."[59] In the vicinity of the Theban necropolis, their primary responsibility was to guard the tombs. And in the investigations concerning the Great Tomb Robberies,[60] it was the *m'ḏ3yw* who were dispatched to probe the tombs under suspicion. In theft cases in particular, the *m'ḏ3yw* frequently served as witnesses at trial. There was also a group called *3ṯw* whose legal function seems to have been something like detectives. Another group identified as the *rwḏw* (usually translated "agents") performed a number of paralegal and quasi-judicial tasks.

§ 5.07 ADJUDICATION BY ORACLE

In addition to using courts for judicial decision making, commencing in the New Kingdom (c. 1552–1069 B.C.), the Egyptians also used divine oracles. In some cases, parties made intricate arguments before an oracle (as they might before a panel of judges). In other instances, however, one party

---

59. McDowell, Jurisdiction 52.
60. *See infra* § 6.05[D][2].

merely posed a simple question to the god. We have half a dozen examples of rather involved written petitions seeking a decsion from the oracle. Tradition has it that Amenhotep I (c. 1526–1506 B.C.) established the workmen's community at Deir el-Medina. Thus, it was the deified Amenhotep I who, as an oracle, rendered judicial decisions there. Besides Amenhotep I at Deir el-Medina, there were at least two other deified pharaohs who were used for oracular quasi-judicial decisions. In Abydos, the citizens took their cases to the oracle of Ahmose I (Amenhotep's father) (c. 1552–1526 B.C.). In the city of This (near Abydos), the deified Ramses II (c. 1279–1212 B.C.) served as the oracle. By the 21st Dynasty (c. 1069–945 B.C.), the oracle of the solar deity Amon-Re at Karnak heard cases.

The procedure for oracular decisions was complex. Priests carried a statue of the god on a litter. Supposedly, the god inspired the priests to move in response to questions posed. By moving backwards, the god indicated a negative response ("no"). A number of Egyptologists have argued that, therefore, forward movement must have indicated a positive answer ("yes").[61] Technically, however, the extant texts use the word *h3n* ("agree") for an affirmative reply. In addition to using forward and backward movement to signify a response, a number of texts state that the oracle spoke. Just as it was the priests (*i.e.,* the priests who carried the image of the god) who manipulated the litter's movements, in all likelihood it was probably also the priests who actually spoke. Thus, in essence, the litter-bearers acted as judges for the oracular decisions. The oracle could also respond in other ways. For example, it could stop moving at a decisive moment.

There seems to have been a division of subject matter jurisdiction in Deir el-Medina. The *ķnbt* decided cases of a criminal nature and either the oracle or the office of the vizier decided cases relating to the ownership of property. The *ķnbt* did not deal with cases of real estate ownership. It is entirely possibile that the reason why the oracle had exclusive jurisdiction to decide cases relating to ownership of real property was because buildings and land may have been considered owned by the State or by the pharaoh. Thus, the oracle decided matters involving the inheritance of real property and it also named thieves and established the value of objects. Other officials could deal with issues concerning real property but only those issues unrelated to ownership. The oracle also decided a number of types of cases other than those related solely to real estate ownership. We have, though, only about a dozen oracle cases that are not related to real estate. Of those non-real estate cases, most either involve establishing the values of goods or

---

61. *See* McDOWELL, JURISDICTION 109. *See also* BEDELL, CRIMINAL LAW 246–247.

the identites of thieves. On those occasions when an oracle was asked to identify a thief, an official read aloud a list of houses in the village. At the instant that the name of the thief was read, the "god" made some sort of movement to signify that that was the name of the thief.

§ 5.08 THE BASICS OF PROCEDURE

I begin this section by describing one lawsuit that provides a curious look at civil procedure and litigation involving a variety of stages. This case provides a partial paradigm and reveals a blend of elements that are typical of ancient Egyptian legal procedure: various officials conducting investigations; witness testimony; the use of documents (some falsified) as evidence; and, persistent retrial of the same issues again and again with diverse results. Although the text of the case that we have focuses on a dispute from the time of Ramses II (*c.* 1279–1212 B.C.), many of the relevant facts stretch back to the beginning of the 18th Dynasty (*c.* 1552 B.C.). This case involves a dispute regarding the ownership of a parcel of land. Actually, several disputes occurred and I begin *in medias res*.

The Great Court sitting in Heliopolis, with the vizier presiding, dispatched a commissioner to the district where the property in question was located. He appointed one of the parties, a woman named Wernero, as trustee to cultivate the land on behalf of her brothers and sisters. One sister objected and apparently convinced the commissioner to change his mind. Now he ordered that the land, which had hitherto been considered indivisible, be split into separate parcels for each of the six heirs. At this juncture, a man named Huy, the father of the principal litigant (whose name was Mose or Mes), and Wernero (Huy's mother) appealed the commissioner's decision to divide the property. When Huy died soon thereafter, his widow, Nubnofre, attempted to use self-help to retake the land by cultivating it. A man named Kha'y ejected her. She then appealed to the Great Court in Heliopolis. That appeal went in favor of Kha'y. Years later, Mose, the son of Huy and Nubnofre (*i.e.,* Wernero's grandson), again appealed to the Great Court. Evidently, the Great Court reversed its prior decision, persuaded by witnesses who testified as to Mose's descent. It seems that, in the earlier case between Kha'y and Nubnofre, a commissioner had colluded with Kha'y to falsify the land records. From this account we can surmise that the Egyptians did not, strictly speaking, adhere to the principle of *res judicata* to the extent that we do today. It is notable that subsequent litigants were able to appeal what appeared to be final decisions to the same court. Regarding the case of Mose, James concludes:

It demonstrates something of the care with which a case of this kind might be pursued; how documents lodged in official archives might be consulted; how legal decisions taken by such high courts could be challenged and, ultimately, reversed by the introduction of fresh evidence.[62]

In Middle Egyptian (the "classic" period of the ancient Egyptian language), the verb *mdw* was used to describe a legal dispute or litigation.[63] To the ancient Egyptian, having a formal dispute resolution process may have been as important as actually winning a case in court. The Egyptians realized that without a formal procedure for resolving disputes, individuals would perceive grave injustice. Thus, they acknowledged the importance of something akin to modern "due process." One Middle Kingdom (*c.* 2040–1674 B.C.) instruction text advises the judge: "The petitioner likes attention to his words better than the fulfilling of that for which he came.... It is not (necessary) that everything about which he has petitioned should come to pass, (but) a good hearing is a soothing to the heart."[64] Having a legal procedure was particularly vital for the poor and disadvantaged. "That the poor and weak could obtain justice was a fundamental object of the legal process in ancient Egypt...."[65]

Scholars have been unable to detect any clear pattern or schedule that might constitute anything like a court calendar. The *knbt* could convene on practically any day. We have texts that show courts in sesion on weekdays, weekends, and even during festival days. Interestingly, there is only one instance where two cases were heard on the same day; and the same person was the plaintiff in both cases. As a rule, though, once a court convened, a typical trial lasted for one day only. In the Great Courts, the same panel of judges usually saw a case from start to finish.

Egyptologists hypothesize that the judges reached their decision together; neither the chief judge nor any one judge had the authority to

62. T.G.H. JAMES, PHARAOH'S PEOPLE: SCENES FROM LIFE IN IMPERIAL EGYPT 97 (1984).

63. *See* McDOWELL, JURISDICTION 20–21 ("The verb *mdw*... is used almost exclusively with the meaning 'dispute' or 'contest.' **** Since in the overwhelming majority of cases the verb *mdw* means to dispute with someone at law, we may fairly translate it with 'to litigate against.'"). *See also* R.O. FAULKNER, A CONCISE DICTIONARY OF MIDDLE EGYPTIAN 122 ("*mdw ḥn* 'dispute with'...*šm r mdt ḥn* 'to go to law with'").

64. WILSON, CULTURE OF ANCIENT EGYPT 93. *See also* GARDINER, EGYPT OF THE PHARAOHS 196 (According to Gardiner, the tomb inscription of Rekhmire, vizier of Thutmose III, has this to say about the job of vizier: "that a petitioner better likes to be allowed to pour out his grievances than that they should be put right."); Théodorides, *Concept* at 308–309.

65. T.G.H. JAMES, PHARAOH'S PEOPLE: SCENES FROM LIFE IN IMPERIAL EGYPT 78.

trump the decision of the group. Courts ordinarily gave specific instructions regarding who was to pay whom and how much (or some other remedy).

§ 5.09 ADHERENCE TO PRECEDENT

Egyptian law was slow to evolve and adhered vigorously to precedent. One factor that contributed to both (*i.e.,* gradual legal evolution and high regard for past decisions) was the typical ancient Egyptian reverence for the past.[66] To some extent, then, partially as a consequence of this esteem for the past, judges relied on both custom and precedent to decide their cases. It seems likely that, at certain periods, they also retained written copies of each judicial opinion.

It was common for litigants in the New Kingdom (*c.* 1552–1069 B.C.) to cite to the "law of the Pharaoh" as authoritative precedent.[67] Thus, the Egyptians discovered the utility of following precedent, a concept that we today refer to by the Latin term *stare decisis*.[68] The vizier Rekhmire was explicitly advised to follow the precedents available: "As for the office in which you hold audience, it includes a large room which contains [the records] of [all] the judgements, for he who must practice justice before all men is the vizier... Do not act as you please in cases where the law to be applied is known...."[69] In practice, we know that in the courts at Deir el-Medina litigants cited precedent when pleading their cases.

By the Middle Kingdom (*c.* 2040–1674 B.C.), the Egyptians ordinarily required that trials be held in public and that records of decisions be kept. In addition to the private accounts of the litigants, some official archives of cases may have been kept at Deir el-Medina (*i.e.,* during the 19th and 20th Dynasties (*c.* 1295–1069 B.C.)). But more than likely, most judicial

66. *See supra* § 4.04[B].
67. *See supra* § 5.03[B].
68. *See* LEXIKON DER ÄGYPTOLGIE, Vol. 5 (1984), "Recht" 186. *See also* Taylor, *Law under the Pharaohs*, 6 POL'Y REV. 66, 67 (1980) ("The principle of *stare decisis* is not a western notion. The Egyptian courts based much of their law on precedent and there are examples of judgements based on decisions many hundreds of years old."); Théodorides, *Concept* 307–308 (Explaining that the Instructions for the Vizier, whose "composition must go back to the 13th Dynasty...", say that "justice is to be rendered in public and in such a way that every individual shall always secure his rights. To this end, appeal is made to a sense of equity and also, by implication, to jurisprudence, since it is pointed out that the records of all judgements are kept in the vizier's archives, where they would certainly have been consulted. ....") (footnote omitted).
69. Théodorides, *Concept* at 309 (elipses in original).

ostraca were private documents preserved by the interested parties whose rights were affected by the litigation. Thus, the prevailing party probably kept a memorandum of the legal proceedings and the decision of the oracle or court.

§5.10 OUTLINE OF LITIGATION PROCEDURE

In most Deir el-Medina criminal cases, we see the same procedural sequence of events. A local official discovers some problem, reports it to the vizier, and the vizier, in turn, dispatches personnel to find out more details. Ordinarily, this involves taking suspects to the riverbank for questioning prior to the time that a decision regarding guilt or innocence is made. Quite a few Deir el-Medina texts note that a suspect is "taken to the riverbank." Although scholars have advanced a number of theories regarding the interpretation of this phrase, McDowell contends, quite plausibly, that it simply means the suspect was brought to the riverbank and interrogated there.[70]

On the other hand, persons who were the victims of civil wrongs had to bring their defendants to court personally. Neither police nor State prosecutors were responsible for bringing these non-criminal cases to trial. The first procedural step for any Egyptian who wished to institute a civil lawsuit against another was to apply to the vizier, who heard petitions daily in the mornings. Originally such complaints may have merely been oral, but the ancient Egyptians probably submitted cases to judges in writing even as early as the Old Kingdom (c. 2700–2200 B.C.). The vizier then had to determine whether the petition was legally suffcient, and, if it was, he then notified the defendant. The defendant next filed a written answer with the vizier. It is possible that the plaintiff in turn was permitted to reply to the defendant's answer and that the defendant was also given an opportunity to respond to the plaintiff's reply (but the evidence is inconclusive). After all of the "briefs" (i.e., written accusations and responses) were filed, the vizier conducted a hearing. He summarized the parties' arguments and asked them both questions. Of course, as is true in modern litigation, the parties also had the option to settle their dispute before the court rendered its decision. As Allam paraphrases the judge's order to Horus and Seth in their

---

70. *See* McDOWELL, JURISDICTION 219–223.

mythological dispute: "Eating and drinking together is by far the best way for opposed parties to negotiate towards a prospective reconciliation."[71]

Although I began this discussion of procedure by stating that the case of Mose was not a perfect or universal paradigm, still, in some respects, it does in fact serve to illustrate a concise summary of basic civil procedure in ancient Egypt. First, the plaintiff filed a complaint with the vizier. That petition explained the basis for the complaint. If the vizier deemed the complaint satisfactory, he next notified the defendant who was then given an opportunity to answer the allegations. After this initial pleading stage, the vizier held a hearing at which he could question the litigants and examine evidence.

There were no professional lawyers who pleaded cases on behalf of clients as advocates, but there were scribes who specialized in legal affairs. These scribes produced legal documents for a fee. Breasted mentions that an ancient Egyptian deceased was expected to "personally represent himself and thus ensure himself the favor of the god in the hereafter."[72] Perhaps the expectation that the dead would plead their own cases merely mirrors the expectation that the living should plead theirs as well.

§ 5.11 PRETRIAL & TRIAL PROCEDURE

In addition to the preliminary steps described in § 5.10, criminal courts routinely took the following measures as part of their pretrial phase. 1) Upon receiving a criminal complaint, officials initiated a preliminary investigation. 2) If the preliminary investigation proved fruitful, the officials intensified their investigation in an effort to identify and arrest suspects. 3) The officials then submitted a list of suspects to the vizier, and they were deposed. Officials questioned the suspects during their depositions in an attempt to locate stolen goods and to discover the identities of other criminals.

Civil trial procedure in the New Kingdom (c. 1552–1069 B.C.) ordinarily followed a prescribed sequence of events. 1) With both litigants standing before the seated court judges, the plaintiff made his complaint. 2) The judges declared the case "heard" and summoned the defendant to answer. 3) The defendant answered. It was crucial for the court to hear the sides of

---

71. S. Allam, *Legal Aspects in the 'Contendings of Horus and Seth', in* STUDIES IN PHARAONIC RELIGION AND SOCIETY IN HONOUR OF J. GWYN GRIFFITHS 137, 141 (Alan B. Lloyd ed., 1992).

72. BREASTED, DEVELOPMENT OF RELIGION AND THOUGHT 287. *See also* GRIMAL, ANCIENT EGYPT 126.

both parties. 4) The court declared its ruling. The litigants then turned to each other and recited ceremonial pronouncements, the winner repeating the court's opinion and the loser agreeing to abide by the court's decision. In some cases, at the close of the proceedings, the losing litigant formally promised not to reopen the case. Courts regularly rendered their decisions in simple terms: A is right, B is wrong: *m3't A 'd3 B.*

At the opening of a trial, the plaintiff usually spoke first. His opening statement laid out the relevant facts of the case and explained the basis for his legal claim. In other words, he described the case and explained what he believed the defendant had done to injure him. This statement contained what the Egyptians called the *smi* (*i.e.,* "the formal charge against a person").[73] There seem to have been no ideosyncratic rules about the form nor prescribed content of the plaintiff's opening argument. Plaintiffs simply gave their version of the dispute as best as they could. We have a number of ostraca that record what appear to have been statements of plaintiffs. These are similar to depositions, or affidavits, that might have been read in court, or, at least, submitted to the court like a plaintiff's brief explaining his version of the facts of the case. In the Great Courts, the plaintiff's opening statement was not required since the judges themselves functioned as prosecutors there.

For criminal trials, the order of proceedings was bascally the same as in civil trials, except that a State official, perhaps the vizier, took the place of the plaintiff. Bedell suggests that the defendant (in a criminal case) was required to plead guilty or not guilty at the opening of the trial—just after the accusation was stated.[74] Apparently, an accused criminal defendant was presumed innocent until proven guilty. Ordinarily, criminal courts in ancient Egypt were legitimate deliberative bodies. They were not kangaroo courts staged merely to lend an appearance of authority to punishments. We know of several defendants in criminal cases who pled not guilty and, indeed, were later set free.

Since there were no advocates who represented the parties, the judges took an active role in litigation. They questioned the parties, often probing with great diligence. They were inclined to ask defendants, especially, numerous questions. It was common for judges to ask a defendant whether he

---

73. *See* BEDELL, CRIMINAL LAW 83–84. *See also* R.O. FAULKNER, A CONCISE DICTIONARY OF MIDDLE EGYPTIAN 227 (1981).

74. *See* BEDELL, CRIMINAL LAW 88–89 ("The first thing the judges wanted was a plea of guilty or not guilty because the nature of subsequent proceedings would depend on this plea."); *Id.* at 145 ("throughout the tomb robbery texts, the term used for innocent was *w'b*, which literally means 'pure.'").

could produce a witness to support his claims. In criminal cases where one defendant confessed, the judges frequently sought evidence (through their questioning) that would advance the case against other co-criminals. The court also hoped to discover the whereabouts of stolen property. In addition, they pressed for details regarding how the criminals had accomplished their crime. In that way, the judges hoped to gain information that could help them prevent reoccurrences. Thus, the judges extensively questioned criminals in an attempt to elicit accomplices, amounts stolen, the modus operandi, and the whereabouts of plunder.

Judges were not confined to asking merely pointed, step-by-step questions (*i.e.,* of the sort that the modern law of evidence often requires on cross-examination). Judges could ask defendants open-ended questions. Such inquiries basically sought a narrative of criminal activity. For example, in one case brought before the Great Court of Thebes, a woman by the name Taaper had witnessed a sale of stolen goods. At trial, one of the judges asked her to tell her version of the blackmarket trafficking: "Come tell the story of this copper which you said was in the possession of…Peikharu…."[75] Thus, the lion's share of the judges' questions were designed to resolve issues of fact. Unlike the cases heard by the oracles, there was very little discussion in the *ḳnbt* relating to applicable laws and precedential cases. In addition to the judges, occasionally scribes—who may have functioned as prosecutors in these cases—also were permitted to ask the witnesses questions.

After the court rendered its decision, the non-prevailing party ordinarily took an oath promising to respect the court's decision. Or, if the court had sentenced the defendant to a punishment, the court itself might implement the penalty (*e.g.,* beatings). For extremely serious cases (particularly in criminal cases), the court usually referred the matter either to the vizier or the pharaoh for final sentencing.

§ 5.12 EVIDENCE

[A] INTRODUCTION

The ancient Egyptians often experienced difficulty obtaining solid, credible evidence. It was burdensome, for example, to discover who stole goods or who vandalized property. But, as Bedell remarks concerning the courts in the Ramesside Period, "there was an attempt to base decisions on human experience, perception, and reason, such as testimony and material evi-

---

75. *See Id.* at 73.

dence...."[76] Judges took into account many kinds of evidence including documents and the testimony of witnesses. In fact, the word used for witnesses, *mtrw*, was used not only for human witnesses but also for other types of evidence, such as written documents (*e.g.*, letters). Egyptian courts preferred the testimony of witnesses to other kinds of evidence.

[B] WITNESSES & OATHS

Parties themselves routinely swore oaths to affirm the veracity of their assertions. In civil trials, witnesses could testify regarding the authenticity of documents, such as wills. One provision in the Law Collection of Hermopolis allows—quite logically—that the testimony of the builders who constructed a house was competent to prove that the party claiming ownership was, indeed, the true owner of the dwelling in question. The ancient Egyptians were very fond of putting a witnesses's testimony into writing. The courts may have considered relevant the sheer number of witnesses who testified for or against a party (in one case we know that six witnesses testified for one party), but the content and credibility of the testimony mattered more than numbers alone.

Sources from the New Kingdom (*c.* 1552–1069 B.C.) confirm that both women and slaves were legally competent to testify in court. Witnesses, however, were not always treated with a great deal of respect. Court personnel often beat or otherwise tortured witnesses. In the case of the famous Great Tomb Robberies under Ramses IX (*c.* 1125–1107 B.C.), officials bound the hands and feet of at least one witness, beat him with a stick, and forced him to swear an oath or else suffer mutilation.[77] And after this cruel treatment, officials incarcerated the witness for further questioning. Some of the thieves who testified were "beaten with sticks, and their feet and hands were twisted."[78] Those who were accused and tortured often confessed—but not always. In some cases, modern scholars believe that an accused may have confessed to a crime not due to actual guilt but instead because of pressure and torture.

Although defendants in criminal trials were permitted to offer the testimony of witnesses into evidence, the witnesses had to swear an oath promising not to commit perjury. The word used for such an an oath was 'nḫ. The witness's oath ordinarily recited that the witness would suffer se-

---

76. *Id.* at 123.

77. *See infra* § 6.05[D][2].

78. J. Capart, A.H. Gardiner, and B. van de Walle, *New Light on the Ramesside Tomb-Robberies*, 22 J. EGYPTIAN ARCHAEOLOGY 169, 172 (1936). *See also Id.* at 187.

vere punishments if he committed perjury. It was common for a witness's oath regarding perjured testimony to invoke the same punishment as the wrong at issue in the case itslf. In the case of Mose,[79] one witness said that he would endure mutilation and banishment ("[I]f I speak falsely, may my [nose] and ears be cut off, and may I be sent to Kush."). A female witness in the Great Tomb Robberies trial summoned banishment as her penalty for perjury: "If I speak falsehood, may I be sent to Ethiopia."[80] It is likely, however, that the penalties recited in the witnesses' oaths were merely formulaic. They served a cautionary function to remind the witnesses of the importance of truthful testimony. It is doubtful that witnesses guilty of perjury actually suffered such severe punishments as a consequence of lying under oath in court.

We know of at least one instance (Papyrus Mayer A) where testimony that modern law characterizes as hearsay was admitted into evidence. In this tomb robbery case, a prosecution witness, a herald named Perpethew, testified that he had *heard* that a butcher named Pennestytauy had been involved in the robberies in some unspecified fashion. Pennestytauy pleaded innocent. Ultimately, the boss of the thieves testified that Pennestytauy had not been involved. Thus, although hearsay testimony appears to have been admissible, in this particular case, it proved to be untrustworthy (and probably just plain false).

[C] DOCUMENTS & OTHER TYPES OF EVIDENCE

Because of the nature of the litigation involved, parties were likely to use documentary evidence in civil cases more than in criminal ones. Documents, in particular, could be important in establishing facts. And as a rule, the testimony of witnesses was rarely used in isolation. It was usually used either to corroborate documentary evidence or to impeach it. Especially in cases involving contract disputes, land ownership, or disagreements over wills, litigants produced the relevant legal document(s) (or sometimes a document purported to be such) as evidence. In the property dispute of Mose,[81] for example, the vizier examined title deeds (documentary evidence). In the same case, other officials examined official records of the granary and treasury at the Northern capital of Pi-Ra'messe. When the officials themselves conspired to falsify those documents, Mose resorted to bringing in witnesses (both men and women) who swore to his lineage and

---

79. *See supra* § 5.08.
80. *See* BEDELL, CRIMINAL LAW 126 (footnotes omitted).
81. *See supra* § 5.08.

swore that his father had cultivated the land in question and had paid taxes. The court changed its mind on the basis of these witnesses and prior written evidence. The Law Collection of Hermopolis required that a plaintiff actually produce an annuity contract in court as a means of proof. Similarly, a valid receipt was considered competent documentary evidence.

In addition to witness testimony and legal documents, the ancient Egyptians also searched homes and visited crime scenes (sometimes producing stolen objects in the process) to obtain evidence. Officials were entitled to search houses of persons who had been accused of theft. But we do not know the scope of the suspects' rights. Nor do we know what degree of suspicion was required before such a search could be made. In short, we have very little idea of whether the Egyptians had any protections for individuals' rights analogous to the American Constitution's prohibitions regarding unreasonable searches and seizures. As a means of acquiring additional evidence, occasionally judges required an accused to accompany them to a crime scene (such as a tomb that had been robbed). There, the court asked questions about the precise nature of the criminal deeds.

§ 5.13 PROCEDURE IN THE SPECIAL COURTS

In those instances where a king appointed a special court to deal with an unusually sensitive case, the procedures followed may have been ad hoc. The earliest example of these extraordinary procedures comes from the 6th Dynasty during the reign of king Pepi I. Pepi, as was mentioned above,[82] appointed one special prosecutor, a man named Weni, who wrote a special report and acted as a single judge for deciding the case.

In an extraordinary criminal case (a plot—hatched and developed from within the pharaoh's harem—to assassinate the 20th Dynasty pharaoh Ramses III), the pharaoh selected a special commission to investigate the matter. Ramses III originally appointed fourteen men to serve on the committee to investigate this infamous harem conspiracy.[83] But in this case, the pharaoh expressly ordered the commission to handle all of the details itself, because he did not want to be involved. Apparently, the matter was so personal that Ramses did not want to let his emotions affect the process and thus he insulated himself from the proceedings. The fact that the same

---

82. *See supra* § 5.03[D]. *See also infra* § 6.05[E].
83. *See infra* § 6.05[E]; BREASTED, HISTORY OF EGYPT 500.

quasi-judicial body in this case was empowered to both determine guilt or innocence *and* also to determine the sentence was unusual. Often in Egyptian legal procedure, one body decided the merits of a case and another (*e.g.,* the pharaoh or vizier) was responsible for sentencing.[84]

In this case, several members of the royal harem originally formulated the plot. Later, members of the military and other officials conspired with them to assasinate Ramses III. Most of the conspirators were attached to the royal household. Their scheme was to kill Ramses and to instigate a coup. The pharaoh wrote special instructions for this ad hoc "court," telling them to execute those who deserved it but not to tell him anything regarding the matter. In order to operate more efficiently, this commission divided itself into two separate subcommittees. A six member subcommittee dealt with one group of conspirators and a five-member subcommittee dealt with the others. Interestingly, in the midst of the investigation, three members of the six-person subcommittee were arrested because they were becoming friendly with the harem women! The members of the commission who were arrested for cavorting with the women were tried, convicted, and punished by having their noses and ears cut off. When the other members of the commission had completed their work, the guilty conspirators were forced to commit suicide.

To investigate the royal tomb robberies (*i.e.,* the Great Tomb Robberies) that occurred under Ramses IX,[85] the pharaoh instructed the vizier to convene a special commission to inspect the pilfered tombs and to report back to the vizier. The commission was empowered to arrest suspects and to hold them pending trial by the vizier and other high officials. The vizier himself personally re-examined the scene of the crime. In these extraordinary cases, the vizier wrote an opinion that delineated which defendants were guilty and which would be acquitted. He then passed his opinion on to the pharaoh who sentenced the guilty.

§ 5.14 APPEAL

The judicial system at Deir el-Medina had no procedure for appeal in its modern sense. We know of no case where a losing party appealed to another authority outside of the community for a second opinion. Nor do our sources indicate—at least ordinarily—that someone who lost a case that had been decided by a court could then appeal the matter to the oracle,

84. *See supra* § 5.03[B].
85. *See infra* § 6.05[D][2].

or vice versa. In fact, a party who lost his case before the *knbt* routinely swore an oath promising not to reopen the issue. For the most part, cases appear to have been adjudicated in a particular forum (*i.e.*, *knbt* or oracle) on the basis of subject matter. Hence appeal to another forum was inconceivable. There are a number of instances, however, where the prevailing party took his opponent to court a second, third, or fourth time. Apparently, these cases illustrate attempts merely to reinforce the initial trial and to apply public pressure to coerce the loser into complying with the court's original order.

Thus, although there is some evidence to the contrary, conventional wisdom teaches that the Egyptian system did not have higher appellate courts. Therefore, parties basically had only one chance to prove their case. Yet, even though appeal was not technically available, the same court could hear the same case again if new evidence came to light. Some Egyptologists maintain that the pharaoh himself could and did act as a kind of appeals court. In one case (Ostracon British Museum 5631 recto) for example, after a man was accused of stealing copper objects, a Delta official sentenced him to penal labor. His father then appealed to the pharaoh who ordered the defendant's release. By the 22nd Dynasty (*c.* 945–715 B.C.), the Egyptians did finally institute changes providing for appeals in their civil and criminal procedure. In civil cases, a right of appeal was granted. In criminal cases involving minor offenses, defendants also were permitted to appeal. Interestingly, the appeal was made to an oracle for judgment. As a practical matter, though, it is doubtful whether this right of appeal actually had a significant effect on the administration of justice.

§ 5.15 ENFORCEMENT

Generally speaking, one of the key weaknesses of Egyptian procedure was its lack of enforcement mechanisms. For example, in a handful of Deir el-Medina cases, the party who was found liable (or guilty) managed to elude the authorities and simply never complied with the court's final order. According to McDowell, "[T]he *knbt* had very little actual power to enforce its decisions. It relied on its prestige for its effectiveness, and on the fact that the entire village was often witness to the legal proceedings, which probably put considerable social pressure on the litigants to abide by the court's decision."[86]

---

86. McDowell, Jurisdiction 117. *See also Id.* at 171 ("Evidently the court could decide where justice lay, but could not ensure that it was done.").

§5.16 CHAPTER SUMMARY

Very early in their history, the Egyptians established courts. Unfortunately, for the Old and Middle Kingdoms we have many obscure references but few clear details. According to tradition, the Old Kingdom kings founded Six Great Courts and employed the Thirty Great Men of the South to serve as arbiters of disputes. Each nomarch, even, may have acted as a judge in his own nome. By the Middle Kingdom, the nomarchs definitely functioned as judges. There was also a legal institution known as the Southern Tens.

By the New Kingdom, our picture becomes clearer. The pharaoh possessed significant judicial authority. He appointed the vizier(s). According to tradition, the pharaoh himslf was responsible for creating a handful of laws. He regularly was the final arbiter of criminal punishments and occasionally he served as a judge himself. Horemhab and Seti I are well known, respectively, for their Edict and Nauri Decree which addressed specific problems and reorganized the court system. The viziers—one in the North and one in the South—were the principal judicial administrators. Known as the "prophets of Ma'at," they heard petitions on a daily basis and reported directly to the pharaoh. The viziers usually acted as chief judges, leading discussion and questioning in their repective Great Courts. For unusual cases, such as the harem conspiracies and Great Tomb Robberies, pharaohs assigned special ad hoc commissions to investigate and adjudicate. These commissions were granted extraordinary powers and authority. Judges on local courts such as the *knbt* at Deir el-Medina ordinarily heard cases in panels, rarely alone. The *knbt* at Deir el-Medina met in a special location, the *htm*, where it conducted its trials in public. The Deir el-Medina court decided cases mostly realted to economic transactions. Interestingly, women were allowed to serve on local courts. Most courts had one individual who—analogous to the viziers in the Great Courts—acted as a chief judge to direct and control discussion. Scribes, given their special training, often served as judges and performed other quasi-judicial services for others. In addition to the judges themselves, there were many other legal and court personnel who assisted the legal machinery in a variety of ways. A number of communities, like Deir el-Medina, used divine oracles for legal decision making to supplement the *knbt*. Priests carried an image of the god on a litter and moved in certain directions to signify the god's judgments. In Deir el-Medina, the deified Amenhotep I made oracular decisions, mostly concerning the ownership of real property.

The ancient Egyptians established fixed procedures for dispute resolution. As is the case with modern American law, they tried to follow precedent, recognized the importance of due process, and kept records of their decisions so that, when similar problems arose, they were able to resolve those problems in a similar fashion. There was no viable appeal procedure until the first millennium B.C.; or if there was a right of appeal earlier, it was extremely limited in scope. The ancient Egyptian had his day in court (so to speak) and that was it. Indeed, most trials lasted only one day. Although there were no professional lawyers, scribes seem to have specialized in preparing legal documents for pleading, and also wrote wills and other documents of a legal nature. Thus, the scribal class, that is the class that was educated in letters, functioned somewhat like lawyers or quasi-lawyers. But scribes did not plead cases for others as advocates. Most of our evidence points to a relatively simple procedural structure. The plaintiff or the State official acting in the capacity of a prosecutor brought his case often by means of a written complaint, argued it, and then the defendant answered, arguing his case; followed by a summation. It is clear that both testamentary evidence (*i.e.*, bringing in witnesses to speak on your behalf) as well as documentary evidence (*e.g.*, contracts, wills, deeds, and tax records) were both admissible as evidence in court. Interestingly, however, the Egyptians preferred to have the testimony of their witnesses written down. The judges took an active role at trial, asking questions and interviewing witnesses. Witnesses were threatened with severe penalties for perjury and sometimes were tortured. Officials had authority to search houses and to seize property as evidence. Although the special courts were not bound by formulaic court procedures, they too relied on traditional judicial mechanisms (*e.g.*, investigation) and standard types of evidence (*e.g.*, witnesses, documents, searches, and visits to the scene of the crime). We are not sure how much power courts had to enforce their judgments.

CHAPTER 6

Substantive Law

§6.01 PERSONAL STATUS

[A] INTRODUCTION

Although some Egyptologists believe that ancient Egypt was a place where people of relatively humble birth could advance in society, there were distinct citizen classes: nobles, middle class merchants, and peasant-serfs. The term *p't*, nobles, was used to describe the citizens who were the civil administrators, priests, and military officers. The term *sr* was also used for an administrator. The terms *rhyt* (Old Kingdom), *nds* (Middle Kingdom), and *nmhy* (New Kingdom) were used for the commoners. Lorton suggests that, for convenience, it may be best to conceptualize ancient Egyptian society as having been divided into two fundamental categories: "elite" and "nonelite": essentially equivalent to the groups represented by the terms *p't* and *rhyt*. But admittedly, there was also a group that was, in many respects, analogous to what we call a middle class.[87] From top to bottom, then, we see the following. First, the king was clearly in a social class unto himself. The nobles (*p't*) ranked highest (other than the king himself). A middle class comprised of artisans and tradespeople prospered in the towns. And the lower class of peasant-serfs (*mrt*) worked on the nobles' estates. According to Katary, "[t]he *nmh* was clearly a smallholder of land rather than a great land-owner. *** [The] *nmhw* were smallholders whose lands were independent of temple lands."[88] By the Middle Kingdom (*c.* 2040–1674 B.C.), all free citizens were routinely listed on rolls and were thereby subject to a draft for military or public service. Foreigners, it

---

87. *See* David Lorton, *Legal and Social Institutions of Pharaonic Egypt, in* 1 CIVILIZATIONS OF THE ANCIENT NEAR EAST 345, 351–52 (Jack M. Sasson ed., 1995); GRIMAL, ANCIENT EGYPT 167.

88. SALLY L.D. KATARY, LAND TENURE IN THE RAMESSIDE PERIOD 211 (1989) [hereinafter "KATARY, LAND TENURE IN THE RAMESSIDE PERIOD"].

should be noted, occasionally received land as rewards for fighting as mercenaries in the Egyptian military.

[B] WOMEN

As the Middle Kingdom (c. 2040–1674 B.C.) approached, the wives of the nobility were moving toward greater equality with their husbands. And, by the 13th Dynasty (c. 1785 B.C.), significant change had occurred. By the New Kingdom (c. 1552–1069 B.C.), women appear to have gained a legal status basically equal to men. Although artistic representations of married couples in the Old Kingdom often portrayed wives as much smaller and less significant figures than their husbands, in the New Kingdom husband and wife generally appear as a balanced pair, with the wife depicted as an equal partner. Thus, in contrast to circumstances in ancient Athens and Rome, women in ancient Egypt—certainly by the New Kingdom—possessed a legal status that was on equal footing with men.[89] Women could participate in legal relations and legal transactions on their own. They could execute wills and enter into binding contracts on their own behalf. They could own, buy, sell, and inherit personal property and real estate. Women could sue and be sued in court, serve as witnesses for contracts and wills, and could testify in court trials. In addition, they were considered competent to serve as jurors. Seti I's Nauri Decree specifically claims that it is designed to protect and promote freedom for both men and women.

Women played a more prominent role in the political developments of the 18th (c. 1552–1295 B.C.) and 19th (c. 1295–1188 B.C.) Dynasties than ever before. To be sure, women had wielded political influence in earlier times, but never before had Egypt seen the likes of Queen Hatshepsut (c. 1478–1458 B.C.), who ruled as "pharaoh" for over twenty years, nor queens Tiy (wife of Amenhotep III (c. 1390–1352 B.C.)) and Nefertiti (wife of Akhenaton/Amenhotep IV (c. 1352–1348 B.C.)). In the Amarna Age under Akhenaton (Amenhotep IV), women actively participated in public life to a degree beyond what Egypt had seen before.

[C] MIDDLE CLASS

During the Middle Kingdom (c. 2040–1674 B.C.), there was a significant increase in the number of persons whom we would label as middle class. This middle class was gradually gaining wealth and prosperity. In particu-

---

89. See infra §§ 9.03[A] and 12.03[A].

lar, we see significant growth in the number of tradesmen, artisans, and artificers. Later, in the New Kingdom (*c.* 1552–1069 B.C.), the more well-to-do of the old middle class climbed into the lower tier of what may be called an "official class." These, along with the relatives and dependents of the landed nobility (who comprised the upper level of the "official class") held administrative offices in local bureaucracies. The tradespeople, merchants, and craftspeople continued to thrive as well.

[D] PEASANT-SERFS & SLAVES

The fundamental social hierarchy that defined ancient Egypt was established and in place early in the Old Kingdom. The nobles operated large agricultural estates and the majority of the population—the landless peasants—worked on those estates. The peasants performed the manual labor and menial tasks. Many historians have analogized the life of an ancient Egyptian peasant to that of a "serf" who worked on a lord's feudal estate in Medieval Europe. Peasants, however, could own property, testify in court, and could marry.

In addition to the class of peasant-serfs, foreign captives came to Egypt as slaves when the kings of the New Kingdom invaded other nations. This influx of foreign slaves resulted directly from the policy of aggression and expansion promoted by the 18th and 19th Dynasty pharaohs. Thutmose III (*c.* 1479–1425 B.C.), for example, brought many foreign slaves to Egypt as captives of war. He rewarded his generals by giving them slaves. And he used many other slaves to work on his estates and to construct his building projects in Thebes. These captive-slaves did not enjoy the technical, legal independence that the peasant-serfs had (at least in theory), although, generally speaking, both slave and serf status usually resulted either from being taken as a prisoner of war, from debt, or from pursuing protection under another's wing. Foreign slaves legally were treated as personal property, chattels. Owners could sell them, rent them, and leave them to another in a will. Many such slaves who worked for the palace or in the households of nobles probably had a more comfortable life than the average peasant. Under Amenhotep III (*c.* 1390–1352 B.C.), in many respects the pinnacle of the New Kingdom, a great many slaves entered Egypt from foreign countries. But at that time the pharaoh's chief scribe was responsible for distributing them throughout Egypt, and for granting them peasant-serf status (*i.e.,* they were liable for payment of taxes). By then, Egypt had become something of a melting pot with more and more intermarriages between native Egyptians and foreigners.

§ 6.02 PROPERTY

[A] INTRODUCTION

Ancient Egypt was chiefly an agricultural society. As a consequence, real property was extremely important. To appreciate the significance of real property, one need only remember the nature of Egyptian topography; there was a limited amount of land which was useful for cultivation. There was really only a narrow strip of land a few miles wide on either side of the Nile that could be farmed. Also every year, after the inundation, property boundaries might have to be redrawn. Indeed, some documents suggest "that every plot in Egypt was measured, its ownership, crop-yields and tax payments recorded, and that very extensive archives once existed...."[90]

In the Predynastic era (c. 4500–3150 B.C.), it is likely that the Egyptians held a tribal, or community sense of property. In the earliest historical times, probably the king, at least theoretically, owned all real property. There has been considerable scholarly debate among Egyptologists regarding the issue of private ownership of real property in pharaonic Egypt. Some argue that the State owned all land while others argue that private individuals were considered owners. Warburton emphatically rejects the theory that the State owned most of the land. He bases his model of the Egyptian economy on the principle that private individuals owned land: "It is... clear that the temples and Pharaoh did not even own a significant portion of the land in ancient Egypt...."[91] According to Warburton, "The agrarian economic system in Egypt was...based on taxation and rent in which people were awarded plots in exchange for services, under the condition that they render up part of the surplus to state authorities."[92] Indeed, as early as the 2nd Dynasty (c. 2925–2700 B.C.) (and perhaps even earlier)[93] the Egyptians *treated* land as if it were privately owned by individuals themselves. No matter what the *legal technicalities* may have been, the Egyptians *treated* real property in a manner basically equivalent to the way

---

90. William A. Ward, *Some Aspects of Private Land Ownership and Inheritance in Ancient Egypt, ca. 2500–1000 B.C., in* LAND TENURE AND SOCIAL TRANSFORMATION IN THE MIDDLE EAST 63, 65 (Tarif Khalidi ed., 1984).

91. DAVID A. WARBURTON, STATE AND ECONOMY IN ANCIENT EGYPT: FISCAL VOCABULARY OF THE NEW KINGDOM 327 (1997) [hereinafter "WARBURTON, STATE AND ECONOMY IN ANCIENT EGYPT"].

92. *Id.*

93. *See* Aristide Théodorides, *The Concept of Law in Ancient Egypt, in* THE LEGACY OF EGYPT 291, 292 (J.R. Harris ed., 2d ed. 1971). *Cf.* WILSON, CULTURE OF ANCIENT EGYPT 21.

that we today treat private property ownership. Land owners could transfer their property by sale, inheritance, or otherwise. Ward maintains that "throughout Egyptian history, private individuals could own farm land and dispose of it as they chose."[94] Manning says much the same thing: "conceptions and terminology in the private documentation suggest very clearly defined concepts of private ownership. *** Whether there was legally defined ownership before the Romans or not, there was much land in private hands that individual holders *treated* as their own and transferred to their heirs."[95] In addition to the outright sale of real estate, we also know of leasing (by means of a document called a *shn*) and sub-leasing as well.[96]

Property could be owned by an individual or jointly by two or more persons (*e.g.,* property that a married couple accumulated while married or property inherited jointly). Women too could legally own, buy, and sell property. Of the many individual (*i.e.,* secular) owners mentioned in the Wilbour Papyrus, whom Katary calls "smallholders", we see quite a diverse mix of persons who were subject to property taxation: slaves, women, goatherds, priests, stablemasters, tenant farmers, soldiers, coppersmiths, embalmers, beekeepers, sailors, scribes, cattle-branders, and various foreigners.[97]

Special attention must be given to the property which the temples owned and also the land owned by officials such as nomarchs. As Lorton notes, "the state and temples were the major landholding institutions."[98]

---

94. William A. Ward, *Some Aspects of Private Land Ownership and Inheritance in Ancient Egypt, ca. 2500–1000 B.C., in* LAND TENURE AND SOCIAL TRANSFORMATION IN THE MIDDLE EAST 63, 72 (Tarif Khalidi ed., 1984). It is perhaps also significant that the each of the laws ascribed to the pharaohs relates directly to property. *See Id.* at 77, n. 24. *See also supra* § 5.03[B].

95. J.G. Manning, *Demotic Egyptian Instruments of Transfer as Evidence for Private Ownership of Real Property,* 71 CHICAGO-KENT L. REV. 237, 267 (1995).

96. *See* KATARY, LAND TENURE IN THE RAMESSIDE PERIOD 11, 16–17, 211, 223 (1989) (Specifically identifying leasing and sub-leasing in P. Wilbour and P. Berlin 3047.); J.G. Manning, *Demotic Egyptian Instruments of Transfer as Evidence for Private Ownership of Real Property,* 71 CHICAGO-KENT L. REV. 237, 239 (1995) (Referring to Ptolemaic Egypt, Manning states: "Many Egyptians took on sub-leases of land that were nominally in the hands of Greek reserve soldiers…."); *Id.* at 241 (Noting that the ordinary number of witnesses for a lease was twelve.); *Id.* at 261 (Describing the land lease provisions of the Law Collection of Hermopolis).

97. *See* KATARY, LAND TENURE IN THE RAMESSIDE PERIOD 71–72; WILSON, CULTURE OF ANCIENT EGYPT 272.

98. David Lorton, *Legal and Social Institutions of Pharaonic Egypt, in* 1 CIVILIZATIONS OF THE ANCIENT NEAR EAST 345, 353 (Jack M. Sasson ed., 1995). *See* William A. Ward, *Some Aspects of Private Land Ownership and Inheritance in Ancient Egypt, ca. 2500–1000 B.C., in* LAND TENURE AND SOCIAL TRANSFORMATION IN THE MIDDLE EAST 63, 64 (Tarif Khalidi ed., 1984) ("It is evident that the major land-holders of Egypt were the temples and government institutions, the royal family, and the rich

Over 90% of the land owners listed on the Wilbour Papyrus are temples.[99] Papyrus Harris (from the age of Ramses III (c. 1186–1154 B.C.)) indicates that the temples at that time held nearly three-quarters of a million acres (about 15% of all useful agricultural land). Additionally, the temples employed about 2% of the country's populace (well over 100 thousand people).[100] Manning describes the operation of temple estates as follows:

> Land was donated by the king on behalf of the god of each temple in order to maintain the cult as well as the priests and dependents. A large part of the priestly income would have been derived from leasing out such land. In addition, plots of temple land were traditionally exchanged for service to the temple estate and they were certainly treated as private land by those who held them because they were passed on to their heirs.[101]

[B] SOME SIGNIFICANT PRINCIPLES OF PROPERTY LAW

The ancient Egyptians appreciated several rather sophisticated concepts relating to property law. For example, one ostracon from Deir el-Medina (British Museum Ostracon 5625)—a text that records a trial by oracle—contains an important concept in property law; namely, a natural rights theory of property (*i.e.,* the supposition that labor begets an ownership interest in property). The oracle decided that the plaintiff, Kenna, should be considered the owner of a particular house. The house at issue had originally been owned by another named Peikharu. The oracle awarded ownership to Kenna (rather than a man named Mersekhmet), because Kenna, by himself, had rebuilt the house after it had fallen into disrepair. This principle—that labor can create a property right—is often associated with principles of Roman law (*i.e., accessio*) and later with theories attributed to John Locke.[102] Thus, it is significant that the Egyptians used this precept hundreds of years earlier than the Romans.

Egyptian bailment contracts shed light on a rather subtle facet of Egyptian law of property. In Roman law, there is a distinction made between the

---

upper strata of the aristocracy") (footnote omitted); KATARY, LAND TENURE IN THE RAMESSIDE PERIOD 93–96.

99. *See* KATARY, LAND TENURE IN THE RAMESSIDE PERIOD 63.

100. *See* BREASTED, HISTORY OF EGYPT 491.

101. J.G. Manning, *Demotic Egyptian Instruments of Transfer as Evidence for Private Ownership of Real Property,* 71 CHICAGO-KENT L. REV. 237, 241 (1995).

102. *See infra* § 12.02[D][6]; J. LOCKE, SECOND TREATISE ON GOVERNMENT ch. 5 (1690).

concept called *usus* and the concept known as *usus fructus*.[103] The distinction is actually rather simple. *Usus fructus* was probably the most significant personal servitude in Roman law. *Usus fructus* allowed a person both to use a thing and to reap the benefits of the "fruits" of that thing (*i.e.,* the products of that thing). For example, someone who had *usus fructus* of an olive orchard would have both the use of the property itself and would also be entitled to reap the benefits of the olives produced by the trees in the orchard (*e.g.,* to press the olives into oil). Roman law did, however, forbid a person with the right of *usus fructus* to destroy or significantly alter the property.[104] A bailee ordinarily has the right of *usus* but not necessarily *usus fructus*. The Egyptians appreciated this same distinction. In one case from Deir el Medina (Ostracon Gard 54), a plaintiff-bailor complains that the person who was renting his donkey (*i.e.,* the bailee) not only failed to return the animal on time but also had confiscated the donkey's foal (*i.e.,* the "fruits" of the donkey), as well. Consequently, we may assume that the ordinary nature of an Egyptian bailment contract contemplated what the Romans would have called *usus* but not *usus fructus* within its scope (otherwise, absent a particular agreement to the contrary, the bailor would not have had grounds to complain).

The ancient Egyptians also recognized the concept of a life estate. This permitted an Egyptian to transfer property for the term of one's life. But the concept of a life estate in essence also creates a trust because the transferee must pass along the subject property to someone else at the end of his (*i.e.,* the trustee's) life.

In addition, Egyptian property law understood the concept of easements. One text (Ostracon Cairo 25555) refers to the right to use a road for entry and egress. The oracle's decision denied a man named Hay (the defendant in the suit) permission to use a road that belonged to the plaintiff, a man named Pentoere. In an earlier court case, the court had "permitted Hay only the right to use the road for access to an undefined place."[105] Bedell explains that the oracle "overruled the court's decision, and granted Pentoere exclusive rights to the access road."[106] Lastly, it should be recalled that the offices of nomarch and vizier were considered hereditary even during the Old Kingdom.[107] One of the significant aspects about offices such as

---

103. *See infra* § 12.02[E].
104. *See* ALAN WATSON, ROMAN LAW & COMPARATIVE LAW 50 (1991).
105. BEDELL, CRIMINAL LAW 267.
106. *Id. See also supra* § 5.14 regarding the right of appeal. This case may be an exception to the general rule (*i.e.,* a case where a litigant does appeal a court decision to an oracle).
107. *See supra* §§ 5.02[A], 5.04.

the nomarchy and vizerate being considered hereditary is that these—like *usus, usus fructus*, and easements—were intangible rights. Thus, in terms of property law, the Egyptians of the Old Kingdom were among the first people to have recognized the existence and alienability of property rights which were intangible.

The Law Collection of Hermopolis contains several provisions that address rights and duties between adjacent landowners. For example, a landowner was required to leave an appropriate amount of space between his neighbor's house and the one that he was constructing. Similarly, a landowner was not permitted to allow his water drain to discharge water onto his neighbor's property, he was not permitted to construct a doorway in a manner that interfered with his neighbor, and he was liable for damage caused when he dug his house foundation too close to his neighbor's house.

[C] SALE & LEASE OF LAND, DEEDS, & RECORDATION OF REAL PROPERTY

[1] SALES

There were detailed laws concerning the sale of real property. Documents relating to real estate sales and wills were routinely executed in the presence of magistrates. The Egyptians used a special term, *imyt-pr*, for a certified deed of conveyance of real property. *Imyt-pr* is the same expression used for a valid will (*i.e.,* another legal document which operates to transfer property).[108] These documents ordinarily contained both the price paid and also a description of the property. The seller usually transferred the written deed to the buyer so that the buyer would then have a document to prove his title.

As early as the 4th Dynasty (*c.* 2625–2510 B.C.), the State required that all *inter vivos* transfers of real estate had to be registered with the vizier in the State archives. Thus, *imyt-pr* (*i.e.,* deeds of sale) for the transfer of real property had to be taken to the office of the vizier, witnessed, and recorded there in order to be considered valid. Once recorded with the vizier, the vizier issued new land titles for the transferee. These records permitted officials to know who was responsible for paying property taxes.[109]

---

108. *See infra* §6.04[B]; R.O. FAULKNER, A CONCISE DICTIONARY OF MIDDLE EGYPTIAN 18 (1981) (Defining *imyt-pr* as "will, testament").
109. *See infra* §6.02[D].

Later, in the Ptolemaic Period (*c.* 304–30 B.C.), a seller ordinarily transferred title by using two documents. One was the "document in exchange for money" and the other was a "document of being far" (*i.e.,* a document in which the seller promised not to contest the buyer's rights). Together these documents functioned as memoranda memorializing the oral agreement for sale. Egyptians routinely executed these documents, like their predecessor the *imyt-pr*, in the presence of witnesses and recorded them in some kind of public archive.

[2] LEASES

The Law Collection of Hermopolis contains numerous provisions regarding the rights and obligations of lessors and lessees. This law collection contemplates the lease of a variety of different kinds of property. For example, it articulates rules for the lease of an agricultural field, a house, a clothiery, a brewery, a hatchery, a cabin, and a garden. Leases were ordinarily executed in writing. A typical lease for an agricultural field began by stating the names of the parties followed by a description of the subject property (*i.e.,* mentioning the adjacent North, South, East, and West plots). It required that the lessor was obligated to provide seed corn (specifying a certain amount of seed corn per aroura (*i.e.,* about two-thirds of an acre) of land) to the lessee and that the lessee was obligated to cultivate the land. Next the lease stipulated the amount of rent that the lessee was required to pay. In many cases, a lessee was allowed to pay his rent (at least in part) with products associated with his lease. For example, a cultivator typically paid his rent in grain from the harvest, a brewer could pay with beer, a clothier could pay with garments, and a gardener could pay with vegetables.

[D] TAXATION OF PROPERTY

[1] INTRODUCTION

Scholars have debated whether the payments made in association with real property should be characterized as "taxes" or "rents."[110] Fundamen-

---

110. *See* KATARY, LAND TENURE IN THE RAMESSIDE PERIOD 172 (Discussing whether the financial transfers recorded in the Wilbour Papyrus should be characterized as "revenue reallocations" or "taxes"); *Id.* at 212 (Noting that "payments...could be termed *either* rent *or* taxes. Documents of this period suggest, moreover, that such a distinction was simply immaterial."); William A. Ward, *Some Aspects of Private Land Ownership and Inheritance in Ancient Egypt, ca. 2500–1000 B.C., in* LAND TENURE AND SOCIAL TRANSFORMATION IN THE MIDDLE EAST 63 (Tarif Khalidi, ed., 1984) ("taxation and rental may not have indicated two different types of payment as they do today") (footnote omitted).

tally, the distinction hinges on whether one considers the land to have been privately owned or owned by the State. As was mentioned above,[111] for purposes of this discussion, we shall consider the land as having been privately owned, and, therefore, the payments made as "taxes" rather than as "rents." Although there were other taxes (*e.g.*, a burial tax), the most common tax levied in ancient Egypt was a property tax. Beginning very early in history, the government conducted a fiscal census. At first it was biennial and later annual. Government agents measured fields (*i.e.*, arable land) and counted assets (*e.g.*, cattle, precious metals, etc.) for purposes of assessing taxes. This inventory of real and personal property established the basis for taxes payable. During the Old Kingdom (*c.* 2700–2200 B.C.), and indeed throughout much of antiquity, the Egyptians paid their taxes not with "money" but with grain, their own labor, or other agricultural commodities. Because the success or failure of crops was linked closely with the height of the annual Nile inundation, Egyptian officials carefully measured and recorded the flood levels and used that information to adjust tax assessments accordingly. By the end of the Middle Kingdom (*c.* 1674 B.C.) and continuing into the New Kingdom, tax lists were compiled on a routine basis and were recorded in the State treasury called the "White House." The Wilbour Papyrus (*c.* 1188–1069 B.C.) records taxes that property owners owed on their farmland. We also have documents that indicate that there was a separate tax paid by a buyer when purchasing real estate.

[2] ADMINISTRATION

The practical aspects of tax collection must have been arduous for the viziers to manage. It is likely that, during the Old Kingdom (*c.* 2700–2200 B.C.), each nome rendered its taxes to the central State government, and that some form of "tax-farming" was used for collection. In the Middle Kingdom (*c.* 2040–1674 B.C.), two districts administered the operations of taxation, census records, and public works: one in the south and one in the north. Because Egyptians routinely paid their taxes in cattle, grain, wine, oil, honey, and other agricultural products, in addition to the staff of scribes required to administer this task, the tax officials of necessity had to build and maintain numerous storage facilities.

The Wilbour Papyrus, which dates from the 20th Dynasty (*c.* 1188–1069 B.C.), furnishes many details regarding real property and taxation.

> Each paragraph begins with the identification of what is apparently the land-owning institution, religious or secular, under which are

---

111. *See supra* § 6.02[A].

ordered a series of assessment lines enumerating plots of various sizes.... Each paragraph specifies the geographic location of each plot.... The assessment lines which follow provide details concerning each plot in question, listing the name and occupation of the responsible party, the size of the plot, and the assessment (if any) levied on the land calculated as a share in the harvest.[112]

Scribes wrote the size of the plots in black ink and the assessed values and tax assessments in red ink. It seems likely that the tax assessors took into account a number of factors when determining property valuation. For example, the location of the property, the owner's occupation (a hint, perhaps, of progressive taxation), the relative irrigability of the land, and "the expected standard yield" appear to have been relevant factors.[113] "[T]he general rate of assessment was actually 30% of the standard average grain harvest."[114] As is usually true in modern real property assessments, the assessed value of property for purposes of taxation was typically "low-balled." For example, for a plot of five arouras (1 aroura ($st3t$) = .66 acres), it was common for the assessed value to be .5 arouras, or 10%.[115]

[3] TAX EXEMPTIONS

Although most residents and business organizations paid taxes, there were some who were tax exempt (*i.e.,* at least exempt to some degree). Nomarchs, judges, and temples paid either no taxes, or at least reduced taxes, at certain times in ancient Egypt. The 18th Dynasty pharaoh, Horemhab (*c.* 1323–1295 B.C.), exempted judges from taxation.[116] Horemhab wanted to provide an incentive for judges to stop taking bribes. In theory, if the judges were permitted to keep their entire income, they would be less likely to accept bribes. We know that, on occasion, kings exempted certain temples from taxation. For example, a 5th Dynasty (*c.* 2510–2460 B.C.) king com-

---

112. Katary, Land Tenure in the Ramesside Period at 1. *Cf.* Wilson, Culture of Ancient Egypt 271 (According to Wilson, even though this document is quite useful, still "we cannot tell whether the figures given are the measures of grain assessed per unit of land or are some kind of data which the assessor would later use to fix the tax.").

113. *See* Katary, Land Tenure in the Ramesside Period at 265–266.

114. *Id.* at 21. *See also Id.* at 22 ("The actual cultivators...had to pay 30% of the yield of their plots to the state.").

115. *See Id.* at 83. In fact, over half of the plots assessed on the Wilbour Papyrus are five arouras in size. *See Id.* at 78.

116. *See supra* § 5.03[B]. Wilson, Culture of Ancient Egypt 237 (Describing the reign of Horemhab, Wilson says: "Pharaoh further made the courts of law free from any tax of silver and gold, in order to prevent an obligation of any kind from being exacted from the courts of Upper and Lower Egypt.'").

pletely exempted the temple at Abydos from all taxes. Evidently, it was the temples that enjoyed the most extensive tax exemption in ancient Egypt.

§6.03 FAMILY LAW

[A] INTRODUCTION

Men generally had only one legal, principal wife and it was she who was considered the mother of his heirs. Numerous sculptures and wall paintings depict husbands and wives together showing respect and love towards one another. Artistic representations depict children also as integral parts of the family unit. One word of caution is in order. A great deal of our information about family law—and especially marriage and divorce—comes from the Ptolemaic Period (c. 304–30 B.C.) and may or may not necessarily reflect conditions during the Old, Middle, and New Kingdoms.

[B] MARRIAGE

Most scholars believe that the ancient Egyptians had no formal, legal requirements for a valid marriage. They had neither a legal nor religious ritual to commemorate marriage. Eyre explains:

> The sole significant act seems to have been…cohabitation, and, in particular, the entry of one party, usually the woman, into the household of the other. Marriage was referred to simply as the founding of a house (grg pr), the entry into the partner's house ('q r pr), or simply living together (ḥmsi irm).[117]

Marriage was, in essence, a private matter that did, however, entail a number of customary social elements. Upon marriage, the man became a hy (husband) and the woman became a ḥm-t (wife). Ordinarily the bride and groom came from the same social class. We do not have a great deal of evidence regarding the customary age for brides and grooms. The texts that

---

117. C.J. Eyre, *Crime and Adultery in Ancient Egypt*, 70 J. EGYPTIAN ARCHAEOLOGY 92, 100–101 (1984) (footnotes omitted). *See also* PESTMAN, MARRIAGE & MATRIMONIAL PROPERTY 29–30 (Describing one specific type of marriage found in the documents, he says "this marriage is exclusively and solely concluded by taking the girl to the house of her future husband, while presents are sent along with her."); *Id.* at 51 ("the outward sign of a marriage is the cohabitation of husband and wife.") (footnote omitted).

we do possess show that males were often around twenty years old and females were younger, some just barely past fourteen (*i.e.*, just past puberty).

Peasants surely could marry. Whether slaves who were captives of foreign conquest had the same right of marriage is doubtful. Although Egyptian nobles ordinarily had only one principal wife (*i.e.*, monogamous marriage was clearly the ancient Egyptian norm), evidence shows that some royalty and nobility had two or more wives; like the 6th Dynasty kings Teti and Pepi (*c.* 2350–2200 B.C.) who each had at least two wives apiece. And, in addition to his legitimate legal wife, a noble could have a harem of women who lived in the household. It was the king's principal wife, however, who legally was considered the mother of the regal line. In this regard, a king's secondary wives essentially constituted a harem. The principal wife could be the king's sister. But the tradition of purity of royal blood began changing in the 18th Dynasty (*c.* 1552–1295 B.C.). Indeed, several 18th Dynasty pharaohs married foreign wives who bore princes who later became pharaohs themselves. There are indications that, on occasion, a king may have married his own daughter. Furthermore, it seems quite clear that royal brothers and sisters intermarried. Other than the royalty, however, sibling marriages and father-daughter marriages were probably quite uncommon. Indeed, commoners probably were not allowed to marry their full sisters. Marriages between uncles and nieces, cousins, and half-siblings (*e.g.*, persons with the same father but a different mother), however, appear to have been legal. It was customary for the bride and groom to exchange certain types of property in association with the beginning of their marriage. Technically speaking, these were not really "gifts" in the strict sense of the modern word, but scholars have occasionally referred to them as such. The groom customarily transferred property–called the *šp*—to the bride's father. Its purpose was to sever, symbolically at least, the link between the woman and her family. Pestman interprets the *šp* as a kind of symbolic "consideration" or price paid for the bride.[118] Later in Egyptian legal history, it appears that the groom gave his bride the *šp* directly. The *šp* was comprised of wealth (we might be tempted to say "money"); often it was a small amount of corn. The bride's father was likely to give gifts to the couple (including something that was essentially a dowry, called the *ḥd n ir ḥm-t*) and a "wedding party" followed. The dowry usually had a much higher value than the *šp*. In addition, the bride typically owned personal items that she brought to the marriage, known as *nkt-w n s-ḥm-t* ("goods of a woman"). These were objects such as ornaments, a bed, mirrors, clothing,

---

118. *See* PESTMAN, MARRIAGE & MATRIMONIAL PROPERTY 19–20.

and sometimes even a musical instrument. Apparently, however, the most important item in this group was some type of special shawl called the *inšn*. Oddly enough, although the wife technically "owned" these articles, the husband was at liberty to dispose of them as he pleased (*e.g.*, he could even sell them). For, in the event of divorce, he was not obligated to return these precise objects to his wife, but only "similar" ones or even other things of equivalent value. In some marriages, the bride also gave her new husband another type of property, known as the *s'nḫ*, which was "money" given in return for the husband supporting her during the duration of the marriage. Apparently, if her husband predeceased her, the *s'nḫ* passed intestate to her directly, while upon her death, her children probably inherited it. In sum, then, there were three types of property that a wife routinely brought to her marriage: 1) a dowry (*ḥd n ir ḥm-t*); 2) her personal effects (*nkt-w n s-ḥm-t*); and, 3) funds intended for her maintenance and the maintenance of her children (*s'nḫ*). The wife technically owned these properties but the husband managed them in any way that he desired. His only obligation with respect to these properties was that, as a rule, he had to give to his wife a comparable sum if the couple divorced.

When a husband acquired property during marriage, Egyptian law—at least by the New Kingdom (*c.* 1552–1069 B.C.)—considered that both husband and wife owned it jointly: two-thirds belonging to the husband and one-third belonging to the wife. Although a husband was permitted to sell or otherwise transfer ownership of property that he jointly owned with his wife, if he did so, he was required to give her equivalent property in its place. The wife did not really have any control over her one-third share during the marriage. It came to her only when the marriage ended—either by divorce or at her husband's death. The same rule operated with respect to any property that the wife had brought to the marriage at its beginning.

Interestingly, we have a number of contracts—most of which date from the Ptolemaic period (*c.* 304–30 B.C.)—that were concluded between husbands and wives that spell out the husband's economic obligations to support his wife and their children. Although some Egyptologists have referred to these as "marriage contracts," they were actually *not* a necessary component of a legal marriage. Thus, Johnson calls these instead "annuity contracts."[119] At their core, the annuity contracts constitute agreements regard-

---

119. *See* Janet H. Johnson, *The Legal Status of Women in Ancient Egypt, in* MISTRESS OF THE HOUSE MISTRESS OF HEAVEN: WOMEN IN ANCIENT EGYPT 175, 180 (Anne K. Chapel and Glenn E. Markoe eds., 1996) ("These so-called marriage contracts, however, concern only economic matters—the husband's responsibility to feed and clothe his wife (and their children), and their children's right to inherit his

ing the disposition of property and property rights related to the marriage (and possible divorce). Indeed, a number of the annuity contracts contemplate the possibility of divorce. Ordinarily, the husband promises that, in the event of divorce initiated by either party, he will give his wife a large sum (an amount equal in value to the property that she brought to the marriage—*i.e.*, her "dowry" (*ḥd n ir ḥm-t*)—plus the value of his bridal gift, the *šp*). If he fails to do so, he will be required to continue to provide, on a monthly basis, a certain specified level of support for his wife and children (*e.g.*, grain, oil, clothing, provisions, silver) until such time that he does, indeed, pay her the preordained sum.

Egyptian law may have recognized a woman's right not to be abused by her husband in marriage. One Deir el-Medina legal text (Ostracon Nash 5 recto) deals with this domestic violence issue, but the text is so badly damaged that we cannot with any certainty state many conclusions. We do know that the court in that instance held that the husband's conduct was wrong. We are unable, however, to tell what consequences befell the man as a result of his conduct.

[C] DIVORCE

Apparently, as is true in modern America, many marriages in ancient Egypt ended in divorce. Both husband and wife had the right to sue the other for divorce. The terms of the annuity contracts[120] (which generally seem to have presumed that a man might eventually desire a younger bride), however, probably had a normative effect, and, thus, discouraged some men from divorcing their wives. To begin with, it was common for these annuity contracts to require that a husband return the *šp* if he decided to divorce his wife. But of greater consequence, upon divorce a husband ordinarily was required to return to his wife her dowry (or its equivalent). Several annuity contracts provide that, if the husband failed to return the dowry to his ex-wife within thirty days, he had to continue to provide maintenance for her until he did return it. Since the cost of maintenance far exceeded the dowry amount, husbands suing for divorce were likely to return the dowry and be done with it. Quite clearly, however, if a wife was guilty of adultery, the husband generally was not required to repay the *šp* nor did he have to make

---

wealth—and are more appropriately called 'annuity contracts.'") (footnote omitted). *See also* MATTHA, THE DEMOTIC LEGAL CODE OF HERMOPOLIS WEST 27–32, 92–103.

120. *See supra* § 6.03[B].

any other sort of payment to her. As a rule, though, upon divorce without adultery, a husband had to pay his wife (either with the original goods or their equivalent) a great deal: 1) the *šp* (or in some cases one-half of it); 2) her dowry (*ḥd n ir ḥm-t*); 3) her personal effects (*nkt-w n s-ḥm-t*); 4) the funds given to him at the beginning of the marriage for her maintenance and the maintenance of her children (*sʿnḫ*); and, 5) one-third of all property that he had acquired during the marriage. In the absence of adultery, a woman who sued for divorce ordinarily did not have to make any sort of payments; although, as was alluded to above, there are some annuity contracts that required a wife to forfeit one-half of the *šp* if she was the one who initiated divorce. In addition to the property already mentioned (*i.e.,* the property to which she was entitled upon divorce), a wife also ordinarily kept any property that she personally owned. If the party who was sued was found to have been at fault, s/he had to surrender their interest in any property that was jointly owned. Presumably "fault" included adultery. We know of a case, for example, finding a wife at fault in divorce where she seized and sold off joint property and even deserted her husband when he was ill.

[D] ROLES OF PARENTS & CHILDREN

Ancient Egyptian children were expected to respect both parents with abiding affection. As early as the 6th Dynasty (*c.* 2460–2200 B.C.), we find the eldest son assumeing the responsibility of administering the funds of the joint property upon the death of the father, and, generally speaking, when a father died, the eldest son became the new head of the family. Children also had a legal duty to care for the funerary rights of their deceased parents.

§6.04 INHERITANCE & SUCCESSION

[A] INTESTATE SUCCESSION

Under the ancient Egyptian laws of intestacy (*i.e.,* inheritance in the absence of a valid will), children inherited equal shares of their parents' estate. Thus, property first passed to a decedent's children. If there were no children, the decedent's siblings were next in line to inherit on an equal basis. If an intestate decedent left neither children nor siblings, our best evidence suggests that the deceased's parents inherited the estate. Generally speaking, husbands and wives did not inherit from one another. It appears that a woman's children inherited her dowry. Thus, upon the death of her husband, an Egyptian wife retained a life estate in her dowry (*i.e.,* after her death the dowry passed to her children) plus one-third of any property acquired by the couple during their marriage.

There seems to have been some degree of preference in inheritance for the eldest son. It was common, for example, for the eldest son to inherit his father's office or position.[121] It was he who was obligated to make funeral arrangements for his parents.[122] Thus, it is likely that he inherited more as a kind of compensation for shouldering extra filial duty.[123] The Law Collection of Hermopolis[124] actually provides that another child could take over the funerary obligations if the eldest son was unable or unwilling to do so. In such a case, the substitute "eldest son" became entitled to the additional inheritance that had been earmarked for the biological "eldest son." This substitute "eldest son" then administered his father's estate and became a guardian for his mother, brothers, and sisters.

Ordinarily, real estate passed undivided in inheritance. As a practical matter, it made more sense to allow houses and agricultural fields to remain intact. Thus, children usually inherited real property jointly. The eldest son normally managed the jointly-owned real estate for the group as a

---

121. *See* GAY ROBINS, WOMEN IN ANCIENT EGYPT 132; C.J. Eyre, *The Adoption Papyrus in Social Context,* 78 J. EGYPTIAN ARCHAEOLOGY 207, 215 (1992). *See infra* §6.04[D].

122. *See* GAY ROBINS, WOMEN IN ANCIENT EGYPT 132–133; C.J. Eyre, *The Adoption Papyrus in Social Context,* 78 J. EGYPTIAN ARCHAEOLOGY 207, 215 (1992); J.G. Manning, *Demotic Egyptian Instruments of Transfer as Evidence for Private Ownership of Real Property,* 71 CHICAGO-KENT L. REV. 237, 259 (1995).

123. *See* Janet H. Johnson, *The Legal Status of Women in Ancient Egypt, in* MISTRESS OF THE HOUSE MISTRESS OF HEAVEN: WOMEN IN ANCIENT EGYPT 175, 183 (Anne K. Chapel and Glenn E. Markoe eds., 1996) ("[T]he child called eldest son bore responsibility for taking care of his parents' funerals and received some of their property in recompense."); J.G. Manning, *Demotic Egyptian Instruments of Transfer as Evidence for Private Ownership of Real Property,* 71 CHICAGO-KENT L. REV. 237, 259 (1995) ("The privileged position of the eldest son derives from the fact that he was legally responsible for both the burial costs and the ritual of burying his parents.") (footnote omitted). *See also* Théodorides, *Concept* at 297 ("On the death of the eldest in a family, the title and duties of 'eldest son' devolved upon the next in age, though in fact a daughter was not called upon to hold a position equivalent to that of 'eldest son', for she was not 'eldest' in relation to her brothers.").

124. *See supra* §4.01.

whole.[125] Still, heirs could (and occasionally did) ask that such property be divided by the administrator of the estate.[126]

[B] TESTATE SUCCESSION

An ancient Egyptian could use the *imyt-pr* (*i.e.*, the same term that refers to the written document used to validate other types of property transfer) as a "will" to transfer either real or personal property and other forms of wealth either to persons or in proportions that differed from the scheme that would have been supplied by intestate succession. A testator had to record his will with the vizier's office in order for the will to be valid. Both men and women could execute valid wills. Egyptian law considered a will revocable, since it did not become effective until the testator's death. A man could revoke his will by means of a second *imyt-pr*, but we cannot be certain whether other methods of revocation were also valid.

As was noted above, under the law of intestate succession, a wife was entitled both to a life estate in her dowry and her one-third share of property acquired by her husband.[127] Apparently, her one-third share came to her upon her husband's death even if he left a will that failed to mention it. As a practical matter, however, a number of wills reveal that husbands routinely left more than the one-third intestate minimum to their wives. For example, one stela (Stela Cairo 34061), dating from the time of Thutmose III (*c.* 1458 B.C.), shows a husband leaving all of his property to his wife first, and then to his children upon her death. It may have been conventional for a father to give his daughter her inheritance as a dowry (we know of situations where this was, in fact, the case). A boy, on the other hand, did not re-

---

125. *See* MATTHA, THE DEMOTIC LEGAL CODE OF HERMOPOLIS WEST 39; Janet H. Johnson, *The Legal Status of Women in Ancient Egypt, in* MISTRESS OF THE HOUSE MISTRESS OF HEAVEN: WOMEN IN ANCIENT EGYPT 175, 184 (Anne K. Chapel and Glenn E. Markoe eds., 1996); GAY ROBINS, WOMEN IN ANCIENT EGYPT 136; C.J. Eyre, *The Adoption Papyrus in Social Context*, 78 J. EGYPTIAN ARCHAEOLOGY 207, 215–216 (1992); J.G. Manning, *Demotic Egyptian Instruments of Transfer as Evidence for Private Ownership of Real Property*, 71 CHICAGO-KENT L. REV. 237, 259–260 (1995). *See also supra* § 6.02[A](joint ownership).

126. *See* MATTHA, THE DEMOTIC LEGAL CODE OF HERMOPOLIS WEST 39; P.W. Pestman, *The Law of Succession in Ancient Egypt* 9 STUDIA ET DOCUMENTA AD JURA ANTIQUI PERTINENTIA 58, 67 (1969); C.J. Eyre, *The Adoption Papyrus in Social Context*, 78 J. EGYPTIAN ARCHAEOLOGY 207, 216 (1992); J.G. Manning, *Demotic Egyptian Instruments of Transfer as Evidence for Private Ownership of Real Property*, 71 CHICAGO-KENT L. REV. 237, 260 (1995) ("To be sure, family land could be split with the consent of the heirs."). *See also infra* § 6.04[C].

127. *See supra* § 6.04[A].

ceive his inheritance until the death of his parents. Parents could leave property to any child, male or female. Likewise, either parent could disinherit children. We have, for example, the "will" of a woman named Naunakhte who disinherited four of her children on the grounds that they had been neglecting her care. Naunakhte says, "But see, I am grown old,…and see, they are not looking after me in my turn.… [H]e who has not given to me, to him I will not give my property.….As for these four children of mine, they shall (not) participate in the division of any of my property."[128] Naunakhte's testamentary disposition is also worthy of note for two other reasons. In addition to disinheriting the four "bad" children, she expressly includes the other children who had taken care of her. Furthermore, she singles out one son, Kenherkhepeshef, for a "special reward" (bequeathing him a particular bronze washing-bowl).[129]

We also have a will of a man named Heti from the 4th Dynasty (c. 2625–2510 B.C.) who gave assets to his children, but with some restrictions on alienability. In addition, Heti's will provided for funerary offerings each day. This will is an interesting one. Heti, in essence, created an endowment. His will created a type of trust administered by his eldest son. He did this instead of contracting directly with the priests. According to the terms of the trust, each family member was to receive only the revenue generated by the trust; and the trust was to remain indivisible forever.

The Egyptians also used adoption as a means to circumvent the laws of intestate succession. In order to validate an adoption, an adopter merely stated, orally, his intent to adopt in the presence of witnesses. We know of a man, a stablemaster named Nebnefer, who lived under Ramses XI (c. 1098–1069 B.C.), who adopted his own wife. Thus, since she was technically his "child," she—not his brothers or sisters and not his parents—inherited his wealth. Interestingly, his wife (i.e., daughter by adoption), then, some seventeen years later, adopted three children who belonged to one of their house slaves, so that they, in due course, could inherit from her. It seems likely that those children—two daughters and one son—were fathered by Nebnefer.

[C] THE CONCEPT OF A TRUSTEE FOR AN ESTATE

The role of an estate administrator was recognized as early as the 6th Dynasty (c. 2460–2200 B.C.). The estate administrator was to "consume

---

128. Jaroslav Černý, *The Will of Naunakhte and the Related Documents*, 31 J. EGYPTIAN ARCHAEOLOGY 29, 31–32 (1945). *See also* PESTMAN, MARRIAGE AND MATRIMONIAL PROPERTY 163 (1961); McDOWELL, JURISDICTION 145.

129. *See* Jaroslav Černý, *The Will of Naunakhte and the Related Documents*, 31 J. EGYPTIAN ARCHAEOLOGY 29, 31, 48–49 (1945).

the fruits of the assets" but without causing any loss.[130] Generally speaking, an administrator was legally bound to preserve the principal of the estate as if he were the deceased father himself. It was also during the 6th Dynasty that it became common practice for the eldest son to assume the responsibility of administering the funds of the joint property upon the death of the father.

The lawsuit concerning Mose[131] (dating from late in the 18th Dynasty — 1552–1295 B.C.), in which the ownership of an estate was contested, provides an example of a woman being appointed trustee for property in dispute. In that case, one of the potential heirs (also a woman) objected to the trustee appointment, and she persuaded the magistrate to remove the trustee and to divide the estate equally among the six heirs instead. Heti's will, mentioned above, also created a trust with his son acting as trustee.[132]

[D] INHERITANCE OF OFFICE

Certain government offices became hereditary as early as the Old Kingdom (2700–2200 B.C.). We have clear evidence for two such offices: nomarch and vizier. Technically, the king retained the right to appoint a successor who was unrelated to a recently deceased nomarch. But as a practical matter, the king rarely ignored the late nomarch's rightful heir. We cannot be entirely certain whether the nomarch's eldest son succeeded to his father's nomarchy or whether the nomarch's eldest grandson—born of his eldest daughter— was the rightful successor (there is conflicting evidence). If it was the latter, it is possible that a nomarch's eldest daughter herself could have ruled a nome as rightful nomarch until her son reached an age at which he could govern in his own stead. Like the nomarchy, the office of vizier seems to have been hereditary even in the Old Kingdom. For example, we know that when the government changed hands at the outset of the 5th Dynasty (c. 2510–2460 B.C.), the vizerate also changed hands and became hereditary with a new family.

---

130. *See* Théodorides, *Concept* at 300. *See also supra* § 6.02[B] regarding the concepts *usus* and *usus fructus*.
131. *See supra* § 5.08.
132. *See supra* § 6.04[B].

§ 6.05 CRIMINAL LAW & TORT LAW (DAMAGE TO PERSONS & THINGS)

[A] INTRODUCTION

There is no compelling evidence to indicate that the ancient Egyptians formally recognized or even abstractly appreciated any general theory of legal recovery remotely similar to modern tort law. Rather, for them, it appears that criminal laws fulfilled some of the functions that modern tort law serves. As is true in many ancient legal systems, the ancient Egyptians did not distinguish between tort and crime in the same fashion that modern societies do. The legal term for "wrong" or "crime" was *bt3*.[133] In many instances, either a victim or his family bore the responsibility to initiate legal action. To be sure, today it is, as a practical matter, virtually impossible for us to distinguish ancient Egyptian tort law from criminal law in any meaningful way. One theoretical means of distinguishing tort from crime is to categorize laws and legal situations based on types of punishments (*i.e.,* the legal consequences). Monetary payments made by a wrongdoer to his victim as compensation are usually associated with torts whereas corporal punishments and fines paid to the State are hallmarks of criminal law. For convenience, this section (like the book as a whole) generally uses modern legal categories as points of reference. Thus, I have relied on modern American legal classifications of crime and tort to discuss analogous conduct in ancient Egypt. Before examining crimes and torts in detail, however, it is probably useful first to consider the consequences of such conduct; namely, punishments and penalties.

[B] PUNISHMENT: AN OVERVIEW[134]

[1] GENERAL

The term used for "punishment" was ordinarily *sb3yt*. More often than not, *sb3yt* involved some form of corporal punishment. In the Old and

---

133. *See* FAULKNER, A CONCISE DICTIONARY OF MIDDLE EGYPTIAN 85 (Defining *bt3* as "wrong, crime."); McDOWELL, JURISDICTION 26 ("In everyday settings *bt3* can mean 'wrong,' 'fault,' or 'harm'; an unpleasant or even offensive action but not necessarily the sort of thing one would take to court. On the other hand, in denunciations, verdicts and the like, *bt3* means 'crime'; at any rate, many of the most blatant crimes are called *bt3* or *bt3 n mwt,* 'crime worthy of death....'") (footnotes omitted).

134. This section provides an overview of punishment for wrongs. I have noted more specifically the punishments associated with individual wrongs in the appropriate sections that follow.

Middle Kingdoms, some criminal penalties were not as physically brutal as later in the New Kingdom. For example, a 5th Dynasty (c. 2510–2460 B.C.) text states that government officials found guilty of misusing their office were removed from office, forced to do labor, and had their property confiscated. Although these were stiff consequences, no bodily mutilation was involved. Other documents from the 6th Dynasty (c. 2460–2200 B.C.) as well as others from the 16th or 17th (c. 1600 B.C.) show officials punished by forfeiting their jobs and property in similar circumstances. Thus, divesting a criminal of his civic status (which included deprivation of ritual burial, and hence loss of status in the afterlife) coupled with forfeiture of property and forced labor were typical of early Egyptian criminal punishments. Beating became a criminal punishment in the Middle Kingdom (c. 2040–1674 B.C.). Later New Kingdom (c. 1552–1069 B.C.) penalties commonly consisted of "a complex set of punishments for various offenses, including beatings, mutilations, and impalement, as well as reduction to unfree status...."[135] Much punishment in the New Kingdom was corporal in nature—and brutal by today's standards; although some economic sanctions did exist, especially for theft. And, in lieu of money damages, since ancient Egypt was really a "non-monetary society," punishment could take the form of conscription for public service.[136] Convicted criminals routinely lost their freedom and their right to inherit office. Evidence suggests that the death penalty was imposed for murder, conspiracy to assassinate the king (treason), robbery of royal tombs, perjury (at least technically), and judicial bribery. In the Nauri Decree of Seti I (c. 1294–1279 B.C.), the punishment prescribed for corrupt judges was 100 blows, removal from office, and to be "placed as a cultivator in the Foundation...."[137] The Edict of

---

135. David Lorton, *The Treatment of Criminals in Ancient Egypt*, 20 J. ECONOMIC & SOCIAL HIST. ORIENT 2, 50 (1977). *See also* McDOWELL, JURISDICTION 29, n. 107 (Referring to death, beating, and mutilation as punishments); *Id.* at 173 (Referring to beating as a punishment). *See also* BEDELL, CRIMINAL LAW 174 ("In the Edict of Horemhab there are crimes for which both mutilation and exile are prescribed."); *Id.* at 175–176 ("[T]here is one recorded case in which cutting off the hand was the specific punishment.") (Bedell also notes that this was a punishment that Diodorus Siculus mentioned, as well.); *Id.* at 178 ("Indeed, the concept of forced labor as reparation for various types of crimes was thoroughly entrenched in Egyptian legal practice."); *Id.* ("The usual number of blows was a hundred, but there were many crimes requiring two hundred blows.") (footnote omitted).

136. *See* T.G.H. JAMES, PHARAOH'S PEOPLE: SCENES FROM LIFE IN IMPERIAL EGYPT 83, 85–87 (1984).

137. William F. Edgerton, *The Nauri Decree of Seti I: A Translation and Analysis of the Legal Portion*, 6 J. NEAR EASTERN STUD. 219, 227 (1947). *See also* BEDELL, CRIMINAL LAW 30–31.

Horemhab punished a corrupt judge with the death penalty ("it shall be (reckoned) to him (for) a great capital crime.").[138] In the Old Kingdom, decapitation was a common method of execution. Although artistic representations from the New Kingdom show prisoners of war being decapitated, there is no similar proof regarding it as type of death penalty. The Egyptians used impalement as a means of execution at least by the 19th Dynasty (c. 1295–1188 B.C.). And, during the New Kingdom, impalement is the only method of State execution for which we have hard evidence. The Nauri Decree of Seti I (c. 1294–1279 B.C.), for example, mentions impalement as a penalty twice. There are also a handful of references to casting convicted criminals to the crocodiles. Death by crocodile may have been used as a literary device to denote either State sanctioned or divinely sanctioned capital punishment. As is true with death by burning or drowning, when a criminal was eaten by a crocodile, he lost the opportunity for a ritual burial.

[2] INCARCERATION

Although prisons existed, they were usually used as means either for detaining suspects before trial or for holding convicted criminals while awaiting their sentences. Even some smaller towns may have had prison facilities. The Egyptians ordinarily did not build prisons but rather used existing buildings for incarceration. Criminals, for example, were routinely held in temples used to serve as makeshift prisons. In Deir el-Medina, it is possible that persons suspected of theft were imprisoned at the ḫtm.[139] It is possible, also, that imprisonment was occasionally a punishment in and of itself; for the prince Merikare (c. 2100 B.C.) was instructed to "punish by beating and imprisonment..." in an effort to maintain order.[140] By the second century B.C., there is more solid evidence. Documents of that time specifically refer to taking convicted criminals to prison.[141]

[C] THE LANDSCAPE OF EGYPTIAN CRIME & TORT

One useful starting point for considering tort and crime is the well-known *Book of the Dead*. By the New Kingdom, scribes routinely produced

---

138. BEDELL, CRIMINAL LAW 152 (footnote omitted).

139. *See supra* § 5.03[C].

140. T.G.H. JAMES, PHARAOH'S PEOPLE: SCENES FROM LIFE IN IMPERIAL EGYPT 73 (1984).

141. *See* S. Allam, *Egyptian Law Courts in Pharaonic and Hellenistic Times*, 77 J. EGYPTIAN ARCHAEOLOGY 109, 120 (1991).

copies of the *Book of the Dead* on papyrus scrolls which were then placed alongside the corpse of a deceased individual at burial.[142] To a certain degree, the *Book of the Dead* is analogous to a legal brief which presents arguments on behalf of the deceased.[143] In the *Book of the Dead*, the speaker—the deceased—claims to have lived an exemplary life and professes not to have done many, many different acts. Presumably, each act that the speaker disclaims represents either a criminal or civil wrong (or both). Among those acts listed are the following: murder; conspiracy to commit murder; diminishing food in the temples; stealing the food offerings of the dead; adultery; "self-pollution in the pure precinct of . . . [the] city god;" misrepresenting the grain measure; misrepresenting measurements of length in commercial transactions; misrepresenting measurements of land in real estate transactions; misrepresenting weights in commercial transactions; stealing cattle; snaring sacred birds; catching fish in pools (*i.e.,* instead of from the river?); diverting water from a neighbor's property to one's own; withholding herds of the temple endowments; "interfer[ing] with god in his payments. . . ."

In addition to the catalogue of wrongs identified in the *Book of the Dead*, there is independent evidence regarding a great deal of criminal conduct in ancient Egypt. As regards "mainstream" or everyday criminal law, there were several aspects of the ancient Egyptian criminal law system that were similar to modern American law. For example, they seem to have established a police force and, as was mentioned above, some kind of a prison system.[144] The prisons do not appear to have been extensive, but there were buildings that functioned temporarily as prisons nonetheless. Officials maintained criminal records. And some laws created specific punishments that were mandatory for certain offenses. Criminal sanctions were available for wrongs as diverse as murder and infanticide, perjury, "treachery," forgery, and judicial misconduct (including bribery).

We also have extensive accounts of several extraordinary criminal trials; trials where special commissions were formed. In these extraordinary criminal trials, special procedures were established for certain high crimes such as treason and robbery of royal tombs.[145] Among the wrongs for which we

---

142. *See supra* §4.02. *See also* GRIMAL, ANCIENT EGYPT 131 ("From the New Kingdom onwards funerary texts were also included in the bandages, fulfilling the same purpose as the amulets and jewels; a *Book of the Dead*, for instance was often inserted between the legs of the mummy.").

143. *See generally* THE BOOK OF THE DEAD: PAPYRI OF ANI, HUNEFER, ANHAÏ (1979) (Commentaries by Evelyn Rossiter). *See also supra* §4.02.

144. *See supra* §6.05[B][2].

145. *See supra* §§5.03[D], 5.13, and *infra* §§6.05[D][2], 6.05[E].

have more extensive evidence are the following: theft; conspiracy/treason and homicide; certain kinds of sexual conduct; judicial misconduct; and, extortion.

[D] THEFT/CONVERSION

[1] GENERAL

The term used for "theft" in our documents from Deir el-Medina is usually *ṯ3wt*.[146] The Deir el-Medina *ḳnbt* handled two especially curious criminal cases involving theft. In one (Ostracon Nash 1), a woman named *Ḥri3* was initially accused of stealing a copper chisel. Then when the court ordered a search of *Ḥri3*'s home, they discovered, in addition to the missing copper chisel, a censer of the god Amon (it had been stolen too). This was notable because the censer was property that the State owned. There is a second case (Ostracon Nash 2) involving chisel theft in Deir el-Medina, but in that case the chisels themselves were State-owned (*i.e.,* "belonged to Pharaoh"). We know that the court conducted a thorough investigation into the matter, but we do not know how the case was resolved. Interestingly, Horemhab's Edict contains several obscure provisions relating to theft of crops (a certain kind of herb, corn, flax, and vegetables).

As a rule, a convicted thief had to return stolen goods to the individual to whom they belonged, and, in addition, pay damages to the victim of double or triple (the cases vary) the value of the stolen goods (what modern law might call "punitive damages"). In some cases of theft, damages were three or four-times the value of the stolen object(s). If, on the other hand, the thief had stolen from the State rather than a private individual, his penalties were far more severe: usually eighty to one hundred-times the value of objects stolen from the State. In one Deir el-Medina theft case (Ostracon Turin 57455), imprisonment was used as a penalty for theft. Apparently, this was a more serious theft than the sort for which a defendant was ordered merely to return the goods and pay an additional two to three-times the value of the stolen goods. For robbery of a *royal* tomb, the penalty was death. Neither the status of the thief nor the status of the victim appears to have been relevant in fixing penalties for theft. Thieves received the same punishments regardless of their social standing.

---

146. *See* McDowell, Jurisdiction 38; Faulkner, A Concise Dictionary of Middle Egyptian 303 (Defining *ṯ3wt* as "theft"; and, incidentally, citing its use in *The Eloquent Peasant* as an illustration).

The Nauri Decree of Seti I (*c.* 1295–1279 B.C.) imposed ear and nose amputation plus forced labor as punishments both for direct and indirect forms of theft: 1) stealing an animal of the estate (an offense to sacred animals); and, 2) moving a boundary marker of the god's estate (an offense to sacred real property). In addition, the thief's family suffered penal servitude on the estate as part of the punishment. Other minor offenses that resulted in a loss of production on the estate (*i.e.,* other indirect kinds of theft) were punished by a specific number of blows (typically 200 or 100), "pierced wounds" (typically five), and forced labor. Also, in the Nauri Decree, one theft crime imposed death as its penalty: when a person who was entrusted with an animal sacred to Osiris allowed it to be offered to a different god or gave it away. Independent evidence shows that theft of a State-owned ox could be punished by exile. Under Horemhab's Edict, a soldier who stole hides from citizens received, as punishment, "one hundred blows, opening five wounds and taking away the hides which he took."[147]

[2] THE GREAT TOMB ROBBERIES

The most celebrated robbery trial—indeed these are often referred to as "the Great Tomb Robberies"—occurred during the reign of Ramses IX (*c.* 1125–1107 B.C.).[148] The court was comprised of "the superintendent of the town and governor" and he was "assisted by two other high officials, the *scribe* and the *speaker* of Pharaoh...."[149] These three "sent out a commission of inquiry" (police officers, scribes, priests, and others) to inspect the tombs in Thebes. Upon investigation, they discovered that, of the ten *royal* tombs that they feared had been broken into, only one had, in fact, been entered. But robbers had also penetrated several private tombs, and they had ransacked the mummies in order to snatch the jewelry contained in the wrappings. The task force sent its written report to the three judges as-

---

147. BREASTED, HISTORY OF EGYPT 404 (footnote omitted). *See also* David Lorton, *The Treatment of Criminals in Ancient Egypt,* 20 J. ECONOMIC & SOCIAL HIST. OF THE ORIENT 2, 25–27 (1977); WILSON, CULTURE OF ANCIENT EGYPT 237 (Wilson describes Horemhab's edict as "not a code of law, but rather a series of police regulations directed against specific malpractices and also a reorganization of the administrative machinery in the land, in order to control future abuses."); GARDINER, EGYPT OF THE PHARAOHS 244–45 (Gardiner describes Horemhab's penalties for theft as follows: "The penalties imposed were of great severity, the malefactors in the worst cases being docked of their noses and banished to the fortress town of Tjel on the Asiatic boarder, and in the lesser cases punished with a hundred strokes and five open wounds."). *See also* McDOWELL, JURISDICTION 158 (Referring to blows as a type of punishment).

148. *See* GRIMAL, ANCIENT EGYPT 289 ("The robberies took place in the sixteenth year of Ramesses IX' reign."). *See generally Id.* at 289–290.

149. ERMAN, LIFE IN ANCIENT EGYPT 131.

signed to the case. The authorities apprehended eight suspects, most of whom were servants in the temple of Amon. Upon being tortured, they confessed that they had broken into the burial chamber. After having confessed, they were compelled to identify the scene of their crime. It was Ramses who then pronounced the sentence for the guilty robbers. Quite clearly, execution—apparently by impalement—was the customary penalty for robbing royal tombs.

Additional evidence soon came to light suggesting that thieves had entered other tombs in the section of the necropolis nearest the tombs of the royal relatives. But upon further inspection, it appeared that none had really been pilfered. And in order to dispel rumors, government officials did their best to inform the public that the tombs had not been robbed. After further threats and squabbling among officials, the whole affair seems to have ended. But thieves continued to loot tombs in the ensuing years. For example, during the first year of Ramses X (c. 1107–1098 B.C.), officials made nearly sixty arrests for tomb robbery. Robbers made their way into the outer chambers of the tombs of Ramses II and Seti I, and later sold the valuables that they had stolen. Thefts continued unabated and officials ultimately gathered the mummies of the most renowned pharaohs and hid them together in one place in an effort to conceal the bodies (at least) of the deceased kings from the rapacious bandits of the necropolis. Luckily for modern scholars, that hiding place at Deir el-Bahri went undiscovered until the late Nineteenth Century A.D. Thus, indirectly, the thievery of ancient tomb robbers caused the royal mummies of the New Kingdom to be preserved. When Gaston Maspero finally discovered the cache of royal mummies in 1881, museum officials were able to collect them and transfer them to the Cairo Museum.

[E] CONSPIRACY/TREASON & HOMICIDE

Records of two ancient conspiracy trials—conspiracies to assassinate an Egyptian king—have survived: one from the 6th Dynasty (c. 2460–2200 B.C.) and the other from the 19th (c. 1295–1188 B.C.). This type of crime necessitated extraordinary procedures, not merely the judicial machinery of routine criminal operations.[150] Interestingly, apart from these cases relating to political assassinations, there is precious little evidence regarding ordinary murder or homicide. As was mentioned above,[151] the *Book of the Dead* indicates that the Egyptians treated homicide as wrongful conduct.

---

150. *See supra* §§ 5.03[D], 5.13.
151. *See supra* § 6.05[C].

McDowell suggests that the one text (Ostracon Deir el-Medina 126) could refer to a murder. But she admits that there is really not much on which to rely.[152] Nevertheless, we have no texts relating to a murder trial from the Ramesside Period.[153] A 21st Dynasty (c. 1069–945 B.C.) stela (Stela of Banishment) shows that the Egyptians punished murder with the death penalty. Hoch and Orel note both that "[t]here is an apparent lack of evidence concerning murder (as distinct from simple homicide) in ancient Egypt"[154] and that "there is no comprehensive discussion...of what constituted murder in that society."[155] Nevertheless, there were specific terms used for murder: sm3 m nf (Middle Egyptian) and hdb m grg (Late Egyptian).[156] "Both phrases may be translated as 'to kill wrongfully.'"[157] As near as we can tell, the ancient Egyptians considered homicide as murder if it was wrongful or unjustifiable. They did not, necessarily, focus on the issue of premeditation as a determining factor.[158] But according to Diodorus Siculus ancient Egyptian law under the Ptolemies (c. 304–30 B.C.) appreciated the difference between premeditated and unpremeditated murder.

When the royal harem hatched a plot to assassinate King Pepi I in the 6th Dynasty (c. 2325 B.C.), Pepi immediately appointed an individual named Weni to act alone as a special prosecutor to hear evidence and to issue a written report of his findings. According to Weni's first-person account:

> When there was litigation in private in the king's harem against the Queen, His Majesty caused me to go to hear (the matter) alone without there being any vizier or any other official there, only myself alone, because of my excellence and of my being firmly planted in the heart of His Majesty, and because His Majesty had confidence in me. It was I who put it in writing alone with one magistrate, though my rank was that of an Overseer of the tenants of the Palace. Never before had the like of me heard a secret matter of the king's harem, but His Majesty caused me to hear it, because I was excellent in the heart of His Majesty beyond any official of his, beyond any noble of his, beyond any servant of his.[159]

---

152. See McDowell, Jurisdiction 225–226.

153. Bedell bluntly asserts: "We do not know how murder was treated in this period." Bedell, Criminal Law 143–143a.

154. See James Hoch and Sara E. Orel, Murder in Ancient Egypt, in Death and Taxes in the Ancient Near East 87 (Sara E. Orel ed., 1992).

155. Id. at 88.

156. See Id. at 92.

157. Id.

158. Id.

159. Gardiner, Egypt of the Pharaohs 95. See Grimal, Ancient Egypt 82–83. See also supra §§ 5.03[D], 5.13.

We know more details of a similar conspiracy that occurred during the reign of Ramses III (*c.* 1186–1154 B.C.). As soon as the scheme was uncovered, Ramses selected fourteen members for a special investigatory commission. When two of the judges and several other court officials were found to have "caroused with" some of the accused harem women, they were immediately tried and found guilty of judicial misconduct. A third judge was accused but was acquitted. The guilty were punished by having their ears and noses cut off. One of the judges immediately committed suicide after having endured his gruesome punishment. The trials of the conspirators proceeded. Each conspirator (including those who merely *knew about* the conspiracy)—thirty-two people in all—received the death penalty.[160]

[F] SEXUAL CONDUCT: HOMOSEXUALITY; PROSTITUTION; RAPE; ADULTERY

Homosexual relations between consenting partners was not subject to legal sanctions in ancient Egypt. Similarly, there is very little evidence relating to any criminalization of prostitution. In addition, unmarried, consenting adults were free to have sex with one another. Both rape and adultery, on the other hand, were considered wrongful conduct. Johnson explains, however, that it is difficult to distinguish rape from adultery in Egyptian law: "In the cases we have, we cannot be certain whether the woman was a willing participant or not—that is, whether it was a case of rape or adultery."[161] It is possible that the Egyptians treated adultery not as an issue for courts to deal with but rather as a family law matter—something that a husband and wife had to resolve privately. Divorce was the most likely consequence of adultery.[162] And, if the wife was guilty of adultery, she forfeited to her husband her one-third share of their marital property, her *šp*, and any dowry.[163]

The Middle Kingdom story, *King Cheops and the Magicians* (Papyrus Westcar), provides a fictional account of adultery. In the second tale in the

---

160. *See supra* § 5.13.
161. Janet H. Johnson, *The Legal Status of Women in Ancient Egypt, in* MISTRESS OF THE HOUSE MISTRESS OF HEAVEN: WOMEN IN ANCIENT EGYPT 175, 216, n. 47 (Anne K. Chapel and Glenn E. Markoe eds., 1996). *See* McDOWELL, JURISDICTION 210 (Referring to "a possible case of rape.").
162. *See supra* § 6.03[C]; C.J. Eyre, *Crime and Adultery in Ancient Egypt*, 70 J. EGYPTIAN ARCHAEOLOGY 92, 98 (1984); PESTMAN, MARRIAGE & MATRIMONIAL PROPERTY 55–56; McDOWELL, JURISDICTION 35–36.
163. *See supra* §§ 6.03–6.04.

narrative, a man named Webaoner discovers that his wife has been committing adultery on a routine basis with a townsman. Without a trial of any sort, Webaoner summons a magical crocodile to attack the townsman. The crocodile snatches the adulterous townsman and descends to the bottom of a lake for seven days. In the meanwhile, Webaoner brings King Nebka for assistance. The king, upon hearing the facts of the adultery, instructs the crocodile to take the body of the townsman away. Thus, the king expressly approves the way that Webaoner handled the situation. This story seems to imply, then, that under Egyptian law, a husband had the right to kill an adulterer whom he discovered with his wife. As for Webaoner's adulteress wife, the king ordered that she be burned alive. In fact, the king, himself, apparently acted as the executioner: "His [Majesty the King of Upper] and Lower Egypt, Nebka, the vindicated, had the wife of Webaoner taken to a plot north of the capital, and he set / fire to her [. . . in] the river."[164] This suggests that capital punishment—in this case, death by burning—could have been the penalty for a woman who committed adultery. Still, one must remember that the example of Webaoner is fictional. Other evidence recommends that "such acts of vengeance" for adultery were *not* common.[165] The later account of the Greek historian Diodorus reports that Egyptian law punished a man convicted of rape by castration; and that a man found guilty of adultery was punished by a thousand lashes, while an adulteress had her nose amputated.

[G] JUDICIAL MISCONDUCT

Judicial misconduct was especially problematic. During the reign of Horemhab (*c.* 1323–1295 B.C.) at the close of the 18th Dynasty, the pharaoh made judicial bribery a capital offense, with a mandatory death penalty. In the case of the harem conspiracy during the reign of Ramses III (*c.* 1186–1154 B.C.),[166] several judges were arrested for becoming friendly with a number of the defendants. As punishment, their ears and noses were cut off.[167]

---

164. SIMPSON, THE LITERATURE OF ANCIENT EGYPT 18.

165. *See* David Lorton, *Legal and Social Institutions of Pharaonic Egypt, in* 1 CIVILIZATIONS OF THE ANCIENT NEAR EAST 345, 358 (Jack M. Sasson ed., 1995) ("While literary texts intimate that a jealous husband might kill his wife and the other man, the 'real life' texts...do not suggest that such acts of vengeance were the norm....").

166. *See supra* §§ 5.13, 6.05[E].

167. *See supra* § 6.05[E]. *See also* Janet H. Johnson, *The Legal Status of Women in Ancient Egypt, in* MISTRESS OF THE HOUSE MISTRESS OF HEAVEN: WOMEN IN ANCIENT EGYPT 175, 215, n. 12 (Anne K. Chapel and Glenn E. Markoe eds., 1996) (Ex-

[H] EXTORTION BY OFFICIALS & TAX COLLECTORS

The Egyptian government in antiquity farmed out taxes.[168] For a fixed sum, the government sold the rights to gather taxes to tax collectors. Nevertheless, the government prohibited tax collectors from overcharging the taxpayers, and made tax extortion a criminal offense. Clearly there were tax collectors who, on occasion, overcharged taxpayers, and kept more than their legitimate share. Thutmose III (c. 1479–1425 B.C.) and Horemhab (c. 1323–1295 B.C.) (both 18th Dynasty pharaohs) are credited with taking exceptional measures to crack down on extortionate tax gatherers. Horemhab, for example, was struggling to reassert pharaonic authority in the wake of the relative laissez-faire laxity that had existed under Akhenaton (c. 1352–1348 B.C.). During the reign of Akhenaton, local government officials had become rapacious. Thus, when Horemhab became king, he took steps to punish the corrupt local officials. In his Edict, Horemhab promulgated a series of laws designed to thwart specific misconduct.[169]

[I] MISCELLANEOUS WRONGS

[1] BATTERY

In modern American law, battery is intentional harmful or offensive contact with another. A few texts suggest that ancient Egyptian law also regarded such conduct as a wrong worthy of punishment. One document

---

plaining that three members of the six-person subcommittee were arrested because they were becoming friendly with the harem women!); ERMAN, LIFE IN ANCIENT EGYPT 144 ("[T]heir punishment was fulfilled by cutting off their noses and ears."). *See also* BEDELL, CRIMINAL LAW 31 ("[T]hree judges, a police chief, and an officer of the infantry were found guilty of carousing with some of the guilty harem women and probably taking a bribe."); *Id.* at 32 (Noting that the guilty judges were punished by dismissal and mutilation (their ears and noses were amputated), and that one judge committed suicide in the wake of his conviction.); *Id.* at 171 (Referring to several of the judges in the harem conspiracy "carousing with" some of the defendants, and being punished by amputation of their ears and noses.).

168. *See supra* § 6.02[D].

169. *See* Kurt Pflüger, *The Edict of Haremhab*, 5 J. NEAR EASTERN STUD. 260 (1944); David Lorton, *The Treatment of Criminals in Ancient Egypt*, 20 J. ECONOMIC & SOCIAL HIST. OF THE ORIENT 2, 24–25 (1977); BEDELL, CRIMINAL LAW 12 (Referring to the decrees of pharaohs (such as Horemhab and Seti I), Bedell states: "These decrees contained criminal statutes for certain crimes against a particular estate of a god."); T.G.H. JAMES, PHARAOH'S PEOPLE: SCENES FROM LIFE IN IMPERIAL EGYPT 81–82 (1984). *See also supra* §§ 4.01, 5.03[B], 5.05, 6.05[B][1], and 6.05[D].

(Papyrus Geneva MAH 15274 verso III), for example, records that a man who struck three others on the head was punished. There are a few other cases in which a person was accused of conduct that we would characterize as battery. In one case (Papyrus Salt 124 2, 17), the wrongdoer, who beat nine different men, received a beating himself as punishment. And in two other instances, including the case of the man who hit three others on the head mentioned above (Papyrus Geneva MAH 15274 verso III and Papyrus Turin 1977), the batterers were punished by forced labor (cutting stone and "compulsory labor" (*h3yt*)).

[2] TRESPASS TO LAND

One case recorded on a papyrus suggests that Egyptian law (at least in Deir el-Medina) recognized the legal theory of trespass to land.

[3] TRESPASS TO CHATTELS/VANDALISM (CRIMINAL MISCHIEF)

One case from Deir el-Medina (RAD 57, 8–58, 6) involves conduct that is analogous to what we might be tempted to call either trespass to chattels (in a civil law context) or vandalism — or criminal mischief (in a criminal law context). A workman named Pn-'nḫt reports "that two workmen... stripped the boulder on top of the tomb of Ramesses II...."[170] Another possible reference to what modern law would consider trespass to chattels, vandalism, or criminal mischief involved a man named P3-nb who was accused of "urinating in a private tomb".[171]

[4] DEFAMATION

Egyptian law had a cause of action for some form of defamation, but we know very little regarding the particulars. In one Deir el-Medina case (Ostracon Cairo 25556), a foreman named *Ḥ3y* complained that a woman and several workmen had slandered him. According to *Ḥ3y*, the defendants said that he had cursed or insulted Seti I (*c.* 1294–1279 B.C.), the reigning pharaoh. Those found guilty of this defamation received a beating as punishment (100 blows). The facts recorded in this case do, however, suggest that truth could be an effective defense in defamation cases; for it was only after the defendants admitted that their statements about the plaintiff were false that the defendants were found guilty. After the defendants admitted that

---

170. *See* McDowell, Jurisdiction 208.
171. *See Id.* at 210; *Id.* at 228.

they had committed perjury, the judges demanded that they take an oath that invoked mutilation (*i.e.,* amputation of nose and ears) if they repeated their defamatory allegations. In another case (Papyrus Deir el-Medina 26 A) that appears to have involved defamation, a foreman named *Ḥnsw* alleged that one of his men had cursed someone (or perhaps something). The defamer was punished with 100 blows of a stick.

§6.06 TRADE, CONTRACTS, & COMMERCIAL LAW

[A] INTRODUCTION

The ancient Egyptians developed extensive domestic and international trade. The Nile facilitated the transport of goods and provided ready access to the Mediterranean. Consequently, at least as early as recorded history (roughly 3000 B.C.), Egyptian merchants actively bought and sold goods throughout the Nile valley and beyond. As Egyptian merchants plied the Nile's waters, they also kept books and accounts, gave purchase orders and receipts, and entered into long term written contracts. The 4th Dynasty King Snefru (*c.* 2600 B.C.) imported wood from abroad. And other evidence indicates that the Egyptians of the pyramid age traded with Lybia, Byblos, the Sudan, Punt, Asia, and even the Aegean world. The government, however, exercised some degree of control over foreign trade on the Nile throughout most of antiquity. During the Middle Kingdom (*c.* 2040–1674 B.C.), more tradesmen, artisans, and artificers were producing and selling their wares than ever before. As might be expected, trade in the Middle Kingdom expanded beyond what would have been imaginable in the Old Kingdom. Foreign markets which the Egyptians had only begun exploring in the Old Kingdom now took on exceptional prominence. Foreign trade during the New Kingdom (*c.* 1552–1069 B.C.) burgeoned. Egyptians bought, sold, and traded goods with foreign lands and peoples such as Nubia, the Sudan, Sinai, Lybia, Babylonia, Assyria, Crete, Mycenae, Rhodes, Palestine, Cyprus, Phoenicia, the Hittites, and other locations throughout the Aegean and Mediterranean. Foreign trade became so extensive under Amenhotep III (*c.* 1390–1352 B.C.) that he established a kind of coast guard or marine police who patrolled the Delta and turned back illegal boats. They also staffed customs houses in the Delta and collected duties for all goods (except those which were being remitted to the pharaoh). With commerce developed to such a degree, it was crucial for Egypt to establish a coherent jurisprudence of business, contract, and commercial law.

[B] BUSINESS ORGANIZATIONS

Early in their legal development, the Egyptians recognized the concept of corporate identity for legal purposes. For example, the State was considered to be its own business entity. There were also associations of people deemed to be business entities, such as the family syndicate created in Heti's will.[172] Heti's family syndicate was an association of individuals comprising a business organization with its own legal personality. Temples and statue cults also were regarded as business entities (although the gods were deemed the actual owners of the temples).[173] Corporate identity in ancient Egypt was important probably in terms of liability in the same way that today we use a corporation as a shield for liability and for accounting purposes. An association had its own life so to speak. Many scholars have asserted that the large estates owned and managed by the government and temples collected taxes—in goods—and channeled their yield to the workers and inhabitants. A number of modern scholars have referred to this as a "redistributive economy."[174] Warburton, however, maintains that this is an erroneous assumption:

> The degree of private enterprise demonstrated by the records stands in clear contrast to the absence of any recorded "redistribution" on a large scale. The state was collecting and constructing, but it does not seem to have been redistributing, primarily because the population had their own sources of income in the private sector.[175]

Indeed, Warburton asserts that "other sources suggest that the ancient Egyptian economy could even be classified as a kind of nascent capitalism,

---

172. *See supra* § 6.04[B].

173. *See supra* § 6.02[A]; Andrea McDowell, *Legal Aspects of Care of the Elderly in Egypt to the End of the New Kingdom, in* THE CARE OF THE ELDERLY IN THE ANCIENT NEAR EAST 199, 204–207 (Marten Stol and Sven P. Vleeming eds., 1998); Théodorides, *Concept* at 294 (Noting that other legal entities/personalities included temples "whose estates are regarded as belonging to the gods to who they are dedicated....").

174. *See* Edward Bleiberg, *The Economy of Ancient Egypt, in* 3 CIVILIZATIONS OF THE ANCIENT NEAR EAST 1373, 1375 (Jack M. Sasson ed., 1995) ("In a redistributive economic organization, all goods are collected by a central authority and channeled to others on the basis of social status or kinship."); David Lorton, *Legal and Social Institutions of Pharaonic Egypt, in* 1 CIVILIZATIONS OF THE ANCIENT NEAR EAST 345, 353 (Jack M. Sasson ed., 1995) ("They collected part of what their tenants raised as taxes and used some of the proceeds to pay their employees, a system that is called 're-distributive.'"). *See also supra* § 6.02[D].

175. WARBURTON, STATE AND ECONOMY IN ANCIENT EGYPT 69. *See also Id.* at 79–80.

for we have wage-labour, a market for land, production for the market, and state involvement."[176]

[C] CONTRACTS

Most early trade (both domestic and foreign) was probably conducted by simple barter, an exchange of one kind of goods for another. Even in the New Kingdom (c. 1552–1069 B.C.), records show that workers at Deir el-Medina continued to transact much of their daily business by simply swapping goods (i.e., barter). Nevertheless, the Egyptians also formulated basic principles of true contracts — that is, mutual exchanges dependent upon bilateral promises for future performance, as opposed to merely a contemporaneous swap. For example, we know of one contract that involved bilateral promises for future performance that was the subject of litigation (in either the late 19th or early 20th Dynasty (c. 1200 B.C.)). This contract provided that a scribe would make a coffin for a woman's dead husband. In return, the woman promised to give the scribe a particular hut. Similarly, the lease agreements detailed in the Law Collection of Hermopolis typically recite, for example, that the lessee promises to pay rent to the lessor and that, in return, the lessor promises that he will permit the lessee to have possession of the premises. As is the case with many aspects of Egyptian law, there was basic equality between men and women; women had legal capacity to enter into binding agreements on par with men.

The term imyt-pr, which even in the Old Kingdom meant "a certified deed of conveyance,"[177] later evolved into a generic term for all kinds of conveyance.[178] The phrase imyt-pr literally translates as "that which is in the house." In most circumstances, the parties saw to it that the imyt-pr was filed in a municipal records facility of some sort. Examples from the Middle Kingdom (c. 2040–1674 B.C.) illustrate the flexibility of this type of document for transfer. These Middle Kingdom imyt-pr typically operate to transfer property to persons such as brothers and wives. The types of prop-

---

176. Id. at 80. See Id. at 92–99 (Refuting Polanyi's theory of a redistributive economy in ancient Egypt.); Id. at 300 ("Egypt can be understood as a pre-capitalist market economy."); Id. at 328 ("There is…not only no 'redistribution', but the market is the primary means of allocating goods.").

177. Théodorides, Concept at 298.

178. See PESTMAN, MARRIAGE & MATRIMONIAL PROPERTY 18; Théodorides, Concept at 304. See also R.O. FAULKNER, A CONCISE DICTIONARY OF MIDDLE EGYPTIAN 18 (entry for imt-pr meaning "will, testament"). See supra §§ 6.02[C][1], 6.04[B].

erty transferred include real property, personal property, and even intangible property, such as the right to live in a house and the right to be buried in a tomb.

In order to form a contract, an offerer orally presented his offer to an offeree in the presence of witnesses. Once the offeree had signified his acceptance, the agreement bound both parties. In one contract for the sale of a slave girl, the offeror states his offer as follows: "Buy this girl and give me a price for her." According to the offeree's own account, he concluded the purchase by doing just that: "And I bought the girl and gave him a [price] for her."[179] In Egyptian sales law, a number of agreements called for an express warranty of title to be made by the seller. Title itself passed from seller to buyer only when the buyer paid the seller. Many of the contracts which have survived were written in the same formulaic pattern:

> Contract concluded between A and B, that B should give x to A, whilst A should give y to B. Behold, B was therewith content.[180]

Menu illustrates "the ancient pattern" of Egyptian contracts with the Cairo Stela from Thebes, dating about 660 B.C.:

> on this day; definition of the juridical act (smn); designation of the contracting parties (the representative of the divine Adoratrice and a Recluse Singer of Amun); description of what is sold (ten arouras of private fields; high lands in Amun's domain in such and such a district); specification of the price received; signature of the scribe and the witness; boundaries of the field sold which seems surrounded by canals; finally the beginning of an imprecatory formula.[181]

Some of the most illuminating examples of Egyptian contracts from antiquity are contracts for funerary services. Typically, such contracts were concluded between a noble and a group of priests. The noble promised to give the priests a fixed payment (of foodstuffs for example) in return for their promise to provide offerings, after the noble had deceased, and to light candles at the noble's tomb on designated days throughout the year. These contracts (which involved a mutual exchange—what we today call

---

179. *See* BEDELL, CRIMINAL LAW 45.
180. ERMAN, LIFE IN ANCIENT EGYPT 145.
181. Bernadette Menu, *Women and Business Life in the First Millennium B.C.*, in WOMEN'S EARLIEST RECORDS FROM ANCIENT EGYPT AND WESTERN ASIA 193, 200 (Barbara S. Lesko ed., 1989); *See also* Andrea McDowell, *Legal Aspects of Care of the Elderly in Egypt to the End of the New Kingdom*, in THE CARE OF THE ELDERLY IN THE ANCIENT NEAR EAST 199, 215 (Marten Stol and Sven P. Vleeming eds., 1998) (Noting the necessity for including dates and party names in legal documents.).

"consideration," a *quid pro quo*) were written, signed, witnessed and, like wills and land deeds, had to be filed in the office of the vizier in order to be valid. Among the best examples of this genre of contracts are a series of ten such agreements that were concluded between a 12th Dynasty (*c.* 1991–1785 B.C.) noble named Ḥapdjefai and the priesthood of the temple of Asyûṭ. In one of these funerary contracts, Ḥapdjefai contracted with "the great priest of Anubis" for the lighting of lamps of Anubis' temple on three specific festival days every year, including New Year's day. According to the contract, Ḥapdjefai promised to give the priests "1000 field measures from the estate of his fathers, as the price for these three wicks...."[182] Other contracts in this Ḥapdjefai series specify amounts of the offering of bread and beer and how they were to be allotted to different priests (staff of the temple).

There are two aspects of the Ḥapdjefai contracts which deserve special comment. First, because Ḥapdjefai himself was a member of the priesthood with which he was contracting (*i.e.,* in one respect he was contracting with himself!), he had to delineate his roles and separate his obligations. As a consequence of this duality, he was able to pay his colleagues, at least in part, with rations from the temple to which he and his heirs would have otherwise been entitled. Second, Ḥapdjefai emphasized that the real property that he promised to give to the priesthood as consideration (in addition to temple rations) was property that derived from his family's inheritance, not property in which he had a life estate by virtue of being a nomarch.[183] These two aspects of the Ḥapdjefai contracts illustrate that the Egyptians reached a sophisticated level of legal abstraction.

Another example of service contracts of a different sort are the contracts of Messuia, a cowherd, which span almost a quarter of a century during the

---

182. ERMAN, LIFE IN ANCIENT EGYPT 146.

183. For more regarding the ancient Egyptian life estate, *see supra* §6.02[B]. *See also* William A. Ward, *Some Aspects of Private Land Ownership and Inheritance in Ancient Egypt, ca. 2500–1000 B.C., in* LAND TENURE AND SOCIAL TRANSFORMATION IN THE MIDDLE EAST 63, at 66 (Tarif Khalidi ed., 1984); J.G. Manning, *Demotic Egyptian Instruments of Transfer as Evidence for Private Ownership of Real Property,* 71 CHICAGO-KENT L. REV. 237, 242 (1995) ("Temple property...may have been transferred by right of the priests' office and not by right of a personal holding of land that the priest would have been able to cede, presumably, permanently."); ERMAN, LIFE IN ANCIENT EGYPT 146–147 (Erman remarks how Ḥapdjefai is careful to declare that his consideration, that is, his payment, is being taken from "that part of his property and revenue which was really hereditary in his family," emphasizing that it was "*not* in any way from the property of the estate of the nomarch." The point here is that the payment is his personal property, not the property that he holds as a life estate by virtue of his official position as nomarch.).

reign of Amenhotep III (c. 1390–1352 B.C.). Messuia ran an agricultural enterprise and weaving industry. These contracts deal mostly with the terms under which Messuia rented slaves for a certain number of days' work; a "hire of services."[184] They basically are "sale of labor" agreements, and include a guarantee, given under oath, that the services will be provided. It may be that this guarantee provision required an accompanying oath because it contemplated future performance rather than merely a contemporaneous swap.

One of the most interesting aspects of the guarantee in the Messuia contracts, at least from the perspective of substantive contract law, is that "[t]he guarantee provides for compensation in case the work cannot be done as agreed."[185] This is equivalent to what we today call "liquidated damages": an express agreement to pay a fixed sum in the event of breach of contract. We see similar liquidated damages provisions in a number of the contracts from Deir el-Medina. In one such contract, a donkey seller promises to replace the beast with another if a third party successfully proves title to it (i.e., in the event the seller breaches his warranty of title). In another, a donkey seller promises double (i.e., presumably two donkeys) if a third party successfully proves title. In yet another agreement, a buyer on credit stipulates that if he fails to pay, he will return the goods and, in addition, pay the court costs of his brothers who had served as witnesses to the transaction. As a general rule, the 18th Dynasty texts, including the Messuia slave-rental contracts, reveal that the breaching party was expected to provide the other party with either equivalent goods or services as compensation. This is often expressed as an equivalent number of work days ("day for day"). As such, this measure of contract damages approximates what modern law calls expectation damages. In other words, the breaching party is obligated to pay an amount to the aggrieved party that will put him (i.e., the non-breaching party) into an economic position equivalent to that which he would have been in had there been no breach. The cases described in the Law Collection of Hermopolis that involve breach of an annuity contract routinely grant specific performance (i.e., the breacher is required to pay the contract amount). This too is a method of achieving what modern law calls expectation damages.

---

184. See Théodorides, Concept at 314–315 (Théodorides speculates that a town may have actually owned some slaves "being then placed at the disposal of the inhabitants at the rate of so many days per month or year. It would then be their right to days of the slaves' work that the inhabitants of the Faiyum were selling to Messuia....") (footnote omitted). See also BEDELL, CRIMINAL LAW 7 (Referring to contracts from the 18th Dynasty that related to rental of a female slave's services.).

185. Théodorides, Concept at 315.

In bailment agreements (such as the rental of a donkey), the term for "rent" was usually *it3y*. Egyptian bailment contracts seem to presume that a bailee was strictly liable (*i.e.,* liable regardless of fault) for loss or damage to bailed property. In particular, in the Deir el-Medina donkey rental cases, the parties accepted that the bailee was always responsible whenever the donkey died while in his possession. A bailee, then, as a general rule, was liable for damage to the bailed property while in his possession. As was mentioned above, in many bailment contracts, the bailor included what modern law characterizes as a liquidated damages provision. This type of contract clause specified the payment that the bailee would make if he failed to return the object that had been bailed. Since these ancient liquidated damages provisions normally imposed corporal punishment (*e.g.,* 100 blows) and two-times the original payment, modern contract law would probably invalidate such provisions as "penalty clauses". Nevertheless, we ought not allow our contemporary sensibilities to cloud our view. It is entirely possible that the Egyptians considered these as reasonable measures necessary to promote their concept of how contracts should operate. It is not, therefore, imperative that we interpret these breach of bailment contract cases as criminal matters rather than civil.

[D] FOREIGN & INTERNATIONAL ASPECTS

We occasionally catch glimpses of both private and public international law in our sources. For example, the extensive foreign trade carried on by Egyptian merchants necessitated a viable law merchant for international shipping and sale of goods. Under Ramses II (*c.* 1279–1212 B.C.), we know that there was an Egyptian law court located in Nubia.

We must always keep in mind that ancient expectations regarding relations with foreign nations were generally not benign. The threat of invasion was a simple fact of life. Aggression was common. Even in the Old Kingdom (*c.* 2700–2200 B.C.), Egyptian kings did not hesitate to attack and plunder foreign nations. By the New Kingdom (*c.* 1552–1069 B.C.), Egyptian militancy was responsible for a tremendous increase in foreign captive slaves.[186] It was also during the New Kingdom that many subjugated countries routinely sent tribute to the Egyptian pharaohs. It was then too that the Egyptians controlled and exploited mines in conquered lands. In contrast to this general acceptance of international aggression is the Hittite peace treaty—an international contract of unique significance.

186. *See supra* §6.01[D].

In the 18th year of his reign, Ramses II (*c.* 1279–1212 B.C.) concluded an international treaty with the Hittites. This treaty with the Hittites marks one of the first international accords between two sovereign nations in the history of human civilization. First, the treaty pledges non-aggression. Each country promised not to attack the other. Secondly, the two nations created an alliance; each promising to come to the aid of the other in the event of an attack by a third party. In addition, they agreed to extradite refugees, and agreed that anyone so extradited would not be subject to mistreatment upon his return to his home country.

[E] GENERAL COMMERCIAL LAW: CREDIT, SECURITY, & STANDARD MEDIA OF EXCHANGE

One important aspect of commercial law in ancient Egypt was that it allowed sales on credit terms. Credit, of course, can facilitate economic growth because it allows buyers to obtain goods without needing the full purchase price immediately, and, as a general rule, it increases business for tradespeople. A concept related to credit, namely, security for loans, was also known and employed in ancient Egypt. The use of security also encourages commercial transactions because it increases the likelihood that lenders will be willing to make loans. As a consequence, more individuals are able to share purchasing power. And at least by the 20th Dynasty (*c.* 1188–1069 B.C.), Egyptian law recognized and permitted suretyship for debts.

As has been mentioned, a significant degree of trade was conducted by means of barter.[187] Beyond this, however, the ancient Egyptians were among the first people to employ fixed standards of economic exchange value. We have a text that describes the sale of a house near the Great Pyramid at Giza in the Old Kingdom (*c.* 2700–2200 B.C.). The buyer exchanged a bed and two different lots of linen for the house. What distinguishes this transaction from ordinary barter is that each item (*i.e.,* the bed and the linen lots) was designated as having a specific, fixed value. The bed was worth four "pieces" and each batch of linen was worth three "pieces." It appears that a "piece" had an established correlation to a particular weight and type of precious metal (of some sort). Thus, the buyer paid a total of ten "pieces" but he paid by transferring property whose total value equalled ten pieces. Wilson observes: "This was an economic advance, and the unit

---

187. *See supra* § 6.06[C].

of value was a precursor of money proper, which would not appear for another two thousand years."[188]

It was during the Old Kingdom that the Egyptians developed the use of copper rings ($\check{s}$ʿt) to use as a medium of exchange. There is evidence showing that there were some high-priced transactions in the Old Kingdom using such rings. In the Middle Kingdom (c. 2040–1674 B.C.), the rings were often silver and, by the New Kingdom (c. 1552–1069 B.C.), gold. In fact, in the New Kingdom under Thutmose III (c. 1479–1425 B.C.), one foreign nation used silver rings weighing almost 100 lbs. each as a means of commercial exchange. Eyre emphasizes the importance of cloth as a medium of exchange also. According to Eyre:

> Cloth is an important form of capital, that the substantial household could itself manufacture on the basis of its lands and household labour. For relatively high value transactions and capital exchanges cloth played as important—if not more important—a role as metal.[189]

Still, Warburton advises that we must be cautious when interpreting units of value in ancient Egypt as anlogous to the modern concept of money:

> Money is assumed to possess three basic attributes, as (1) a unit of value, (2) a store of value, and (3) an exchange value. In ancient Egypt, the copper *deben* was a unit of value and evidently a store of value, but it was not normally employed in transactions, and thus fails to meet all three criteria. The *khar* of grain was used both as a unit of value and a unit of exchange, but storing grain is not a realistic method of keeping one's savings, so that it likewise fails to meet all three criteria. Beds and other articles could be used for exchange purposes, and perhaps as a store of value, but they could not be regarded as a unit of value. In any case, there was no government controlled money or currency, which could be used as a tool of monetary policy....[190]

---

188. WILSON, CULTURE OF ANCIENT EGYPT 83 (footnote omitted).

189. Christopher J. Eyre, *The Market Women of Pharaonic Egypt, in* LE COMMERCE EN ÉGYPT ANCIENNE 173, 180 (Nicolas Grimal and Bernadette Menu eds., 1998) (footnotes omitted). *See also Id.* at 182–83 ("The local records of transactions [in Deir el-Medina] frequently include cloth among the commodities used to make payments....") (footnote omitted). *See also* WARBURTON, STATE AND ECONOMY IN ANCIENT EGYPT 68 (Citing Roth for the proposition that "cloth was used 'as compensation for labor'" "'with well-known values'."); *Id.* at 330 ("in the peculiar nature of the Egyptian economy, precious metals and textiles, etc. were both 'money' and 'articles'....").

190. WARBURTON, STATE AND ECONOMY IN ANCIENT EGYPT 116.

Warburton concludes, however, that grain was Egypt's principal medium of exchange:

> Egypt was...basically on the grain standard, and this particular commodity was the basis on which the entire economy flourished. It was grain which was used to pay the workers who built the monuments of the land, and by withdrawing labour from the agricultural sector, demand was actually increased, along with employment.[191]

[F] CUSTOMS TAX & TAX ON MUNICIPAL OFFICE

In addition to the ubiquitous property tax and the tax on real estate sales,[192] there were two other kinds of taxes routinely collected by the Egyptian government, namely, a customs tax and a tax on holding municipal office. At the time when commerce on the Nile was waxing—especially during the New Kingdom (c. 1552–1069 B.C.)—the government established customs houses in the Delta region at the mouths of the Nile. Thus, merchants ordinarily paid a customs duty on most imported goods. The tax on holding municipal office was basically a tax for having the privilege of being an official. The amounts appear to have been substantial.

§ 6.07 CHAPTER SUMMARY

[A] PERSONAL STATUS

The king was clearly at the apex of the legal and social pyramid in ancient Egypt. After the king, there was a significant group of persons whom historians usually call nobles. The nobles constituted an elite circle who were the principal land owners. An appreciable number of merchants, craftspeople, and, eventually, local government administrators comprised what came to be a thriving middle class. The peasant-serfs typically worked on large estates owned by nobles. During the New Kingdom, foreign slaves were brought into Egypt as captives of war. In contrast to many other an-

---

191. *Id.* at 120; *Id.* at 122 ("[A]lthough most people interested in Egyptian economics would not claim that Egypt had money, many economists could be persuaded to believe that emmer and barley were in fact money...."); *Id.* at 326 ("The evidence of P. Louvre E 3226 suggests that during the 18th Dynasty the state organs used grain as a medium of exchange to acquire other goods.") (footnote omitted).

192. *See supra* § 6.02[D][1].

cient civilizations, women in ancient Egypt—at least by the New Kingdom—enjoyed a status that was the legal equivalent of men.

[B] PROPERTY

Because ancient Egypt was so heavily dependent upon agricultural pro-
ductivity, real property was a vital concern. Although the king may have
been considered the legal owner of all land in the early stages of Egyptian
history (and, perhaps, technically, later too), by the New Kingdom the
Egyptians *treated* real property as if the individuals who occupied the land
were its owners. Thus, individuals sold, leased, and bequeathed their land
in a manner commensurate with legal ownership. In addition to individual
ownership, it was common for certain kinds of property to be owned
jointly, by two or more persons. The State and many temples owned and
operated large estates, functioning essentially as corporations managing
immense tracts of agricultural land.

The vizier(s) maintained records of sales and the taxation of real property.
Our data indicates that the government conducted a census for purposes of
collecting taxes on real property. Documents such as the Wilbour Papyrus
provide a great deal of information relating to property and property taxes.
For example, we know that the size, location, irrigabilty, yield, and owner's occupation affected the rates of taxation. Tax law exempted (at least to some extent) certain entities and individuals, such as nomarchs, judges, and temples.

Egyptian law recognized a number of sophisticated concepts and principles relating to property law. For example, the Egyptians appreciated: 1) a
natural rights theory of property law (*i.e.,* the understanding that labor
may create a property interest); 2) a distinction between *usus* and *usus fructus*; 3) life estates; and, 4) easements.

[C] FAMILY

The nuclear family was important to the ancient Egyptians. Most Egyptians were monogamous. Royalty and nobles occasionally had a harem of
secondary wives. Only royalty, however, practiced marriage between fathers
and daughters or between siblings. There were no legal formalities required
for a valid marriage. There were, however, a number of traditions and customs associated with the creation of marital relations. The groom ordinarily
gave property called the *šp* to the bride's father. The bride usually brought
three special kinds of property to the marriage: 1) a dowry (typically given
by her father); 2) certain personal effects—the most important of which

was a type of shawl called the *inšn*; and, 3) funds for the bride's maintenance and the maintenance of her children (property known as the *sꜥnḫ*). It was the husband, however, who had legal control of the properties during the marriage. The husband and wife shared property that they acquired during the marriage—the husband owned two-thirds and the wife owned one-third. Many Egyptian couples entered into annuity contracts that were, in some respects, similar to modern prenuptial agreements. Both husband and wife had legal capacity to sue for divorce. Unless the wife was guilty of serious misconduct (such as adultery), upon a divorce the husband was required to return the three properties to the bride and pay for her support.

[D] INHERITANCE & SUCCESSION

When an ancient Egyptian died without a will, the laws of intestate succession dictated to whom his property would pass. As a rule, a decedent's children inherited equal shares of his estate. Ordinarily, real estate passed to the heirs as undivided property which they then owned jointly. If there were no children, the decedent's siblings inherited the estate. In the event that the decedent had neither children nor siblings, his parents inherited instead. Husbands and wives did not inherit from one another. A woman's children inherited her dowry. The eldest son had both more rights and obligations than his siblings. He inherited his father's office (especially in the case of a nomarch or vizier), he may have been entitled to select his share of the estate first, he bore the burden of caring for the funeral and cult obligations for his deceased parents, and he served as administrator of his parents' estate. In some instances a child who was not the biological eldest son assumed the eldest son's rights and responsibilities.

The Egyptians recognized the validity of wills. They used a document called the *imyt-pr* to function as a will, and the testator was required to record the *imyt-pr* with the vizier in order for it to be considered valid. Wills were considered revocable and served to dispense property to designated legatees in just about any manner that the testator desired. A testator could even disinherit children by means of a will. Some Egyptian wills operated to create rather sophisticated trusts. The Egyptians also used adoption (as a type of substitute for a will) as a vehicle for creating an heir.

[E] CRIME & TORT

There was little if any distinction between criminal law and tort law in ancient Egypt. Typical punishments that did not entail abject brutality included forced labor, confiscation of property, loss of office (*i.e.*, civic status), and loss of ritual burial. Punishments progressively became more brutal and included some grotesque penalties in the New Kingdom. Among the more harsh penalties that convicted criminals suffered were beatings, mutilation (*e.g.*, amputation of nose and/or ears), branding, and death by impalement. The Egyptians used prisons mostly as places either for confining the accused while they awaited trial or for holding convicts for sentencing. The *Book of the Dead* enumerates a long list of wrongful conduct recognized by Egyptian society such as murder, commercial fraud, theft, waste, adultery, rape, and battery.

For ordinary theft, a thief had to return the stolen goods and pay double or triple their value, as a kind of punitive damages. The punishment was markedly more severe if the stolen objects were either sacred or owned by the State, and the penalty was death in the case of theft from a royal tomb. We have very little evidence relating to ordinary homicide. But those found guilty of conspiracy to assassinate a monarch (*i.e.*, treason) received the death penalty (*e.g.*, the harem conspiracies to assassinate Pepi I and Ramses III). Judicial misconduct could be punished by death. Rape was treated as a crime, but there is less conclusive proof regarding adultery—which may have been considered more of a private, family law matter to be worked out between husband and wife. Tax collectors and other government officials guilty of extortion were banished to remote areas and could also suffer amputation of their ears and nose. The Egyptians usually punished battery by beatings or forced labor. They also recognized trespass to land, vandalism (or trespass to chattels/criminal mischief), and defamation (*e.g.*, the case involving Ḥ3y) as wrongful conduct.

[F] TRADE, CONTRACTS, & COMMERCIAL LAW

Beginning even before the historical period, Egypt developed an active trade, both foreign and domestic. A number of business entities, such as the State, temples, and various associations of individuals prospered. Ancient Egyptians used the *imyt-pr* to formalize bilateral agreements (*i.e.*, contracts) in which both parties promised mutual exchanges. Archaeologists have unearthed many different types of contracts, including contracts for funerary services, slave sales, slave rental, donkey rental, and sales of houses and sales of goods. In bailment agreements, Egyptian law seems to have presumed that bailees were strictly liable for damage to bailed property. Some contracts included provisions for liquidated damages and warranties of title. In a number of circumstances, damages for breach of contract approximated what we today would call expectation damages (giving the non-breaching party the benefit of his bargain). The Hittite Peace Treaty provides an example of a contract of international proportions. As regards general commercial law, we know that the Egyptians allowed sales on credit and established standard values for purposes of exchange. And, in addition to property taxes, there were also import or customs taxes

Unit III

Law in
Classical Athens

CHAPTER 7

Background and Beginnings of Athenian Law

§ 7.01 INTRODUCTION

Scholars who specialize in ancient Greek law often observe that Greek law has failed to significantly influence the law of later societies. They have, in short, apologized for Greek law; concluding that "ancient Greek law has had a negligible influence on posterity."[1] Nevertheless, as MacDowell remarks in his influential book, *The Law In Classical Athens*, "[T]he attempt to understand the subject is worth making. Law is the formal expression of a people's beliefs about right and wrong conduct, and no people in the world has had more interesting and original beliefs about conduct than the ancient Greeks."[2] Besides, the Romans, who are world-famous for their influence on subsequent legal development, read and studied Greek philosophers who wrote about law. Thus, the ancient Greeks had a profound effect on legal progress and evolution, albeit in an indirect manner.

Much of what we know about the particulars of ancient Athenian law itself comes from over one hundred forensic speeches of the late 5th and early 4th centuries B.C. These speeches were written with the intention that they would be presented orally in court. In terms of our understanding of legal philosophy, we can turn to the abstract discussions of law in the writings of Greek philosophers. Especially relevant are Plato (*Laws, Republic*), Aristotle (*Nicomichean Ethics*), and Theophrastus, Aristotle's pupil, (*Laws*). But before we turn our attention to the main focus of this Unit, the laws of

---

1. S.C. Todd, The Shape of Athenian Law 4 (1993) [hereinafter "Todd, Shape"]. *See also Id.* at 3 ("Law is one of the very few areas of social practice in which the ancient Greeks have had no significant influence on subsequent Societies.").
2. Douglas MacDowell, The Law In Classical Athens 8 (1977).

Classical Athens during its Golden Age in the 5th and 4th Centuries B.C., we shall first examine its antecedents in the 8th through 6th centuries B.C.

§ 7.02 THE EARLIEST GREEK LAW

Our earliest evidence for law in ancient Greece comes from the poetry of Homer and Hesiod.[3] In Homer's *Iliad* and *Odyssey*, it is not unusual for individuals to resolve their conflicts simply by fighting. Quite often in the Homeric poems, persons seek vengeance as a means to redress wrongs, and that pattern of violent self-help was formative in early Greek law. Despite legendary traditions (which held that early Greek lawgivers were guided by gods), there is no historical evidence that early Greek law was founded on religious rules or divine commandment to restrain or remedy violence.[4]

In classical mythology, *Dikē* was a virgin daughter of Zeus. Early in Greek literature, writers began using the word "*dikē*" to refer to an orderly means of dispute resolution. Both Homer and the 8th Century B.C. poet, Hesiod, frequently refered to "*dikē*." Homer and Hesiod used the word *dikē* to refer to "law," "judgment," or in a more abstract sense "justice." Hesiod said that "*dikē* is a distinctive feature of human societies...."[5] According to Sealey in his book *The Justice Of The Greeks*, "the goal of *dikē* or of law is to resolve disputes without violence."[6]

In Homer we do see evidence that the archaic Greek society was beginning to explore an orderly means of dispute resolution. There are a number of instances, for example, in the *Iliad* where quarrelling individuals appeal to an impartial outsider in order to resolve their differences. On several occasions, a king acts as arbiter. There are, of course, a number of reasons why a king is the logical person to resolve disputes. First, a king is likely to be

---

3. Although Professor Gagarin himself frequently uses Homer and Hesiod as evidence for early Greek law, he cautions: "[W]e do find a few explicit rules of behavior...[in Homer and Hesiod]. But these rules concern a broad range of human behavior, and none of them is singled out as having a special status, not even those rules that we might be tempted to call laws." MICHAEL GAGARIN, EARLY GREEK LAW 11 (1986) [hereinafter "GAGARIN, EARLY GREEK LAW"].

4. *See* GAGARIN, EARLY GREEK LAW 15–16 ("A common view of law...is that the earliest law...is strongly religious, only becoming fully secular in its later historical development. Whatever validity this view might have with respect to other societies,...religious factors are of little significance in the earliest stages of Greek law.") (footnote omitted).

5. GAGARIN, EARLY GREEK LAW 49.

6. RAPHAEL SEALEY, THE JUSTICE OF THE GREEKS 102 (1994) [hereinafter "SEALEY, JUSTICE"].

older and therefore have considerable experience. Second, as a rule, kings are thought to have received divine inspiration. Third, kings hold authority by consent of the aristocracy whom they rule. In addition, a king ordinarily has the power, the brute force, to enforce his judgments.

Hesiod's poetry makes a strong plea for justice, and argues that "without an effective legal process the social order will disintegrate."[7] In his work entitled *The Theogony*, Hesiod noted that kings succeed when they give "straight judgments," provide "restitution," and speak with "soft words." In his poem called *The Works and Days*, Hesiod described the ordinary judicial procedure as one where individuals take their disputes to a king who then renders his decision.

In addition to kings giving judgments in Homer's *Iliad* and *Odyssey*, both epics depict instances where groups of elders—rather than an individual king—make judicial decisions. In those situations, the elders make their judgments in public; therefore public opinion presumably influenced the decision of the judges. One remarkable example of this procedure appears in Book 18 of Homer's *Iliad* when the god Hephaestus forges a new set of armor for the Greek hero Achilles. Among the many scenes that he fashions on the face of Achilles' shield, he engraves a trial scene; apparently at a tense moment in the midst of litigation.

> The people were assembled in the marketplace, where a quarrel had arisen, and two men were disputing over the blood price for a man who had been killed. One man promised full restitution in a public statement, but the other refused and would accept nothing. Both made for an arbitrator, to have a decision, and the people were speaking up on either side, to help both men. But the heralds kept the people in hand, as meanwhile the elders were in session on benches of polished stone in the sacred circle and held in their voices. The two men rushed before these, and took turns speaking their cases, and between them lay on the ground two talents of gold, to be given to that judge who in this case spoke the straightest opinion.[8]

This scene depicts a formal public dispute resolution mechanism at work. Sealey contends that the two litigants are actually arguing about different things: one argues that he has paid the price while the other maintains that he will not accept the payment. Thus, the dispute is really about

---

7. Gagarin, Early Greek Law 50. For a general discussion of Hesiod's views on justice and the legal implications of his poetry, *see Id.* at 46–50.

8. Homer, *Iliad*, bk 18, 497–508, at 388 in *Iliad of Homer* (R. Lattimore trans. 1976).

whether the payment by the former is effective to make the other's argument irrelevant.[9] Apparently, then, the defendant has been accused of homicide but there is some argument about whether the payment, the "*poine*," either has been paid, or is, for some other reason, not acceptable. According to the text, the two talents of gold had been set aside for a judge whom the people chose as having pronounced the most acceptable resolution to the dispute. It seems that each of several judges would have his chance to render an opinion, but that the public's opinion influenced the outcome. Thus, we can see (even as early as Homer) that Greek culture established a decidedly democratic approach to law.[10]

Gagarin envisions the Greek protoliterate judicial system as follows:

> A judge who satisfied both litigants most of the time would gain a reputation for "justice," and once such a judge became well known, all those who basically accepted the social order and wished to have their disputes with their neighbors settled peacefully would naturally resort to this judge.[11]

In both Homer and Hesiod, it appears that using the procedure for dispute resolution was voluntary. Each litigant had to agree to submit his case to an arbitrator. It is not until later that dispute resolution evolved into a mandatory process. In addition to being voluntary, the procedure took place in a public forum, involved a judge or group of judges who tried to fashion a compromised settlement acceptable to both parties, and often involved the swearing of oaths. Furthermore, the formal, public dispute resolution procedure was in place long before any substantive laws regarding conduct were established.

§ 7.03 THE FIRST "LAWGIVERS" & WRITTEN LAWS

[A] INTRODUCTION

The first written laws began to appear in the Greek world in the mid-7th century B.C., and, by the close of the next century, many Greek cities had

---

9. *See* SEALEY, JUSTICE 104.

10. It is probably unwise for us to assume that all early Greek communities used an orderly procedure for dispute resolution like the one described on the Shield of Achilles. We must, rather, admit that this is merely one poet's representation. *See* TODD, SHAPE 33–35.

11. GAGARIN, EARLY GREEK LAW 22.

followed suit. Zaleucus is the Greek who, according to tradition, first wrote laws in 662 B.C. His laws were for a Greek colony in southern Italy. He was supposedly a shepherd who learned his laws (*nomoi*) from the goddess, Athena. Some scholars have argued that Mesopotamian laws influenced Zaleucus' laws, but the evidence is inconclusive. He is known for simplifying contracts, for creating several procedural laws, and for providing stiff penalties for anyone who tried to change his laws. Legend has it that if someone wanted to suggest a change to his laws, that individual had to present his proposal with a noose around his neck. Thus, if the preferred amendment was rejected, the person making the proposal would be hanged immediately. This law illustrates the significance of legal procedure. In fact, it is important to emphasize that procedural laws predominate during this era when the Greeks first began writing laws. Gagarin accentuates this point: "By far the largest area of innovation...was legal procedure, which...was the area of greatest concern to the early lawgivers."[12]

The city of Dreros on the island of Crete in the 7th century also had written laws. And as the 6th century dawned, many other large Greek cities had begun to embrace written laws as well. Athens, Mytilene, Cyrene, and Greek colonies in southern Italy and Sicily enacted written laws. There was a distinct pattern for the cities that adopted written laws during this period. According to Gagarin:

> [I]n a time of civil strife a city would call for a special person, not currently a member of the ruling class (who would presumably be too partisan) and in some cases a foreigner, to write a set of laws for the city.[13]

In addition to Zaleucus, literary tradition has preserved the names of several other early Greek lawgivers; for example: Minos and Rhadamanthys of Crete (probably fictitious); Charondas of Katane; Philolaos of Corinth (who wrote laws for Thebes); Diokles of Syracuse; and, Demonax of Mantinea. Charondas supposedly prohibited sales made on credit; requiring that only cash payments would be permitted for sales transactions. He de-

---

12. *Id.* at 78.
13. *Id.* at 60. *See also Id.* at 137 ("[T]he appointment of a lawgiver was an act of negotiation and compromise—the result of a long period of struggle in which all factions in the city came to understand that if a law code was to have public authority, it could not be enacted by a single group."). *See also* SEALEY, JUSTICE 25 ("A Greek city suffering internal strife sometimes invited a man or men from another city to come and draw up rules.").

manded that citizens serve as jurors and may have enacted a law of *lex talionis* (retribution).

The Gortyn Code from southern Crete represents an exceptional early attempt to codify ancient Greek law. This code was inscribed in twelve rather large columns that comprise part of a wall. There are over 500 lines of text dealing with various legal subjects such as marriage and family, inheritance, debtors, and procedure. Other shorter 6th century legal inscriptions have been found on Chios (*c.* 575–550 B.C.), at Argos, Thessaly, and Eretria (*c.* 550–525 B.C.). In addition to the most prevalent type of law, namely, legal procedure (often restricting the powers of magistrates), these inscriptions also show a great deal of concern for matters relating to family, property, and inheritance.

Sparta and Athens, the two city states that eventually came to dominate life on the Greek mainland during the Classical period of the 5th Century B.C., had distinctly different experiences at this critical time when written laws were sweeping through Greece. In Sparta, tradition maintained that Lycourgos was the lawgiver who, among other things, forbade the use of gold and silver coinage. Ironically, according to tradition, Lycourgos also prohibited written laws. One of the reasons that he did not want laws to be written was to afford flexibility for change in the future. In Athens, on the other hand, two famous lawgivers, Draco and Solon, initiated a strong tradition of written law. Their importance merits separate treatment.

[B] DRACO

According to tradition, Draco promulgated the first written laws in Athens in 621 B.C. Draco's laws were important and influential. If for no other reason, they were important because they were in writing. The ancient biographer Plutarch relates that death was the penalty for nearly every one of the offenses proscribed by Draco. But this reputation for severity probably arose because Draco provided for lethal self-help (not execution) for various offenses. However, our evidence today is actually very weak regarding the particulars of Draco's laws. Although his laws were concerned with other offenses as well, one principal subject with which Draco's laws dealt was homicide. Even as late as the 4th century B.C., the Athenians attributed their laws relating to homicide to Draco, who had written them two centuries earlier. Draco's homicide law contained both substantive and procedural elements. Gagarin summarizes Draco's homicide law by saying that it "establishes exile as the penalty for homicide and then deals largely with procedural matters: the trial, the obtaining of pardon, and the protection of the killer from the threat of retaliation by self-help."[14] Draco recognized the procedures called *apagogē* and *endeixis*, which permitted the arrest of certain criminals as a substitute for unrestrained self-help.[15] Draco's laws helped to achieve two primary social objectives: 1) to curb violent conduct, particularly revenge; and, 2) to establish a judicial procedure that was mandatory rather than voluntary.

[C] SOLON

In 594 B.C., Solon abolished most of Draco's laws but not those relating to homicide. Solon's laws were inscribed on wooden *axones* (four-sided wooden structures that could be rotated to facilitate the reading of the laws). Many orators of the 4th century B.C. frequently refer to the laws of Solon. These laws appear to have been extensive, covering many different substantive topics of law. Broadly speaking, for the sake of convenience, we may categorize his laws as: 1) Procedural; 2) Private; 3) Political; 4) Economic/Commercial; and, 5) Religious.[16] His greatest contribution to Athenian law appears to have been in procedural matters. Solon was responsible for inventing several important institutions of Athenian legal procedure: 1) the public cause of action that later came to be called *graphē* (permitting a third person to bring suit on behalf of another in certain circumstances)[17]; 2) the procedure known as *dikē exoulēs* (permitting a creditor to sue on a rendered judgment (or verdict) that forced the defendant to pay a double penalty);[18] 3) *eisangelia* (providing impeachment for tyranny);[19] and, 4) *ephesis* (permitting a right of appeal to the popular courts).[20] In addition to these innovations, like several other early lawgivers, Solon decreed some fixed penalties. For example, he established a 100-drachma punishment for rape (apparently without abrogating the cus-

---

14. GAGARIN, EARLY GREEK LAW 63. For greater detail *see Id.* at 86–89.

15. *See infra* § 8.02.

16. But we cannot be certain just what *his* categories were nor how broad his scope. *See* TODD, SHAPE 55.

17. *See infra* § 8.02.

18. *See* GAGARIN, EARLY GREEK LAW 74. Professor Gagarin notes that *dikē exoulēs* was designed "to remedy one of the greatest weaknesses in Athenian (and other Greek) law, the difficulty of enforcing a verdict...." *Id.* Technically, *dikē exoulēs* did not require that a defendant pay double damages to the plaintiff/prosecutor. Rather, he paid the amount owed to the plaintiff/prosecutor plus the same amount as a fine to the State. *See also infra* § 8.14.

19. *See* GAGARIN, EARLY GREEK LAW 76. *See also infra* § 8.02.

20. *See* GAGARIN, EARLY GREEK LAW 73 (quoting Aristotle).

tomary rule of self-help). Also relating to procedure, Solon enacted laws appertaining to witnesses and oaths.

Solon was responsible for a number of private family laws relating to matters such as adoption, marriage, dowries, inheritance, and the behavior of women. Under Solon's laws, private individuals were required to survey their real property, and were restricted in the manner in which they could build houses, dig wells, locate a beehive, and plant trees. Laws that regulated political activity concerned affairs such as citizenship, qualification for political office, taxes, and public meals. His laws also controlled many components of economic activity in Athens. In particular, some of Solon's economic laws dealt with mortgages, suretyship, debt slavery, interest rates, and agricultural exports. In the sphere of religion, Solon drafted rules regarding public festivals and sacrifices.

[D] THE IMPACT OF WRITTEN LAWS

The early lawgivers were both recorders and innovators. To a certain extent, they merely codified a community's customs. But in doing so, they must have endeavored to harmonize inconsistencies and clarify ambiguities. In addition, they occasionally originated novel legislation to solve new problems. The mere fact that laws were written affected Greek communities in at least four profound ways: 1) it promoted equality in law; 2) it increased the use of the judicial system because it made legal procedure mandatory instead of voluntary; 3) it diminished the power of individual magistrates (by providing innovations such as term limits and a right of appeal); and, 4) it increased the authority of the *polis* over its citizens and all who lived there.

§ 7.04 THE EVOLVING VOCABULARY OF "LAW"

The Athenians never formulated precise legal definitions with the exactitude that we strive to achieve today in contemporary American law. Todd remarks: "Athenian law never developed a fully technical vocabulary precisely because there was no way for words to be legally defined."[21] In most cases there were no recognized experts to explicate the law. Well informed laymen, though, could recognize and explain technical vocabulary.

---

21. TODD, SHAPE 205; *also see* SEALEY, JUSTICE 53.

In the 4th century B.C., jurors swore an oath at the beginning of every year; not at the outset of each individual trial. Demosthenes gives the substance of the jurors' oath: "I will judge according to the laws and the decrees of Athens, and matters about which there are no laws, I will decide by the justest opinion."[22] The Greek word that was used for "laws" in the jurors' oath, "*nomos*", means "custom, way of life." It is "a term of a norm of action recognized by a society, what is agreed to be the right thing to do."[23] By the early 4th century B.C., the word "*nomos*" was adopted at Athens to mean "statute" or "written law." Early lawgivers, Draco in particular, used the word "*thesmos*" for their laws. The *Liddell & Scott* lexicon defines "*thesmos*" as "that which is laid down, law, ordinance."[24] Some scholars have argued that the gradual shift in terminology from "*thesmos*" to "*nomos*" illustrates a shift to a more democratic definition of law (*i.e.*, that which is acknowledged to be customary in society). As Plato argued in *The Laws*, community acceptance supersedes "the power of the ruler."[25]

§ 7.05 THE "REINSCRIPTION" OF LAWS

Near the end of the Peloponnesian War, the great war between Athens and Sparta, in about 410 B.C., a special commission called the *Anagrapheis* was appointed to inscribe Solon's laws on stone. Shortly thereafter, the *Anagrapheis* were given the task to inscribe Draco's homicide law also on stone. Between 410 and 404 B.C., the *Anagrapheis* reinscribed the laws of Solon and Draco, and thus made Athenian law more accessible, at least to the literate. According to Sealey:

> [T]he recorders were merely to transcribe the laws, that is, collect the scattered records with a view to stocking a central archive. Where contradictions were discovered, they were to be resolved by the council and assembly or from 403/2 B.C. for reasons of economy, by the board of lawgivers. Consequently, some measures, such as the law of Draco on homicide, were published anew on stone. But

---

22. MacDowell, The Law in Classical Athens 44 (footnote omitted). *See also infra* § 8.08.
23. MacDowell, The Law in Classical Athens 44. The standard Classical Greek dictionary, *Liddell & Scott*, defines "*nomos*" as "that which is in an habitual practice, usage, custom." H.G. Liddell and R. Scott Comps., A Greek-English Lexicon 1180 (1977).
24. H.G. Liddell and R. Scott Comps., A Greek-English Lexicon 795 (1977).
25. MacDowell, The Law in Classical Athens 44.

it is concluded there was no general publication of the whole list of laws.[26]

After the chaotic year of 404 B.C., and rule by "The Thirty," a special group, the *Nomothetai* ("law givers"), along with the *Boulē* ("council") established a new beginning of legal order in Athens. Initially the *Nomothetai* were selected from a portion of the jurors for that particular year. MacDowell states that: "no law passed before 403/2 was valid, henceforth unless it was included in the new inscriptions in the years from 410–403; no uninscribed law was to be inforced; no decree could override a law; and no prosecution could be brought henceforth for offences committed before 403/2."[27] From that time forward, the Ionic alphabet was used for all legal inscriptions. At that time (if not earlier), the Athenians established a central records office for keeping copies of the laws. It was also at this same time that a new procedure for enacting laws was established. Henceforth, the *Nomothetai* had to review and vote on every proposed change to a law that the citizen assembly, the *Ekklēsia*, handed down.[28] Furthermore, any new law first had to be proposed in writing and read aloud at three meetings of the *Ekklēsia*, (only at certain times of the year). As the 4th century progressed, both the restriction that laws could only be proposed at certain times of the year and the requirement that they had to be read aloud three times at the *Ekklēsia* fell into disuse.

§ 7.06 JUSTICE & JURISPRUDENCE: THE ROLE OF LAW

It is well beyond the scope of this book to treat Athenian jurisprudence fully. Briefly, however, a surface-level glimpse into a few of the more salient works of Sophocles, Plato, and Aristotle is instructive. In them we see principles such as natural law, equality, and community as paramount legal influences. In Sophocles' play, *Antigone*, the character Antigone challenges King Creon by burying her brother in contravention of Creon's law. She argues that unwritten, immutable laws of god and heaven take precedence over mortal edicts. By traditional reading, her sympathetic position illus-

---

26. SEALEY, JUSTICE 47.
27. MACDOWELL, THE LAW IN CLASSICAL ATHENS 47 (footnote omitted).
28. The Classical Athenian assembly of citizens was called the *Ekklēsia*. It was comprised of all male citizens who were at least 18 years old and older. It met about every nine days. TODD, SHAPE 294.

trates the Athenian ideal; namely, that there existed certain natural laws that superseded the positive legislation of humans.

A similar concept is discernable in Plato's (429–348 B.C.) *Republic*, in his metaphor of the shadows in the cave. The people in the cave perceive only one aspect of truth—like a ruler who enacts statutes—whereas the world outside the cave represents complete truth—like Antigone's universal, higher law. It is also in the *Republic* that Plato proposes that law's purpose is to benefit all people in a society not just any one class. According to Plato, law either persuades or compels citizens to unite, and it helps them to share the benefits that each individual is able to give the community. Plato asserts that one important function of law is to establish peace and unanimity in the midst of strife.[29] Plato believed that law was essential for a society to thrive. In the *Laws*, his last dialogue, Plato emphasizes two tenets: 1) that laws must apply equally to all; and, 2) that the voluntary acceptance of citizens to the rule of law is what gives it its force—not the government's foisting it upon citizens. In terms of equality, Plato insists that no one group can be permitted to acquire too much wealth nor can poverty be tolerated. Plato proposes that proper education should encourage citizens to desire the rule of law. This explains how law's strength will emanate from the voluntary acceptance of the citizens. In the *Laws*, then, Plato stresses that elective consent to law is important. For law to function properly, citizens must rationally believe that the laws are correct. Voluntary acceptance is preferable to coercion. And, for Plato, voluntary acceptance is natural law.

In the *Nichomacean Ethics*, Aristotle (384–322 B.C.) takes the position that an unjust man is one who either breaks the law or one who appropriates for himself more than his fair share. Therefore, for Aristotle, justice is something that should be both lawful and equal. Aristotle believed that natural law controlled ethical and political life. He postulates a distinction between natural law (that retains its validity in all times and places) as opposed to man-made laws (that are merely conventions adopted by communities with individual differences). Thus, although government creates positive law that is subject to change, natural law is universal and immutable. Aristotle also explains that there were two kinds of justice: 1) distributive justice; and, 2) corrective justice. Distributive justice relates to equality. Distributive justice operates to reward individuals for the benefits that they confer upon society. In simple terms, those who are equals receive equal rewards while those who are non-equals receive unequal shares. Corrective justice, on the other hand, relates to lawfulness. Judges exercise corrective

---

29. *Plato, Laws* 627–28.

justice when they punish criminals, award damages, or impose injunctions to settle disputes. For Aristotle, law is the operation of judgment in deciding right and wrong. Magistrates are the ones responsible for creating and adminstering law to bring about order for the community.

Thus, in the writings of Sophocles, Plato, and Aristotle, we recognize several different jurisprudential concepts. The distinction between natural law and positive law is prominent, as is the notion of equality. These writers saw law as an instrument to benefit society by supplying peace, equality, and unity.

§ 7.07 CHAPTER SUMMARY

The law of ancient Greece is interesting in and of itself. In addition, because of its influence on the Romans, it indirectly helped to shape a great deal of later legal thought. Our most important sources for the particulars of ancient Athenian law are the forensic speeches of 4th century orators and, for information concerning abstract principles of the philosophy of law, Plato, Aristotle, and Theophrastus provide our best picture. Some of our earliest evidence for Greek law may be found in the poetry of Homer and Hesiod. They used the word *dikē* to refer to "law", "judgment", and "justice". They also depicted kings serving as judges. In addition, Homer shows a council of elders making judicial decisions. The famous trial scene in book 18 of the *Iliad* suggests that public opinion could play some role in the legal dispute process. Still, what is remarkable is that the Greeks in the protoliterate period seem to have employed a formal legal procedure for resolving differences.

A number of cities in the Greek world began adopting written laws as early as the middle of the 7th century B.C. Among the earliest to adopt written laws were the Athenians, cities in southern Italy, and communities on Crete, Mytilene, and Sicily. Typically, an individual "lawgiver" was responsible for producing a series of laws; and usually procedural laws received the most attention. Of particular importance was the Gortyn Code from southern Crete. In Athens, Draco is notorious for the severity of his laws (especially dealing with homicide), but that is probably because he legitimized potentially lethal self-help. Solon is best known for giving Athens a number of procedural, private, commercial, and religious laws (including *graphē*, *dikē exoulēs*, *eisangelia*, and *ephesis*). As regards substantive law, Solon's laws related to matters such as family law, inheritance, property, politics, commercial law, and religion. Written laws promoted equality, encouraged the use of the judicial system, placed additional power in the hands of ordinary citizens, and increased the power of the *polis* over its citizens. Lycourgos of Sparta, on the other hand, purposely chose not to adopt written laws, relying instead on unwritten laws for the sake of preserving flexibility.

Even though the Athenians did not develop an extensive legal vocabulary, they used two words to refer to law in different contexts. Both Draco and Solon used the word *thesmos* ("ordinance") for their laws. *Nomos* initially meant "custom" but gradually evolved to mean "statute" or "written law". At the close of the 5th century B.C., a special commission called the *Anagrapheis* collected the laws of Draco and Solon—the so-called "Reinscription of the laws." After the Reinscription, the *Nomothetai* ("law givers") had to approve every law after the *Ekklēsia* (citizen assembly) had first voted on it.

The works of the playwrights and philosophers suggest that the ancient Athenians viewed law as a natural force and that law should promote social justice. Sophocles' character Antigone, for example, steadfastly believed that unwritten, universal natural laws were more important than man-made legislation. Plato argued that citizens must voluntarily accept the rule of law and that law should apply equally to all persons regardless of wealth and social standing. Aristotle recognized a distinction between natural law and man-made law. He also contrasted "distributive justice" (based on notions of equality) and "corrective justice" (based on notions of punishment).

CHAPTER 8

Legal Procedure, Institutions, & Organization

§ 8.01 PRIVATE & PUBLIC ARBITRATION; DĒME JUDGES

As is true in modern American law, ancient Athenians could submit a dispute to independent (*i.e.,* non-judicial) arbitration. Such arbitrations could be legally binding even prior to the Reinscription of the laws (410–403 B.C.). In order to be binding, the parties had to agree in advance: 1) who would serve as arbitrator(s); and, 2) what was the content of the question for the arbitrator(s) to resolve. Like other contracts in Classical Athens, an agreement to arbitrate did not have to be in writing. The only other requirement was that the arbitrator(s) had to take an oath before the arbitration began.

One of the best known examples of private arbitration in ancient Athens comes from Menander's comedy, *Epitrepontes.* A character named Daos finds a baby and gives it to another, Syriskos, to rear. Daos, however, wishes to keep the baby's valuable necklace. Syriskos objects. They waste virtually no time arguing but instead accost a total stranger on the street, Smikrines, and convince him to arbitrate their dispute. In a humorous scene, Smikrines ultimately decides in favor of Syriskos; and although Daos is displeased, he does, nevertheless, acquiesce and accepts the arbitrator's decision. In theory, private arbitration sounds great. But in practice, parties often had difficulty agreeing who should arbitrate. That is why public arbitration also came to be an important part of Athenian law. In the 4th century B.C., most disputes first went to a public arbitrator who sought to mediate a settlement.

At age 59 all male citizens were required to perform the civic duty of serving as public arbitrators. A plaintiff was responsible for paying the arbitrator's fee of one drachma. Arbitrators heard cases in public as the litigants argued their sides and presented evidence. Under Athenian law, a litigant could not produce evidence later at trial unless he had produced it first at the arbitration. Thus, litigants were compelled to take the compulsory public arbitration seriously and assembled whatever evidence they could. On many occasions, an arbitration itself must have consumed several days. When an arbitrator made his decision, he related it forthwith to the four tribe judges who had referred the case to him in the first place. According to MacDowell, "[i]f both disputants accepted the arbitrator's judgement, it was final. But either could appeal against it."[30]

By the middle of the 5th century B.C., there were 30 *dēme* judges who rotated throughout Attica. There is insufficient evidence about them to know how they were appointed or anything of substance about their procedures or the disputes that they heard. In about 400 B.C., the number of *dēme* judges was increased to 40. Each of the ten tribes now picked four judges by sortition. "The Forty" (as they came to be called) heard the majority of private cases brought by means of a *dikē* (except cases under the jurisdiction of the *archon* or *thesmothetai*).[31] A plaintiff first took his complaint to the four judges from his own tribe. If the amount in dispute was ten drachmas or less, they could decide the matter by themselves. If the amount in controversy was more than ten drachmas, the tribe judges were required, after 399 B.C., to refer the case to a public arbitrator. And this is the only way that a public arbitrator got a case.

§ 8.02 THE VOCABULARY OF ATHENIAN LEGAL PROCEDURE

In order to understand Athenian procedure, it is worthwhile to be familiar with several terms. The word used for a law case ordinarily is *dikē*. Although technically speaking a private case was called a *dikē idia* and the term for a public case was *dikē demosia*, the word *dikē* evolved to mean basically a private case and the most common procedure for bringing a public case came to be called *graphē*. As has been noted,[32] tradition credits Solon with having introduced the procedure by which a volunteer could instigate a case on behalf of a third party or regarding matters that affected the community at large. This is the procedure that came to be called *graphē*. Thus,

---

30. MacDowell, The Law in Classical Athens 209.
31. For more regarding the *archon* and *thesmothetai, see infra* § 8.05.
32. *See supra* § 7.03[C].

as early as the laws of Solon (594 B.C.), the Athenians recognized certain wrongs that should be punished in the public interest. In this way, Solon's laws made it possible for an individual, in certain circumstances, to bring a law suit to avenge wrongs committed against a third party. This "volunteer prosecutor" could only act in certain types of cases. Nevertheless, this innovation of Solon's laws became an important component in Athenian law thereafter. A number of scholars have also noted that this "volunteer prosecutor" aspect of Athenian procedure, in Cohen's words, "enhanced the opportunities for individuals to manipulate legal institutions to serve private purposes."[33] In fact, a great deal of Athenian litigation appears to have been the result of the upper classes using the court system as a tool that was integral in advancing their personal enmities and feuds.[34] "[M]uch litigation should be viewed as a form of feuding behavior, and...it was acknowledged as such by Athenian judges and litigants."[35]

In addition to the general term *graphē*, which literally means "writing," the Athenians had several other specialized terms for different types of public cases which volunteer prosecutors could bring; often called "summary procedures." Different types of cases permitted different procedural avenues. The most prominent of these procedures were as follows. 1) *Apagogē*: The volunteer prosecutor arrests the defendant first and then brings him to the competent official (forcibly if necessary). 2) *Ephegesis*: The volunteer prosecutor leads the magistrate to the defendant for arrest. 3) *Endeixis*: The volunteer prosecutor first explains the charge to the magistrate and is then authorized to make the arrest. 4) *Apographē*: The volunteer prosecutor lists property wrongfully held by the defendant, property that rightfully belongs to the State. 5) *Eisangelia*: First the volunteer prosecutor denounces the defendant to the *Ekklēsia* or *Boulē* or to the Archon—the latter in cases concerning mistreatment of an orphan or "heiress"[36]. 6) *Probolē*: A preliminary hearing at the *Ekklēsia* regarding official misconduct. 7) *Dokimasia*: A hearing where a candidate might be disqualified from citizenship, public office, or speaking in the assembly (*Ekklēsiu*). 8) *Euthynai*: Review of performance in public office.

As was mentioned, very often private cases were simply called *dikē*. The word *dikē* was used to refer to a case concerning matters that did not relate to the community as a whole but rather only to an individual: "a private or-

33. DAVID COHEN, LAW, VIOLENCE AND COMMUNITY IN CLASSICAL ATHENS 21 (1995) [hereinafter, "COHEN, LAW, VIOLENCE AND COMMUNITY IN CLASSICAL ATHENS"].
34. *See Id.* at 23, 72, 83, 87, 101, 112, 183, 188, 194.
35. *Id.* at 87.
36. *See infra* §§ 9.03[B], 9.04[A].

dinary prosecution, as opposed to a *graphē*."[37] In the case of a *dikē*, only the individual himself who actually had been wronged could act as the plaintiff/prosecutor. Cases involving homicide were *sui generis*, since the victim, himself, was unable to prosecute. Nevertheless, homicide was still considered a *dikē* (*dikē phonou*), and the term *graphē* was not used in homicide cases of this type (though some homicides could be prosecuted by *apagogē* or *endeixis*).

This multiplicity of procedures led to considerable confusion and overlap. For example, theft could be prosecuted by *apagogē*, *ephegesis*, *graphē*, or *dikē*. However, only the established procedures could be used.

In addition to the cases which could be brought by "volunteer prosecutors," some cases could be brought by public prosecutors called *Synēgroi* ("supporting speakers").[38] The *Synēgroi*, as a rule, only brought actions against men who were acting in an official capacity. The *Synēgroi* were ten citizens selected by lot who were paid one drachma per day.

§8.03 LITIGATION PROCEDURE

The ancient Athenians had a reputation for being extremely litigious. In Aristophanes' comedy *The Clouds*, when someone points to a city on a map of Greece and claims that it is Athens, the character, Strepsiades, protests that it cannot be Athens because he does not see courts in session. Although there was a great deal of litigation, it is curious to modern sensibilities that "neither judges nor litigants had any formal legal training and the system as a whole relied almost entirely upon the initiative of private citizens."[39]

Although a few types of legal claims could be filed on any day of the year, many could only be instituted on particular days and only in particular months. Therefore, a would-be plaintiff/prosecutor had first to consult the judicial calendar to make sure that he was filing his suit during the right kind of month and on the right kind of day. Generally speaking,[40] a plaintiff/prosecutor's first formal step was to issue a summons (*prosklesis*) to the

---

37. TODD, SHAPE 100.
38. *See* MACDOWELL, THE LAW IN CLASSICAL ATHENS 61.
39. COHEN, LAW, VIOLENCE AND COMMUNITY IN CLASSICAL ATHENS 61.
40. Some notable exceptions include cases brought by the following procedures: 1) *Apagogē* (the procedure by which an accuser personally arrested a thief and escorted him to The Eleven); 2) *Ephegesis* (the procedure by which an accuser went directly to The Eleven and notified them of the whereabouts of a thief); and 3) *Endeixis* (the procedure by which an accuser alleged that a disenfranchised man had gone into a prohibited area). *See* MACDOWELL, THE LAW IN CLASSICAL ATHENS 238.

defendant, in the presence of a witness.[41] This summons alerted the defendant to three crucial facts: 1) the specific date on which the defendant was to appear; 2) the magistrate(s) before whom the defendant was to appear; and, 3) the alleged wrong for which the defendant was to appear.

On the established day, the plaintiff/prosecutor filed his claim in writing and paid a filing fee (*prytaneia*) of 3 or 30 drachmas (depending on the amount in dispute). If the plaintiff/prosecutor prevailed at trial, the defendant had to reimburse him for the *prytaneia*. The magistrate who heard the initial complaint (on that day when it was originally filed) also then scheduled another formal hearing, a pre-trial conference (*anakrisis*). At the *anakrisis* the magistrate read the complaint aloud and asked the defendant to admit or deny the allegations. Both parties vowed that they were telling the truth and the magistrate questioned them. If the defendant wished to raise a procedural challenge to the claim by *paragraphē*, this was the time to do so.[42] The Athenians used this pretrial conference to delineate and clarify the triable issues. At the conclusion of the *anakrisis*, the magistrate then assigned a trial date (unless it was a case before the four tribe judges, in which case the matter went directly to a public arbitrator).[43]

At a trial's beginning, a court clerk announced the case and recited the complaint for all to hear. If one of the parties was absent and had a legitimate excuse (*e.g.*, he was sick, or, he was out of town for some appropriate reason), a friend could appear on his behalf and swear an oath as to the party's justification for his absence. The jury then voted either: 1) to postpone the trial due to the party's excused absence; or, 2) to grant the party in attendance a default judgment. Of course, if one of the parties failed to appear and no one offered an excuse on his behalf, the jury automatically granted the party in attendance a default judgment. A party who was the victim of a default judgment could, however, resuscitate his case if within two months he could demonstrate good cause for his failure to appear on the original trial date.

The Athenians managed to finish almost all of their trials in one day or, very often, less than a full day. After the clerk's reading of the complaint, the

---

41. Todd notes: "The exception was the threefold procedure of *apagoge, endexis,* and *ephegesis,* where summons (and sometimes also indictment) were replaced by summary arrest." TODD, SHAPE 125 n. 3. *See also* MACDOWELL, THE LAW IN CLASSICAL ATHENS 238.

42. *See infra* § 8.04 [B].

43. *See supra* § 8.01. Another exception to this general rule was for homicide cases where the Basileus scheduled three *prodikasia* (pre-trial conferences) for three straight months. *See infra* § 9.05 [B][3].

plaintiff/prosecutor spoke first, followed then by the defendant. Evidently, in private cases (*i.e.,* those brought by *dikē*), the plaintiff and defendant each made a second speech as well. But in public cases (*i.e.,* those brought by *graphē*), the prosecutor and defendant were limited to just one oration per speaker (though several might speak on each side). Athenian law restricted the time allowed for speeches and, thus, court personnel timed them with a water clock (*klepsydra*).[44] The permissible duration of a speech varied depending upon the type of case (*i.e., graphē* or *dikē*) and also depending on whether it was the litigant's first or second speech in the trial.

Each litigant represented himself and pled his own case on his own behalf (*i.e.,* without an advocate).[45] Litigants, however, routinely hired speech writers, called *logographoi,* to construct their written arguments for them. Each *logographos* acted like a ghost writer attempting to forge a compelling story of facts, laws, logic, reason, and proof. In effect, these were the Athenian trial lawyers (or nearest approximation thereof). Most scholars believe that litigants memorized and recited the speeches written by their *logographoi*—rather than reading them aloud—in an attempt to give an impression of spontaneity, candor, and sincerity. In addition to presenting logical argumentation and proof, Athenians were not above using pure sympathy and emotional appeals. For example in Aristophanes' play *The Wasps,* a juror describes a litigant who "drags his children out in front—all his little girls and boys" who "all grovel in a heap, bleating."[46] The litigant then implores the jury to "hear the cry of my son" and "let my daughter persuade thee."[47] The juror even admits, "And after that, perhaps, I relax my severity a little."[48]

The jury voted without deliberation as soon as the litigants concluded their speeches. Unlike modern American trial procedure, the presiding Athenian magistrate did not provide the jury with a summation nor did he impart jury instructions to advise the jury how they should apply legal rules to the facts of the case. Each juror individually had to decide how to vote. Because the jurors, the *dikastai,* did not articulate the reasons for their decisions, it is doubtful that any given case could really have precedential

---

44. The *klepsudra* "was allowed to flow during the speech itself and was blocked up for the reading of evidence." TODD, SHAPE 130. *See also* MACDOWELL, THE LAW IN CLASSICAL ATHENS 249.

45. Occasionally a litigant also asked a close friend or relative to speak on his behalf as a "supporting speaker." *See* MACDOWELL, THE LAW IN CLASSICAL ATHENS 250–51.

46. ARISTOPHANES, WASPS 58 (David Barrett trans. 1964).

47. *Id.*

48. *Id.*

force for a subsequent case—certainly not in the modern common law sense of precedent. However, in one speech involving an accusation of *hubris*,[49] Demosthenes did encourage his jury to set a precedent.

Although the precise physical mechanics of voting did change during the Classical period, throughout both the 5th and 4th centuries jurors recorded their votes by using small tokens that they dropped into urns. In the 5th century, jurors voted by placing a pebble or shell into one of two urns; one marked for the prosecutor/plaintiff, and the other marked for the defendant/accused. In the 4th century, jurors went to court with two kinds of tokens in their possession: a bronze disk with a solid shaft in the middle and a bronze disk with a hollow shaft in the middle. Jurors voted for a *plaintiff/prosecutor* by placing the bronze disk with the *hollow shaft* in its middle into an urn for registering votes; and voted for a *defendant/accused* by placing the bronze disk with a *solid shaft* in its middle into an urn for registering votes. They dropped their other bronze disk (*i.e.*, the one that they did not intend to count) into a different urn designated as the urn for invalid votes. When each juror had recorded his vote by placing his token(s) into the appropriate urn(s), the votes were counted and a simple majority decided the case (a tie going to the defendant/accused).

If the plaintiff/prosecutor had prevailed, the jury's last duty was, then, to assess the defendant's/accused's penalty or damages owed to the plaintiff/prosecutor.[50] Ordinarily, the jury simply picked between two alternatives that the litigants each offered in yet another (much shorter) speech: one penalty proposed by the successful plaintiff/prosecutor; and the other penalty submitted by the vanquished defendant/accused. Obviously, it was in the defendant's/accused's best interest not to suggest a penalty that was *too* lenient lest the jury reject it in a perfunctory manner in favor of the plaintiff/prosecutor's (obviously harsher) proposal.

§ 8.04 PLEADING & FORMS OF ACTION

[A] *DIAMARTYRIA*

In some cases a litigant could assert his rights simply by having a witness affirm decisive facts before the magistrate. In one instance, a defendant was

---

49. *See infra* § 9.05[F].
50. "In some types of trial, no decision was required, because it was already fixed by statute; in others, the law permitted a range of penalties...." TODD, SHAPE 133–134.

able to bar a suit for damages simply by having a witness affirm that the case was already settled. This procedure was called *diamartyria*.[51] MacDowell says, "*Diamartyria* was a formal assertion of fact by a witness who was in a position to know it."[52] According to Todd, "It is normally produced on behalf of the defendant, to show reason why the case must be halted; but in one case it is used for the plaintiff, to show why it must continue...."[53]

[B] *PARAGRAPHĒ*

In about the year 400 B.C., the Athenians began to realize that not all challenges to jurisdiction or other procedural flaws could be resolved simply by relying on someone's bare assertion of fact (*diamartyria*). Thus, one of the most important procedural devices in Athenian law came into being: *paragraphē*. *Paragraphē* became the commonest way for a defendant to mount a procedural challenge to a plaintiff's case in the 4th century B.C. "*Paragraphē* probably means 'prosecution in opposition', 'counter-prosecution'; and the procedure was essentially a separate trial in which the original prosecutor was himself prosecuted for bringing a prosecution in a way forbidden by law."[54] "The original case was postponed until the *paragraphē* case was decided; the result of the *paragraphē* trial settled whether the original case should proceed or not."[55] In short, the *paragraphē* was a technical, legal mechanism employed by defendants in an effort to short-circuit a plaintiff's case. In the 4th century, defendants used *paragraphē* to assert what modern American law recognizes as a variety of procedural defenses. For example, it was used to assert the same as the following modern procedural challenges: 1) *res judicata* (*i.e.*, an assertion that another court has already adjudicated the same issue); 2) statute of limitations (*i.e.*, the period of time within which a claim of the nature at issue should have been brought has already passed); 3) lack of subject matter jurisdiction (*i.e.*, the court is not authorized to adjudicate claims of the nature at issue); and, 4)

---

51. If a defendant tried to claim that the court lacked jurisdiction to decide a case (for example, arguing that the plaintiff was an alien, and, thus, that the polemarch (*See infra* § 8.05) should be hearing the case instead of the tribe judges), the plaintiff could produce a witness to counter such an assertion. For example, a witness could claim that the plaintiff was in fact an Athenian citizen.

52. MacDowell, The Law in Classical Athens 212.

53. Todd, Shape 136(citation omitted).

54. MacDowell, The Law in Classical Athens 215. *See also* Todd, Shape 136 ("It is a counter-prosecution, by means of which the original defendant charges his opponent with attempting to bring an illegal prosecution.").

55. MacDowell, The Law in Classical Athens 215.

statute of frauds (*i.e.,* certain types of contracts must be in writing in order to be considered valid). *Paragraphē* was, however, not without financial risk. The unsuccessful party in the *paragraphē* had to pay one-sixth of the amount in dispute.

§8.05 ORGANIZATION & PERSONNEL: JUDGES, COURTS, & CALENDARS[56]

Although Athens may have been ruled by kings at some early point, by the Classical period she was ruled by nine archons. The Archon Eponymous (who gave his name to the year) controlled property and family matters. Another archon, called the "Archon Basileus," was responsible for laws regarding religion, homicide, and acts of deliberate wounding. A third archon, called the "Archon Polemarchus," was responsible for law dealing with non-Athenians. In addition to these three, there were six *Thesmothetae*. They were in charge of many other types of cases. The Board of Generals, the *Strategoi*, had jurisdiction in military affairs. In addition to these, there were a number of additional officials responsible for many other aspects of Athenian legal life. For example, the officials called the *Agoranomoi* and the *Sitophylakes* settled commercial disputes in the marketplace.

In the 7th and 6th centuries B.C., as written laws and juries became commonplace throughout the Greek world,[57] the power of each individual magistrate decreased. The existence of written laws and the presence of a jury as a decision-making body curtailed the discretion of the magistrates.

In Athens in the 7th century B.C., the aristocratic council called the *Areopagus* held virtually unlimited power; particularly with respect to serious offenses such as intentional homicide, wounding, arson, the destruction of sacred olive trees, and tyranny.

The complexity of Athenian society increased as the Athenian Empire grew during the 5th century B.C. Along with heightened complexity came the need for a more organized legal system. Thus, the Athenians began formulating a judicial calendar. They assigned certain types of cases to be heard during certain months. It is possible that by scheduling cases in this manner, they hoped to make attending trials more convenient for those who were from the member states of their Delian League.[58] A decree from

---

56. *See generally* MacDowell, The Law in Classical Athens 25–28, 224–233.

57. *See supra* §7.03[A].

58. Following the Persian Wars (*c.* 479 B.C.) the Athenians formed the Delian League; an association comprised of Athens, herself, and numerous island states that

445 B.C. mentions for the first time a group of magistrates called *nautodikai* ("judges of sailors"). The *nautodikai* handled cases involving Athenians who either lived overseas or sailed as mariners or merchants. During the 5th century, Athens formed a board called the *xenodikai*, judges of foreigners. We know precious little about how the *nautodikai* and *xenodikai* operated in the 5th century. Nevertheless, their mere existence attests to the Athenian desire to construct a more organized legal framework in the wake of their burgeoning empire.

Around 350 B.C. the Athenians abolished both the *xenodikai* and *nautodikai*. Presumably, persons with commercial interests in Athens (both citizens and foreigners) had become exasperated with the sluggishness of the legal machinery. The *thesmothetai* henceforth maintained jurisdiction to hear cases involving merchants and shipmasters; the *dikai emporikai* ("mercantile cases"). A new law permitted litigants to bring *dikai emporikai* on a monthly basis, from the Athenian months called "*Boedromion*" through "*Mounikhion*" (roughly September-April).[59] Thus, sea merchants and other traders could conduct commercial business during good sailing weather and resolve their legal differences during the time of year when it was precarious to venture out to sea anyway. In terms of administrative efficiency, it is significant that the *dikai emporikai* were available to, and applied to, both citizens and non-citizens. The *dikai emporikai* were, however, narrowly defined. These cases could only be initiated if the dispute at issue pertained to an alleged breach of a *written* contract that either: 1) had been concluded in the Athenian Market itself; or, 2) related to a transaction that involved shipping either into or out of the Athenian Market.

The success of categorizing a group of cases and scheduling them to be heard by a certain adjudicative body at specific times was not lost on the ancient Athenian lawmakers. Soon they began establishing other case categories with their own judicial schedules. For example, there was a category comprised of tax-collecting cases, a category comprised of mining cases, and a category for financial/banking cases.

By the late 4th century, the Athenian court system was divided into distinct jurisdictional classifications dependent upon either the subject matter of the dispute or the status of one of the litigants. However, as Todd puts it, "[a]lthough they presided over the court, they [*i.e., the presiding magis-*

---

pooled their financial and naval resources in an effort to provide protection and to serve as a deterrent to further Persian aggresssion. *See* CYRIL ROBINSON, HISTORY OF GREECE 127 (1965).

59. But some legal historians theorize that the months should be transposed; thus meaning that the cases were brought only *during* the summer. *See* TODD, SHAPE 335.

trates] had no right of jury direction, no right to rule evidence or arguments out of order, and no power of summing up."[60] The magistrates and their respective jurisdictional spheres were as follows:

1) **Archon Eponymous.** Cases involving inheritance and other matters among family members. Cases relating to particular religious festivals.

2) **Basileus.** Homicide cases. Cases pertaining to religion.

3) **Polemarch.** Cases relating to metics (*i.e.,* resident aliens).[61]

4) **Thesmothetai.** *Dikai emporikai* (mercantile cases), cases regarding treaties with other states, and a variety of other public cases.

5) **The Eleven.** Cases involving *kakourgoi,*[62] and cases that required a defendant to be incarcerated while awaiting trial.

6) **Agoranomoi.** Cases involving disputes brought in the Agora (the Athenian Market).

7) **Sitophylakes.** Cases concerning grain and grain sellers.

8) **Epimelētai Tou Emporiou.** Cases involving the sale of grain in the wholesale market that was conducted in the Athenian port, the Peiraeus, at the *Emporion.*

9) **Eisagogeis.** Pecuniary cases related to loans and banking.

10) **The Forty.** The majority of private cases brought by means of a *dikē* (except cases under the jurisdiction of the Archon, *Thesmothetai,* or some other specialized court).

§ 8.06 CASES INVOLVING NON-CITIZENS

Originally, the Polemarch probably was responsible for initiating cases involving a non-citizen (*i.e.,* when the non-citizen was either prosecutor or defendant). By the mid-5th century the Polemarch was too busy to handle all cases involving foreigners. Thus, new magistrates called *Xenodikai* were created to handle certain kinds of cases pertaining to foreigners. Later, somewhere around 400 B.C., most public cases relating to aliens were transferred from the Polemarch and the *Xenodikai* to the same courts as public cases involving citizens. By the middle of the 4th century, there were probably few procedural distinctions between a case involving a metic versus a case involving a citizen.[63]

---

60. TODD, SHAPE 79.
61. *See infra* § 9.01[B].
62. *See infra* § 9.05[C].
63. *See infra* § 9.01 regarding metics and citizens.

§ 8.07 *GRAPHĒ PARANOMĒN*

In order to keep their laws conservative and devoid of rash changes, the Athenians used a procedure called *graphē paranomēn* ("prosecution for illegalities"). This was in use by the late 5th century to block decrees that contradicted or conflicted with established laws. A person found guilty of *graphē paranomēn* three times was punished by *atimia* (*i.e.*, a kind of disenfranchisement).[64]

In the early 4th century, when *laws* were significantly distinct from *decrees*, improper laws could be challenged by a suit "for submitting unsuitable law." Simply stated, when an individual proposed a law, he was subject to the accusation that his proposal conflicted with an existing law. If the proposer was found guilty, his new law was invalidated and he was fined. In the year 382 B.C., one jury even imposed the death penalty. There was, however, a statute of limitations of one year, after which the legislator could no longer be punished, but his law could be invalidated.

§ 8.08 JURIES

In 594 B.C., Solon redirected judicial decision-making authority from the magistrates[65] to the people. The assembly of all Athenian citizens (*i.e.*, all Athenian males over the age of 18) was called the *Ekklēsia*.[66] However, when the *Ekklēsia* was convened for a judicial purpose, it was referred to as the *Heliaia*. Solon's new law permitted a citizen to appeal a magistrate's decision (at least regarding some types of decisions) to the *Heliaia*. The *Heliaia* then could hear the case *de novo* and render a judgment in the matter. However, a citizen's right of appeal was not absolute and was probably only available in certain types of cases. Because Solon gave citizens a right of appeal, the entire judicial process ultimately changed. By the 5th century B.C., magistrates simply held an initial hearing and then arranged for the *Heliaia* to conduct a trial. At that trial, the magistrate presided and then pronounced the jury's verdict. We cannot pinpoint an exact date for this change. It was probably evolutionary during the 6th and 5th centuries B.C. Simply stated, since an appeal became certain, it became pointless for a magistrate to render a decision. This change was firmly in place by the end of the 5th century B.C.

---

64. *See infra* § 9.01[A].
65. *See supra* §§ 7.03[C] and 8.05.
66. *See infra* § 9.01[A] regarding citizenship.

Because the *Ekklēsia* was such a large group, it was impractical for it to convene on a regular basis to function as a jury. Therefore, by the middle of the 5th century B.C., Athens began using a representative jury system. In the 450's B.C., Pericles instituted pay for jury service. In order to serve on an Athenian jury, one had to be at least 30 years old and a male citizen. Six thousand jurors were selected by lot every year. They did not, however, sit every day on jury service. In order to be eligible to serve as a juror for the coming year, at the beginning of every year, each *dikastes* was required to swear the "dikastic oath." As it has been preserved for us, the dikastic oath states: "I will vote in accordance with the laws and decrees of the people of Athens and of the council of five hundred, and on matters where there are no laws, I will vote in accordance with the most just opinion."[67] A juror was paid two *obols* per day for his work. In 425 B.C., payment for jury service was increased to three *obols* per day. Some historians have suggested that pay for jury service may have helped representation of the poorer classes. Many who served on juries were old men for whom jury pay was like an old-age pension. The playwright Aristophanes painted a rather comic portrait of jury service in his play, *The Wasps* (422 B.C.). By the 4th century B.C., juries were customarily comprised of 500 jurors. In addition to the normal number of 500, we know of certain special occasions when juries consisted of 1,000, 1,500 and 2,000 jurors.

The system of jury selection was elaborate. When the system began, jurors were selected by lots drawn from containers on the morning of their prospective jury duty. At the beginning of every year, jurors were assigned to a panel designated by a particular letter of the alphabet. All jurors who had the same letter would go to the same court on any given day. Based on evidence in the plays of Aristophanes, it appears that this system was still in place in the 390's and 380's B.C. By the 370's B.C., the system of jury selection was changed to a far more complicated system. The new system involved selection using black and white balls (or cubes) as well as a *pinakion*. A *pinakion* was a wooden or bronze "ticket" that had each juror's name on it and one of the first ten letters of the alphabet, as well. The black and white balls were sorted in an allotment machine called a *kleroterion*. In addition to the use of the balls and the *pinakion*, colored sticks were also used

---

67. SEALEY, JUSTICE 51. According to Todd, "The opening words of the oath promise to give a verdict 'in accordance with the *nomoi* (laws) and the *psephismata* (decrees) of the Athenian *demos* (i.e., the *Ekklēsia* or assembly) and of the *Boulē* (council)." TODD, SHAPE 54. *See also Id.* at 83. Apparently, the jurors had two tasks: 1) to apply laws and decrees; and, 2) to decide what was most just in the absence of laws and decrees. SEALEY, JUSTICE 51–52.

to determine which court (if any) a particular juror might go to on a given day. This elaborate system was necessary to prevent bribery.

The fact that the Athenians chose their jurors by lot is a clear indication of their tremendous faith in democracy. The Athenians devoted substantial resources to this elaborate jury selection system. The confidence that the Athenians placed in their jury system is also illustrated by the fact that there was no appeal from a decision of an Athenian jury.

§ 8.09 EVIDENCE

If a public arbitrator had heard a case first, then the litigants could not offer into evidence anything that they had failed to use as evidence before the arbitrator.[68] There were basically two kinds of evidence that an Athenian might offer to prove his case: 1) evidence of relevant laws; and, 2) evidence of facts. Athenian litigants were responsible for bringing copies of germane laws to the court's attention.[69] A court clerk might have read aloud the actual text of a law furnished by a party. Many statutes are quoted in the speeches of the Attic orators. Parties also presented the facts of their cases by means of witnesses (testimony), documents (*e.g.,* contracts, wills, deeds), and other exhibits (*e.g.,* an article of clothing, a piece of jewelry, a weapon). In the 5th century B.C., witnesses usually testified orally. Then, in about 375 B.C., the law was changed to require that a witness's testimony be transcribed ahead of time and then simply read aloud for the jury at trial.[70] The witness was, however, ordinarily present at the trial to attest to the veracity of his written statement. In fact, a litigant could demand, by means of a summons, that a witness appear; and if the witness refused to make a statement to be recorded, the litigant could write his own version of the testimony (*martyria*) and then demand that the reluctant witness either confirm it or else swear an oath that it was untrue.

Either party could challenge the veracity of the opposing side's witness by bringing a *dikē* for false testimony. In fact, it is clear that many witnesses testified falsely themselves. Demosthenes recognized that perjury was common. Witnesses, according to Demosthenes, lied because they were bribed,

---

68. *See supra* § 8.01.

69. "It was not the task of the court to know or to discover what law or laws applied in particular circumstances; rather it was the litigant's right to bring forward any law(s) which he felt would support his case...." TODD, SHAPE 59 (citation omitted).

70. Sealey states that the date for this change was 389 B.C. SEALEY, JUSTICE 138.

because they were friends with the party for whom they were testifying, or because they were personally at odds with the party against whom they were testifying. At certain points in Athenian legal history, it was also possible for anyone to bring a *dikē* for false testimony (*pseudomartyrion*). Nevertheless, a litigant's speech was far more important to his case than the testimony of witnesses. Interestingly, there was no cross-examination nor did "experts" testify to evaluate evidence.

At least three kinds of evidence were *in*admissible in Athenian trials: 1) testimony by the litigant himself; 2) hearsay (*i.e.*, statements by a witness regarding what some third party had said); and, 3) the testimony of certain persons (*i.e.*, women, children, and citizens who had otherwise been disenfranchised). A party himself could not testify on his own behalf. Even though it was he who argued the case in court, he was not permitted to offer his own written testimony of the facts. Like modern American rules of evidence, the Athenians, generally speaking, disallowed hearsay evidence; that is, evidence of statements made out of court that are offered for the purpose of proving the truth of the matter asserted. One notable exception to the exclusion of hearsay was that statements made by slaves (even female slaves!) under torture were admissible. According to Isaios in his speech *On the Estate of Ciron*, although regular witnesses habitually lie, when witnesses testify under torture, they tell the truth. Interestingly, however, even though they might have had pertinent things to say about an incident, Athenian rules of evidence routinely barred the testimony of women,[71] children, and the disenfranchised.

No matter what evidence was offered, we know that on many occasions—perhaps most—litigants and witnesses simply told opposite stories. Consequently, juries often were forced to make decisions based upon the comparative reputations and societal contributions (both prior and anticipated) of the litigants rather than on a dispassionate analysis of facts.

§8.10 LEGISLATION

After the Athenian democracy was established in about 509 B.C. by the reformer Kleisthenes, it was the *Ekklēsia* that enacted laws. During the Classical period, a law was passed in the following manner. A citizen could pro-

---

71. Women were permitted to serve as witnesses under certain circumstances. *See* RAPHAEL SEALEY, WOMEN AND LAW IN CLASSICAL GREECE 43, 151 (1990) [hereinafter "SEALEY, WOMEN AND LAW"].

pose a law to the *Boulē*.[72] If approved by the *Boulē*, the *Boulē* then took the matter to the *Ekklēsia*. If approved by the *Ekklēsia*, it would then become a law. A law enacted in this manner was called a *psephisma*. During much of the 5th century B.C., the words *nomos* and *psephisma* functioned as overlapping terms for "laws." Later, after the Reinscription of the Laws in 403/2 B.C.,[73] the Athenians formally distinguished the two: a *nomos* ("law") was thereafter intended to be universal and permanent; whereas, a *psephisma* ("decree") was intended to have limited effect, or, in other words, to be ephemeral.

New laws were inscribed in either wood or stone and displayed in a public place. Although we know that some public officials kept copies of individual statutes that bore a direct relationship to their own sphere of influence, there is conflicting evidence as to whether there was a central collection of laws prior to the 5th century B.C. It is certain, though, that the Athenians did not impose any kind of comprehensive and/or macroscopic organization on their statutory corpus until late in the 4th century B.C.

By the 5th century B.C., written laws began with an identification of the year date and the procedure by which the law had been enacted. This information was called the "prescript." Following the prescript, the law identified what conduct it prohibited. The language was relatively plain and simple, with no definition of terms. Some laws also contained preestablished penalties for their violation.

§ 8.11 SYCHOPHANCY

Sycophancy was one interesting by-product of the Athenian system that allowed volunteer prosecutors. Since volunteer prosecutors often received a percentage of a convicted defendant's fine, some persons found that it was profitable to make a living suing others in hopes of financial gain. Aristophanes ridiculed these *sycophants*, or legal bounty hunters, in his play *The Acharnians*. A sycophant brought cases hoping either to win a percentage of the judgment or hoping to bribe the accused into settling the case. In order to discourage sycophancy, the Athenians enacted laws providing that, when an unsuccessful prosecutor failed to gain at least 20% of the jury's vote in a

---

72. The *Boulē* was a citizen council comprised of 500 members (50 from each of the 10 tribes), appointed by a quota system. The minimum age for *Boulē* membership was 30, just like for jury duty and for other public offices. The *Boulē* determined the agenda for the *Ekklēsia*, and performed other miscellaneous executive duties.

73. *See supra* § 7.05.

public case, he was punished with a 1,000 drachma fine. In some cases, a sycophant could be punished by disenfranchisement (*atimia*)[74] as well. This 1,000 drachma fine could be assessed when an unsuccessful prosecutor failed either to get 20% of the jury's vote or when he abandoned a case once it had been initiated (apparently to discourage settlement blackmail). By the 4th century B.C., the penalty for sycophancy included both the 1,000 drachma fine as well as loss of the right to bring cases of the same type in the future. Once a year it was possible to bring charges of sycophancy to the *Ekklēsia* by the procedure called *probolē*. At the *probolē*, the *Ekklēsia* held a hearing first and a jury trial followed. It was also possible to prosecute sycophancy by *graphē* or *eisangelia*.[75] At least three different activities were deemed serious enough to warrant prosecution for sycophancy: 1) paying another to prosecute a case; 2) threatening to prosecute another unless paid to forbear (bribery); and, 3) prosecuting a case when one did not actually believe his charges. Although the Athenians tried, apparently they were quite unsuccessful in their efforts to deter sycophancy.

§ 8.12 REMEDIES, DAMAGES, & PUNISHMENTS

Some Athenian statutes fixed precise penalties for their violation while, in many other instances, the possibilities for punishment appear to have been virtually limitless. A litigant could suggest "any penalty he thought suitable, however unusual."[76] In most cases, the guilty defendant had to pay a sum or sums of money. For most private cases (brought by *dikē*), a defendant paid damages to the plaintiff/prosecutor; although in some cases he also had to pay a fine to the State. For most public cases (brought by *graphē*), a defendant paid a fine to the State; and in some cases the plaintiff/prosecutor got to keep a percentage as a bounty.

---

74. *See infra* § 9.01[A].
75. *See supra* § 8.02.
76. MacDowell, The Law in Classical Athens 254. Todd emphasizes that: Punishment at Athens was designed neither to fit the crime nor to fit the criminal, but rather to reorder the relative position of the two litigants. It is for this reason that Athenian law granted to the would-be prosecutor a wide range of procedures for use in a given case; and also that the latter's choice of procedure (inevitably in some sense a political choice) determined both the penalty faced by the defendant and the risk faced by the prosecutor. Todd, Shape 163.

The death penalty was carried out either by: 1) hurling the convicted individual into a pit (*barathron*); 2) exposing the convicted individual by securing his neck, wrists, and ankles to a vertical wooden plank (*apotumpanismos*); or, 3) forcing the convicted individual to drink hemlock. Short of death, the ancient Athenians could also, depending upon the defendant and the offense committed, impose punishments such as: exile; fine; confinement in stocks; confiscation of property; enslavement; disenfranchisement (*atimia*); and, imprisonment (relatively rare). Although many of these punishments appear brutal to modern readers, Todd explains: "Societies which catch very few criminals tend to punish these very severely, and this may be one of the reasons why Athenian judicial penalties were so savage."[77]

§ 8.13 APPEALS & THE FINALITY OF JUDGMENTS

A jury's decision was, as a rule, final. There were, however, exceptions. For example, if a defendant had been found guilty by a default judgment,[78] he could (provided that he had justification for his absence at trial) secure a new trial within two months.[79] Similarly, where a defendant had been found guilty due to a witness's false testimony, he could then be acquitted. In addition, the family of a victim of *unintentional* homicide could pardon an exile. "Otherwise retrials and appeals against a jury's decision...were not allowed."[80] Other than the special exceptions applicable to default judgments, perjury, and a family pardon for unintentional homicide, it is difficult to imagine any way to overturn a jury's determination.

§ 8.14 *DIKĒ EXOULĒS*

Because of the difficulty of enforcing judgments, Athenian law provided a means by which a defendant (*i.e.,* a defendant whom a jury had found liable for damages) would have to pay an extra fine to the State if he failed to pay the plaintiff what was due. This was accomplished by a unique procedure called *dikē exoulēs*. Sealey interprets judicial enforcement as involving a party's right to rely on self-help. A successful plaintiff, for example, "had

---

77. TODD, SHAPE 79.
78. *See supra* § 8.03.
79. *See Id.*
80. MACDOWELL, THE LAW IN CLASSICAL ATHENS 258.

the burden of executing the judgment; that is he resumed his act of self-help."[81] According to Sealey:

> If in executing the judgment he tried to seize property and was impeded, classical Athens would do no more than offer him the "action against being kept out" (*dikē exoulēs*). If he won this action, the person impeding him was ordered to pay twice the value that had been at issue.[82]

§8.15 CHAPTER SUMMARY

Even as early as the 5th century B.C., Athenian citizens could agree by contract to have an arbitrator (under oath) resolve private disputes. Parties could orally agree to submit to arbitration so long as they agreed both on who would serve as arbitrator(s) and precisely what issue they expected to be resolved by arbitration. In the 4th century, public arbitration became mandatory for many cases. All male citizens were required to serve as public arbitrators at age 59. Because a litigant was prohibited from introducing evidence into court unless that same evidence had been introduced first in arbitration, Athenians approached public arbitration seriously. The first *dēme* judges appeared in the 5th century B.C. But in the 4th century, each of the ten tribes randomly selected four *dēme* judges each; and these came to be called "the Forty". Thereafter, the Forty heard the majority of private cases brought by *dikē*.

Dikē was the most common term used to describe a private case. Interestingly, even homicide was considered a private matter to be resolved legally by *dikē*. *Graphē*—a procedure attributed to Solon—was the usual term for a public case. A volunteer prosecutor could bring suit by *graphē* in cases where the community's interests were affected. Volunteer prosecutors could also initiate lawsuits using a number of other procedures, such as *apagogē*, *ephegesis*, *endeixis*, *apographē*, *eisangelia*, *probolē*, *dokimasia*, and *euthynai*. Because so many procedural forms existed, there was, indeed, room for considerable overlap. A plaintiff/prosecutor had to choose which procedural mechanism he wished use to pursue any given claim.

As Aristophanes' play *The Clouds* suggests, the Athenians had a reputation for being exceedingly litigious. In order to initiate a lawsuit, a plaintiff/prosecutor had to issue a summons (*prosklesis*) to the defendant, file a

---

81. SEALEY, JUSTICE 110.
82. *Id.*

complaint, and pay a fee (*prytaneia*). After a pre-trial conference (*anakrisis*), the matter went to trial. If one of the litigants (usually a defendant) failed to appear at trial without a legitimate excuse, the judge could enter a default judgment against him. Ordinarily, however, when both parties were present, a clerk read the complaint and the parties made separate speeches; the plaintiff/prosecutor spoke first. The number of speeches and their lengths varied depending on whether the case was brought by *graphē* or *dikē*. A water clock (*klepsydra*) kept track of the time allotted for each speech. The litigants represented themselves but typically relied on professional speech writers, called *logographoi*, to serve as legal counsel. After the final speeches, the jurors (*dikastes*) voted immediately, without the benefit of anything even remotely similar to the modern jury instructions. Without deliberating, juries voted, using special tokens that they placed into specific urns. Jurors also determined penalties; selecting from alternatives proposed by the plaintiff/prosecutor and defendant.

The Athenians had a special form of pleading—*diamartyria* (*i.e.*, summary judgment on decisive evidence)—that they used, for instance, to contest a court's jurisdiction. In the 4th century B.C., the most common way that an Athenian defendant challenged the procedure used by a plaintiff/prosecutor was by means of the *paragraphē*. The Athenians used *paragraphē* to contest issues that modern American law would characterize as *res judicatae*, statute of limitations, subject matter jurisdiction, and the statute of frauds. A variety of groups were responsible for different asects of legal administration in Athens. The Archons (who handled matters relating to property, family, religion, homicide, and non-citizens), *Thesmothetae*, *Strategoi* (who dealt with internal military disputes), *Agoranomoi* and *Sitophylakes* (who judged commercial issues) and the Council of the *Areopagus* (who adjudicated claims involving arson, sacred olive trees, and intentional homicide), exercised considerable authority. In the middle of the 4th century B.C., they began scheduling their court cases in a systematic manner for administrative efficiency. Certain types of courts heard cases only at specific times. And specific bodies adjudicated cases related to particular subjects; such as the *Nautodikai* (judges of sailors), *Xenodikai* (judges of foreigners), and, later in the 4th century, the *Thesmothetae* heard suits involving *dikai emporikai* (mercantile cases). By the close of the 4th century B.C., the Athenian court system was divided into distinct jurisdictional classifications, dependent upon either the subject matter of the dispute or the status of one of the litigants. Although originally, the *Archon Polemarchus* was responsible for cases involving non-citizens, eventually, the *Xenodikai* assumed that jurisdiction until the time that such matters were assimilated into the mainstream of public cases involving Athenian citizens. Also, in the late 5th and early 4th centuries, the Athenians developed the conservative devices, *graphē paranomēn* and related devices in an effort to inhibit the passage of laws that contradicted existing law.

The Athenian jury system seems to have its roots in Solon's reforms. Tradition credits Solon for giving the citizen assembly—the *Ekklēsia* (referred to as the *Heliaia* when convened to serve as a jury)—the authority to review decisions of magistrates. Because the *Ekklēsia/Heliaia* was such a large group, it was impractical for it to convene on a regular basis to function as a jury. Therefore, by the 5th century, Athens instituted a representative jury system. Jurors were selected randomly by elaborate procedures designed to prevent bribery. A combination of black and white balls, a "ticket" (*pinakion*), alphabetical assignment, and the use of a sorting machine (*kleroterion*) helped to ensure a neutral jury selection. All jurors were male, at least thirty years old, and were paid for their service. In the 4th century B.C., it was customary to impanel 500 jurors to serve in a typical trial. Litigants were responsible for providing relevant statutes to the court as evidence. Litigants also brought witnesses to testify (or—later in the 4th century—written statements prepared by witnesses) and pertinent documents and exhibits to help prove the facts of their case. Ordinarily, either party could challenge the veracity of a witness by bringing a *dikē* for perjury and, at certain points in Athenian legal history, it was possible for anyone to bring a *graphē* for perjury (*pseudomartyrion*). At least three kinds of evidence were inadmissible in Athenian trials: 1) testimony by a litigant; 2) hearsay; and, 3) testimony of women, children, and the disenfranchised.

Statutes first approved by the *Boulē* and then enacted by the *Ekklēsia* were called *psephismata* (*psephisma*, singular). Sometimes the Athenians inscribed them on wood or stone to be publicly displayed, but they had no central collection and organization of statutes until the late 4th century. Typically, a *psephisma* begins with a prescript that identifies the year of enactment and the procedure used to bring about enactment, followed by the prohibited conduct and prescribed punishment.

In order to discourage *sychophancy* (*i.e.,* paying another to prosecute a case, threatening to prosecute unless paid to forbear, or prosecuting without believing the truth of the charges), the Athenians enacted laws that severely punished volunteer prosecutors who failed to gain at least 20% of the jury's votes.

Defendants found guilty/liable ordinarily paid money damages as compensation (or fines). In criminal cases, the guilty also could be punished with death, exile, loss of property, enslavement, disenfranchisement (*atimia*), and imprisonment. Once a jury had decided a case, appeal to higher authority was virtually unknown in the Athenian legal system. As an incentive to encourage compliance with a court's order, Athenian law, through a procedure called *dikē exoulēs*, imposed on those found liable an additional fine paid to the State.

CHAPTER 9

Substantive Law

§ 9.01 PERSONAL STATUS

[A] CITIZENSHIP

All legal rights in Classical Athens depended on an individual's citizenship status. Until the mid-5th century B.C., persons whose fathers were Athenian citizens automatically received Athenian citizenship regardless of their mother's citizenship status. The great Athenian statesman, Pericles, initiated a significant legal change about 451/50 B.C. whereby citizenship depended on *both* parents being Athenian citizens—not just the father.

> Two laws were passed. By the first a foreign man who was convicted of living with an Athenian woman as her husband was to be sold into slavery, his goods confiscated, and one-third of the proceeds given to his accuser; a foreign woman convicted of living with an Athenian man as his wife was liable to the same penalty, and in addition the man had to pay a fine of 1,000 drachmai. By the second law anyone ('any Athenian' must be meant) who was convicted of giving a foreign woman in marriage to an Athenian man representing her as related to him (viz., related in such a way as entitled him to give her in marriage) is to suffer *atimia*, his goods are to be confiscated, and a third of the proceeds to be paid to his accuser.[83]

This new citizenship law, however, did not operate retroactively; therefore it did not nullify the citizenship of persons already born of an Athenian father but a non-Athenian mother. The chaotic circumstances that prevailed during the Peloponnesian War (431–404 B.C.) prevented the Athenians from enforcing Pericles' citizenship law strictly. But after the war, the Rein-

---

83. A.R.W. Harrison, The Law of Athens (Vol. I) 26 (1968) [hereinafter "Harrison, The Law of Athens (Vol. I)".

scription of the laws[84] reaffirmed Pericles' citizenship law and it again became effective in 403 B.C.

Citizenship was originally organized around and based upon the four traditional tribes (*phylae*) of Attica. In his reforms (*c.* 508 B.C.), Kleisthenes reorganized citizenship so that a person's citizenship depended on the small village units called *dēmes*. There were over 150 *dēmes*. After the time of Kleisthenes, *dēme* membership was hereditary. Thus, even when someone relocated to another part of Attica, he retained his *dēme* membership in the *dēme* where his family had been in 508 B.C. All Athenian males whose parents were both citizens could join their *dēme* during their 18th year. In a process called *dokimasia*, the *dēme* members voted whether to accept a boy's membership. Primarily, the *dēme* had to determine—in a culture without marriage certificates or birth certificates—whether the boy was old enough and of appropriate parentage to qualify for membership. After the *dēme* had voted to accept a boy, the *Boulē* reviewed the *dēme's* determination. If the *Boulē* was of the opinion that the boy was not qualified (and thus that the *dēme's* decision had been erroneous), the *Boulē* fined the *dēme* members themselves. Since girls were not registered in *dēmes*, apparently, the Athenians had to rely on oral testimony regarding a woman's (*i.e.,* mother's) citizenship. It was possible to challenge the validity of another person's citizenship by *graphē*.[85] The accused was imprisoned to await trial, and the penalty for impersonating a citizen was enslavement to the highest bidder.

Although some legal historians doubt Plutarch's (the Greek biographer of the late 1st and early 2nd century A.D.) veracity on this point, Plutarch states that Solon's laws permitted a foreigner to become a citizen: 1) if he had been exiled from his own country; or, 2) if he relocated his entire family to Athens and established a trade there. If Plutarch's claim is inaccurate, then until about 370 B.C. (by which time the *Ekklēsia* could vote to confer citizenship on a foreigner), Athens had no routinized naturalization process by which a foreigner could become an Athenian citizen. There were, on occasion, extraordinary means by which some foreigners were granted citizenship, but those situations were usually limited to a grant of citizenship to an illustrious foreigner for political reasons or a grant to military volunteers during times of war when the Athenians needed additional soldiers or oarsmen to fill their ranks. According to Harrison, "[t]here is good evidence that Athens had conferred this right on certain cities in Euboia towards the end of the 5th century, and in 401/400...."[86]

---

84. *See supra* § 7.05.
85. *See supra* § 8.02.
86. HARRISON, THE LAW OF ATHENS (Vol. I) 29.

Citizenship was a bundle of rights and obligations. Among the rights in the bundle were the following: 1) the right to vote; 2) the right to enter temples; 3) the right to enter the Agora; 4) the right to hold public office; 5) the right to marry an Athenian citizen; 6) the right to own property; 7) the right to serve on a jury; 8) the right to speak in the *Ekklēsia*; and, 9) the right to speak in a law court and exercise legal remedies (in one's own person). Among the obligations were military service and payment of taxes. Tradition credits Solon and Draco with establishing a law that even required all citizens to maintain a job or be subject to a 100 drachma fine. But, generally speaking, adult male citizens enjoyed remarkable freedom in Classical Athens. They were not subject to anyone else's control; they could own property and were the masters of their own *oikoi* (households).

All Athenian male citizens and metics[87] ages 18–60 had mandatory military service. Whenever Athens needed its army or navy, the *Strategoi* (the board of ten generals) called on those eligible to serve. There were some valid excuses for avoiding service; such as illness and the performance of some other types of public service. Anyone could prosecute another for evasion of military service (by *graphē*) for the offense called *deilia* (draft dodging). The penalty for draft dodging was *atimia* (the loss of many— but probably not all—of a person's citizenship rights). The *Strategoi* reserved the authority—with broad discretion—to punish soldiers and sailors (once they were active) for misbehavior in the line of duty.

As a penalty for certain wrongdoings, a citizen could be punished by *atimia*. The complete picture is unclear but *atimia* probably entailed the loss of the right to vote, the right to hold public office, the right to serve on juries, the right to speak in the *Ekklēsia* and courts, and the right to enter the Agora and temples. Thus *atimia* probably did not erase a citizen's rights to own property and to marry; nor did it relieve him of his responsibilities to perform military service and to pay taxes.

[B] FOREIGNERS & METICS

Foreigners in Athens could neither own property nor marry an Athenian woman. Foreigners were, however, required to pay taxes if they wished to transact mercantile business in the Agora. Interestingly, a foreigner was permitted to speak in Athenian law courts.

If a foreigner resided in Athens for a particular period of time, he could qualify for status as a *metic*. Metics were "resident aliens" who were ac-

---

87. *See infra* § 9.01[B].

cepted into the fabric of Athenian society. A slave who had been given his freedom also became a metic under Athenian law. According to Todd, "Broadly speaking, a metic was liable to all those obligations which would have been imposed on a citizen of equivalent wealth, together with some additional responsibilities."[88] They were obliged to pay a special metic's tax (*metoikion*) and had to serve in the military if called.[89] Metics were also required to maintain a *prostates*, an Athenian citizen to serve as something like a guardian. It is unclear exactly how the *prostates* functioned in reality, but it appears that the *prostates* served more of a symbolic than a practical function. As Harrison puts it: "[w]e are unfortunately almost wholly in the dark on the duties of a *prostates* beyond that of appearing in court."[90] Nevertheless, metics did receive a certain measure of legal protection. Specifically, the *Archon Polemarchus* was given jurisdiction over cases involving metics. The exact details, however, of a metic's legal capacity are unknown. Unfortunately our sources often fail to distinguish between metics and other non-resident aliens when describing legal status. We do know, however, that, as a general rule, metics could not own real property unless they had received a special exemption called *enktesis*. In addition to the privilege of *enktesis*, it was also possible for a metic to be granted *isoteleia*, an exemption from the obligation of paying the metic's tax. It also seems likely that, on some occasions, a metic could be exempted from the obligation of maintaining a *prostates*. A census taken around 315 B.C. placed the number of metics in Athens at about 10,000.

[C] SLAVES & FREEDMEN

Most slaves in ancient Athens were considered personal property (chattel slavery), and therefore, they could be bought and sold. But, as Harrison advises, "we should recognize that there was a pervasive ambiguity about the legal status of a slave which made him both a chattel and something more than a mere chattel."[91] Scholars estimate the number of slaves in Classical Athens between 20,000 and 75,000. Athenian slaves were usually foreigners. We may classify slaves in ancient Athens as either public or private. There were only a handful of public slaves. Caretakers of public buildings, the public "coin-tester," and a group of slaves who functioned somewhat

---

88. TODD, SHAPE 196.
89. The metic's tax was twelve drachmas per-year for a man and six drachmas per-year for a woman. *See also infra* § 9.07[F].
90. HARRISON, THE LAW OF ATHENS (Vol. I) 193.
91. *Id.* at 163.

like a police force (the Skythian archers) were the public slaves. Most private slaves were slaves by virtue of having been captured in war or by having descended from a war captive. Tradition has it that Solon abolished debt slavery in Athens. It is possible that a child's status as a slave depended on the mother. If a child's mother was a slave, the child would be a slave, but not otherwise.

Theoretically speaking, Athenian slaves had no rights. For example, Athenian law did not recognize their family relationships. A slave could not own property in Athens. Slaves could not sue in court and could not enter the *gymnasia* (exercise grounds) *palaistrai* (wrestling grounds) reserved for citizens. But some slaves routinely worked outside of the owner's home and could earn money. Those slaves working outside of the household were required by law, however, to pay their owners an established payment called *apophora*. Some evidence suggests that it was illegal for owners to kill their slaves; although the law did not prohibit severe corporal punishment. Using a legal theory substantially similar to our modern *respondeat superior* (*i.e.*, vicarious liability), one of Solon's laws made slave owners liable for the offenses committed by their slaves against others. It is also likely that owners were responsible for debts incurred by their slaves as well. Harrison, however, is cautious on this point: "Where an obligation had arisen out of contractual dealings by a slave the rules are far from clear, and they had certainly not been worked out at Athens with anything like the detail and subtlety that obtained in Roman law."[92] Occasionally a slave owner freed a slave in his will. Otherwise, a slave owner could also manumit a slave during his lifetime without going through any formal procedure. According to Harrison, "[i]t was probably fairly common practice for a slave to purchase his freedom out of accumulated earnings."[93] Freedmen were generally permitted to attain only *metic* status, not citizen status. Thus, for example, a freedman could not own land in Attica. Furthermore, a patron had to represent freedmen in judicial proceedings, and the Polemarch had jurisdiction in cases relating to them.

§ 9.02 PROPERTY

[A] INTRODUCTION

Harrison relates that "the Athenians of the 4th century were still at a relatively simple stage in their legal thinking about property; so much so

---

92. *Id.* at 174. *See also infra* § 12.01[C].
93. HARRISON, THE LAW OF ATHENS (Vol. I) 182.

that they had no general term which could describe this branch of the law."[94] Real property was especially important in ancient Athens.[95] An owner of real property also *ipso facto* owned any improvements (such as buildings), any crops, and any animals on the land. Aliens were not allowed to own real property in Attica. In addition to real property, Athenian law also authorized ownership of various kinds of tangible personal property (household items, clothing, tools, *etc.*). But it is clear that Athenian law never refined legal categories of property to a degree even remotely similar to that of Roman law.[96] Still, some ancient writers distinguish between property that was visible *versus* invisible and between property that was ancestral (*patrēia*) *versus* acquired (*epikēta*). Generally speaking, there seem to have been some restrictions on the alienability of ancestral property even as late as the 4th century B.C. Since, slaves were considered personal property, it was only logical that slaves themselves could own neither real nor personal property.[97] Slave owners could sue for injuries inflicted on their slaves by others (*e.g., dikē aikeias*). An owner could also sue someone who murdered a slave (*dikē phonou*). Although the Athenians "had no abstract word for ownership,"[98] corporate entities (*e.g., dēmes, phratries,* religious bodies, and the State) were, nevertheless, legally capable of owning any kind of property that an individual could own. According to Aristotle, the benchmark of ownership was the capacity to alienate. Two or more people could own property jointly; but in order to sell—or otherwise alienate—property that was jointly owned, all joint owners had to agree. If they were unable to concur on the proposed disposition, a joint owner who wished to alienate his property could bring suit to request that the property be divided for purposes of sale. Athenian property owners could transfer possession—as opposed to outright ownership of property—by a loan or lease.[99] And Harrison asserts that "the Athenians were fully aware of the judicial importance of the distinction" between possession and ownership.[100]

---

94. *Id.* at 200.

95. *See* MacDowell, The Law in Classical Athens 133. *Also see* Todd, Shape 236 ("Astonishingly few surviving speeches, however, are concerned generally with property or obligations involving property.").

96. *See infra* § 12.02[A].

97. *See supra* § 9.01[C].

98. Harrison, The Law of Athens (Vol. I) 201.

99. *See* Todd, Shape 250. MacDowell, however, notes that there was "no Greek noun for ownership as distinct from possession...." MacDowell, The Law in Classical Athens 133.

100. Harrison, The Law of Athens (Vol. I) 204.

According to Sealey, "[t]he law of property is mainly concerned with ways of acquiring property."[101] In the first instance, we presume (and that is all it is, a presumption) that Athenian law acknowledged original occupation as a source of ownership. Indeed, Aristotle specifically asserts that one could acquire property by fishing, hunting, and seizing in wartime. Otherwise one of Solon's laws allowed that someone who left an object—for example, at a roadside—remained the owner of it so long as he could be identified as the owner. In addition, Athenians could transfer ownership of property by gift, sale, or by operation of inheritance. During the 5th and 4th centuries, a man was not permitted to leave his property in a will to whomever he wished. Instead, the laws of succession established immutable inheritance rights during the Classical period.[102]

In the 6th century B.C., the Greeks first began using coinage as a medium of exchange. The introduction of coinage had a profound effect on the Greek economy and, therefore, on the transfer of property. The availability of metal coins as a medium of exchange greatly facilitated all conveyance of property.

[B] REAL PROPERTY

Because agriculture dominated the ancient Athenian economy, many unique laws governed the ownership and use of real property. However, there was neither a collection of public records nor a registration system that evidenced a person's title to his real estate. In 5th century B.C., Athenian citizens could legally sell real property. An alien could only own real estate under exceptional circumstances; if he was granted a special privilege called *enktesis*.[103] Generally speaking, an owner of real property was legally permitted to do whatever he wished with his own land. One exception to a land owner's freedom had to do with olive trees. Because olive oil was such an important commodity in the Athenian economy, property owners were limited to cutting no more than two olive trees per year. A violation of this restriction gave rise to a fine of 100 drachmas per tree. In addition, some olive trees (even some on property that was otherwise considered private property) were designated as sacred to the goddess Athena. Even at the beginning of the 4th century B.C., if someone cut down a sacred olive tree, he could face trial before the *Areopagus* and the death penalty. Technically, the

---

101. SEALEY, JUSTICE 60.
102. *See infra* § 9.04.
103. *See supra* § 9.01[B].

olives of the sacred trees belonged to the Athenian State, and the landowners in the late 4th century still paid a royalty of a little less than 3/4 of a pint of olive oil per tree per year.

Property owners also were not permitted to plant trees or excavate ditches so close to their boundary lines that it would hinder their neighbor. Because of the scarcity of fresh water on the Greek mainland, several laws controlled the manner in which land owners could use water on their property. Solon is credited with establishing laws that permitted citizens to obtain water either from public wells or from their neighbors, depending on availability. Thus, under certain circumstances, one citizen was obliged to allow neighbors to enter his property and take specified amounts of water on a daily basis. This type of law is roughly analogous to what modern law might characterize as an easement appurtenant; that is, a right, based on the proximity of two parcels of land, to enter another's land. In order to protect landowners downstream, laws prohibited polluting the rivers upstream. In addition to pollution, Athenian law also imposed penalties (damages of at least 1000 drachmas) on upstream owners who diverted water in such a way that it harmed the property of a downstream owner.

[C] MINES

Attica had valuable silver mines. According to Harrison, issues relating to the ownership and use of mines are complex:

> In what sense the state owned minerals under Attic soil and how precisely it exploited this ownership are highly controversial issues. There is a fair amount of evidence in connection with the silver mines at Laureion, but it has not yet produced clear and generally accepted conclusions. The main question is whether the Athenians achieved the abstraction of separating out from rights of ownership in the soil the right to exploit the minerals below the surface and vesting this latter right as such in the state.[104]

A great deal of evidence suggests, however, that the State claimed ownership of the subterranean sections of mines. As owner, the Athenian State routinely, through a formal registration process, leased mines to others who then quarried them. The normal lease period for a mine was ten years. When a mine was located underneath the surface of land that was privately owned, it is possible that the State paid a percentage of its lease

---

104. HARRISON, THE LAW OF ATHENS (Vol. I) 234.

payment (*i.e.*, the payment from the individual who had registered and was working the mine) to the surface property owner. A special "catch-all" mining law, called *nomos metallikos* forbade anyone from interfering with mining operations.

[D] RESOLVING OWNERSHIP DISPUTES RELATING TO PERSONAL PROPERTY

In contemporary American law, when one person claims that a particular property is rightfully his but another person has possession of it, the rightful owner (*i.e.*, the person who does not have possession) can sue for "replevin," thereby asking the court to order the wrongful possessor to return the goods to him (*i.e.*, the rightful owner who for one reason or another has lost possession). When two or more persons disputed a claim to an *inheritance* in classical Athens, one of the disputants could petition the *archon* and the conflict would be resolved in a process called *diadikasia* using a jury trial.[105] Harrison explains *diadikasia*:

> The primary function of the court is to decide which of the two has a better right to own the thing....This gave to the procedure its characteristic features: there was no plaintiff and no defendant; the two parties stood side by side, trying each to show that his relation to the thing or duty gave him a better right to own the thing or to escape the duty than his opponent....[106]

Otherwise, it seems that Athenian law generally permitted A to bring suit against B when A believed that B possessed money or property that A believed was rightfully his. It is likely that such a suit was brought as a *dikē*, and that additional words were used alongside the word "*dikē*" to designate the nature of the property that was in dispute (*e.g.*, *dikē khreōs* (debt), *dikē ousias* (property)). Here, as is the case in a modern action for "replevin," the alleged rightful owner merely was asking that the subject property be returned to him. If the possessor alleged that he had purchased the disputed property from a third party, the defendant/possessor could subpoena the seller to appear at trial. If the court found that the possessor had, in fact, bought the item from a third party, the third party was obligated to repay the possessor/defendant his purchase price, and the possessor had to return the property to the plaintiff who rightfully owned it. Modern American

---

105. *See infra* §§ 9.03[B], 9.04[A].
106. HARRISON, THE LAW OF ATHENS (Vol. I) 215.

commercial law reaches a different result (allowing the buyer to retain possession but mandating that the seller—presumably the original crook—pay the initial owner compensatory damages) if the possessor legitimately bought the property in good faith.

§ 9.03 FAMILY LAW

[A] INTRODUCTION: POWER & CONTROL

In Classical Athens, the family centered on the *oikos*, the household unit of production and consumption. Adult men were responsible for the protection and well-being of their *oikoi*. Women and children were dependent on their *kyrios*, the adult male who was legally responsible for them. The term *epitropos* is often used for the guardian of boys. The *kyrios* for a child was typically his/her father, the *kyrios* for an adult woman was usually her husband.[107] Upon marriage, a woman's *kyrios* changed from father to husband. When a woman's husband died, she could decide whether she wished to return to her former *oikos* under the control of her father (or her father's successor as *kyrios*), or she could remain with her married family under the supervision of her husband's heir (typically her own son). This is unusual in Athenian law because, in this special situation, *a woman had an option to make a decision that had legal consequence for herself.*

Otherwise, Athenian law typically treated women like children who needed a guardian to administer their property and transact business on their behalf at all times. Women could not make a valid will but apparently could, under certain circumstances, testify on legal matters, although not as a court witness.[108] Women could be tried in court as defendants. Women could own personal property and could buy and sell it if the value of the transaction was below a certain modest amount. And, although much evidence suggests that a woman was not legally capable of owning real prop-

---

107. Speaking in general terms about all ancient Greek women—not just women in classical Athens, Professor Sealey remarks:

> Her *kyrios* might be her father, her brother, her grandfather, or her uncle; in consequence of marriage her *kyrios* would be her husband or eventually her adult son or son-in-law. But in any one city at any one time the degree of authority exercised by the *kyrios*, whoever he might be, was uniform. A Greek woman was subject to *kyrieia* solely because she was a woman.

Sealey, Justice 82.

108. Sealey, Women and Law 43 (Sealey gives an example of women testifying regarding the authenticity of a document in an arbitration).

erty, Sealey argues that a woman was capable of "owning" real property such as her dowry and inherited real estate.[109] Her "ownership" was restricted in the sense that it was technically administered by her *kyrios*. Nevertheless, the *kyrios* may have functioned something like an agent for the woman (*i.e.,* the principal) who legally owned the property.

[B] MARRIAGE & DIVORCE

Harrison warns that "there is no single Greek word which can be taken to stand for 'marriage.'"[110] Ancient Athenian law recognized two very different kinds of marriage: *enguē* and *epidikasia*. Marriage by *enguē*, which required no formal government sanction, was the more common type. *Enguē* involved "a transaction between the bride's father and the bridegroom of which the bride [was] the object."[111] In many respects this type of marriage resembles a contract between the prospective father-in-law and the groom. *Epidikasia*, which did require government sanction, was a marriage of a female who had become an *epiklēros*.[112]

As a rule, the law did not allow a man to marry his mother, grandmother, daughter, granddaughter, sister, or half-sister (by his mother). He could, however, marry his half-sister (by his father), an adopted sister, niece, cousin, and, by the mid-5th century B.C., anyone else who was a citizen. Neither *enguē* nor *epidikasia* was available when one party was free and the other was a slave. According to Harrison, "[w]here one of the parties was Athenian and the other a foreigner or metic, the rule differed at different periods."[113] At some point in antiquity, there seem to have been certain legal drawbacks to being a bachelor under Athenian law but the evidence is thin and unclear. Girls were usually about fourteen when they were married and men were much older. A groom probably had to be at least seventeen in order to take part in a valid contractual arrangement, like *enguē*. And, although we have no direct evidence for a statute prohibiting polygamy, Athenian law seems not to have permitted it.

In a typical marriage by *enguē*, the man first had to reach a formal agreement called *engyesis* (*i.e.,* an oral contract) with his intended bride's *kyrios*, typically her father. Indeed, it was this formal agreement process between

---

109. *See Id.* at 43–49.
110. HARRISON, THE LAW OF ATHENS (Vol. I) 1.
111. *Id.* at 2.
112. For a brief discussion of the peculiarities involving an *epiklēros, see infra* this section and *infra* § 9.04[A].
113. A.R.W. HARRISON, THE LAW OF ATHENS (Vol. II) 24 (1968) (footnote omitted).

the would-be husband and the girl's father that was called *enguē*. Primarily, the *enguē* consisted simply of the father's formal declaration to the suitor that he (the father) was giving his daughter to the suitor. The girl's wishes were irrelevant to the *enguē*. Later, the actual transfer, *ekdosis*, took place. The *ekdosis* occurred when the woman physically relocated to her husband's *oikos*. It was also possible, though not legally required, for the couple to have a more formal ceremony called *gamos*. And the *ekdosis* and the *gamos* often may have occurred simultaneously.

A bride's father was not legally required to provide a dowry (*proix*) to his son-in-law. Nevertheless, upon divorce, a husband was obligated to return any dowry that had been given. This law, requiring a divorced husband to return any dowry received, had a normative effect. Because the law discouraged divorce when a dowry had been given, it encouraged fathers to give a dowry. In fact we know of no actal instance where there was *engyesis* but no dowry. The dowry served as the functional equivalent of the bride's inheritance. "It was property of any kind, whether money, chattels, land, or claims, made over by a woman's *kyrios* to a man in contemplation of their marriage by *enguē*."[114] Thus, a husband was not completely at liberty to alienate the property that comprised the dowry. If a husband refused to return the dowry upon divorce, his ex-wife's *kyrios* could sue him for its return (*dikē proikos*) and for income or "alimony" reckoned at 18% interest (*dikē sitou*). Otherwise there were few legal impediments to obtaining a divorce if initiated by the husband. Basically, the husband merely had to send his wife away in order to obtain a divorce (*apopempsis*). Divorce was probably more difficult for a wife to secure (*apoleipsis*). She had to leave her husband's house, appear before the Archon with her *kyrios* (*i.e.,* the *kyrios* to whom she returned upon leaving her husband—typically either her father or a brother), and give a written notice. Otherwise, "[v]oluntary dissolution of marriage might arise from agreement to separate between the husband and wife."[115] If a married woman died without surviving children or grandchildren, her husband was required to return the dowry to her *kyrios*. However, if she had any children, the children inherited the dowry.

In addition to the ordinary marriage by *enguē*, an Athenian marriage was also legally valid when accomplished through *epidikasia*. The necessity for this kind of marriage arose in cases where a father died leaving no male heirs—no sons, no grandsons, and no great-grandsons. If, however, such a man did have a daughter, granddaughter, or even a great-granddaughter, it

---

114. *Id.* at 46.
115. Harrison, The Law of Athens (Vol. I) 39.

was theoretically and practically possible for her to give birth to a male child who would thereby become the deceased's grandson, great-grandson, or great, great-grandson. The ancient Athenian legal term for a woman in such a position was *epiklēros*; a term that some legal historians have translated "heiress." In order to facilitate the deceased's inheritance lineage, the closest male relative of the deceased was entitled to marry the *epiklēros*. He (the closest male relative) could, if he wished, decline the opportunity to marry the *epiklēros*. However, at the other extreme, he could also legally force her to divorce her current husband. The orator Isaios claims, indeed, that the nearest male relative commonly invoked this privilege, and required the *epiklēros* to divorce and remarry. The Archon was responsible for ensuring that the *epiklēros* married an appropriate husband. Frequently, more than one relative laid claim to marry the *epiklēros*, and a legal proceeding (*diadikasia*) was necessary to select a husband. Once a male relative had married the *epiklēros*, the court was required to ratify the marriage (*epidikasia*). According to tradition, one of Solon's laws required that an *epiklēros*' husband have intercourse with her a minimum of three times a month for the purpose of producing legitimate heirs. And anyone could prosecute (by *eisangelia*) a person who mistreated an *epiklēros*.

Athenian law regarding fidelity was extremely sexist by today's standards. According to Demosthenes, prostitutes were available for a man's "pleasure" and concubines were necessary for the daily needs of a man's body, but the purpose of wives was to bear legitimate children and to tend the house. During marriage, a man was not required to be faithful to his wife, but a wife was required to be faithful to her husband. Elsewise, as Harrison puts it, "her misconduct might introduce an adulterine bastard into the family."[116] A husband was even allowed to have another woman actually live in his *oikos* and have sexual relations with him. Such a woman was called a *pallakē*. The term *pallakē* was also used for a woman who lived with a man more or less permanently (but in circumstances where there had been no *enguē*). Nevertheless, a woman who was divorced or widowed could legally remarry if she desired.

[C] CHILDREN

As a rule, in order to be considered legitimate, a child had to be born of parents who were married either by *enguē* or *epidikasia*. When one parent was a citizen and the other was not, or if a child was born when the parents had not been married by *enguē* or *epidikasia*, such a child was called a

---

116. *Id.* at 32.

nothos. Although *nothoi* clearly did not enjoy the rights of full citizens, they had some rights superior to metics and foreigners (*e.g.,* certain rights of inheritance). A citizen boy remained under the control of his *kyrios* (usually his father) until his 18th year. A girl remained under her *kyrios'* control until marriage. "Until a son came of age his father represented him in every kind of legal transaction, whether procedurally before a court or in matters of contract, since a minor was incapacitated from entering into any contract."[117]

Children's rights were few. Parents were legally permitted to practice population control by exposure of an infant. "He could...expose the child, that is, abandon it in some place where there was a chance of its being found and nurtured by another person. There seems no reason to doubt that the father had this absolute discretion and that the right of exposure was more than a purely formal one."[118] Parents could also, before the time of Solon, sell or pledge their children (*e.g.,* for a debt). Solon's laws subjected a son to prosecution for neglecting or mistreating his parents in their old age. The punishment for such neglect or abuse was *atimia.*[119]

When a child's father died, the Archon was responsible for appointing a substitute *kyrios* to serve as guardian. It was common for the Archon to appoint several guardians who shared the responsibilites. A guardian was responsible for the ward's food, clothing, housing, and education. Guardians also had to maintain their ward's property and represent him in matters relating to taxes and law. The guardian-*kyrios* was required to keep careful financial records and accounts of his management of his ward's estate. At the end of the term of guardianship, a ward could bring a private action against his guardian for mismanagement of the estate. Technically speaking, there were several different kinds of legal theories which a ward might advance, and we have evidence for at least three different types of lawsuits—the details of which need not concern us here—(*dikē epitropes, dikē sitou,* and *phasis*). Furthermore, a public cause of action, *eisangelia,* was available against a guardian-*kyrios* (or anyone else for that matter) who mistreated a youth whose father had died.[120] But the details of such a prosecution are uncertain. We do know, however, that a volunteer prosecutor who brought suit in an effort to protect the rights of a child in this manner did not risk the fine that ordinarily accompanied the failure to garner one-fifth of the

---

117. *Id.* at 73.
118. *Id.* at 71.
119. *See supra* § 9.01[A].
120. *See supra* § 8.02.

jury's votes.[121] This exception to the one-fifth-vote-of-the-jury rule illustrates a paternalistic desire on the part of the State to protect the interests of children whose fathers had died.

§ 9.04 INHERITANCE & SUCCESSION

[A] INTESTATE SUCCESSION

Although there are many fundamental rules of inheritance that we can discern from the speeches of orators, nevertheless, many inheritance disputes degenerated into unfettered fabrication and self-serving testimony, as relatives and pseudo-relatives presented false testimony, forged wills, and forged adoption documents, while they jockied for a piece of a decedent's property. "Athenian inheritance cases should not be treated as the product of a system where clear rigid rules of kinship are authoritatively interpreted and mechanically applied."[122]

When a man died—without a will and without having adopted an heir[123]—and only one legitimate son survived him, that son inherited all of his father's assets and liabilities (public debts in particular). In the case of more than one son, the sons inherited equally, without preference for the eldest. Although the inheriting sons could agree to share and keep their inheritance jointly in an undivided whole, brothers under such circumstances usually physically divided and separated their father's goods and property (*i.e.*, the estate, or *klēros*) as equitably as possible. When a son predeceased his father, his sons (*i.e.*, the grandson's) were entitled to inherit their deceased father's share (*i.e.*, his share of their grandfather's estate) on a *pro rata* basis.

One of the more interesting problems of Greek inheritance law occurred in situations involving an *epiklēros*.[124] In the circumstance of an *epiklēros*, marriage by *epidikasia* ensured that the *oikos* of the deceased would continue and that his estate would be secure. When a man died leaving no sons, grandsons, great-grandsons, and no female descendant eligible to be an *epiklēros*, Athenian inheritance law then permitted the man's nearest living relatives, his *anchisteis*,—in a predetermined order of prefer-ence—to inherit his property. Brothers (and his brother's descendants) were first in line,

---

121. *See supra* § 8.11.
122. Cohen, Law, Violence and Community in Classical Athens 176.
123. *See infra* § 9.04[B].
124. *See supra* § 9.03[B].

along with half-brothers by the same father. Sisters (and his sister's descendants) followed, along with half-sisters by the same father. After brothers and sisters, inheritance law defaulted to the following: 1) All other relatives on the father's side of the family "as far as the children of cousins";[125] 2) half-brothers (and their descendants) by the same mother; 3) half-sisters (and their descendants) by the same mother; 4) all other relatives on the mother's side of the family "as far as the children of cousins." The real losers in the Athenian inheritance scheme were the widow (she could not become an *epiklēros*), parents, and grandparents, who, because they had no inheritance rights whatsoever, were not even left holding an empty bag, but no bag at all. In 403 B.C., a new law prohibited illegitimate children from inheriting.

Athenian inheritance law did not function with the rule of primogeniture. Thus, sons of the deceased inherited equal shares without regard to birth order. In addition, inheritance was *per stirpes* not *per capita*. For example, suppose the deceased, for purposes of illustration, let us call him Aeschylus, had two sons named Sophocles and Euripides. Now suppose that one of the sons, Sophocles, had predeceased his father, Aeschylus. Suppose also that, prior to his own death, Sophocles had had two sons of his own, Aristophanes and Menander. In this scenario, there would be three individuals, a son, Euripides, and two grandsons, Aristophanes and Menander, who stand to inherit the estate of Aeschylus. The ancient Athenian *per stirpes* system gave Euripides 50% of Aeschylus' estate and gave Aristophanes and Menander 25% each (representing an equal portion of what would have been Sophocles' 50% share had he not died before his father, Aeschylus). A *per capita* system, which the Athenians did *not* use, on the other hand, would have divided Aeschylus' estate equally according to the total number of heirs (three in this hypothetical). Thus, a *per capita* system would have given Euripides, Aristophanes, and Menander each 33⅓% of Aeschylus' estate.

Sons and grandsons were permitted simply to take possession of any property that was rightfully theirs (by inheritance laws) without having to resort to any formal or legalistic procedure. Anyone else who might claim an inheritance right had to petition the Archon in writing and give notice of his alleged claim through the *Ekklēsia*. This process was called *epidikasia*. If, for some reason, an individual's claim was disputed by another, the claim

---

125. In ancient Athenian law, the word "cousin" probably means "first cousin." But even ancient cases disputed the actual meaning of this word. *See* MACDOWELL, THE LAW IN CLASSICAL ATHENS 106–07. *See also* COHEN, LAW VIOLENCE AND COMMUNITY IN CLASSICAL ATHENS 178.

was called a *diadikasia*. Of course, it was entirely possible that more than one person could emerge to dispute an inheritance claim. As a consequence, a *diadikasia* might prove to be an exceptionally complicated process. Further confounding this process was the prospect that a man's estate might pass through an *epiklēros*.[126] Several speeches of the orator Isaios, an orator who appears to have specialized in Athenian estates law, reveal just how intricate this field of law was. One well known contested inheritance lawsuit was still raging in the courts more than 50 years after the decedent's demise.

In those instances, when inheritance claims were disputed (*diadikasia*), the legal machinery struggled with profound problems of proof. A jury needed sound evidence to serve as a basis for its factual determinations. Because there were neither marriage nor birth certificates, any claimant necessarily had difficulty proving genealogy and/or legitimacy. Whenever someone offered into evidence a document purporting to be the deceased's will, there was the distinct possibility that it was a forgery. Credible and persuasive oral testimony from witnesses obviously made or broke many inheritance cases in ancient Athens.

[B] ADOPTION & WILLS

Even prior to the laws of Solon (*c.* 594 B.C.), men who had no biological sons had begun the practice of adopting a son during their lifetime. They adopted a son in order to create an heir. According to Harrison,

> Solon seems to have made two closely related rules; he allowed a man who had neither son nor daughter to choose an heir, whom he adopted; and he allowed a man who had only a daughter to choose for her a husband, whom he adopted. There seems now little doubt that this was the essence of what was later regarded as a law conferring complete freedom of testament on a man who had no legitimate issue.[127]

In order to adopt, an adopter had to be a male adult citizen who had no living sons. In Athenian law, adoption was an institution designed primarily to benefit the adopter not necessarily the adoptee. Adoption was a contractual mechanism used to preserve the adopter's *oikos*. "[T]he normal effect of any adoption was to make the adopted son...heir to the whole of the es-

---

126. *See supra* §9.03[B].
127. Harrison, The Law of Athens (Vol. I) 82.

tate of the adopter."[128] Therefore, most adoptees were adult males, and most adopters were so old or so infirm that they considered themselves incapable of siring a son. Upon adoption, an adoptee legally acquired the same rights as if he had been a natural child of the adopter (except that he, himself, was not permitted to adopt children). During the 4th and 5th centuries B.C., adoption was the only means by which an Athenian could transfer his estate to a person other than those persons designated in the inheritance laws. An ancient Athenian could not, as we can today, bequeath property to anyone whom he pleased in his will. If he wished to do so, he had to adopt that person as a son. Interestingly, even a man who already had a natural son was permitted to adopt a son in his will. In the event that the natural son predeceased his father (or died simultaneously—in a common accident, for example), the testate adoption became effective. Otherwise, the adoption by will was considered merely contingent, and was thus deemed invalid (*i.e.,* in cases where a natural son outlived his father). It was not until centuries later that Athenian law permitted testamentary disposition in a manner roughly analogous to modern wills and estates practice. When an Athenian did make a will—for example in order to posthumously adopt an heir—he usually did so in writing. Witnesses were ordinarily present and the testator commonly sealed the document too. Nevertheless, neither a writing, witnesses, nor seals seem to have been required in order to give legal effect to an Athenian will. Instead, those formalities were often used for the purpose of deterring forgeries.

§ 9.05 CRIMINAL LAW

[A] INTRODUCTION

Most scholars who specialize in Athenian law agree that criminal law, in its modern sense, did not exist in Classical Athens.[129] Although there was a group of Skythian archers who performed some of the duties of modern police, and although the "Eleven" "had charge of prisons and executions... [and] also had the power summarily to arrest offenders...," the State on the whole lacked the basic institutions necessary to operate a criminal jus-

---

128. *Id.* at 95–96.
129. "[I]t is widely agreed among scholars that the concept of crime cannot be properly applied to Athens at all, where prosecutions were almost invariably brought by private individuals acting on their own behalf even for offences committed directly against the state." TODD, SHAPE 263.

tice system.[130] There were no district attorneys, no criminal courts, and no categories of "crimes" per se. Nevertheless, there were many laws that were designed not only to remedy a wrong but also to punish offenders, and also laws that required the guilty to pay fines to the State. Indeed, modern criminal law scholars recognize punishment as one of the paradigm purposes of criminal law. Furthermore, the Athenians had numerous laws designed to protect the interests of the community as a whole; a goal also frequently found in modern criminal laws. Therefore, although criminal law may not have existed in ancient Athens in a technical sense, it is useful for modern readers to consider, as a group, those Athenian offenses that are most closely analogous to and that correspond with the objects of our modern criminal laws; such as homicide, theft, sexual offenses, and criminal battery.

[B] HOMICIDE

[1] GENERAL

Undoubtedly the most famous Athenian law relating to homicide was Draco's (*c.* 621 B.C.). Well into the 4th century B.C., the Athenians still claimed to be applying Draco's homicide law. Athenian homicide law had at least three objectives: 1) deterrence; 2) revenge; and, 3) religious purification. As to the third, the ancient Greeks believed that a killing itself precipitated a "pollution" sent by the gods, *miasma*. MacDowell explains: "[p]ollution was a kind of supernatural infection, which was liable to spread from the killer to others who consorted with him, and to the whole community, unless they took steps to bring him to justice."[131]

[2] CATEGORIES

Classical Athenian law differentiated between intentional and unintentional homicide. Like contemporary American law, Athenian law recognized that a person who kills another on purpose commits a more culpable act than one who kills accidentally. Consequently, the Athenians punished someone who killed by design more severely than one who killed through some unforeseeable mishap. A slayer's state of mind at the moment of the lethal act, then, determined the manner in which Athenian law treated any given homicide. Modern jurisprudence distinguishes varying degrees of an accused's state of mind. We use terms like premeditation, intent, recklessness, and negligence to classify diverse kinds of mental states. To better ap-

---

130. *Id.* at 79.
131. MacDowell, The Law in Classical Athens 110.

preciate the Athenian law, it is useful first to summarize how modern criminal law treats the different mental states that a killer may have.

In contemporary homicide law, "premeditation" is ordinarily considered the most blameworthy state of mind; encompassing both the notions of planning and deliberation prior to killing. A person is usually said to kill with "intent" when he either desires to cause death or serious bodily harm, or when he acts while being substantially certain that his act will produce death or serious bodily harm. A person kills "recklessly" when he kills knowing that his conduct will produce an unusually high degree of probability that it will cause death or serious bodily harm. And, a person kills "negligently" when his conduct fails to conform to that of a reasonably prudent person.

The ancient Athenians used at least three terms that may be translated "intentionally": 1) *ek pronoias* ("with forethought," "with design," "purposely"); 2) *hekōn*; and, 3) *hekousios* ("voluntarily"). Scholars disagree about the precise nuances of these terms. Nevertheless, it is clear that homicide that could be described by any one of these terms was treated differently from a negligent or otherwise accidental homicide. A homicide that could be described as *ek pronoias, hekōn,* or *hekousios* was punishable by death and the confiscation of the murderer's property. Athenian law punished unintentional homicide by exile (permanent, pending pardon). But, in the case of unintentional homicide, the victim's family retained the right to pardon the killer. Punishment for killing a slave was less severe than for killing a citizen.

Athenian law appreciated certain mitigating factors that modern criminal law characterizes as affirmative defenses. The affirmative defenses that are most evident in Athenian homicide law are assumption of risk, self-defense, defense of property, and "heat of passion." For example, when an athlete killed a competitor while wrestling or boxing, such a homicide was excused. Today we would say that the victim had assumed the risk of death or serious bodily harm simply by voluntarily engaging in such a violent and inherently dangerous sport. Curiously, the same rationale apparently applied to doctors and their patients. When a patient died, the doctor was not held responsible. Perhaps, in such a primitive state of medicine, a patient was considered to assume the risk of death when being treated by a physician. Interestingly, this exception stands in stark contrast to several ancient Mesopotamian law collections that severely punished doctors under similar circumstances.[132] In situations where a victim actually was the initial aggressor (*i.e.,* the first to strike a blow) and the killer responded in self-defense, Athenian law permitted the killer a complete defense. If a man killed

---

132. *See supra* § 3.06[G].

a thief who was either using force or attempting to rob the accused at night, he was excused under the theory that a man is entitled to defend his property in such circumstances (*i.e.*, forceful or nocturnal attempts of robbery). A complete defense was available for a man who killed another *in flagrante delicto* with his mother, sister, daughter, or a concubine kept "with a view to free children."[133] One other kind of justifiable homicide was the murder of a person who had been declared a "public enemy."

Abortion was, technically speaking, not treated as a kind of homicide. In many respects the Athenians considered abortion a wrong committed against the father. Thus, it was possible for a father to bring an action for abortion by *dikē*. But a *graphē* was also possible. Harrison notes, "the fact that a *graphē* was available might suggest that abortion was regarded as a public wrong...."[134]

[3] PROCEDURE

There was no district attorney who initiated criminal proceedings against an alleged killer. Rather, a victim's family bore the responsibility of starting the trial process. Generally, a close male relative introduced the legal proceedings against an alleged killer. If the victim was a slave, then it was the owner who brought suit.

The prosecuting relative was first required to make an accusation against the alleged killer in the Agora. As part of that allegation, he demanded that the accused "keep away from things laid down by law." The prosecuting relative next brought his accusation to the Archon Basileus, the official principally responsible for religious matters. The Archon Basileus also proclaimed that the person charged with the homicide must stay away from the things laid down by law. This formulaic prohibition—that the accused had to "keep away from things laid down by law"—required that he must refrain from entering temples, public religious ceremonies, the Agora, all public meetings, and the law courts. If someone charged with homicide violated the terms of this prohibition—for example, if an accused entered the Agora—, he was subject to the procedure called *apagogē*. Using *apagogē*, anyone was authorized to make what amounted to a citizen's arrest, and could escort the accused to "the Eleven," the prison wardens, who then incarcerated the accused until he could be tried on the homicide charge. If

---

133. *See* HARRISON, THE LAW OF ATHENS (Vol. I) 13 (Harrison refers to this "concubine" as a *pallakē* "whom a man had taken to himself with the purpose of breeding free children from her.").
134. *Id.* at 72.

he did not violate the terms of the prohibition, the accused seems to have been free to go about as he pleased while awaiting trial.

There were primarily two adjudicative bodies that tried homicide cases: the *Areopagus* and the *Ephetai*. The *Areopagus* was the council composed of ex-*archons* (perhaps as many as 200 members at times during the 5th and 4th centuries B.C.) who were given life-tenure. Because of the status of its members, the *Areopagus* maintained an outstanding reputation for sound opinions (although there were some notorious exceptions). It generally heard cases where a defendant was accused of intentional homicide. Interestingly, the *Aereopagus* was known for considering and analyzing the facts of cases more than other ordinary courts. The *Areopagus* held court only on the last three days of every month. The *Ephetai*, a special court of 51 men over the age of 50 — perhaps a subgroup of the Areopagus —, tried other homicide cases in four distinct courts: 1) the *Delphinion*; 2) the *Palladion*; 3) the *Prytaneion*; and, 4) the *Phreatto*. Homicide cases were tried in the *Delphinion* when the defendant was asserting an affirmative defense (*i.e.*, arguing that the homicide was excused on grounds of assumption of risk, self-defense, defense of property, *etc.*). Cases were heard in the *Palladion* when the homicide was clearly unintentional and when the victim was a slave or a foreigner. The *Prytaneion* was the site for cases where a death was caused either by an unknown person (*i.e.*, the victim's family had no suspects), an animal, or an inanimate object. There the Basileus conducted a special trial accompanied by the four kings of the tribes.[135] This unique court officially denounced the undetermined killer. In the case of death by animal, the court denounced it and then either killed it or drove it from Attica. Similarly, if the homicide had been caused by a lifeless object, they physically ejected it outside of Attica's borders. Presumably, this process achieved a cleansing and ritualistic function. Lastly, the *Phreatto* was the location where cases were heard when the accused had already been convicted and exiled for a prior homicide. Thus, the defendant had to plead his case from a boat while the judges sat on the beach. The defendant was not permitted on Attic soil lest he pollute it. As was noted, it was the victim's family that was responsible for instituting legal proceedings against an accused killer. The procedural stages of an Athenian homicide trial, then, were roughly as follows.

> 1) The victim's relative, in the role of prosecutor, files a charge against the accused with the Basileus, and proclaims that the accused must henceforth keep away from things laid down by law.

---

135. *See supra* § 8.10.

2) The Basileus formally and officially proclaims that the accused must keep away from things laid down by law.

3) The Basileus holds three separate pre-trial conferences (*prodikasiai*) in three successive months.

4) In the fourth month immediately following the three *prodikasiai*, the Basileus convenes and presides over the actual trial on the merits.[136]

During the trial on the merits, the prosecutor presented his case first. The accused was next allowed to make his speech in reply. After the accused had completed his first speech, he was allowed to go into exile voluntarily rather than proceeding to judgment. Thus, if the accused perceived that the case was going poorly and acquittal seemed unlikely, he could at least save his skin by choosing exile rather than risking death as a result of conviction. If the accused chose not to go into exile, then the prosecutor made his final speech followed again by the defendant's closing argument. Both parties swore oaths attesting to the veracity of their respective statements. And, unlike other trials, women, children, and slaves could testify as witnesses in homicide cases. The jury voted immediately after the defendant's closing, and the Basileius announced the jury's verdict.

[C] THEFT CRIMES

Even in modern American law it is difficult to distinguish tort theory from criminal law theory in situations where one individual takes personal property that belongs to another without permission. When one person takes another's property, criminal law regards the former's conduct as "theft" and tort law considers his conduct "conversion." For purposes of this chapter, we shall consider such conduct as criminal.

When a property owner caught a thief red-handed, he could employ the procedure known as *apagoge* to take him before the Eleven for punishment. The cause of action for theft in classical Athens was called *dike klopes*. Common street thieves probably were tried before the Eleven using "summary procedures and punishments" rather than having a trial on a grand scale

---

136. The same Basileus was required to preside at all four hearings (*i.e.*, the three pre-trial conferences and the trial itself). Therefore, since archons were only in office for one calendar year at a time, a homicide trial could only be started during the first nine months of the year—not during the last three months. Otherwise, the Basileus would be unable to see the trial through to completion. *See* MacDowell, The Law in Classical Athens 118.

repleat with *logographers* and extensive procedures.[137] Athenian law required a person found guilty of theft to return the object stolen and to pay the plaintiff twice its value. One speech of Demosthenes suggests that the guilty defendant paid the plaintiff and the State equal amounts. In today's terms, then, we would say that the remedy for theft involved both a civil and a criminal element (compensation and a fine). A jury could also penalize a thief with confinement in the stocks; a form of public humiliation. A more serious degree of theft was *dikē biaiōn* (theft by force). A defendant found guilty of *dikē biaiōn* paid damages to the plaintiff in any amount that the jury deemed appropriate. In addition, the guilty defendant paid the same amount to the State as a fine. Finally, the most serious degree of theft was a kind classified by the Athenians as having been committed by the *kakourgoi* ("malefactors"): those thieves who: 1) stole at night; 2) stole from a gymnasium or other location where men disrobed to exercise; 3) stole more than ten drachmas from a harbor; or, 4) stole more than fifty drachmas from anywhere else. Those thieves found guilty as *kakourgoi* received the death penalty.

In addition to these three private causes of action (*dikē*) for theft, Athenian law also permitted a *graphē* to be brought against someone accused of stealing from a sacred treasury (for example by embezzlement). Furthermore, robbing from a temple (*hierosylia*) was punishable by death.

[D] SEXUAL CONDUCT

If a man forced a woman to have extramarital sexual intercourse against her will, the woman and her *kyrios* could bring a private case against the rapist. A *kyrios* might bring an action before the thesmothetai called *graphē moicheias* or an action before the Forty with the suit known as *dikē biaiōn* (the same type of suit that a person brought if his property had been stolen through violent means). Unfortunately, we are certain of precious few details about the laws dealing with rape in ancient Athens. Solon established the compensation for rape at 100 drachmas. By the 4th century B.C., the penalty for rape had acquired aspects that today we would characterize as both civil and criminal. The jury used its discretion to determine the money damages that a rapist had to pay; but he paid an equal amount to the victim (compensatory damages) and to the State (a fine). Of course, the victim, since she was unwilling, was not criminally liable.

---

137. *See* COHEN, LAW VIOLENCE AND COMMUNITY IN CLASSICAL ATHENS 139.

Evidently the *kyrios* had the right to kill anyone caught in the act of sexually violating a member of his household. Our sources, however, emphasize this remedy against the adulterer, not the rapist. If a man had extramarital sexual intercourse with a woman who was not forced but instead seduced, Athenian law, at least according to Lysias, treated the seducer more harshly than a rapist.[138] The rationale for punishing a seducer more severely than a rapist was that a rapist only abused and injured a female's body but a seducer perverted her mentally. This distinction is roughly analogous to the difference between taking an enemy as a prisoner of war *versus* convincing an enemy to desert and join the other side as a turn-coat. As was noted, if a woman's *kyrios* caught the seducer in the act, he (the *kyrios*) legally was entitled to kill the seducer on the spot without being subject to penalty for murder. If the *kyrios* so desired, instead of killing the seducer, he could seize him and demand money as compensation. He could even subject him to torture. "[T]he husband could inflict on the adulterer various bodily humiliations, or he could accept compensation from him, holding him a prisoner until he could provide sureties for the payment of the sum agreed."[139] According to Cohen, "we possess no references to actual prosecutions (*graphai*) brought for adultery."[140]

There is evidence that Athenian law punished a woman who willingly had extramarital sexual relations. A husband immediately divorced his wife if she was found guilty of adultery, and an Athenian woman found guilty of adultery was automatically denied access to public religious ceremonies. If, after a successful prosecution for adultery, a man still refused to divorce his wife, he suffered *atimia*.[141] In addition, the laws prohibited the adulteress thenceforth from wearing any adornments. Some legal historians have hypothesized that this prohibition was intended to decrease the likelihood that other men would find her attractive. But female prostitution itself was not illegal,[142] and so extramarital intercourse with a prostitute was not considered seduction. Similarly, slave owners could (and frequently did) have sex with their female slaves without violating any laws.

---

138. *See* Lysias 1.32–33. *See also* Harrison, The Law of Athens (Vol. I) 34.

139. Harrison, The Law of Athens (Vol. I) 33.

140. Cohen, Law, Violence and Community in Classical Athens 155.

141. *See supra* § 9.01 [A].

142. Athenian law permitted homosexual activity. Male prostitution was legal for a non-citizen. A male citizen who was a prostitute, however, could be punished by a loss of certain citizenship rights, *atima*. *See* MacDowell, The Law in Classical Athens 125–126; Cohen, Law, Violence and Community in Classical Athens 155; Harrison, The Law of Athens (Vol. I) 37–38.

As a final note, it is worthwhile to appreciate that, as Cohen states, "adultery, rape, and seduction all would have fallen within the purview of the law of hubris because they all involve insults to the honor of the family to which the woman belongs."[143]

[E] CRIMINAL BATTERY

A kind of battery serious enough to classify under criminal law rather than tort was called *trauma ek pronoias* ("wounding with intent" to kill). In fact, *trauma ek pronoias* was probably similar to the modern criminal offense of aggravated assault. Speeches of Demosthenes and Lysias suggest that *trauma ek pronoias* was battery with a weapon—not just with fists. Procedurally, a suit for *trauma ek pronoias* was brought by *dikē* before the *Areopagus*, and if found guilty, the defendant was punished with exile and his property was confiscated.

[F] HUBRIS

According to Demosthenes, it was technically possible to prosecute someone, by *graphē*, for *hubris*. A legal cause of action for *hubris* could be predicated on behavior that had been directed toward any man, woman, or child (free or slave). As a practical matter, however, very few cases for *hubris* were ever brought to trial. The paucity of cases brought alleging *hubris* was probably due, in part, to the difficulty of defining *hubris*. The Hellenic concept of *hubris* was complex. No single English word functions as an appropriate synonym. *Hubris* combines a number of unsavory characteristics. For purposes of law, the ancient Greeks considered a person's conduct to be hubristic if it was arrogant, self-righteous, irresponsible, indulgent, taunting, and insulting. *Hubris* often also involved a measure of sexual oppression, domination, aggression, and degradation. Cohen characterizes "essentially unproblematic," "standard cases" of *hubris* as "[a]busive and humiliating public assaults and rape (whether heterosexual or homosexual)...."[144] It was easier, nevertheless, in most cases, simply to prove that a defendant had committed battery or slander, and to obtain redress using those simpler legal theories. Otherwise, to prove *hubris* a plaintiff needed to prove that the defendant had displayed

---

143. COHEN, LAW, VIOLENCE AND COMMUNITY IN CLASSICAL ATHENS 151. For a brief description of *hubris, see infra* § 9.05[F].

144. COHEN, LAW, VIOLENCE AND COMMUNITY IN CLASSICAL ATHENS 153.

an arrogant, self-righteous, irresponsible, *etc.* attitude at the moment that he had injured the plaintiff.

[G] RELIGIOUS OFFENSES

[1] INTRODUCTION

In the 4th century B.C., religious officials, called *exegetai* ("expounders"), had memorized sacred laws so that they could advise others about them. Unlike today, persons accused of violating religious laws could be prosecuted in the State court system.

[2] LAWS RELATED TO FESTIVALS

When someone violated a rule of conduct regarding religious festivals, anyone else could prosecute the transgressor using the procedure called *probolē*. A person conducting a prosecution for *probolē* brought his case to the *Ekklēsia*, but the *Ekklēsia's* vote was merely a straw vote. After the *Ekklēsia's* vote, a *probolē* prosecutor had to bring the case to another jury in the court of the *nomothetai*. "Any 'wrong action concerning the festival' could be the subject of a *probolē*; this expression was not defined in the law, and it was for the *Ekklēsia* and subsequently the jury to decide whether the defendant's behavior should be so described."[145] It was, for example, illegal to try to collect debts during festivals. In fact this was a particular problem.

[3] IMPIETY

In the 5th and 4th centuries B.C., a prosecutor generally used the *graphē* procedure to prosecute someone for *asebeia* ("impiety"). *Asebeia* included offenses such as the following: 1) the wrong person performing a sacrifice; 2) battery, violence, or other misbehavior in a temple; 3) performing magic; 4) honoring religions other than those traditionally recognized by the State; 5) mutilation of statues of deities; and, 6) parodying secret religious ceremonies (*e.g.*, those of the Eleusinian Mysteries).

For cases that were especially serious, a prosecutor alleging impiety might use *eisangelia* before the *Ekklēsia* and *Boulē* instead of using a *graphē*. *Asebeia* was probably not carefully defined. Thus, juries were left to interpret it on an ad hoc basis; determining whether any given conduct should be construed as impious. The famous trial of the philosopher Socrates in 399 B.C. was a *graphē* for "impiety." The penalty was usually severe; either

---

145. MacDowell, The Law in Classical Athens 195.

death or permanent exile coupled with confiscation of property. Apparently, a plaintiff/prosecutor often brought a charge of impiety in an attempt to destroy a political rival.

[4] ATHEISM

Prior to the 430's B.C., it was probably not a punishable offense for a person simply to express that he did not believe in the traditional gods. Then, in the 430's, the Athenians passed the Decree of Diopeithes, a decree which forbade both stating a disbelief in the traditional gods and the teaching of astronomy. The procedure contemplated to enforce these prohibitions was *eisangelia*. At least two well-known ancient philosophers were prosecuted under this law: Anaxagoras and Protagoras. This law is probably best understood as a prohibition of "atheistic speech."[146]

[H] MISCELLANEOUS CRIMES

[1] ARSON

To recompense injury by arson, it is likely that an individual whose property had been damaged by fire brought a *graphē* before the *Areopagus*. But perhaps cases only went before the *Areopagus* if the blaze had actually injured a person (in addition to merely property).

[2] *PRODOSIA* (BETRAYAL)

An Athenian general could be subject to prosecution for *prodosia* for the loss of ships, troops, or territory.

[3] DECEPTION OF THE PEOPLE

If someone persuaded the *Ekklēsia* to make a particularly bad decision, that person could be prosecuted for deception of the people and receive a death sentence.

[4] *EISANGELIA*

It is possible that, as early as the 5th century, *eisangelia* was a procedure used for "new wrongs"—things that were arguably wrong, but for which no rule or law yet existed. It was also used for some other offenses, like treason, that were pretty well defined. In the late 4th century B.C., *eisangelia* was the procedure used to prosecute three distinct types of conduct that

---

146. *Id.* at 200.

were considered injurious to the State: 1) subverting the democracy; 2) betrayal; and, 3) (an orator) misleading the people. This, in many respects, sounds like a basic law against treason. It is probable that during the Reinscription (c. 410–403 B.C.) the custom of using *eisangelia* for treason was codified. At about this time, *eisangelia* may also have been used *only* for treason and *not* (like before) for any wrongs committed for which there was no adequate cause of action.

§9.06 TORTS

[A] INTRODUCTION

Modern American law recognizes tort as a distinct field of substantive law. Although there is no one unifying principle of modern tort law, most lawyers are content to think of torts as non-contractual civil wrongs. In contemporary tort doctrine, defendants, generally speaking, become subject to liability when they intentionally cause harm, or when their conduct causes foreseeable harm (negligence), or when their conduct causes harm in such a manner that they will be deemed strictly liable (*i.e.*, usually for reasons of public policy and risk management—without regard to whether the consequences of their conduct were either intentional or reasonably foreseeable). There was no directly analogous group of laws in ancient Athens, yet many *dikai* seem roughly similar to modern tort categories; such as battery, false imprisonment, and defamation. In addition to these, the Athenians of the classical era used a particular cause of action, *dikē blabēs*,[147] as a legal mechanism for redressing several kinds of conduct that we today would classify as tortious.

[B] BATTERY

Modern tort law clearly distinguishes assault from battery. Battery is the act of intentionally causing harmful or offensive contact with another person. Assault occurs when a person intentionally causes another to apprehend that harmful or offensive contact is imminent. Athenian law in the 5th and 4th centuries B.C. did not really recognize so fine-tuned a distinc-

---

147. *See infra* §9.06[E].

tion. An Athenian committed battery (*dikē aikeias*) when he struck another. If a fight ensued between the two, only the initial aggressor (*i.e.,* the one to strike the first blow) was subject to liability for battery. Generally, intentional personal injury did not occur in isolation. Cases such as these were ordinarily the result of an extended feud, or ongoing enmity between the parties. In any event, the jury assessed compensation to the victim with money damages.

[C] FALSE IMPRISONMENT

Although details are few, it appears that Athenian law recognized a wrong akin to the modern tort of false imprisonment. This cause of action was called *dikē heirgmou*,[148] and we can only guess that the jury used its discretion in fixing damages for each such case.

[D] DEFAMATION

Solon's laws prohibited maligning anyone who was deceased. Solon's laws also punished speaking ill of anyone while in a temple, in court at trial, in public offices, or while at festival contests. Damages for these types of slander under Solon had both civil and criminal components: the slanderer had to pay five drachmas; three to the person slandered and two to the State.[149] By the end of the 4th century B.C., the Athenians had modified and updated the law of slander, *dikē kakēgorias*. From the speeches of Lysias and Demosthenes we know that it was considered slander to allege falsely that someone had beaten or killed his father or mother, and it was also deemed slanderous to allege falsely that someone (presumably while a soldier in battle) had thrown away his shield. Furthermore, it was defamatory to deprecate the work of a citizen in the Agora. Although some recent scholarship has cast doubt on whether truth was a defense as it is in modern doctrine,[150] most legal historians have believed that such statements were re-

---

148. Or it was also called *graphē adikēs heirkhthēnai*. This would be the remedy in cases where the husband has wrongly seized a supposed adulterer.

149. But Professor Sealey doubts whether the payment to the State was really a criminal fine. He suggest instead that it may have been a payment to the State officer as recompense for the plaintiff wrongfully requesting the officer's protection. *See* SEALEY, JUSTICE 127.

150. *See* TODD, SHAPE 260 ("Independent evidence, however, tends to confirm that 'truth' was not admissible as a defence in cases of defamation at Athens.").

garded defamatory only if they were false.[151] Thus, if an Athenian accused of slander could prove that his assertion was true (for example, if the plaintiff had, in fact, beaten his father as the defendant had alleged), then he (*i.e.*, the defendant) had a complete and effective defense. At any rate, the plaintiff certainly argued that the assertions were false.

Athenian law in the late 4th century fixed damages for slander at 500 drachmas. But we do not know whether the guilty slanderer paid the entire 500 drachmas to the plaintiff or whether the same 60%–40% ratio established by the laws of Solon still operated (in which case a slanderer would have been required to pay 300 drachmas to the plaintiff and 200 to the State as a fine).

It is likely that the laws regarding slander applied with equal force to false statements that were written (*i.e.*, not only words merely spoken). The Athenians apparently had no *dikē* for libel that was distinct from slander.

Modern American defamation doctrine has had to be sufficiently flexible to accommodate our First Amendment right to free speech. Courts have afforded considerable latitude, for example, to political satire. In a similar manner, Athenian defamation law seems, generally speaking, to have exempted the playwrights of Old Comedy during the 5th century (at least prior to 414 B.C. when, evidently, the scope of this exemption was severely narrowed). Some of Aristophanes' characters, for example, say things about contemporary politicians that clearly would have been slanderous had there been no "comedy exception."

[E] *DIKĒ BLABĒS*

Dikē blabēs was a cause of action used to redress a wide variety of civil wrongs, many of which involved an allegation by the plaintiff that the defendant's conduct (*i.e.*, either action or failure to act) caused him (plaintiff) some type of harm. The torts that modern American law labels as "trespass to chattel" and "conversion" were, in part, addressed by *dikē blabēs*, because the property owner (*i.e.*, the owner whose property had been damaged) had suffered an economic loss—in these cases, the loss was a reduction in his property's value. *Dikē blabēs* also was the most common cause of action for breach of contract.[152] In addition, it was used in circumstances where modern doctrine would employ nuisance, both intentional and unintentional harm, and even strict liability.

---

151. *See* MacDowell, The Law in Classical Athens 128.
152. *See infra* § 9.07[D].

§ 9.07 TRADE, CONTRACTS,[153] & COMMERCIAL LAW

[A] INTRODUCTION

In the *Iliad*, characters use oxen as a medium of exchange. Homer refers to objects as being worth X-number of oxen to describe their value. Once coinage was invented by the Lydians in the 7th century B.C., the Athenians found that the sale of goods was much easier using coined money. Under Athenian law, title passed from seller to buyer at the moment when the buyer physically gave cash to the seller. Many historians have maintained that ancient Athenian law did not sanction sales on credit. However, we know of at least one instance when a seller of slaves loaned the purchase money for the sale to the buyer. Obviously, this arrangement was functionally the same as a sale on credit. Todd explains that "freedom of contract" was a powerful principle in ancient Athens:

> The doctrine of freedom of contract was so strong at Athens that it was possible to contract out of the protection of the law, or to agree that a contract should take precedence over law, or to expect a court of law to uphold a contract which is publicly admitted to have constituted a conspiracy to commit an unlawful act.[154]

In order to make a valid contract, Athenian law required the existence of four elements: 1) the parties had to agree; 2) their agreement had to be voluntarily; 3) their agreement had to be made in the presence of witnesses; and, 4) their agreement had to be just. Contracts did not have to be in writing. Evidence is strong that Athenian contract law bound buyers and sellers from the moment of their agreement onwards. For example, once a buyer had paid a deposit (*arrabon*) to his seller, the seller was legally obligated to hold the property secured by the deposit until the time fixed by their agreement for final payment.

There were several laws that proscribed misrepresentation in sales transactions. First, sellers in the Agora were not permitted to say things about their goods that were untrue. In a more particularized context, slave sellers were legally obligated to declare to their buyers any of the slave's bodily

---

153. Todd maintains that it is "inappropriate" to refer to "contract" as a category of law in classical Athens. TODD, SHAPE 72, 263–67. With all due respect, as someone who regularly teaches contract law in an American law school, I find his "arguments" (for a lack of contract theory in classical Athens) unpersuasive.

154. TODD, SHAPE 264 (footnote omitted).

faults. A buyer could return for a refund any slave whom he (*i.e.,* the buyer) later discovered had a defect that the seller had not identified at the time of the original sale. Prior to selling real estate, Athenian law required that a prospective seller give 60-days' written notice (to a State official) of his intent to sell. Since there was no land registration procedure in Athens to protect prospective buyers, this requirement of a written notice gave the public an opportunity to catch a swindler in advance.

[B] LEASE CONTRACTS

In ancient Athens a landowner could lease his property to another (this could be done either orally or in writing). A lease arrangement might include a payment schedule for lease payments and specific provisions detailing a lessee's obligations. Landowners routinely leased agricultural property to be farmed. We have some examples of leases—from public entities to private individuals—that were actually recorded on stone. One such lease required the lessee to whitewash the building's walls, to husband the trees on the leased property, and provided for liquidated damages in the event that the lessee failed to fulfill his obligations under the lease. When a lessee did breach a lease agreement, the lessor could bring suit (*dikē enoikiou* or *dikē karpou*).

[C] LOANS

It was lawful for one Athenian to loan money to another. But of the hundreds of loans that we know about from ancient documents, only about a dozen are loans borrowed from a banker, the rest are from private individuals. Although it was common for creditors to charge interest at a rate of 1% per month, the law dictated neither the amount of interest nor the duration of a loan. And, although Solon abolished debt slavery, a creditor could, nevertheless, confiscate his debtor's property in the event that the debtor failed to pay back his loan. In order to foster the making of loans, for the benefit of debtors, while at the same time providing protection for the benefit of creditors, debtors soon discovered the utility of giving their creditors collateral (*enekhuron* or *hypothekē*) as security for loans. We know of Athenians using items both of personal property (*e.g.,* a gold cup, a horse, slaves) and real property (*e.g.,* land itself or a house) as collateral for loans. Shipmasters, for example, routinely used their ships and cargo as collateral for loans. Scholars have identified no less than four distinct types of collateral arrangements; each with its own peculiar rules relating to the nature of the collateral and the ownership and possession of it. It would be an understatement to to say that the "law" on this topic is both complex and ambiguous. According to Harrison, however, "sale with right of redemption is, for the classical period, the predominant and typical form of real security."[155] Archaeologists have even unearthed stones (*horoi*) that were placed on land that had been used as collateral for loans. These stones have inscriptions detailing the conditions of the loan agreements. Some texts also show the use of sureties (*enguētai*), people who promised to pay in the event that the debtor defaulted. *Dikē khreōs* was the cause of action for failure to repay a debt. *Dikē parakatathēkēs* was the cause of action for refusal to repay a deposit.

[D] BREACH OF CONTRACT

Dikē blabēs was used as a cause of action to recover, as a general theory, for any kind of economic loss that one might incur.[156] Thus, plaintiffs could and did use *dikē blabēs* as a theory to recover for breach of contract (*e.g.,* failure to repay a loan). If a plaintiff could convince the jury that the defendant had caused the economic loss *intentionally*, the defendant had to pay twice the amount of the loss. Thus, *dikē blabēs* was a popular cause of action with Athenian plaintiffs.

[E] COMMERCE

Most commerce was retail and most took place in the Agora. As a rule (except during part of the 5th century B.C.), an alien could not trade in the Athenian Agora unless he paid a special tax (*xenika*). The "controllers of the market" (*agoranomoi*) served as a specialized court to arbitrate disputes brought in the market. There were five *agoranomoi* in the Agora and five in the Athenian port, the Peiraeus. Some particular laws that the *agoranomoi* applied in their court were laws that: 1) prohibited misrepresentation; 2) prohibited selling adulterated goods; and 3) prohibited fish sellers from sprinkling water on their fish in an effort to fool prospective buyers into thinking that the fish were more fresh than they really were. Some fish prices also seem to have been established by law.

The "guardians of grain" (*sitophylakes*) were a specialized panel, consisting of 5–20 men selected by lot, that enforced laws concerning the sale of grain. Some grain laws dealt with prices and others pertained to the quanti-

---

155. HARRISON, THE LAW OF ATHENS (Vol. I) 271.
156. *See supra* § 9.05 [E].

ties of grain that any one seller was allowed to stockpile. Another unique judicial authority was that of the *epimelētai tou emporiou*, a commission that superintended the sale of grain in the wholesale market that was conducted in the Peiraeus at the *Emporion*.[157]

The board called the *metronomoi* (ordinarily five board members in the Agora and five in the Peiraeus) inspected measures and weights. In addition to the *metronomoi*, Classical Athens had a State-owned slave who held the position of "official coin tester." He sat in the Agora and inspected any suspect coins to judge their authenticity. The penalty for making counterfeit coins was death. But clearly death was not the penalty for merely *trying* to use a counterfeit coin. Any person attempting to use an imitation coin could always allege that he had received the fake from some third party.

For some violations of market laws, an offender could be subject to a legal procedure called *phasis*. Details of this process are not complete, but apparently *phasis* was initiated simply by denouncing or exposing contraband or illegal gains. The procedure was then similar in some respects to *graphē*. For example, anyone could bring suit (*i.e.*, not just the individual injured), and a successful prosecutor received a bounty of half of the fine that the offender had to pay.

[F] TAXES

[1] INTRODUCTION

The ancient Athenians considered the imposition of direct taxes on citizens the act of a tyrant. Therefore, the only taxes that they levied on citizens were indirect taxes, such as harbor dues, and irregular taxes, such as a tax on the wealthy only imposed when there was a severe financial shortage. The purchaser of a house had to pay a real estate sales tax of 1% of the purchase price.

Metics paid a special metic's tax, the *metoikion*. The *metoikion* was a direct and regular tax on metics of one drachma per-month for men and one-half drachma per-month for women.[158] During the 5th and 4th centuries B.C., one drachma, the monthly *metoikion*, equalled, on average, a day's pay or less for a skilled laborer.

As a rule, the State auctioned off tax collection rights annually to the highest bidder. Legally, then, the State assigned its collection rights to the tax collector. Thus, the tax collector owed the State and the taxpayer owed

---

157. *See supra* § 8.05.
158. *See supra* § 9.01 [B].

the tax collector. The collector paid the State and kept whatever surplus he could as profit.

[2] LITURGIES (FORCED PHILANTHROPY)

Athenian law required the wealthiest citizens to foot the bill for a number of expensive public services. This forced philanthropic duty was called a "liturgy." For example, public officials appointed wealthy men, on an annual basis, to: 1) support public religious festivals; 2) maintain an Athenian warship (which included serving as its captain); and, 3) pay taxes for a group of taxpayers (and then the individual who had been appointed had to try to collect taxes from his designated citizens in order to reimburse himself). If an appointee wished to challenge his appointment to a liturgy, he could claim that another man was in a better financial position to take on the task. In so doing, he had to suggest a replacement (*i.e.*, another, more wealthy, Athenian to take his place) and challenge the person whom he had proposed to a procedure called *antidosis*. If the proposed substitute refused to accept the liturgy, the *antidosis* would compel him to exchange all of his property with the original appointee. Demosthenes once was involved in an *antidosis* action, and he decided to accept the liturgy rather than to transfer estates. It is doubtful whether anyone ever swapped property instead of taking on the liturgy.

§ 9.08 CHAPTER SUMMARY

[A] PERSONAL STATUS

After Pericles in the middle of the 5th century, in order to be considered an Athenian citizen, an individual's mother and father both had to have been Athenian citizens. Kleisthenes reorganized Athenian citizenship so that a person's citizenship depended on local *dēme* membership (which thenceforth became hereditary). Athenian boys—at age 17—gained citizenship status only after a formal review process called *dokimasia*. Among other things, citizenship entitled a person to vote, to hold public office, to conduct business in the Agora, to own property, to participate in the legislative process and court proceedings, and to marry. Citizens were obligated to serve in the military and to pay taxes. Foreigners may have been granted citizenship in limited circumstances, but that was a rare occurrence. Foreigners could acquire "resident alien", or *metic*, status, which provided them with some of the rights (*e.g.*, access to law courts) and obligations (*e.g.*, military service and liturgies) of a citizen. Most slaves in ancient

Athens were foreigners and were treated, theoretically speaking, as personal property. But there were aspects of slavery that reflected a limited degree of individual freedom and responsibility. Upon manumission, a former slave was considered the legal equivalent of a metic.

[B] PROPERTY

The ancient Athenians developed advanced property law concepts. For example, they understood various notions regarding real estate, tangible personal property, joint ownership, and possession—as opposed to ownership outright. Aristotle says that the capacity to alienate property is the distinguishing feature of ownership. Athenian law appreciated multiple ways by which one could transfer or acquire property rights, such as fishing and hunting, seizure in war, gift, sale, and inheritance. The advent of the use of coinage in the 6th century B.C. facilitated property conveyance.

Because agriculture dominated the ancient Athenian economy, many unique laws governed the ownership and use of real property. Owners of real property generally had great freedom to do as they wished with their land, but they were forbidden to cut down olive trees. Due to the scarcity of fresh water, there were special laws that regulated the use of wells, rivers, and streams. Although we are unaware of many details regarding the laws as they related to mines, a great deal of evidence suggests that the State claimed ownership of the subterranean portions of all mines. Athenian law also provided formal mechanisms for persons to resolve ownership disputes regarding property (*e.g., diadikasia*—for inheritance, *dikē khreōs*—debt, *dikē ousias*—personal property).

[C] FAMILY LAW

The physical center of the Athenian family was the *oikos*. The father was often the principal adult male who served as *kyrios* (legal guardian) for his wife and children. Women had few rights, and could not, as a rule, participate in legal affairs. Women were required to have a guardian who could act on their behalf. They could own personal property, and probably, some types of real estate.

Ordinarily, Athenian law did not recognize marriage between close relatives and had certain minimum age requirements for marriage. *Enguē* was the typical type of marriage in ancient Athens. This marriage occurred simply by virtue of an agreement (*engyesis*) between the bride's father and the groom. Later, the bride physically relocated (*ekdosis*) to the groom's *oikos*.

The bride's father usually gave a dowry (*proix*) to his son-in-law. Ordinarily, however, upon divorce, a husband was required to return the dowry. Husbands could divorce their wives by simply sending them away (*apopempsis*) but wives had to use a formal, State-sanctioned procedure (*apoleipsis*) to effectuate a divorce. When a father died leaving a female heir (*epiklēros*) but no male heir, Athenian law provided for a special kind of marriage called *epidikasia*. In this circumstance, a close male relative usually married the *epiklēros* in order to preserve the family and its property. A husband was not legally required to be faithful to his wife but a wife was legally required to be faithful to her husband. Societal custom permitted men to visit prostitutes and even to have a live-in mistress (*pallakē*).

As a rule, in order to be considered legitimate, a child had to be born of parents who were married either by *enguē* or *epidikasia*. Children lived under their father's control and enjoyed little independence. When a child's father died, the Archon was responsible for appointing a substitute *kyrios* to serve as guardian. A guardian had strict legal duties and was held legally accountable for his management of his ward's affairs.

[D] INHERITANCE & SUCCESSION

Although the speeches of the orators have preserved a number of legal principles regarding Athenian inheritance, many inheritance disputes degenerated into ugly, mendacious quarrels that were waged by means of perjured testimony and forged documents. As a rule, sons — without regard to their order of birth — inherited their father's estate equally, and they ordinarily divided his estate (*klēros*). In the circumstance of an *epiklēros*, marriage by *epidikasia* ensured that the deceased's *oikos* would continue and that his estate would be secure. When a deceased man had no sons and no *epiklēros*, there was a strict order of inheritance: brothers and half-brothers by the same father; sisters and half-sisters by the same father; the father's other relatives; half-brothers by the same mother; half-sisters by the same mother; all other relatives on the mother's side. Athenian inheritance was based on a *per stirpes* system; allowing a deceased's grandchildren to inherit their father's share. The procedure called *epidikasia* permitted persons who had uncontested inheritance claims to petition the Archon. The procedure known as *diadikasia* was used to resolve contested claims. Athenians who had no living sons routinely adopted sons to secure heirs. Ordinarily ancient Athenians used what we might call a "will" only to adopt an heir, but not to bequeath property.

[E] CRIMINAL LAW

The ancient Athenians did not have a body of law that technically was analogous to modern criminal law. Nevertheless, they did have some laws—laws that imposed punishment or fines—relating to homicide, theft, sexual conduct, and the infliction of injury that were similar in many respects to modern criminal law. Draco is famous for establishing the foundational principles of Athenian homicide law. In addition to a desire for revenge and deterrence, the Greeks punished homicide because they believed that homicide caused a pollution (*miasma*) that damaged an entire community. Thus, formal, legal resolution was needed for homicide. Athenian law punished intentional homicide that was characterized as *ek pronoias*, *hekōn*, or *hekousios* (we might say "murder") by death and loss of property, but treated unintentional homicide ("manslaughter") less severely—with exile. They accepted self-defense, defense of property, assumption of risk, and "heat of passion" as justifiable excuses for homicide.

Although abortion was, technically speaking, not treated as a kind of homicide, in many respects it was treated as an offense against the father. Using a specific legal process (including a formal declaration made in the Agora, requiring the accused to "keep away from things laid down by law"), a close relative of the homicide victim ordinarily prosecuted the case. As a rule, the *Areopagus* tried a person accused of intentional homicide and the *Ephetai* heard all other cases of homicide. The *Ephetai* tried cases in four distinct venues: 1) the *Delphinion* (when a defendant asserted an affirmative defense); 2) the *Palladion* (cases involving a homicide that was clearly unintentional, or when the victim was a slave or foreigner); the *Prytaneion* (when the death was caused by an unknown person, an animal, or inanimate object); 4) the *Phreatto* (when the defendant had already been convicted or exiled for a prior homicide).

An Athenian homicide trial ordinarily proceded through four distinct stages: 1) a relative of the victim initiated the complaint with the *Basileus*, proclaiming that the accused must "keep away from things laid down by law"; 2) the *Basileus* made the same formal pronouncement; 3) the *Basileus* held three pre-trial conferences (*prodikasiai*); and, 4) the *Basileus* presided over the trial on the merits. At trial, the prosecution presented its case first, followed by the defense. Prior to making their final arguments, the accused was given the opportunity to go into exile rather than proceeding to the jury.

The punishment for theft varied, depending upon the amount stolen, the location of the theft, and whether force was involved. For simple theft (*dikē klopēs*) a thief had to return the stolen object and pay the victim twice its value. For theft by force (*dikē biaiōn*) a fine paid to the State was usually imposed as well. The death penalty was given for more serious types of theft (*kakourgoi*) and theft from the treasury or a temple.

Rape was punished by payment of money damages to the victim (100 drachmas under Solon's laws) and also a fine to the State. A *kyrios* might bring an action before the *thesmothetai* (*graphē moicheias*) or an action before the Forty (*dikē biaiōn*). Seduction, because it entailed mental subversion, was supposedly more heinous than rape. The victim's *kyrios* was permitted to kill or torture a seducer who was caught in the act; or he could seize him and demand a payment of money damages. Adultery committed by a married woman was considered wrongful, but we possess few details regarding it. The husband was required to divorce an adulteress, and she was, thereafter, forbidden to wear jewlry and forbidden attendance at public religious ceremonies. Female prostitution, however, was both legally and socially permissible.

Trauma ek pronoias was a kind of criminal battery involving either unusual force or the use of a weapon with intent to kill. One of the more enigmatic wrongs that may be considered criminal was *hubris*. The Athenians categorized certain types of abusive behavior as *hubris*. *Hubris* has no modern analogue, but it encompassed a broad range of activity that included arrogant, insulting, and sexually aggressive acts. The most obvious kinds of wrongs relating to religion were offenses committed in connection with a religious festival, impiety (*asebeia*), and atheism. For offenses committed in connection with a religious festival (*e.g.*, collecting a debt at a festival), a prosecutor brought his case using the procedure known as *probolē*. A prosecutor could use *graphē* to prosecute someone for impiety (*asebeia*). Since *asebeia* was not well defined, juries had broad latitude to interpret it as they wished on an ad hoc basis. After 430 B.C., a prosecutor could use *eisangelia* to allege atheism.

In addition to these "crimes" clearly there were others recognized in Athenian law, such as arson, betrayal by a general, and "misleading the people." The procedure called *eisangelia* was perhaps once used to prosecute a variety of "new" wrongs, but by the beginning of the 4th century, *eisangelia* was the procedure used in cases alleging treason.

[F] TORTS

As was the case with criminal law, the Athenians did not distinguish a discrete category of tort law. Many types of *dikē*, however, were analogous to "wrongs" that modern law catalogs as torts; and courts typically imposed money damages for these wrongs. *Dikē aikeias* was similar to the modern concept of battery (*i.e.* intentionally striking another), *dikē heirgmou* was similar to what we call false imprisonment, and *dikē kakēgorias* was an action for defamation. The laws regarding defamation were more specific than general. Solon's laws prohibited maligning anyone who was deceased, anyone while in a temple, court, public office, or at a festival. Other laws punished (*i.e.*, by the 4th century B.C., damages were fixed at 500 drachmas) those who falsely alleged that someone had beaten or killed his parents or that he had discarded his shield in battle. The political satire of Attic Comedy seems to have been permitted without recourse to the law of defamation. *Dikē blabēs* was a rather broad cause of action that the Athenians used in circumstances where modern litigants would bring suit for property damage of one sort or another.

[G] TRADE, CONTRACTS, & COMMERCIAL LAW

The Athenians had tremendous faith in freedom of contract; permitting individuals to fashion many kinds of agreements. Although parties did not have to write down an agreement in order for a contract to be considered valid, they did have to voluntarily agree to a just deal in the presence of witnesses. Specific laws concerning the sale of slaves, sales in the Agora, and sales of real property were designed to curb fraud and various forms of misrepresentation. Other laws governed a lessee's obligations to his lessor, and we have a number of examples of lease contracts (*e.g.*, for farming agricultural land). Creditors (mostly private individuals) loaned money and charged interest. Although Solon abolished debt slavery, a creditor could, nevertheless, confiscate his debtor's property when the debtor defaulted. Collateral (*enekhuron* or *hypothekē*) was often given as security for loans. Scholars have identified no less than four distinct types of collateral arrangements; each with its own particular rules relating to the nature of the collateral and the ownership and possession of it. *Dike blabēs* was the cause of action used for most breach of contract cases. For intentional breach, a breaching party had to pay double damages.

The Athenians established unique institutions to handle commercial disputes that occurred in the Agora. The *agoranomoi* ("controllers of the market"), *sitophylakes* ("guardians of grain"), *epimelētai tou emporiou*, and *metronomoi* (inspectors of weights and measures) adjudicated controversies arising from fraud, grain prices, and weights and measures in the marketplace. For some violations of market laws, an offender could be subject to a legal procedure called *phasis* which allowed a successful prosecutor to recover half of the offender's fine as a bounty.

The Athenian government imposed little in the way of direct taxes on its ordinary citizens. The State usually gathered the taxes that were collected by farming them out to independent tax collectors (who kept a portion for themselves as profit). There were some indirect taxes and sales taxes (*e.g.*, on real estate). And metics paid a special tax called the *metoikion*. Otherwise, a great deal of govenment expense (*e.g.*, funding for public religious festivals and maintenance of war ships) was borne by the wealthy by means of liturgies.

Unit IV

Law in
Ancient Rome

CHAPTER 10

Background and Beginnings of Roman Law

§ 10.01 INTRODUCTION

[A] PUBLIC LAW & PRIVATE LAW

One traditional way of studying Roman law is to divide its contents into public law (*ius publicum*) and private law (*ius privatum*). In Roman law, criminal law and administrative law were categorized as *ius publicum*. The *ius privatum* included rules of property, succession, contracts, and laws relating to the family.[1] According to the Roman jurist Ulpian,[2] the *ius publicum* is that which deals with the interests of the entire community whereas *ius privatum* deals with the interests of separate persons. Indeed, even if a crime victim were to forgive the criminal, we today believe that the interests of the entire community have been infringed by a crime, and thus must be vindicated. On the other hand, it is merely a private matter, for example, when a borrower fails to return money that he owes to his lender.[3]

---

1. It is common for students to study the Roman *ius privatum* rather than the *ius publicum*, because many scholars and legal historians have taken the position that Roman lawyers did not really create anything worth borrowing in the realm of *ius publicum*. *See e.g.,* HANS JULIUS WOLFF, ROMAN LAW: AN HISTORICAL INTRODUCTION 53 (1951) [hereinafter "WOLFF, ROMAN LAW"] (According to Wolff, Roman private law is the law that has most influenced the Western legal tradition. "Criminal law and procedure were slow in their development and never attained the importance comparable to that of private law and civil procedure.").

2. *See infra* § 10.04[B].

3. This distinction between public and private law exists in most European continental countries (but not in the United Kingdom). The United Kingdom countries reject this distinction because of its peculiar legal history. Specifically, the manner in which appeals were originally heard and appealed to the king affected the United Kingdom's approach: only when the king had an interest in a case was it deemed pub-

One of the greatest gifts that ancient Rome has bequeathed to the world is its private law. Although the Roman Empire eventually collapsed, Roman private law has survived and still permeates many legal systems in the world. In particular, Roman law is the basis for all of the laws in western Europe (including Scotland), except England and Scandinavia. There is even a significant influence in English law.

[B] PERIODS OF ROMAN LAW: PRE-CLASSICAL; CLASSICAL; & POST-CLASSICAL

Modern scholars traditionally classify Roman legal development into three stages: 1) Pre-Classical; 2) Classical; and, 3) Post-Classical. The Pre-Classical period lasted from the beginning stages to the 1st century B.C. This was a time when the pontiffs (priests) kept law as a secret. The pontiffs hid the law, in part, because it was profitable for them. Later, laws were codified and published, and the priests lost their monopoly. The Classical period of Roman law began in the 1st century B.C. and lasted through the 3rd century A.D. This is probably the most important and interesting period of Roman law. Roman jurists developed legal forms that were abstract and, many have argued, universal (*i.e.,* capable of being applied at any time in any society). The Post-Classical period runs from the beginning of the 4th century A.D. through the 6th century A.D. From the end of the Classical period to Justinian, the law was characterized by bureaucratic administration more than the ingenuity or consideration of jurists. Some have called this the bureaucratic period of Roman law.[4] Few if any significant new legal ideas developed during this period but it is still engaging because this is when the Romans organized, classified, and wrote down a great deal of their law. Thus, students customarily consider the Post-Classical period because of the important codification that occurred during the 6th century A.D.[5] At this juncture it is useful also to mention that Roman history itself is marked by three major periods: 1) Monarchy (753–509 B.C.); 2) Republic (509–27 B.C.); and Empire (27 B.C.–5th century A.D. in the Western Empire and 27 B.C.–1453 A.D. in the Eastern Empire).

---

lic. But the Roman law public *versus* private distinction is still important in most western European countries.

4. *See* WOLFF, ROMAN LAW 130 (Citing Schultz).

5. *See infra* § 10.05.

§ 10.02 EARLY ROMAN LEGAL HISTORY

[A] LAWS OF THE KINGS

Prior to any codification, the earliest Romans seem to have prospered using custom as the basis for law. According to the ancient Greek authors Plutarch and Dionysus of Halicarnassus, the seven kings who ruled Rome from 753–509 B.C. enacted quite a bit of law dealing with family law and sacred law (*i.e.*, relating to religion). Although many scholars doubt the veracity of Plutarch and Dionysus, others take the position that there may be a fair degree of truth to their assertions.[6] Romulus, the first king, required that each plebeian had to select a patrician to serve as his patron. Each patron was responsible for the legal affairs of his plebeian-client (bringing lawsuits and explaining laws). There were other legal rights, duties, and obligations between a patron and his client as well. Romulus prohibited a wife from divorcing her husband. It was also Romulus who formulated the law that decreed that a son was considered to have been freed from his father's paternal power if his father sold him three times. Numa, the second king, decreed that individuals were to mark the boundaries of their property. He also differentiated between murder and manslaughter. Servius Tullius, the sixth king, established that manumitted slaves automatically became Roman citizens. He also set up different trial procedures, depending upon whether they were public or private.

[B] THE LAWS OF THE TWELVE TABLES

[1] TRADITIONAL BACKGROUND

In the first half of the 5th century B.C., Rome saw the beginnings of what came to be known as the "struggle of the orders": a conflict between the patricians (originally the upper class) and plebeians (originally the lower class). Many plebeians believed that it was unfair for the priests to keep the laws secret and for the judges to put themselves above the law. In 462 B.C., a tribune of the Plebs named Gaius Terentilius Harsa proposed that a commission be established to codify laws to bind the consuls. After a period of stalling and inactivity, tradition has it that the Romans then sent a committee to Athens to research Solon's laws (written about 594 B.C.).[7]

---

6. *See e.g.*, ALAN WATSON, ROMAN LAW & COMPARATIVE LAW 9 (1991) [hereinafter "WATSON, ROMAN LAW & COMPARATIVE LAW"].

7. *See supra* § 7.03[C].

The second century A.D. jurist, Gaius, identifies some laws that he says reflect influence from Solon; but few modern scholars are convinced of such a connection.[8] There is no mention of it in the Greek sources and the Romans had very little contact with the rest of the Mediterranean world at the time.[9] Nevertheless, when the committee returned from Greece, in 451 B.C., ten patricians, the decemvirs, were elected to write new laws for Rome. The decemvirs produced ten tablets of laws written on either bronze or wood. Supposedly, they allowed the populace to comment on their laws and then amended them accordingly. In the next year, another ten decemvirs (including some plebeians) were elected, and they wrote two additional tablets of laws. These decemvirs, however, expressed the desire to remain in power, and after the plebeians seceded in protest, the people ejected the decemvirs. Their work, however, was retained. Many have observed, nevertheless, that the Laws of the Twelve tables are extremely well written. They are so succinct and clear that the drafters must have had considerable legal expertise.

[2] CONTENT OF THE LAWS OF THE TWELVE TABLES

The ancient Romans considered that the Twelve Tables were the basis for their laws. According to Cicero, schoolboys memorized them. We do not possess the original copies. Tradition has it that the originals burned when the Gauls sacked the city in 390 B.C. Because we no longer have the first bronze (or wooden?) tablets, historians have had to piece the laws together from various alternative sources.

The provisions in the Twelve Tables tend to be concerned with unusual circumstances rather than ordinary ones. The beginning parts of the Twelve Tables contain numerous statements about suitable legal procedure. Indeed, procedural laws are prominent. The laws provide that, in cases of conflicts between statutes, the most recently enacted controls. The Twelve Tables establish procedures to substitute for self-help or outright retaliation. In some instances, private vengeance is allowed by retaliation in kind (*lex talionis*), but only in the form of pure retaliation in the event that the wrongdoer and his victim are unable to agree on financial terms. Otherwise, many laws provide for public punishments for a wrongdoer or require that the wrongdoer compensate his victim. It is significant that the laws reflect an appreciation of the subtle distinction between intentional and acci-

---

8. *See* WATSON, ROMAN LAW & COMPARATIVE LAW 13–14. *Cf.* WOLFF, ROMAN LAW 60 ("It is not impossible that the decemvirs consciously took over some Greek ideas.").

9. *See* WATSON, ROMAN LAW & COMPARATIVE LAW 11.

dental homicide. The laws establish guardians for persons incapable of taking care of themselves and their concerns (such as children, women, "prodigals", and those who are mentally unstable). The Twelve Tables grant a man the right to make a will to control the distribution of his things upon death. There are laws that fix predetermined payments as compensation for personal injuries. The Twelve Tables also give effect to the *stipulatio* form of contract (a face-to-face contract that originally required one party to ask *Spondesne?*—"Do you promise?"—and the other to respond *Spondeo*—"I promise").[10] And, there is a law concerning the settlement of boundary disputes.

§ 10.03 THE ROLE OF THE PRAETOR & AEDILE IN THE DEVELOPMENT OF ROMAN LAW

The praetors, who were second in magisterial rank and power only to the consuls, were responsible for much of the operation of the judicial system. The aediles were in charge of the streets and marketplace. When these magistrates issued their edicts—usually at the beginning of their terms in office—they ordinarily explained how they intended to carry out the laws, and in so doing, changed the face of Roman law. Roman praetors did more for the development of Roman law than any other Roman officials. Simply stated, they were responsible for matters relating to justice. Praetors were not judges themselves but were officials who administered the legal system and instructed judges concerning how to resolve certain questions of law.

The Romans established the office of praetor in 367 B.C. Because the State was interested in dealing with foreigners and in further developing foreign trade, the Romans added a second praetor, called the *praetor peregrinus* in 242 B.C. From that point forward, the *praetor urbanus* (city praetor) took charge of matters concerning Roman citizens and the *praetor peregrinus* (foreign praetor) concerned himself with matters relating to disputes between citizens and foreigners or strictly between foreigners. But in addition to these few facts, we know precious little about the distinctions between the urban praetor and the peregrine praetor. But after 242 B.C., there were two praetors: peregrine and urban.

The praetor urbanus, however, was actually the more important of the two. Each praetor served for just one year. Upon entering office, he promul-

---

10. *See infra* § 12.07[B].

gated an *edictum* (edict). His edict gave judges general instructions about how to resolve cases. Although each edict of the new praetor urbanus repeated much of what his predecessors had said, he inevitably implemented a little addition, subtraction, and modification. Praetors were not actually empowered to change laws, but because of their office, they could control a great deal of legal interpretation. The praetor urbanus, in his discretion, had the authority, therefore, to waive various formalities in the law and to recognize new or variant causes of action, and to disregard others.[11] Legal historians refer to the laws that resulted from the praetors' edicts as the *ius honorarium*. Thus, by adaptations through their edicts, the urban praetors molded Roman law and created the law that has come to be known as the *ius honorarium*. It was the final century of the Republic (*i.e.,* roughly 140–40 B.C.) that was the most active and significant period for the development of the *ius honorarium*.

The *ius gentium* (law of peoples/nations) that the praetor peregrinus administered was not used between different states but only between a Roman citizen (*civis*) and a foreigner (*peregrinus*) or between two foreigners who were involved in a dispute on Roman soil. Thus, in a restricted and limited sense, the *ius gentium* was the Roman predecessor of International Law.

As Rome's influence and territory expanded, the State added more praetors for the provinces (Sulla [Dictator 82–79 B.C.] raised the number to eight in 81 B.C.) and six additional praetors in Rome itself to handle the increased caseload.

In the course of their duties, Roman praetors created several notable legal institutions. For example, the praetors were responsible for the procedural device called the *exceptio* (exception). The *exceptio* was actually a method of protecting rights indirectly as a kind of defense to an action. Indeed, in a contract where a seller sells goods to a buyer for a certain price, if the contract is silent as to when payment is to occur, the law implies that payment will be simultaneous with delivery of the goods. If the seller sues the buyer for payment, the buyer, rather than denying the existence of the contract, might, by *exceptio*, plead that the seller failed to deliver the goods. In essence, it is easier for a buyer to wait for the seller to sue him (and then defend by *exceptio*) than it is for the buyer to sue the seller and plead that the seller failed to perform. Another example of the praetor's invention is *restitutio* (restitution), by which the law forced a party who had been unjustly enriched to return the unjustly-obtained money. For example, very early in Roman Law, even a contract entered into under duress was consid-

---

11. *See infra* § 11.01 regarding causes of action.

ered valid. The Romans said "*Coactus voluit, tamen voluit*" ("Although he was coerced when he assented, nevertheless, he assented"). Eventually, the praetors realized the injustice of this approach to contract interpretation. To mitigate the harshness, then, the praetors determined to acknowledge the existence of the contract, but also decided that it could not be enforced as written, given that the agreement was concluded under duress. Hence, the praetors invented the concept of *restitutio* so that the party who had been coerced could be entitled to restitution. In terms of the big picture, however, the two most significant things that the praetors did to affect the substance of Roman law were: 1) to fashion their edicts (on an annual basis); and, 2) to fashion formulae—as part of what was known as the formulary system of procedure—(on a daily basis).[12]

In addition to the office of praetor, the office of *aedile* was also created in 367 B.C. The four *aediles* kept the State archives, and supervised the streets, aqueducts, buildings, bridges, and the public marketplace. Because of their role in maintaining order in the market, the aediles gradually influenced laws relating to the sale of goods. Like the praetors, the aediles issued edicts at the outset of their terms. Thus, they too had a certain degree of flexibility to adapt the laws of the marketplace by creative interpretation through the *ius honorarium*.

During the Empire, the praetor's edict brought about very little in the way of significant change. Ultimately, the jurist Julianus, under the Emperor Hadrian (117–138 A.D.), put the praetorian and aedilician edicts into their final, frozen forms. Later the classical Roman jurists referred to Julianus' version of the praetor's edict as the *edictum perpetuum*, and considered it established law.

§ 10.04 LEGAL INTERPRETATION: ADVOCATES, JURISTS, & EMPERORS

[A] BACKGROUND

Very early in Rome's history, only the pontiffs (*pontifices*) had access to the archives containing the specialized legal forms and phrases that were necessary to conduct a lawsuit. They regulated the specialized rules for initiating and carrying out lawsuits. Only patricians were allowed to serve as pontiffs until the passage of the *lex Ogulnia* in 300 B.C. The first plebeian

---

12. *See infra* § 11.03[B].

pontifex maximus was elected in 253 B.C. The pontiffs could interpret laws broadly or narrowly to suit their own purposes. Thus, they had a monopoly on legal advice and law. The pontiffs eventually lost their exclusive grip on legal interpretation. Tradition has it that they lost that grip all at once in 312 B.C. when Gnaeus Flavius, the secretary of Appius Claudius (the famous censor) stole (aided by the collusion of Appius) and published the forms of action.

[B] ADVOCATES & JURISTS

The wealthiest young Romans generally selected one of three careers: military; politics; or, law. These three professions were closely related. According to Cicero, the jurists of the first century B.C. had three functions: 1) *ad respondendum* (answering legal questions and giving legal advice); 2) *ad agendum* (preparing a case for court); and, 3) *ad cavendum* (drafting documents). The function called *ad respondendum* ("to respond") was the private function of a lawyer—perhaps the ancient jurist's most important task—explaining to a praetor, aedile, judge, or layperson what a particular law meant. Since all legal disputes assumed personal participation by the parties, one needed an attorney for consultion. This was the role known as *ad agendum* (literally "to drive/perform"). *Cavere* actually is Latin for "to warn." Because early Roman procedure was very formal,[13] one needed to use proper legal language in order to create valid documents. *Ad cavendum* was the process of drafting written formulae (either using a standardized form or creating a new one) for lawsuits or business transactions.

Roman advocates were those who were more likely to conduct the business of court cases (*ad agendum*) whereas jurisconsults (jurists) were more like academics who rendered opinions (*ad respondendum*). Advocates were not allowed to accept payment—at least theoretically—for their services. Jurists did not receive fees for their advice either, but rather performed their services as a contribution to society. The jurists tended to be conservative in their approach. They ordinarily were from families that were of the senatorial class, and thus they were highly respected. Since the *praetors* and *aediles* were politicians who were usually not trained in law, they relied heavily on the *responsa* of jurists. From the time of Hadrian (*c.* 117–138 A.D.) forward, Roman jurists thought of themselves as a special, privileged class who were above the advocates in the courtrooms.

---

13. *See infra* Chapter 11.

The early Roman jurisconsults (*i.e.*, those in the Pre-Classical period) developed the essential principles of Roman law mostly during the second and first centuries B.C. There were a number of early attempts to impose a semblance of order on Roman law. The *Ius Flavianum* (*c.* 312 B.C.) consisted of a collection of formulae for lawsuits. The *Ius Aelianum*, another collection of formulae, was issued by Sextus Aelius Paetus (consul, 198 B.C.). He also published the first attempt at a systematic treatment of Roman law: a major legal work called the *Tripertitia*. In the *Tripertitia*, Paetus presented first the text of each provision of the Twelve Tables, second, the interpretations by pontiffs and jurisconsults of these provisions, and, third, written formulae appropriate for lawsuits applicable to each provision (*i.e.*, the written words necessary to bring a cause of action under that law). Around 150 B.C., Manius Manilius published forms for sales transactions. The consul Quintus Mucius Scaevola (95 B.C.) is given credit for having divided civil law into *genera* (classes). He wrote an 18-book commentary about the civil law which was the first legal treatise that attempted to impose structure on Roman law. Scaevola organized the text into sections based on related legal principles. His students continued his tradition. The consul Servius Sulpicius Rufus (51 B.C.) wrote the first commentary on the praetorian edict.

The Emperor Augustus (27 B.C.–14 A.D.) granted certain jurists a right called the *ius respondendi* (*ius respondendi ex auctoritate principis*—the right of responding based on the authority of the emperor). Although we do not know precisely what the *ius respondendi* entailed, it apparently entitled the jurist on whom it was bestowed to give his opinion on legal questions. Clearly the opinions of the jurists who possessed *ius respondendi* were given great weight. The opinion did not, in actuality, bind a judge, but as a matter of practice, judges typically adhered to the opinions rendered by jurists with *ius respondendi*.

The jurist Marcus Antistius Labeo (who died about 10 A.D.) is credited with being the first great jurist of the Classical period. He supposedly wrote over 400 works (though very little of his work has survived). Also in the Classical period, Gaius wrote the *Institutes* or *Institutiones* (composed about 161 A.D.). The *Institutes* served as a relatively short and direct introduction to law for students. Indeed, law students in the Empire used the *Institutes* as their principal handbook for learning substantive law. When the Emperor Justinian had his *Institutes* written in the 6th century A.D., the drafters closely followed Gaius' *Institutes*.

Domitius Ulpianus (Ulpian) and Iulius Paulus (Paul) are known for their great legal works on Sabinius and the Edict. Wolff describes their works as follows:

Ulpianus's and Paulus's commentaries came to be considered as final statements of *ius civile* and *ius honorarium* and thus became the standard works of the post classical period. A very large part of Justinian's Digest consists of fragments taken from these four commentaries. Showing Roman law as it was after two centuries of incessant and intensive development by a group of outstanding jurists, Paulus's and Ulpianus's commentaries are therefore our primary sources for classical law.[14]

Supposedly, the Emperor Hadrian (117–138 A.D.) expanded the *ius respondendi*. Under Hadrian, if the jurists who were questioned agreed—naturally these were jurists with *ius respondendi*—, then their opinions were binding. If they were inconsistent, then the judge was free to adopt whichever jurist's opinion he wished. The last of the great jurists of the Classical period was Aemelius Papinianus (died 212 A.D.).

In 426 A.D. Theodosius II and Valentinian III enacted the "Law of Citations," which regulated the use of citations in court of the classical jurists and Gaius. Simply stated, this law provided that the writings of Papinianus, Ulpianus, Paulus, Modestinus, and Gaius could be used as precedents. Judges were directed to follow the majority opinion of these writers. If there was a tie among these authors on a point, the position of Papinianus controlled. If Papinianus was silent on the issue, then the judge was to apply his own judgment.

[C] THE "SCHOOLS": SABINIANS & PROCULIANS

Two schools of jurists dominated the first 150 years of the Empire: the Sabinians and the Proculians. Labeo[15] is considered the founder of the Proculians and Gaius Ateius Capito is considered the founder of the Sabinians. We know very little about the operation or structure of these schools. It is likely that these "schools" were not schools in the strict sense; that is, they were probably not actual teaching institutions *per se*. Rather, they were probably loose associations of jurists and their pupils. Presumably they met and discussed various topics and questions of law as a means of instruction. Interestingly, although these are the two traditional "schools," and there are isolated instances of differing opinions on specific points of law, scholars have been unable to pin down any general, overarching theoretical disparity between the two. Apparently, shortly after Hadrian, the schools no

---

14. WOLFF, ROMAN LAW 122.
15. *See supra* § 10.04[B].

longer operated, and ultimately no longer influenced Roman jurisprudence.

[D] THE ROLE OF THE EMPEROR

By 150 A.D. it was taken for granted that the emperor was empowered to issue legislation of his own accord. Even before then, emperors affected law in four distinct ways. First, an emperor could issue edicts (*edicta*). Second, an emperor could actually take a case himself—acting as judge and jury. By giving *decreta* (legal decisions rendered by the emperor in any given case that had been brought before him), the emperor's decision (*decretum*) superseded all other decisions, and became precedent. The Emperor Claudius (41–54 A.D.), in particular, enjoyed exercising this power, and did so regularly. Third, emperors influenced law by answering, in writing, legal questions for officials and private citizens. This answer was called a *rescriptum* (rescript) or *epistula* (letter). Lastly, emperors routinely issued *mandata*, the emperor's orders to officials (*e.g.*, provincial governors). In these four ways, the Roman emperors themselves exerted significant influence over the development of law. Eventually, the law developed by the emperors superseded even the *ius honorarium*.

§ 10.05 JUSTINIAN & THE *CORPUS IURIS CIVILIS*

After one initial false start, a commission appointed by Theodosius II compiled a code of Roman law, the Codex Theodosianus, in 438 A.D. Theodosius made the code effective in the Eastern Empire at the beginning of 439 A.D. and soon thereafter Valentinian III adopted it in the Western Empire as well.

In 528 A.D. the Roman emperor, Justinian, created an ad hoc commission to codify all of Roman law. Justinian appointed a lawyer named Tribonianus (Tribonian) to take charge in producing what we know today as the *Corpus Iuris Civilis*. It took Tribonian and his commission seven years (528–534 A.D.). Justinian endeavored to strike a balance between the old, time-honored jurisprudence of the classical jurists and the practical requirements of the sixth century A.D. The *Corpus Iuris Civilis* is divided into four parts. In ascending order of relative importance, they are as follows. 1) *Codex Iustiniani*. First, the least important is the *Codex Iustiniani* (Justinian's Code), promulgated in April of 529 A.D. The *Codex* consists of constitutions of emperors (*i.e.*, bureaucratic legal regulations and various legal acts). 2) *Novellae*. Next are the *Novellae*. Justinian added various amendments, called *novellae* (new laws adopted after the entire *Corpus Iuris* had been written). His successors also issued *novellae* of their own. 3) *Institutiones*. Of penultimate importance were the *Institutiones*, or *Institutes* (535 A.D.). Justinian's *Institutes* were intended as a first-year student textbook but the text was actually enacted into law by imperial statute. Thus, the *Institutes* served both as an official textbook on Roman Law and as a functional code that could be consulted for subsequent decisions (*i.e.*, it had the force of law). 4) *Digest*. Most scholars consider the *Digest* the most important part of the *Corpus Iuris Civilis*. It became effective as law at the end of December, 533 A.D. It consists of approximately two thousand fragments (quotations) of works of 39 different Roman jurists going as far back as the 1st century B.C. Over half of the quotes are from Ulpian and Paul (about 33% are from the former and nearly 20% from the latter). Justinian's codification of Roman law provided a brief but comprehensive summary of Roman law. His synopses served as useful prototypes for later generations to imitate.

§ 10.06 THE RECEPTION OF ROMAN LAW (RECEPTIO)

One of the principal reasons that it is worthwhile for us to study Roman Law today is its importance to and incorporation in modern legal systems. Scholars traditionally refer to this incorporation by the countries of the world as the "reception of Roman law."

After the Barbarian invasions at the close of the 5th century A.D., the invaders retained the Roman law for their relations with Romans and retained their own *lex Barbarorum* only for relations among themselves. Of course, there was a gradual amalgamation of these, and then, for the next two to three centuries, Roman law began adjusting and taking on new qualities as times changed. Roman law thus evolved into a different form in the 7th, 8th, and 9th centuries A.D. In the 11th century A.D. in Bologna, Italy, two professors (one of whom was especially important—Irnerius 1055–1130 A.D.) found a copy of the Justinian Code under another text. They studied and commented upon these laws (explaining and cross-referencing). These comments came to be called *glossa*, and thus the scholars who created these comments were called *glossators* (this was primarily an academic enterprise). The work of the *glossators* continued from the 11th to the 13th centuries A.D. By the 14th century, lawyers had to reinterpret and add further comments in addition to what the *glossators* had done. These scholars were called the *post-glossators* or *commentators*. They further modified Roman law to adapt to new circumstances and an expanding capitalistic system.

Before the French Revolution (1789 A.D.), France did not have its own code, even though at the time it was probably the most developed capitalistic society. France was officially divided by north and south. The south was *le pays du droit ecrit* ("the country of the written law") and the north was *le pays des coutumes* ("the country of customs"). When Napoleon ascended, he created an ad hoc commission to draft a civil code. On the commission there were representatives of both north and south. According to tradition, when Napoleon was a young officer just over twenty years of age, he read and virtually memorized the *Corpus Iuris Civilis* (while serving a brief stint in a military stockade). Thus, Napoleon relied on Justinian's laws for his French law. Of course, today the Napoleonic Code has been expanded and modified, and there have been many attempts to do away with it entirely, but the only substantial change has been that dealing with family law. In Belgium and Luxembourg (and for a time in Italy and other countries) the Napoleonic Code has been adopted.

Early Prussian emperors adopted Roman law. Thus, it became the basis for German law. Even when the German civil code was rewritten in 1900 A.D, almost two-thirds of the new code mirrored Roman law. In 1942, Italy borrowed a great deal from that German code for its laws.

The United Kingdom is the most notable exception to the Reception of Roman law. English law was not as greatly affected by Roman law as were Germany and France. The king's judges invented the Common Law beginning in about the 11th century when the judges heard cases for the Crown and resolved disputes according to their understanding of equity. This created the Common Law system and *stare decisis*. The English system was not a system of general abstract rules, but primarily case law. Roman law, on the other hand, is mostly statute law. But in the 10th century A.D., two important books were published in England; one by Bracton and the other by Glanvill. Both were dedicated exclusively to Roman law and described Roman law, in a systematic way. Later, when the kings' judges came across difficult cases, they appealed to Bracton and Glanvill for authority (not Roman sources directly). Thus, Roman law became integrated into the law of the United Kingdom rather indirectly. Therefore, the tradition that English law avoided the influences of Roman law is patently untrue. Roman law has also had a major influence on the laws in Scotland, Quebec, and Louisiana (thanks to its French roots).

It is especially important for lawyers to study Roman law today. It is virtually impossible to survive in isolation, using purely domestic legal thinking. We must understand the legal systems of other nations in order to exist (especially concerning economic and cultural aspects of other nations). Foreign law affects the world. As has been seen, the general principles of Roman law permeate many of the laws of the world.

§ 10.07 JUSTICE & JURISPRUDENCE: THE ROLE OF LAW

Watson takes the position that custom was relatively unimportant "as a source of new law" during both the Republic and Empire.[16] Most legal historians agree, nevertheless, that laws ordinarily are rooted in custom.[17] The Romans did segregate secular law from law relating to religion. Thus, there was not necessarily a strong correlation between law, religion, and morality. And, although the Roman jurists had studied philosophy and rhetoric, their principal interest in law was practical not theoretical.

Still, many of the classical jurists were strongly influenced by the philosophy of Stoicism. Zeno (350–260 B.C.), the founder of the Stoics, made nature the key to his philosophy. For Zeno and the Stoics, a pervasive reason dominated and controlled the universe. Equality was an integral precept in the Stoic concept of natural law. In his *Institutes*, Gaius states that natural reason establishes laws that men follow. These laws, brought about by natural reason, constitute the *ius gentium* (law of nations) whereas the laws created by state legislation are *ius civile* (civil law).

Cicero (106–43 B.C.) held fast to the Stoic ideal of a natural and universal law. In his *De republica*, he described true law as right reason that works in concert with nature. It exists among humans and is constant. True law's principles encourage citizens to perform their duties while discouraging illegal acts. According to Cicero, law is the same everywhere and it governs all people. It is everlasting and immutable. In *De Legibus*, he says that law is the highest reason. It emanates from nature and dictates what men should do and prohibits those things that they should not. Natural law depends on intelligence and human reason. It is a higher law that began before governments and the written law of mortals. As Wolff states, Cicero believed that

---

16. WATSON, ROMAN LAW & COMPARATIVE LAW 15.
17. *Id.* ("Of course, if one goes back to the beginning, one will find that most fundamental rules derive from custom.").

there were certain "legal institutions and conceptions inherent in human nature and therefore reasonable and shared by all mankind."[18] In sum, for Cicero, justice is a single nature-based unity that governs all people. It is right reason applied to command and prohibition.

§ 10.08 CHAPTER SUMMARY

The Romans considered criminal and administrative laws as public law (*ius publicum*) and laws relating to individuals — such as property, contracts, and family laws — as private law (*ius privatum*). The private law of the ancient Romans has significantly influenced a great deal of modern law. We traditionally categorize Roman legal development in three major periods: 1) Pre-Classical (up to the 1st century B.C.); 2) Classical (1st century B.C. through the 3rd century A.D.); and, 3) Post-Classical (4th century A.D. to the 6th century A.D.). During the Monarchy (753–509 B.C.), the seven kings of Rome established laws relating to matters such as legal procedure, religion, the patron-client system, property, family law, and citizenship. According to tradition, in 451/450 B.C., the Romans sent a delegation to Athens to study Solon's laws. As a result of that research, two groups of decemvirs produced the Laws of the Twelve Tables. In addition to many procedural rules, the Laws of the Twelve Tables also address issues such as punishments, compensation for personal injury, homicide, guardianship, wills, and contracts.

Praetors were the officials in charge of the judiciary — the legal system as a whole. By the middle of the 3rd century B.C., the Romans had established two praetors: 1) the *praetor peregrinus*, who administered disputes that involved foreigners; and, 2) the *praetor urbanus*, who was responsible for law relating to Roman citizens. Through their annual edicts, the praetors played a significant role in the development of both Roman law, the *ius honorarium*, and also the antecedent of international law, the *ius gentium*. By the 1st century B.C., there were more than a dozen praetors in Rome and the provinces. The praetors were responsible for numerous legal innovations that allowed procedure and business to operate more smoothly. In addition to the praetors, the aediles — who were in charge of the marketplace — directly affected laws relating to the sale of goods. Under the Emperor Hadrian, the jurist, Julianus, polished the praetorian and aedilician edicts into their final forms.

Although the patrician pontiffs originally controlled legal procedure through secrecy, at the close of the 4th century B.C., plebeians became eli-

---

18. WOLFF, ROMAN LAW 83.

gible to serve as pontiffs and, thus, henceforth had access to the rules governing lawsuits. Eventually, Roman jurists developed distinct roles: 1) *ad respondendum* (answering legal questions and giving legal advice); 2) *ad agendum* (preparing a case for court); and, 3) *ad cavendum* (drafting documents). As a rule, the advocates (who were not permitted to accept fees) litigated cases in court and the jurisconsults (who, likewise, received no fees) gave legal advice to praetors, aediles, and judges. During the 2nd and 1st centuries B.C., a number of jurists (such as Paetus, Manilius, Scaevola, and Servius Sulpicius Rufus) began organizing and summarizing the fundamental principles and rules that were developing in Roman law. Augustus granted the *ius respondendi* to certain jurists—giving them the authority to render non-binding, but highly influential opinions to judges. Later the Emperor Hadrian made such opinions binding. In the Classical Period, Gaius composed his *Institutes*, which were later used by law students and subsequent scholars as a basis for study and as authoritative statements of the law. Soon thereafter, Ulpian and Paul wrote important commentaries that later were used extensively in the preparation of Justinian's *Digest*. Early in the 5th century A.D., the Emperors Theodosius II and Valentinian III formally elevated the writings of the jurists Papinian, Ulpian, Paul, and Modestinus to that of binding authorities.

Labeo, whom many consider the first great jurist of the Classical Period, is thought to have been the founder of the Proculians; while Gaius Ateius Capito is regarded as the founder of the Sabinians. These—the Proculians and Sabinians—were the two most prominent "schools" of Roman jurisprudence. The emperors themselves influenced the direction of law by issuing edicts (*edicta*), by writing opinions in cases brought before them when acting as judges (*decreta*), by giving formal written opinions on legal questions (*rescripta/epistula*), and also by issuing orders to administrative officials (*mandata*). The Emperor Theodosius II appointed a commission that compiled a law code (*Codex Theodosianus*) which became the rule of law in 439 A.D. Nearly a hundred years later, the Emperor Justinian enlisted the aid of several jurists (most notably Tribonian) who produced the *Corpus Iuris Civilis*; comprised of four important works which constituted the most comprehensive codification of Roman law: 1) *Codex Iustiniani* (529 A.D.); 2) *Novellae*; 3) *Institutes* (535 A.D.); and, 4) *Digest* (533 A.D.).

From the 5th to the 13th centuries A.D. various European nations adapted and used Roman law. The glossators (11th–13th centuries) and post-glossators/commentators (14th century) renewed interest in Roman law by trying to explain it and trying to put it to use in the context of a changed Europe. In France, Napoleon used Justinian's laws as the basis for his Code, which, in turn, profoundly influenced the later development of law in Italy, Belgium, and Luxembourg. German law also employed Roman law as its foundation. Even the United Kingdom—with its reliance on Common Law—indirectly borrowed from and absorbed a great deal of Roman law through its reliance on authorities such as Bracton and Glanvill. Thus, even today Roman law and legal thinking permeate much of the law in the Western World.

Roman law was dependent, to a degree, on both custom and practicality. Nevertheless, Greek philosophy, such as Zeno's Stoicism, influenced Roman jurisprudence and its reliance on the concept of natural law. Cicero, for example, shows in his writing an adherence to immutable, universal natural laws shared by all humans.

CHAPTER 11

Legal Procedure, Institutions, & Organization

§ 11.01 INTRODUCTION

In American law, the possession of a right is considered a prerequisite to beginning a legal dispute. In ancient Rome, the opposite was true. The procedure was the cause of the right. In some respects, this is similar to the old English writ system. Prior to William the Conqueror, all legal disputes in England were resolved by local custom. Before the King became involved in a dispute, he had to have some sort of interest in it (*i.e.,* an interest for the Crown). Then and only then, did the King become involved by using a proper document, the "writ." The commonplace was "where there is no writ, there is no right." Therefore, the King's judges heard a case only if the plaintiff had a writ (*i.e.,* the writ gave the party the right to sue). The same was true under Roman law. Suits in Roman law were called *actiones* (*actio* in the singular). A person's rights came from the *actiones*. One might have said in ancient Rome, "where there is no *actio*, there is no right."

For civil cases between citizens, litigants took their cases to the court of the Urban Praetor. Civil cases involving foreigners were heard by the Peregrine Praetor. Criminal cases in the Republic were heard by various *quaestiones perpetuae* that were established by specific legislation to address particular kinds of criminal conduct. As an antecedent, however, to understanding the nuts and bolts of legal procedure, it is helpful to appreciate something about the nature of the legislative bodies that created laws. Thus, this chapter begins with an overview of the Roman constitution and important early laws that established the basis for much of later Roman law. As regards procedure itself, in early Roman law, it was important that a litigant use the proper form of action. Without a pre-set form of action, a litigant would have no remedy. Therefore, the second section of this chapter examines the three traditional chronological phases of Roman legal procedure: 1) Pre-Classical (*Legis Actiones*); 2) Formulary (*Per Formulam*); and 3) Extraordinary (*Cognitio*). Lastly, we survey the specialized field of criminal procedure and briefly consider the Roman law of evidence.

§ 11.02 THE ROMAN CONSTITUTION & SIGNIFICANT REPUBLICAN LEGISLATION

[A] INTRODUCTION

When historians speak of the "Roman Constitution," they do not mean a document *per se* like the American Constitution, but rather they mean the totality of customs, principles, and separate legislation that in sum delineated the powers and functions of the Roman government. Scholars have speculated that the Romans borrowed some concepts in their constitution from the Etruscans. Scholars have also speculated—with very little corroborating evidence—that they also borrowed Etruscan concepts as part of their private law. For the purposes of the present study, it is necessary to consider the Roman Constitution in order to understand the nature of the officials and legislative bodies responsible for the development of Roman law.

As has been observed, Roman law originally was a monopoly of the priests, the *pontiffs*. During the Monarchy (*c.* 753–509 B.C.), the early Roman kings created laws that dealt with family law and sacred law. In the 5th century B.C., the Laws of the Twelve Tables constituted the first codification of Roman laws (*c.* 451/450 B.C.). Apparently, the Twelve Tables presented the only expression in writing of old Roman customs that heretofore had been kept secret by the priests.

In addition, two other legal sources supplemented the Twelve Tables in earliest Rome: *leges* and *senatus consulta*. *Leges* were statutes adopted by the *populus Romanus*. A statute generally was binding because it resulted from a positive vote of an assembly of the people. Some ancient Roman *leges* survive in original texts (such as inscriptions on stone) while others have come down to us as quotations in ancient authors. Over 800 are extant. Given that these laws span many centuries, this is actually a rather small number. In many respects the Roman *leges* were designed to honor the *mos maiorum*, the customs of their ancestors. *Senatus Consulta* were not really laws but "advice" from the senate. The Twelve Tables, *leges*, and *senatus consulta*, technically speaking, only applied to Roman citizens.

We often find Roman statutes that have at least two parts: 1) *praescriptio* (a general comment concerning the wrong); and, 2) *sanctio* (the negative consequences which resulted from a person's violation of the *praescriptio*). Thus, theoretically speaking, there can be four basic types of laws based on the relationship between the *praescriptio* and the *sanctio*: 1) *lex imperfecta* (a law which provides a rule without a sanction); 2) *lex perfecta* (here the *sanctio* merely invalidates the act which has been performed but prohibited by the *praescriptio*, *i.e.*, the *praescriptio* is "protected" by the *sanctio*); 3) *lex plus quam perfecta* (here the *sanctio* both invalidates the act that has been performed and prohibited by the *praescriptio* and it also exacts other negative consequences (*e.g.*, fines)); and, 4) *lex minus quam perfecta* (here the *sanctio* does not invalidate the act prohibited by the *praescriptio*, but instead imposes negative consequences—for example, when a master frees a slave without observing the proper formula, the slave is still considered free [the act was not invalidated], but the former owner has to pay a fine.).

[B] LEGISLATIVE BODIES

The entire Roman citizenry gathered, as an assembly for political purposes, in several different groups. Each such assembly was called a *comitia*. It was the citizenry gathered as a *comitia* that initially enacted statutes. There were three such assemblies worthy of note: 1) *comitia centuriata;* 2) *comitia tributa*; and, 3) *comitia curiata*. The *comitia centuriata* was the assembly comprising all Roman citizens organized into "centuries", or one-hundreds. It was arranged by a wealth-classification. Because of the order of voting in the *comitia centuriata*, the wealthiest citizens could always outvote the poor. The *comitia tributa* was established on an old tribal/territorial basis. During the Monarchy, Rome was divided into four districts called *tribus* (tribes). Gradually, tribes were added in the surrounding countryside until there were thirty-one rural and four urban tribes as of 241 B.C. All Roman citizens were considered members of one of these tribes for voting purposes. Eventually, they abolished the geographic distinctions, and instead made membership in the tribes hereditary. We have very little precise knowledge about the *comitia tributa* and its operation. The *comitia curiata* operated in some fashion during the Monarchy but the details are far from clear. By the Republic it served mostly to witness (and perhaps to authorize) wills and adoptions.

The *concilium plebis* was originally an assembly of all plebeians. The *lex Hortensia* of 287 B.C. decreed that the enactments of the *concilium plebis*, called *plebiscita*, had the force of law over all Roman citizens. Prior to 287

B.C., *plebiscita* had legally bound only plebeians. The tribunes of the plebs were the officials who presided over the *concilium plebis*.

In order for the *comitia centuriata*, the *comitia tributa*, or the *concilium plebis* to convene legally, a magistrate had to call the assembly. A consul could call a meeting of the *comitia centuriata*, only a "patrician" magistrate could call a meeting of the *comitia tributa*, and a tribune of the plebs could convene the *concilium plebis*. After the end of the 1st century A.D., neither the *comitia centuriata* nor the *comitia tributa* enacted legislation.

Two *censors* were elected every five years for the purpose of conducting the census. By virtue of their position, they were able to determine the political and social status of all Roman citizens. In addition, they acquired the role of evaluating both public and private moral behavior. Technically speaking, the *censors* selected senators. As a rule, the censors only picked former magistrates to serve as senators. Senators served for life. During most of the Republic, there were 300 senators. In 81 B.C., Sulla increased the number to 600. Usually the senate (which, during the Republic, technically had no power to pass laws itself) debated a bill first. Then, after it had been worked out in the senate, a magistrate presented it to an assembly. The assembly only had the power either to accept or reject the bill as presented by the magistrate. As a practical matter, however, the assemblies respected the wisdom and *auctoritas* of the advice given by the senate. The legislative power of the senate waxed during the Empire—a time when decrees of the senate, *senatus consulta*, acquired the force of law. Initially a clause in the praetor's edict was required to elevate *senatus consulta* to the level of statute, but in time— certainly by the time of Hadrian (117–138 A.D.) (*senatus consultum Tertillianum*)—this was no longer necessary. By the 2nd century A.D., the emperor routinely sent bills to the senate for its approval or rejection.

[C] LEGISLATION

Watson asserts that "most legislation was political and…there are in fact few statutes concerned with private law."[19] But there are a few statutes from the Republic that influenced Roman law to such an extent that they should, at least, be mentioned. The *lex Canuleia*, passed in 445 B.C., gave plebeians the right of intermarriage with the patricians. In 367 B.C., the Licinian-Sextian law provided that one of the two consuls elected every year had to be a plebeian. A very important piece of legislation during the Republic was

---

19. WATSON, ROMAN LAW & COMPARATIVE LAW 18. *See also* WOLFF, ROMAN LAW 67 ("Roman legislation served the purpose of adapting the structure of state and law to changed conditions, but never that of radically altering it.").

the *lex Aquilia*, passed by the *concilium plebis* in 287 B.C. The *lex Aquilia* governed most of the law related to damage to property. It established the rights of a master against someone who injured his slaves or animals. Also in 287 B.C., the *lex Hortensia* provided that measures passed by the plebeian assembly (*plebis scita*—plebiscites) were binding on all Romans, and thus, had the force of law. Although we do not know the specifics of the *lex Aebutia* (passed in the latter part of the 2nd century B.C.), we do know that it brought about changes to Roman legal procedure.

§ 11.03 THE THREE CHRONOLOGICAL PHASES OF ROMAN PROCEDURE

[A] LEGIS ACTIONES

In the early stages of Roman procedural development, lawsuits were conducted by means of the *legis actiones* ("suits of law"). These were unalterable and only existed in a few forms. The praetor and the judge (*iudex*) were the two most important officials involved in the development of the *legis actiones* system. The praetor was the person to whom a plaintiff first appeared for the initial stage of procedure. This initial stage was called *in iure* ("in accordance with law"). The praetor did not really affect the substance of the case but instead characterized the dispute. In particular, it was he who determined whether a particular type of action addressed the particular dispute in question. He rejected the case if there was no applicable cause of action. If the praetor decided that there was a cause of action, logically, that meant that the praetor had decided that there was, in fact, a protected right which existed. The praetor then spoke directly with the plaintiff and defendant. If the praetor determined that there was a valid cause of action (*i.e.*, he determined that the *in iure* stage had been successful for the plaintiff), the matter then proceeded *apud iudicem* (*i.e.*, the time at which the case would be heard by the judge (*iudex*) on the merits). The opinion of the *iudex* was called a *sententia*. The *legis actiones* system, therefore, involved a relatively passive role by the praetor. He merely decided whether the case could be heard by a judge. Thus, the praetor actually had little impact on the substantive law itself.

[B] FORMULARY PROCEDURE (PER FORMULAM)

The formulary system, a more flexible system of procedure, eventually— perhaps as early as the beginning of the 2nd century B.C.—replaced the *legis actiones*. The *formulae* were less formal and less rigid. This newer legal process permitted expansion of fresh legal concepts and innovative ideas. In the formulary system, the praetors began taking an active role in shaping the substantive law.

We are not sure of the precise date of the *lex Aebutia* that legitimated the procedure *per formulam*, but it was probably passed between 150 and 125 B.C. Much later, the *lex Iulia* (17 B.C.) of Augustus established the formulary procedure as the mandatory procedure for virtually all kinds of lawsuits under Roman law. The distinction between *in iure* and *apud iudicem* still existed. In fact, there was no significant change in the *apud iudicem* phase. There were, on the other hand, major changes in the *in iure* step. In essence, this system did away with the rigid *in iure* stage and, instead, substituted the use of a *formula* (written instruction) that delineated the facts and law for the judge. Praetors still concluded whether the dispute was sufficiently significant to warrant being heard by a judge. The parties appeared before the praetor to initiate a suit. This appearance was the *litis contestatio*. It was here that the praetor, if he decided that there was a cause of action, wrote the formula that then went to the judge. The praetor's formula summarized the claims and defenses of the parties. The judge was required to make his decision based on the praetor's written formula. It was the formula that, in effect, created the legal rule which the judge was to apply in any given case. Because the formula was not bound by the strictures of the *leges actiones* and the *in iure*, the praetor had a new-found flexibility when considering the claims and defenses of the parties.

A typical formula consisted of three different parts: 1) *iudicis nominatio* (nomination of a judge); 2) *intentio* (the statement of the plaintiff's claim— the most important section of every formula); and, 3) *condemnatio* (the instruction to judge to either find the defendant liable or not, based upon an application of the formula to his findings of fact). The *intentio* made clear exactly what the action was. It could claim either a specific claim (*certum*) or an unspecific one (*incertum*). In terms of later jurisprudence, it was aspects of the formulary procedure which survived (specifically, the distinction between determinations of law and fact as in the distinction between *in iure* and *apud iudicem*).

Almost any adult male could serve as a judge (often called an arbiter). Eminent jurists frequently served as judges. Surveyors often judged cases involving land division and boundaries. The parties could also appoint their own arbiter, extra-judicially, to decide their case. Praetors could appoint a small jury of *recuperatores* (recoverers), usually three to five judges instead of a single *iudex*. We also know of large juries especially for disputes involving inheritance of large estates of nobles or the rich. These were called *centumviri* (100 men). The writer Pliny describes a case where there were actually 180 jurors not just 100.

If a defendant, who was found liable, failed to comply within 30 days, the plaintiff could bring an "action on the judgment." The plaintiff then could seize the defendant, personally imprison him, and seize his property and sell it to satisfy the judgment. Otherwise, especially during the Republic (509–27 B.C.), there really was no appeal. The best that a defendant could do was to argue that the judge had not issued an opinion, that the judge had been coerced or fraudulent, or the defendant could sue the judge for "corruption."

[C] EXTRAORDINARY PROCEDURE (COGNITIO)

The final chapter of Roman procedure was the stage called *cognitio*, or as Justinian referred to it, "extraordinary" (*extraordinaria*) procedure. This was the procedure used in the Post-Classical period (certainly the principal process used by the mid-2nd century A.D.). In many respects, it was a regression, falling well below the achievements of the Classical period. Because the Roman Empire had expanded to such an extent, administration was complex. In simple terms, an emperor was incapable of handling everything. The emperor's bureaucrats managed litigation on the emperor's behalf. As was noted, under the formulary system the *in iure* phase was distinct from the *apud iudicem* phase. The *in iure* consisted of the praetor deciding what legal rules would apply to a case. The *apud iudicem* involved the judge who dealt with the facts in order to assess the proofs gathered by the parties, and thus to resolve the problem (of course the hearing itself was subordinated by specific rules of presenting evidence and the other party's explanation of any potentially damaging evidence). In the end, the judge had to give an opinion along with his conclusions and explanations to articulate his reasoning and support his conclusions. By contrast, in the extraordinary procedure, there was no distinction between the *in iure* and *apud iudicem*. The two were combined. The same official decided both the legal prerequisites and the facts as well. Robinson describes *cognitio* as having been "trial before an official (such as the Urban Prefect or a provincial governor) sitting alone as a judge...."[20] The implementation of a lawsuit was in writing, expounding both the plaintiff's demands and also the testimony of witnesses.

---

20. O.F. ROBINSON, THE CRIMINAL LAW OF ANCIENT ROME 7 (1995) [hereinafter "ROBINSON, CRIMINAL LAW"].

§ 11.04 CRIMINAL PROCEDURE

[A] INTRODUCTION

[1] THE EARLY CRIMINAL COURTS— QUAESTIONES PERPETUAE

We know very little about the earliest Roman criminal law and procedure. It is not until the time of Plautus and Terence (*i.e.*, during the 2nd century B.C.) that we begin to get a reasonably clear picture. Roman law ordinarily dealt with many types of conduct that modern legal systems treat as criminal (such as theft, battery, and injury to property) instead as torts.[21] Criminal courts were established during the Republic. In 149 B.C. the *lex Calpurnia* instituted a permanent criminal court comprised of senators as jurors. This court decided cases concerning extortion by officials in the provinces. In the period following the *lex Calpurnia*, the Romans began establishing new permanent jury courts for handling criminal matters, known as *quaestiones perpetuae*.

The Dictator Sulla set up a system of *quaestiones perpetuae* in 82/81 B.C. As a rule, any given permanent criminal court was established by the vote (a *lex*) of one of the citizen assemblies. We know of at least one pre-Sullan *quaestio perpetua* that was formed as a result of the *lex repetundarum* (law concerning extortion) of the *tabula Bembina* (formerly referred to as the *lex Acilia*—perhaps from about 120 B.C.). The courts that Sulla established tried cases dealing with a variety of topics such as homicide, forgery, counterfeiting, assault, treason, extortion, and embezzlement. Other permanent criminal courts followed during the next thirty years.[22] Augustus created the last of the permanent criminal courts. Augustus' *quaestiones perpetuae* dealt with matters such as election practices, adultery, violence (*vis*), and treason. Sulla saw to it that, in addition to the Urban Praetor and Praetor Peregrinus, other, additional praetors managed the business of the various *quaestiones perpetuae*. Occasionally a former aedile served as a *iudex quaestionis* in the absence of a praetor.

[2] EVOLUTION OF THE COURTS AND CRIMINAL JURISDICTION

Although a number of *quaestiones perpetuae* continued to operate until the mid-2nd century A.D., they ceased to have their former, Republican sig-

---

21. *See infra* §§ 12.05, 12.06.
22. *See* ROBINSON, CRIMINAL LAW 3.

nificance. In their place, courts convened by the Urban Prefect took precedence. The *quaestiones perpetuae* did not perish wholesale. Indeed, many functioned, and in fact, thrived for at least the first hundred years of the Empire. The Urban Prefect had broad-sweeping jurisdiction in criminal cases. The emperor and the senate also exercised a degree of criminal jurisdiction.

In the 1st century A.D., the senate itself acted as a court for public crimes of the sort that the *quaestiones perpetuae* had heard during the Republic. By and large, the senate only heard cases involving non-political charges when the cases themselves involved either a senator or a senator's family. In the early Empire, the senate took over the legislative functions that had previously belonged to the citizen assemblies. The emperors also wielded a fair degree of personal power in criminal matters. At some point, it appears that the emperor had to approve all death sentences. And, until Hadrian put a stop to it, emperors had the power to put an end to trials and to reverse the senate's verdict. The emperor even conducted some trials on his own. But it is nearly certain that jurists who acted as his advisers actually wrote the emperor's *decreta* (judicial decisions) and rescripts (written responses to legal questions).

The Urban Prefect initially controlled criminal jurisdiction within the city of Rome proper. By 200 A.D., his jurisdiction extended outward from Rome to a radius of 100 miles. Other prefects also acquired criminal jurisdiction during the Empire. The Prefect of the Night Watch, the Prefect of the Grain Supply, and the Praetorian Prefects all supervised criminal cases that pertained to their respective subject matter. Although we are not completely certain, it seems likely that the *tresviri capitales* of the Republic and the Urban Prefect or Prefect of the Night Watch during the Empire would have been in charge of criminal law as it related to foreigners in Rome. In the late Empire (*i.e.*, the Dominate—the Empire after 284 A.D.), the senate ceased to function as a standard court. Instead the Urban Prefect presided over a court of five senators (*iudicium quinquevirale*) to hear capital cases in which a senator had been charged. There was no general right of appeal from a decision of the Praetorian Prefect. In addition, other bureaucratic imperial officials were given jurisdiction over criminal courts at various levels in Rome and the provinces.

[B] JURIES & JURORS

The earliest jurors in the permanent criminal courts were senators. For a time, after changes wrought by Gaius Gracchus (122 B.C.), equestrians took the place of the senators. Sulla gave the juries back to the senators. The *lex Aurelia* (70 B.C.) established the system that, with minor adjustments, prevailed for the balance of time during which the *quaestiones perpetuae* operated. The scheme of the *lex Aurelia* took prospective jurors from three groups: 1) senators; 2) equestrians; and, 3) *tribuni aerarii* (*i.e.*, probably the citizens whose census wealth was just below that of the equestrians). In order to be eligible, a prospective juror had to reside either in the vicinity of Rome or in Rome itself. In addition, jurors had to be between the ages of 30 and 60. Originally, each law that established a court also established the size of its jury. We know of at least one jury that had 32 jurors in a criminal trial in 74 B.C. After the *lex Aurelia*, most criminal juries appear to have been comprised of 75 jurors—25 senators, 25 Equestrians, and 25 *tribuni aerarii*.

[C] CRIMINAL PROCEDURE & AFFIRMATIVE DEFENSES

Ordinarily, any male citizen could initiate proceedings upon application to the president of the court. The prosecutor swore an oath that his prosecution was in good faith. Roman law considered it a criminal offense for an accuser to bring false charges (*calumnia*), to hide legitimate charges (*praevaricatio*), or to abandon charges once formally begun (*tergiversatio*). The legal institution of the prosecution began with the *nominis delatio* (*i.e.*, a kind of initial hearing, or arraignment). The person who was being accused was required to attend the *nominis delatio*. The court president then wrote down an *inscriptio* for the prosecutor to sign. After signing the *inscriptio*, the prosecutor could not turn back without facing severe penalties himself. Thereafter, the prosecutor had a reasonable period of time (a minimum of 10 days) within which to ready his case for trial.

At trial, the prosecutor made a lengthy introductory statement in which he explained the charges against the defendant (or in some cases several speakers were involved). Next, the defendant—or usually an advocate (or advocates) speaking on his behalf—responded to the charges. Thereafter, each side, beginning with the prosecution, presented its evidence. Evidence could be in the form of oral or prepared written testimony by witnesses or documents.[23] It is clear that jurors in Republican courts considered the oral testimony of witnesses as the most reliable evidence. In particular *laudatores*, character witnesses, were often pivotal. In addition to giving direct testimony, witnesses were also cross-examined by the opposing side.

The jurors voted by secret ballot using wax-covered tablets. Each juror had a two-sided wax tablet. One side of the tablet was inscribed with the

---

23. *See infra* § 11.05.

letter "A" for *absolvo* (*i.e.,* acquittal) and the other was inscribed with the letter "C" for *condemno* (*i.e.,* conviction). In order to convict, a prosecutor needed a simple majority of the jury's votes. But even a 50–50 deadlock yielded an acquittal for the defendant. If convicted, a defendant was sentenced either automatically by the terms of the relevant statute itself or by the jury in cases where the statute did not provide a compulsory penalty. The most common penalties were fines, banishment (*interdictio aquae et ignis*—denial of water and fire), death, infamy, and forced labor.

Before Augustus, there were, apparently, no statutes of limitations for crimes. As part of his legislation on *quaestiones perpetuae*, Augustus did introduce a statute of limitations of five years for adultery and *peculatus* (embezzlement).[24] About 300 A.D., a twenty-year statute of limitations was imposed for the crime of *falsum* (forgery).[25] Otherwise, there appear to have been few, if any, statutes of limitations for other crimes.

Roman law recognized a number of viable affirmative defenses. For example, self defense could justify homicide. Similarly, a man who killed someone engaged in sexually assaulting a family member had a complete defense. In the appropriate circumstances, duress could also furnish an affirmative defense to conduct that otherwise would have been criminal. The "heat of passion" could function as a defense for a man who killed his wife when she was caught in *flagrante delicto* in adultery. However, Roman law treated "heat of passion" in these circumstances not as an affirmative defense *per se* but rather as a mitigating factor that could reduce his punishment.

§ 11.05 EVIDENCE

"To the Roman lawyer evidence, as a separate division of the law, was unknown.... [T]he Roman law of evidence is scattered throughout Code, Digest, and Novellae."[26] Roman law did not have rules regarding admissibility of evidence. Advocates could introduce nearly any kind of evidence, including what modern law characterizes as hearsay. Quintillian recognized a distinction between oral *versus* documentary evidence. Public documents, for example, were afforded great evidentiary weight. Private documents

---

24. For more on adultery, *see infra* § 12.05[E][1], on *peculatus, see infra* § 12.05[G][3].

25. *See infra* § 12.05[G][5].

26. Carr Ferguson, *A Day in Court in Justinian's Rome: Some Problems of Evidence, Proof, and Justice in Roman Law,* 46 Iowa L. Rev. 732, 740 (1961).

(*e.g.*, letters) were considered equal in evidentiary value to oral testimony. There was a preference for original documents (as the "best evidence").

Quintillian noted a difference between what he called "artificial" and "inartificial" evidence. This latter distinction is roughly analogous to what modern law identifies as the difference between circumstantial evidence (*e.g.*, the discovery of footprints in the snow) and direct evidence (*e.g.*, the direct testimony of an eyewitness who testifies that he saw an individual walking in the snow). In certain circumstances, Roman law gave evidentiary weight to various oaths taken by parties. Statements that a party made that contradicted his own interests and outright admissions by a party were given added evidentiary weight.

Originally the direct testimony of witnesses provided the most important evidence in Roman law courts. It was not until late in the Empire (*i.e.*, perhaps late in the 4th century A.D.) that documentary evidence came to be regarded as more reliable than a witness's testimony. Justinian's corpus reveals a clear distrust towards witnesses and a marked preference for evidence established by documents. As a rule, a lone witness's testimony was insufficient to prove a fact. Some form of corroboration was needed to supplement a single individual's statements. The number of witnesses, also, could be crucial. For example, in order to validate a gift, a contract of *depositum* (gratuitous loan for safekeeping) or *mutuum* (loan of fungibles),[27] prove adultery, or legitimize a child, it was necessary to have three witnesses. One needed five witnesses to validate the contract of *mancipatio* (transfer of *res mancipi*—*e.g.*, Italic land, slaves, cattle, horses, mules, donkeys, and the four praedial servitudes),[28] an amendment to a will, or the manumission of a slave. Both a divorce and a will needed seven.

Certain persons were not permitted to serve as a trial witness. For example, a party, himself, could not testify. For obvious reasons of conflict of interest, husbands and wives, parents and children, and patrons and freedmen could not testify in matters concerning one another. In order to testify in a civil trial, a witness had to have reached puberty, for a criminal trial, he had to be at least twenty years old. Slaves could only testify under torture. Occasionally, Roman courts relied on expert witnesses. For example, handwriting experts could detect forgeries, surveyors could assist in boundary disputes, and doctors could offer testimony relating to illnesses or death. It is a matter of some interest that Roman jurists frequently remarked that men of higher wealth and rank were to be regarded as more trustworthy witnesses than the poor and those of lesser rank. Roman law provided a

---

27. See *infra* § 12.07[D].
28. See *infra* § 12.02[D][1].

certain measure of flexibility for the sake of convenience: it permitted a witness who lived a distance from the situs of a civil trial to give his testimony in writing (*i.e.*, such as by an affidavit or deposition). Thus, he was not forced to travel a great distance to testify. For a criminal case, however, he had to appear personally. Perjury was a serious offense. Depending on the circumstances, a witness who lied in court could be put to death, or receive a number of lesser punishments.

§ 11.06 CHAPTER SUMMARY

In the beginning stages of formal law in Rome, a litigant had to have and use a pre-established form of action in order to obtain legal redress. In addition to the Twelve Tables, the advice of the senate (*senatus consulta*) and laws passed by the people (*leges*) comprised the backbone of early legislation. A number of statutes have a *praescriptio* (a general comment concerning the wrong) and a *sanctio* (the negative consequences that resulted from a person's violation of the *praescriptio*). Originally, the citizens gathered into an assembly (*comitia*) to enact legislation. The *comitia centuriata, comitia tributa*, and *comitia curiata* were the three principal assemblies responsible for legislation in the very early Republic. After the *lex Hortensia* (287 B.C.), the *concilium plebis* (under the direction of the tribunes of the plebs) was legally empowered to pass binding laws. The censors selected senators (who served for life). During the Republic (509–27 B.C.), the senate first debated legislation and then presented it to one of the assemblies where it could be enacted into law. During the Empire (27 B.C.–mid-5th century A.D.), the senate itself made law, primarily by means of *senatus consulta*. Among the most significant Republican laws passed were the following: 1) *lex Canuleia* (445 B.C.—plebeian right of intermarriage); 2) the Licinian-Sextian law (367 B.C.—one consul must be plebeian); 3) *Lex Aquilia* (287 B.C.—rules regarding property damage); 4) *lex Hortensia* (287 B.C.—made plebiscites binding); and, 5) *lex Aebutia* (2nd century B.C.—laws governing procedure).

The traditional chronological phases of Roman legal procedure are: 1) Pre-Classical (*Legis Actiones*); 2) Formulary (*Per Formulam*); and, 3) Extraordinary (*Cognitio*). In the Pre-Classical period, the praetor, during a procedure called *in iure*, assessed the dispute brought before him and initially determined whether the plaintiff's suit had any merit. If he decided that it did, he then sent the matter forward to a judge for a decision (*apud iudicem*). In the Formulary system, the praetor took on a more significant role. He evaluated the parties' claims and defenses, and then wrote a formula—a summary of the facts and a statement of the applicable laws—

which the judge had to follow when deciding the case. Ordinarily, a praetor's formula consisted of three parts: 1) *iudicis nominatio* (naming of a judge); 2) *intentio* (a statement of the plaintiff's claim); and, 3) *condemnatio* (an explanation of how the judge was to apply the facts to the law). In the Extraordinary Procedure of the Empire, an imperial bureaucrat alone performed the roles that had hitherto been executed separately by the praetor and the judge. In essence, the bureaucrat conducted both the *in iure* and *apud iudicem* functions in the same procedure (presumably in an effort to achieve greater efficiency of process).

The first criminal courts—such as those designed to address extortion by provincial officials—were established in the middle of the 2nd century B.C. Sulla devised a system of permanent criminal courts (*quaestiones perpetuae*) to adjudicate cases involving various matters, and Augustus also was responsible for creating additional permanent criminal tribunals. During the Empire, the courts administered by the Urban Prefect gradually replaced the *quaestiones perpetuae*. The senate and the emperor, probably relying on the advice of jurists, decided a number of criminal cases. The role of the Urban Prefect and other prefects evolved during the Empire. Eventually, the various prefects oversaw the lion's share of all Imperial criminal cases. Although originally only senators were eligible to serve on criminal juries, after the *lex Aurelia* (70 B.C.) criminal juries usually had seventy-five jurors (each between the ages of thirty and sixty): twenty-five senators; twenty-five equestrians; and, twenty-five persons from the class just below the equestrians.

Any male citizen could initiate a criminal prosecution; beginning the process with an arraignment (*nominis delatio*) before the president of the court. After opening arguments by the prosecutor, first, and next, an advocate on behalf of the accused, each side presented evidence. Jurors in criminal trials voted secretly, using wax tablets. A simple majority was all that was necessary to convict. Even though Augustus implemented some statutes of limitations, as a rule there were few. Self defense, defense of a third party, duress, and, to a lesser extent, "heat of passion" operated as valid defenses for certain crimes (especially homicide).

Roman courts produced very little regarding the law of evidence. Although Quintillian did note both the distinction between oral *versus* documentary evidence as well as the difference between circumstantial and direct evidence, advocates generally introduced nearly anything that they wished (including hearsay) in attempting to sway a jury. As the law matured, judges gradually placed greater trust in documents than in the testimony of witnesses. In time, certain types of proof required a specific number of witnesses in order to be considered competent. Due to a presumption of bias, parties themselves, their relatives, and patrons and freedmen were not allowed to testify. Ordinarily witnesses had to be of a certain minimum age, and expert witnesses occasionally gave their professional opinions at trial.

CHAPTER 12

Substantive Law

§ 12.01 PERSONAL STATUS

[A] INTRODUCTION

In ancient Rome, only persons who had "legal capacity" could be rights-holders and obligors (*i.e.*, those capable of having legal rights and duties). The notion of "legal capacity" was known as *caput* (literally "head"). According to the Roman jurist Paul, there were three kinds of status which determined legal capacity: 1) *civitas* (citizenship); 2) *libertas* (freedom); and, 3) *familia* (family).[29] At its most elementary level, the scope of rights and duties of any individual depended on whether he was a citizen or a foreigner, free or slave, and the head of his family or a subordinate.

[B] CITIZENSHIP

[1] GENERAL

In many respects, citizenship (*status civitatis*) was the most empowered legal capacity. Those who were born as Roman citizens had three very important legal rights: 1) *ius honorum* (the right to hold governmental office); 2) *ius connubium* (the right to marry another citizen); and, 3) *ius commercium* (the right to participate in commercial and property transactions). In early law, these three rights were strictly observed as the province of Roman citizens only. Foreigners (*peregrini*) were required to secure a citizen, as patron, in order to transact business. Eventually the law evolved, primarily for two reasons. First, economic relationships with foreigners rose to such a level that legal capacity for foreigners to contract was needed for foreign

---

29. In § 12.01 I discuss *civitas* and *libertas*. The discussion of *familia* appears *infra* in § 12.03.

trade. Thus, in the Classical period of Roman law, foreigners received *ius commercium* with certain restrictions. But foreigners received neither *ius connubium* nor *ius honorum*. Second, because the Roman Empire expanded to such a broad geographic extent, in order to function effectively as a state, Rome needed to have more citizens than non-citizens. In the early Republic, the Latins and Junian Latins received varying degrees of citizenship. During the first two centuries of the Empire, army veterans often received Roman citizenship. This altered the nature of Roman citizenship. Then in 212 A.D., the Emperor Caracalla granted Roman citizenship to nearly all of the free persons in the vast Roman empire. Eventually all adult male inhabitants of the Empire were declared citizens. Hence, the adult men within the boundaries of the Empire received all three rights of citizens.

There is yet another interesting aspect of the Roman law of legal capacity that should be noted. One way that jurisprudence classifies legal capacity is as two distinct types: 1) "legal capacity"; and, 2) "dispositive capacity." "Legal capacity" is the capacity which arises at birth. It is, in essence, a passive capacity that entitles a person to have certain rights and duties. On the other hand, "dispositive capacity" is the capacity which allows an individual independently to acquire and exercise rights and duties (*i.e.*, not merely arising at birth, but rather as an active pursuit). Law ordinarily requires that a person attain a certain age (*e.g.*, eighteen) and be of sound mind in order to acquire dispositive capacity. Although Roman law did not employ the terminology of "legal" and "dispositive" capacity *per se*, the Roman concept of *caput* actually included both types. Consider legal regulations concerning children. There is a clear distinction between adults and minors. Roman adults could exercise all rights and perform all duties but minors could not. For example, under Roman law, children under the age of seven could exercise no commercial rights and had no commercial duties; all of their transactions were invalid. Parents or guardians executed all contracts for children under the age of seven. When a child was between seven and fourteen (for boys) or seven and twelve (for girls), s/he could enter into transactions and contracts. But these could only be transactions or contracts that were favorable to the child (*e.g.*, a child of this age could receive gifts). At age fourteen (for boys) and twelve (for girls) Romans were no longer considered children but adults, and thus could fully execute all commercial transactions and contracts.[30] Thus, by birth a Roman child may

---

30. There were certain exceptions. For example, ordinarily, a person had to be at least twenty-five years old to sell or buy a slave. Or an adult under twenty-five could do so with the consent of his curator (*i.e.*, a person who acted as a guardian for an adult—*see infra* §12.03[E]).

have received the legal capacity of a citizen but he could not exercise many of his citizenship rights (or perform many of his citizenship duties—such as military service) until he had acquired dispositive legal capacity through the process of aging and attaining or retaining a sound mind. In Roman law, the insane had no dispositive capacity. Insane persons always had a guardian of some sort, and only their guardians could execute contracts for them. Roman Law did, however, permit a person who was *lucidiae intervalis* (*i.e.,* someone who had periods of mental clarity) to have dispositive capacity during his periods of lucidity.

[2] CAPITIS DEMINUTIO

The legal capacity (*caput*) of Roman citizens could, however, be restricted for a number of reasons. If events warranted it, Roman Law could reduce (or diminish) a person's legal capacity. This reduction in status was called *capitis deminutio*. It could occur on three levels: 1) *maxima*; 2) *media*; and 3) *minima*. *Maxima capitis deminutio* resulted from loss of freedom (becoming a slave). This entailed losing one's freedom and all other status. Fundamentally, one could receive *maxima capitis deminutio* in three ways. First, an individual might become a captive of a foreign war. Second, some criminal punishments resulted in *maxima capitis deminutio*. For example, some punishments for crimes required that a person go into exile "across the Tiber River" (*trans Tiberim*) and others dictated that a convicted criminal be sold as a slave to a foreigner. Lastly, a free woman who had sex with a slave could also receive *maxima capitis deminutio* by being sold as a slave *trans Tiberim*. A Roman citizen who suffered *media capitis deminutio* lost only some of his rights as a citizen. Ordinarily, such a person lost his *ius honorum* (the right to hold political office) and *ius connubium* (the right of marriage) but retained his *ius commercium* (the right to enter into business transactions). Thus, a person who suffered *media capitis deminutio* acquired essentially the legal status of a foreigner. Generally, *media capitis deminutio* resulted from criminal punishment where the individual was exiled but not sold into slavery (for example he might be forced to move to a colony). The term *minima capitis deminutio* refers to a reduction in status with respect to family. Specifically, the expression is only used when a person who had previously been a *persona sui iuris* (person of his own right) became a *persona alieni iuris* (person of another's right).[31] For example, a man could experience *minima capitis deminutio* as a result of

---

31. *See infra* § 12.03[A].

adoption. A woman could experience it by marriage *cum manu*.[32] To explain further, suppose that a husband and wife were married and had no sons. If the husband then died, the widow would have become a woman *sui iuris*. Then upon remarriage *cum manu*, she would undergo *minima capitis deminutio*. This reduction in legal capacity entailed important legal consequences. For example, all personal property immediately became the property of the new *paterfamilias*, and indeed, all other legal consequences of being a *persona alieni iuris* arose.[33] Nevertheless even a person who had endured *minima capitis diminutio* still retained his *libertas, civitas, ius honorum, ius connubium,* and *ius commercium* — all, of course, within the limits of subordination to his *paterfamilias*.

[C] SLAVES AND FREEDMEN

The most important distinction in terms of legal capacity was that between freedom and slavery. In essence, the Roman jurists said *"servi res sunt"* ("slaves are things"). Slaves were considered means of production, not persons themselves. Legally speaking, however, slaves had attributes of both property as well as attributes of human beings. When a slave made something, it belonged to his master. Slaves were, in essence, *res mancipi*.[34] Slaves did not have legal standing either to sue or be sued. In the Republic (509–27 B.C.), masters had free reign to treat their slaves however they wished. In the Empire (27 B.C.–mid-5th century A.D.), certain laws restrained a master's unmitigated command. In particular, the Emperor Hadrian (117–138 A.D.) prohibited a slave owner from killing a slave unless a magistrate first approved the execution.[35] By the time of Constantine (272–337 A.D.), the State could prosecute a master for murder if his inhumane discipline caused his slave's death. By the time of the Emperor Justinian (527–565 A.D.), a Roman master was only permitted to exact punishment on his slaves that was regarded as "reasonable."

There were three principal ways that someone could become a slave. One could become a slave as a result of: 1) being a prisoner of war; 2) birth;[36] or, 3) debt. In addition, there were certain crimes that could be

---

32. *See infra* § 12.03[B][2].

33. *See infra* § 12.03[A].

34 *See infra* §§ 12.02[A], 12.02[D][1].

35. *See* WATSON, ROMAN LAW & COMPARATIVE LAW 40.

36. *See Id.* at 39 (1991) (Watson explains that a child born to a slave woman could legally be considered free (*i.e.*, not slave) if the mother had been free at any point between the child's conception and his birth.).

punished by enslavement. The Twelve Tables declared that a thief who was caught red-handed could be punished by enslavement. Moreover, if a person tried to dodge the census (*i.e.*, trying to escape military duty), he too could be punished with enslavement. Furthermore, the *senatus consultum Claudianum* (52 A.D.) provided that a freewoman who lived with another's male slave (without the slave owner's permission) automatically became a slave to that owner. Any children born of that union also became his slaves. If an individual was a slave because of any of these reasons, his *caput* was non-free. Interestingly, if a Roman citizen became a prisoner of war in a foreign country, but subsequently was freed, the praetors developed an institution—known as *postliminium* (literally "beyond the threshold")—whereby that Roman was deemed to be free, not a slave. In fact, Roman law considered that such a man had *never* been a slave.

Originally, Roman law treated all offspring of a female slave as slaves themselves, even if their father had been a free man. This was true if the mother had been a slave even temporarily while she was pregnant. Eventually the rule was turned on its head. If the mother had been free even temporarily, the child was considered free. By an interesting twist of legal logic, the children of slaves were not technically considered "fruits" of the slave. This did not mean that a slave's child was not a slave—she certainly was. It simply meant that when a third party had the use of a slave and the slave's fruits (for example by contract), if the slave gave birth during that time, the child became the property of the owner of the slave-mother, not the usufructary.[37]

Because many slaves served in responsible positions (such as herding sheep or captaining a ship), there had to be some legal way for such slaves to execute valid contracts. To a limited extent, a slave could act on behalf of his master as an agent would. But the analogy to principal and agent is imperfect in many respects. Thus, a distinction was drawn between a "legal obligation" and a "natural obligation." An *obligatio naturalis* created a relationship similar to the type of obligation in modern American law where an adult contracts with a minor. An adult cannot enforce a contract against a minor but a minor can enforce it against an adult if he so desires. Similarly, after the statute of limitations has run on a cause of action, there may still exist an *obligatio naturalis*, even though there is no legal obligation due to the statute of limitations. For example, American law recognizes a natural obligation in the case of a debtor who pays his creditor after the statute of limitations has run: the law will not force the creditor to return the payment to the debtor. Roman law used this same concept of natural obliga-

---

37. See *infra* § 12.02[E] regarding the concepts *usus* and *usus fructus*.

tion to permit slaves to enter into binding contracts. This gave slaves a semblance of quasi-legal capacity (not an *obligatio stricti iuris* but an *obligatio naturalis*).

Another legal problem relating to slaves was their relationship to torts (*i.e.,* injuries to persons or property).[38] For example, when a slave caused damage, who was responsible? Technically, a slave could not be responsible for damage that he caused because he had no legal capacity (*caput*). Thus, as a rule, a slave's owner was responsible for (*i.e.,* vicariously liable for) damage caused by his slave. But this liablity was only limited liability up to the value of the slave. Once the amount of liability rose to or above the value of the slave, himself, the master could choose simply to give the slave as compensation instead of paying money. The basic rule is that of *respondeat superior*. The Romans also used the term *culpa in custodiendo* (guilty in supervising). A master could escape liability in such situations only if he could prove that he had done virtually everything in his power to prevent his slave's damage.

Another institution peculiar to the Roman law relating to slaves—and, in fact, pertinent to their tort liability—is the *peculium*. The *peculium* was a stipend of money or property that a master customarily gave to his slave for the slave's use. It legally belonged to the owner. As a rule, however, a slave owner—and everyone else—dealt with the *peculium* as if it belonged to the slave. Technically speaking, a slave was only allowed to use the *peculium* in accordance with the wishes of his owner. The legal significance of the notion of *peculium* is actually rather subtle. When a master transferred property to his slave as *peculium*, the master was only liable for the slave's actions (*i.e.,* actions relating to the *peculium*) to the extent of the *peculium*. The same general concept operates today in the notion of limited liability in modern corporations law. When an individual buys stock in a company, if the company causes damage or goes bankrupt, the stockholder can only be liable up to the amount of his investment.

Another group with special legal rules was the *libertini*, freedmen (*i.e.,* slaves who had been manumitted or freed in an appropriate manner). During the Republic, there were three legally recognized methods of freeing a slave: 1) manumission by will (very common in the late Republic); 2) *manumissio censu* (a master allowed his slave to enroll in the census); and, 3) *manumissio vindicata* (This was accomplished by collusion whereby a third party—ordinarily a friend of the master—brought a legal action against the master and falsely alleged that the slave was, in fact, free. The owner, playing his part in the collusion, simply failed to contest the suit

---

38. For more about the Roman law of torts, *see infra* § 12.06.

and the slave became free thereby.). Using an interesting bit of legal fiction (since technically slaves could not enter into binding agreements) a master could agree to free his slave in exchange for the slave's promise to work a specified number of days every year (*operae*) for the master. The only limitation on this type of agreement was that the amount of days could not be unreasonable.

In addition to manumission by will, *manumissio censu*, and *manumissio vindicata*, in time, other less formal methods of manumission came to be accepted as a matter of custom. For example, a master could free a slave by means of a letter or by a declaration in the presence of friends (as witnesses). These methods of manumission, although not technically considered legal, were recognized by praetors as a practical matter. Augustus enacted legislation—the *lex Fufia Caninia* (2 B.C.)—to limit the number of slaves that any one owner was permitted to manumit. The *lex Aelia Sentia* (4 A.D.) invalidated manumission in circumstances where the slave owner was under the age of twenty. This same law provided that if the manumitted slave was not yet thirty, he was not considered a Roman citizen. In addition, the law invalidated a slave's manumission if it had been done in an attempt to defraud the master's creditors.

Manumitted slaves acquired both freedom and partial Roman citizenship. They became clients of their former masters and the former masters became their patrons. A freedman (*libertinus*) could never be truly equal to a person who was free by birth in the eyes of Roman law. Once freed, the freedman and the patron each owed the other certain duties. As former slaves, freedmen—at least up to the time of Justinian—were expected to do some work *gratis* for their former owners. A freedman could obtain neither *ius honorum* nor *ius connubium*. However, he did obtain *ius commercium* as a result of gaining his freedom. Still, this was a somewhat restricted *ius commercium*, since he was unable to make a valid will. In some respects, then, the *libertini* lived as free people but died as slaves (*vivunt liberi moriuntur servi*). At death, a freedman's property went to his former owner. Finally, in the 6th century A.D., Justinian gave freedmen full Roman citizenship upon manumission.

§ 12.02 PROPERTY

[A] INTRODUCTION: THE MOST SIGNIFICANT CATEGORIES

One of the most striking things that one notices when first studying the Roman law of property (*i.e., res*, "things") is the incredible degree of classification. Roman jurists categorized property *ad nauseam*. We will examine the most significant categories of property first. Gaius divided property into two parts: 1) *res divini iuris* (things under divine law); and, 2) *res humani iuris* (things under human law). Roman law further subdivided things under divine law (which, incidentally, were incapable of human ownership) into *res sacrae* and *res religiosae*. The former were things such as temples that the Roman people had consecrated for the celestial gods. The latter were things such as graves that were dedicated to the gods of the netherworld. There was also a third branch of *res divini iuris* known as *res sanctae*, such as a city's walls and gates.

Roman jurists subdivided things under human law into two categories: 1) *res publicae* (public things); and, 2) *res privatae* (private things). *Res publicae* could not be owned by any one individual. Examples are roads, harbors, and rivers—all of which, of necessity, had to be accessible for all to use. A similar category was *res communes*. These were also things that could not really be owned, such as the air, the seas, and flowing water.

Gaius also classified property as either corporeal (*res corporalis*) or incorporeal (*res incorporalis*) (*i.e.,* tangible and intangible). Most civil law countries did not keep this ancient distinction, but the Common Law countries (*e.g.,* England) did borrow it from Roman Law. The principal import of this differentiation was that only tangible property could be— legally speaking—transferred by the method known as *traditio* (the most common method of property transfer).[39] This was because *traditio* required a physical conveyance in order to be valid. With intangible property (*res incorporalis*), a different mode of legal transfer had to be used (usually *in iure cessio*).[40]

In addition, Gaius classified property as *res mancipi* and *res nec mancipi*. Property which was classified as *res mancipi* could only be sold by the method called *mancipatio*.[41] *Mancipatio* involved a very specific, formal, and formulaic method of transfer. It is often said that the things that were *res mancipi* were things that were essential for a rustic agricultural subsistence. Examples commonly given of *res mancipi* are slaves, oxen, horses, donkeys, real property, and the four praedial servitudes (*iter, actus, via,* and *aquaeductus*).[42] For example, to sell a slave by *mancipatio* the following had to be present: five witnesses; a person to hold a scale (*libripens*); the owner of the

---

39. *See infra* § 12.02[D][2].
40. For more about *in iure cessio, see infra* § 12.02[D][3].
41. *See infra* § 12.02[D][1].
42. *See infra* § 12.02[E].

slave; the buyer; and, the slave. The purchaser placed precious metal—often copper—(later a coin) on the scale and one hand on the slave's shoulder, and said "I declare that this is my slave." Simply stated, in order to validly transfer ownership of things that were *res mancipi*, one had to use the formulaic method of transfer known as *mancipatio*.[43] One could transfer things that were *res nec mancipi* using less formal methods such as *traditio*[44] and *in iure cessio*.[45]

Eventually, as Roman society increased in complexity and size, *mancipatio* fell into disuse. In the late Empire the differentiation between those things that were *res mancipi* and those that were not vanished. Justinian officially eradicated the distinction. Nevertheless, some of the formulaic vocabulary of *mancipatio* continued to be used although the procedure itself was not. According to Justinian, however, mere delivery was not sufficient to legally transfer ownership of a *res* unless the buyer first either paid the price or gave security for it.

[B] ADDITIONAL CATEGORIES

Roman jurists separated property into many, many other classifications. Some additional categories of Roman property (all of which are still used in some fashion in modern legal systems) are the following.

1) *Res in commercio* as opposed to *res extra commercio*. *Res in commercio* were those things in economic circulation. Anyone was able to buy and sell these types of things. *Res extra commercio*, on the other hand, were things excluded from economic circulation. The majority of things were *in commercio*. Of the very few things that were considered *extra commercio*, the most common was probably the *ager publicus*, the land owned by the Roman State which could not be bought or sold.[46]

2) *Res mobiles* as opposed to *res immobiles*. *Res mobiles* were all things in Rome except land. All else, at least theoretically, could be moved. Thus only land, the most valuable type of property in ancient Rome, was considered a *res immobilis*. In nearly every country where plots of land can be sold today, the legal system classifies land as *immobilis*, and thus, as such, the sale and purchase of land must follow a specific form (*e.g.,* the transaction must be registered and/or recorded with the local government). As a general rule,

---

43. For more on *mancipatio, see infra* § 12.02[D][1].
44. *See infra* § 12.02[D][2].
45. *See infra* § 12.02[D][3].
46. This is not too dissimilar to the public squares, parks, or commons in many modern cities today (*e.g.,* the Boston Common).

only the registered landowner can be considered the rightful owner of such real property. A party who buys from a registered owner is considered a bona fide purchaser, and thus gains title to the land. These registration systems for land and the related rules about the sale of land which have evolved from this Roman distinction (*res mobliles/res immobiles*) constitute the principal significance of this distinction in the modern world.

3) *Species* as opposed to *genera*. *Species* were specific things with certain unique peculiarities that made it possible to distinguish them from other things (*i.e.,* things which could be identified by sight or appearance). Legally, *species* could not, for example in a contract, be replaced by another similar thing. If a *species* was destroyed, the contract to sell it immediately became unenforceable due to impossibility. *Genera*, on the contrary, were fungible items which did not have peculiarities that distinguished them from other like or similar items. Therefore, *genera* were considered replaceable. Hence, even if the object of a sales contract were destroyed, the contract was still enforceable if the object of the contract was an item classified as *genera*. The applicable Latin maxim was *genera perire non consentur* (*genera* are not considered to perish). The distinction between *species* and *genera* is roughly the same distinction that exists between non-fungible (*i.e.,* unique) and fungible goods in many modern legal systems today.

4) *Res quae usu consumatum* (things which are consumed by use) as opposed to *res quae usu non consumatum* (things which are not consumed by use). *Res quae usu consumatum* are those things which, in the process of their use, are consumed (even if the consumption is little by little). Food, for example is a *res quae usu consumatum*. *Res quae usu non consumatum*, however, are those things which are not consumed by use, but instead remain intact (*e.g.,* an ox). They retain their uniformity. One may well wonder why this distinction is significant. In Roman law, it was considered impossible to lease or rent consumables (*i.e., res quae usu consumatum*). This is so, because, by definition, a lessee is required to return the property that he leases. Thus, leases can only occur with *res quae usu non consumatum*.

5) *Divisible things* as opposed to *non-divisible things*. This distinction was a purely legal distinction, not a physical one.[47] For example, grain is divisible because it retains its peculiar identity even if individual granules are physically separated from one another. On the other hand, a chair is non-divisible because, if it is physically split into parts, it loses its identity as a chair. In other words, a thing was deemed non-divisible if, when broken, it

---

47. Unlike the case of *res mobiles* and *res immobiles* where the distinction is physical.

was no longer what it started out as. Clearly, that type of thing—in order to retain its integrity—should never have been divided in the first place.

[C] LEGAL TITLES CONNECTED WITH THINGS

A person is legally entitled to keep property because of some type of legal "title" to that thing. Different titles entail different legal consequences. The three most important types of legal title defined by Roman jurists are: 1) *dominium*; 2) *possessio*; and, 3) *detentio*.[48]

Dominium was basically what we today call "ownership." This type of title differs distinctly from all others. The Romans described it as yielding *plena in re potestas* (complete power with respect to the thing). One who had *dominium* of an object (its "owner") had unlimited power over the thing within the bounds of the law.

Possessio (possession) was a very complicated concept. When an ancient Roman had *possessio*, he kept a thing at his disposal; though not necessarily "physically." In order to have *possessio* of a thing, a person had to have it available for his control. There were two principal features of *possessio*: 1) a person kept a thing; though not necessarily physically; and, 2) not only did the person keep the thing, but he kept it *as his own thing*. Possession could be accomplished personally or through an agent. Interestingly, a tenant in a Roman lease was not considered to possess the property. Instead, the landlord was deemed to have *possessio* through the tenant.

At this point, it may be helpful to consider the legal difference between *dominium* and *possessio*. In basic terms, when a person who has *dominium* keeps a thing, he keeps it because he *really* owns it (with complete, unfettered power over it). However, when a person keeps something *merely thinking* that he owns it—but in reality he does not—he has mere *possessio*. When a person has *possessio*, he is entitled to the legal presumption that he, the possessor, is the owner unless proven otherwise. Thus, a possessor is considered the owner of a thing, unless someone else succeeds in proving that he is not.[49] The same presumption exists in most legal systems today. This presumption is important for people who are the genuine owners of things, because it puts the burden of proof on a non-possessing claimant.

---

48. Of course these three did not exhaust all possible titles (*e.g.*, abstract title—which may be broad enough to include nearly all others).

49. This distinction between *proprietas dominium* and *possessio* is significant also for the concept of *usucapio* (adverse possession or "usucaption"). Third parties must be capable of dealing with an adverse possessor just as if he were the true owner. *See infra* § 12.02[D][7].

Of course, in some cases a true owner will use self-help to "steal" back an item which another person has somehow obtained (as a possessor). Thus the unjust possessor, in order to get the item back (short of stealing it back yet again) would have the burden of proof of his ownership in court. This would, no doubt, be a difficult task if the true owner can produce—which he probably could—witnesses who could testify as to his rightful ownership (*dominium*) of the item in question.

Detentio (detention) is a type of title that occurs when a person keeps a thing; but he is not the owner and, in fact, he does not think or even contend that he is the owner. Instead, an individual with *detentio* simply maintains that he has a legal right (of some sort) to possess the thing. Our modern concept of bailment is quite the same as *detentio*. A person keeps another's property but does not claim or imagine ownership. Unlike *possessio*, *detentio* can never ripen into ownership through adverse possession. As far as Roman law is concerned, all property disputes required an analysis of the type of title involved: whether the claimants had *dominium*, *possessio*, or *detentio*.

[D] METHODS OF ACQUISITION OF PROPERTY

[1] MANCIPATIO

In Roman law, a person could acquire the right of ownership (*dominium*) in a number of ways. For example, a purchase and an inheritance are two rather obvious means of gaining ownership of things. But many ways existed, and some of them still exist in modern legal systems. As has been mentioned above, the earliest and most formal method of acquiring ownership through transfer of a thing was *mancipatio*.[50]

In early Roman law, *mancipatio* was the only valid means of transfer for *res mancipi*[51] (*e.g.*, Italic land, slaves, cattle, horses, mules, donkeys, and the four praedial servitudes; namely, *iter*, *actus*, *via*, and *aquaeductus*). There were a number of formalities that were required. There had to be five witnesses present (all Roman citizens who had reached puberty) and a sixth was needed to hold the scale. The transferee held the *res*, struck the scale with a bronze or copper ingot, and proclaimed the object to be his. Presumably the bronze was symbolic of an earlier incarnation of this ritual when that would have been the actual "money" exchanged for the *res*. The

---

50. *See supra* § 12.02[A].
51. *Id.*

transferee probably also stated aloud the purchase price. The transferor, for his part, remained silent as a way of demonstrating that he did not contest the transferee's ownership.

Mancipatio automatically entailed an unwaivable warranty of title. If the true owner successfully sued a good faith purchaser, then the purchaser's damages against the fraudulent seller were twice the price that had been stated during the *mancipatio*. Buyers and sellers soon found a way around this rule by stating a ridiculously low (fictitious) price in the *mancipatio*. In addition to the verbal statements made during the *mancipatio*, it was common for a written record to be made that stated both the genuine value of the *res* as well as the price that had been recited in the *mancipatio*.

[2] TRADITIO

Traditio was the most common method of transferring tangible personal property, and it was available for both Romans and foreigners. Apparently *traditio* was recognized as early as the Twelve Tables. It was perhaps the most commonly recognized mode of transfer for *res nec mancipi*. And later, in Classical Roman Law, it was accepted as a valid means of transferring even *res mancipi*. *Traditio* was a much more simple (and thus more practical) method of ownership transfer than *mancipatio*. Three elements were necessary to effectuate a transfer by *traditio*: 1) the actual, physical transfer of the thing; 2) the intent by the transferor to bestow all of his rights in the thing to the transferee; and, 3) the intent by the transferee to accept both the thing and all of the transferee's rights. These elements (*i.e.,* physical delivery, intent of the transferor to transfer, and intent of the transferee to accept) operated to transfer *dominium*. By the end of the Republic (*c.* 27 B.C.), *traditio* was even accepted by law at the moment that a buyer simply affixed his seal to the goods.

In addition to "ordinary" *traditio*, Roman law also recognized three legitimate variations ("soft" versions) of it: 1) *traditio longa manu* (*traditio* by the long hand); 2) *traditio brevi manu* (*traditio* by the short hand); and, 3) *constitutum possessorium*. If the nature of the goods to be sold made physical transfer impractical (*e.g.,* tons of cut stone stored in a warehouse), Roman law legally admitted *traditio longa manu* (long-handed *traditio*) when the seller, in view of the warehouse, gave the buyer a key to that warehouse. Thus, a person transferred *dominium* by *traditio longa manu* when he (the transferor) pointed out to the transferee the object to be "transferred" under conditions that could enable him (*i.e.,* the transferee) to take it at once. For example, *traditio longa manu* would take place if, while they were standing next to the granary, a seller of corn (*i.e.,* corn that was in the granary) were to give the granary keys to the transferee. A person transferred *dominium* by *traditio brevi manu* when he (the transferor) merely authorized the transferee to keep an object (*i.e.*, an object owned by the transferor) that the transferee already had under his control (*i.e.*, by *detentio*).[52] Thus, in circumstances where a buyer already had possession of the *res*, the law recognized *traditio brevi manu*. For example, *traditio brevi manu* would take place if a lender of a tool were to tell the borrower that he (*i.e.*, the borrower) may keep it for himself. Gaius referred to this type of *traditio* as transfer by *nuda voluntas* (bare desire). *Constitutum possessorium* was, essentially, the opposite of *traditio brevi manu*. A person transferred *dominium* by *constitutum possessorium* if he (the transferor) physically kept the object but *his* power over that object transformed from *dominium* to *detentio*. In other words, the transferor retained physical control of the thing but, without actual movement, his control turned into a mere holding for the transferee's benefit. For instance, a seller could sell an ox to a buyer with the understanding that the buyer would actually pick up the animal at an agreed upon future date. In the interim, the seller could retain physical control of the beast by *detentio* but the buyer obtained *dominium* by means of *constitutum possessorium*.

[3] IN IURE CESSIO

Another method of transfer of ownership (a method that could be used to transfer both *res mancipi* and *res nec mancipi*) was *in iure cessio*. In some respects, *in iure cessio* was similar to a modern quiet title action. The transferor and transferee would arrange to meet before a magistrate. The transferee then declared that the *res* to be conveyed belonged to him. Playing his part, the owner/transferor simply remained silent. Thus, the magistrate ruled that the thing did, indeed, belong to the transferee. This was an unwieldy way to transfer goods. Consequently, the Romans tended not to use it if other means were readily available. It was, however, practically the only way to transfer certain incorporeal property, such as personal servitudes.[53]

[4] OCCUPATIO

[A] GENERAL

Occupatio was the acquisition of *dominium* of a thing just by seizing possession of it. *Occupatio* was possible in the case of *res nullius* (things that

---

52. For an explanation of *detentio, see supra* § 12.02[C].
53. *See infra* § 12.02[E].

no Roman had previously owned) or *res derelictae* (things abandoned by their owners). For example, objects that one found on an ocean beach (*e.g.*, pearls and shells) were *res nullius*. Wild animals (*ferae naturae*) are the paradigmatic example of *res nullius*; capable of ownership by *occupatio*. In Roman law, the first person to take possession of a *res nullius* with intent to keep it as his own (*i.e.*, the first occupier) was considered the owner (*res nullius primo occupanti*). As regards *res derelictae*, the Sabinians advocated that, once abandoned, things immediately were considered *res nullius*, and, thus, capable of ownership by someone else through *occupatio*. But the Proculians argued that the former owner did not cease to own an abandoned object until a finder actually seized it. In any case, to become the object of *occupatio*, the original owner must have sincerely forsaken it. If a person merely lost an item, he did not lose his ownership unless and until he gave up trying to find it. This is why cargo that a ship captain jettisoned in the midst of a storm was not capable of new ownership by *occupatio*. Presumably, he tossed his freight wanting to save his ship and those on board, not wanting, necessarily, to abandon it.

[B] THESAURI INVENTIO

Roman law took special interest in what was known as *thesauri inventio* (found treasure). Apparently, the underlying legal justification for acquisition of *thesauri inventio* was *occupatio*, and hence, that is why we consider it here. The jurist Paul defined it as a deposit of money the remembrance of which has been lost, so that it now has no owner. Although Paul only refers to money, it apparently also encompassed many other types of valuables such as jewels and precious metals. The laws regarding *thesauri inventio* evolved over the centuries. As of the 2nd century B.C., the jurists had decided that treasure belonged to the landowner on whose property it was discovered. In the early Empire it was deemed to be property of the Imperial Treasury. The precepts relating to the ownership of treasure that Justinian ultimately embraced were embodied first in laws passed under the emperor Hadrian. Under Justinian, the rules of ownership of treasure were as follows. 1) A person was permitted to keep treasure that he discovered on his own property. 2) A person was permitted to keep half of the treasure that he inadvertently discovered on another's property (the landowner kept the other half).[54] 3) If a person was either willfully searching for treasure on

---

54. If the land was public land, half of the treasure went to the Imperial Treasury.

another's property or employing magic to find it, he was not permitted to keep any of the treasure that he found (the landowner kept it all).[55]

[5] SPECIFICATIO

A person secured ownership (*dominium*) of a thing by *specificatio* when he created something completely new (*nova species*) from materials that someone else initially[owned. Suppose, for example, that A owns a stone and that B makes it into a sculpture. The simple question in such a circumstance is whether A or B should be considered the owner of the statue?

Roman jurists observed that the sculpture in this case was actually a *nova species*, a new kind of thing. The two prominent juristic schools, the Sabinians and the Proculians,[56] initially adopted different points of view on ownership in these situations. The Sabinians gave ownership to A, the owner of the materials. The Proculians gave ownership to B, the person who made the sculpture, the *nova species*. Under Justinian, if the creator had owned part of the materials used to create the new thing, then he was the owner of it. A third approach (*media sententia*) was approved in Justinian's *Corpus Iuris Civilis*. Under the theory of the *media sententia*, if it was practical to return the *nova species* to its original condition, then the owner of the component element(s) was deemed the owner of the new thing. If, on the other hand, the *nova species* could not be reduced to its former state, then the creator became the owner, but he was required to compensate the person who had originally owned the materials for their value. Thus, in our example, since it would be impractical to piece the stone back together, B, the creator, would be deemed the owner of the sculpture. Presumably, the opposite result would be reached if A had owned a bronze ingot, and B had melted and molded that into a sculpture. In that case, it would be practical to melt the sculpture back into an ingot.

In modern law, the relative values of the materials and the *nova species* often determine who will be deemed the owner. In a number of jurisdictions (*e.g.*, France and Germany) whichever (*i.e.*, the raw materials or the new thing) is the more valuable—monetarily speaking—controls. So, if the raw materials are more valuable than the new thing, then the original owner of the materials is considered the owner of the new thing, but, if the value of the new thing is greater than that of the raw materials, then the creator is considered the owner of the new thing.[57]

---

55. If the land was public land, all of the treasure went to the Imperial Treasury.

56. *See supra* § 10.04[C].

57. Still the maker/owner in such a scenario must compensate the owner of the raw materials for their value.

[6] ACCESSIO

In rudimentary terms, if B joins a minor object to A's major object (such as painting on a wooden board), the law of *accessio* determines the ownership of the entirety. One of the more interesting debates in Roman law centered around acquisition of property by *accessio*. The Roman juristic controversy took the following form. Imagine that A owns a parchment and that B, in good faith (*e.g.*, without knowing that A owns it), writes a poem on it. Or, suppose that A owns a canvas and that B, in good faith (*i.e.*, not knowing that the canvas belongs to A), paints a picture on it. The simple question is whether A or B is considered the owner of the poem on the parchment and the painting on the canvas? Roman jurists gave answers that appear somewhat inconsistent if not illogical.

It is difficult to justify the inconsistent approaches that Roman jurists took in these situations. The first inconsistency can be seen in the different treatment afforded to writing *versus* visual art. In the case where a writer writes on another's parchment, the general Roman law rule was that the owner of the parchment became the owner of the entirety. On the other hand, in the case where a painter paints on another's canvas, the general rule was the opposite: the painter became the owner of the whole.

In sum, then, a person could obtain ownership of one item of property by *accessio* when it (*i.e.*, that item of property) became incorporated into another item of property that that person already owned. In order for a valid *accessio* to occur, however, two essential elements had to exist: 1) the thing acquired had to have been assimilated with the object already owned in such a way that it was no longer recognizable as what it had been; and, 2) the thing acquired had to be inseparably incorporated.[58] Thus, the newly acquired article ceased to exist in its previous form, due to its merger into the other, already owned, thing. Therefore, for example, since a new leather strap attached to a horse's bridle could be separated without much difficulty, the strap in such a situation would not be acquired by *accessio*. The general rule of *accessio* is clear, the owner of the principal thing gained ownership of the incorporated thing.[59] Hence, the fate of the principal thing determined the fate of the adjoining thing. But as the examples of the writing on parchment and painting on canvass illustrate, it is not always simple to determine which thing should be considered the principal and which the accessory.

---

58. This is also the general the rule that applies in most legal systems today.
59. The applicable Latin maxim was *accessoria cedit principalis* (an accessory yields to a principal thing).

[7] USUCAPIO

Usucapio was a method of acquiring ownership of property that was similar to the modern concept of adverse possession. In its simplest terms, *usucapio* entitled a person to acquire ownership of property by using that property when its original owner had apparently abandoned it. In terms of public policy, the principle encourages persons to make productive use of property and discourages "sleeping on one's rights" while allowing otherwise productive property to go to waste.[60] In order for a person to acquire ownership of a *res* by *usucapio*, several criteria had to be fulfilled. First, the thing had to be the kind of property capable of human ownership. Second, because, by definition, *possessio* ordinarily required good faith on the part of the possessor,[61] stolen items could not be acquired by *usucapio*. Third, the person claiming ownership by *usucapio* had to have started his possession in good faith (*i.e.,* thinking that he was entitled to possession).

A person acquired ownership of a thing by *usucapio* by virtue of uninterrupted *possessio* for a designated amount of time. In Roman law, the time period necessary for *usucapio* to mature into *dominium* was relatively short (especially when compared to modern adverse possession which often takes 15–20 years of possession): two years for land and one year for other property.

[E] IURA IN RE ALIENA (RIGHTS IN THE THING OF ANOTHER)

Roman law recognized certain rights with respect to the things that belonged to others. In particular, Roman law admitted servitudes both that were connected to land (similar to what modern American law calls easements appurtenant) and servitudes that were personal (similar to the American law easements *in gross*).

As early as the Twelve Tables (451/450 B.C.), there were four servitudes that "ran with the land." In order for these to be applicable, the two parcels of land at issue had to be adjacent to one another. These four *praedial* servitudes were: 1) *via* (the general right of passage through a neighbor's property); 2) *iter* (the right to walk through a neighbor's property); 3) *actus* (the

---

60. *See generally* ROGER CUNNINGHAM, WILLIAM STOEBUCK, & DALE WHITMAN, THE LAW OF PROPERTY, § 11.7, at 814 (1993).

61. *See supra* § 12.02[C]. There were, however, a few exceptions to the requirement of good faith in *usucapio*.

right to drive animals through a neighbor's property); and, 4) *aquaeductus* (the right to conduct water from one's own property across a neighbor's property). These servitudes were basically intangible rights that were dependent upon an association with land.[62] They could be established either by *mancipatio* or *in iure cessio*—but not by *traditio*.[63] Because the praedial servitudes ran with the land, they were not tied to individuals. Accordingly, if the parties who created a right of *iter*, *actus*, *via*, or *aquaeductus* were to die, the servitude itself endured; the demise of the mortals who established it being irrelevant.

Eventually, in addition to these servitudes related to land, Roman law also recognized personal servitudes (somewhat similar to modern easements in gross) that were not tied to real property. The Roman personal servitudes, then, were associated only with specific persons for limited periods of time. There could be any number of such personal servitudes (*e.g.*, a life estate, fishing privileges, fruits of an orchard, living in a house). In particular, Roman jurists categorized the following: 1) *usus fructus* (the right to use another's property and its fruits); 2) *usus* (the right to use another's property, but not its fruits); 3) *habitatio* (the right—for life—to live in another's house); and, 4) *opera servorum vel animalium* (the right to have slaves or animals perform work).

Probably the most significant personal servitude in Roman law was *usus fructus*. *Usus fructus* allowed a person both to use a *res* and to reap the benefits of the "fruits" of that thing (*i.e.*, the products of that thing). For example someone who had *usus fructus* of an olive orchard would have both the use of the property itself and would also be entitled to reap the benefits of the olives produced by the trees in the orchard. Roman law forbade a person with the right of *usus fructus* to destroy or significantly alter the property. It was common for a man—in his will—to leave his real property to his children but to leave the right of *usus fructus* to his wife for her life.[64] The other two most important personal servitudes were *usus* and *habitatio*. When a person had *usus*, he had the right to use a property but did not have the right to appropriate its fruits. A person who had *habitatio* had the prerogative to live in a specific residence, usually for life.

---

62. In this regard they were similar to our easements appurtenant—such as the right to light and the right to the support of a common wall or roof.

63. *See supra* §§ 12.02[D][1]–[3].

64. For more on Roman wills, *see infra* § 12.04[C].

§ 12.03 FAMILY LAW

[A] POWER & CONTROL: *PATERFAMILIAS*

Probably the most significant feature of the family in Roman law was the institution of the *paterfamilias*. The Roman *paterfamilias* was ordinarily the father and husband who held the right of life and death over his entire family. Legally speaking, a wife was considered "in place of the daughter." In essence, all family members were either: 1) a *paterfamilias* (an independent person of his own right — *persona sui iuris* — who could resolve all issues of a legal nature with his own discretion and without restriction); or, 2) members of the family (persons who were considered *personae alieni iuris* — persons of another's right [*i.e.*, dependent upon the *paterfamilias*]). Family members could not participate in any legal relationships without the permission of their *paterfamilias*. The *paterfamilias* owned all of the family's property. As Roman law and society developed, the institution of the *peculium* came to be used by family members.[65] Family members did have *ius honorum*[66] which was considered a *quasi-peculium* that the State, not the *paterfamilias* granted.

Patria potestas was the power that a Roman father held over his subordinates (*e.g.*, wife, children — both biological and adopted —, grandchildren). A Roman male — if his own father, grandfather, *etc.* were dead — acquired *patria potestas* when he entered into a valid marriage. As long as the father was living, he retained his *patria potestas*. Technically, by virtue of *patria potestas*, a Roman father had complete power over his children. He had the power of life and death. He decided whether to expose an infant at birth. He could, before the Empire, sell them into slavery. His consent was needed to marry and, generally speaking, he could force them to marry and also forbid them to marry. Before Antoninus Pius (138–161 A.D.) changed the law, a father's *patria potestas* even permitted him to dissolve a son's marriage — even a happy one — without his son's consent. A Roman *paterfamilias* owned his children's possessions; although a child might have a *peculium* (a fund nominally owned by them).

The Emperor Augustus (27 B.C.–14 A.D.) created an exception for sons who were in the army but technically still under their father's (or grandfather's) *patria potestas*. Augustus granted a son in the army the power to make a will, and to distribute — in any manner that he wished — any money

---

65. A family member's *peculium* was similar in many respects to the *peculium* of a slave. *See supra* § 12.01[C].
66. *See supra* § 12.01[B][1].

or property that he had obtained as a soldier. This money and/or property was called his *peculium castrense*. The Emperor Hadrian (117–138 A.D.) amended Augustus' law by simply granting complete ownership, outright, of the *peculium castrense* to the soldier-son.

[B] MARRIAGE & DIVORCE

[1] GENERAL CONSIDERATIONS

The earliest marriage contracts were in the form of a *sponsio* (*i.e.*, an early form of formulaic oral contract),[67] and were supposedly actionable. By the 2nd century B.C., Roman marriage contracts were no longer actionable. Generally speaking, an agreement of the *paterfamilias* of both the bride and groom was needed to make a marriage valid. Before the Empire (*c.* 27 B.C.), what the girl wanted made little difference. A prospective husband or his father made the marriage contract. The *paterfamilias* of the prospective wife always conducted the contract negotiations for her—unless she was no longer under the control of her *paterfamilias*—in which case one of her relatives took the place of her *paterfamilias*. Once a marriage contract was concluded, sex with another man was deemed adultery.[68]

Marriage was defined simply as the joining of a man and woman; the incidence of all life (*matrimonium est coniunctio maris et feminae consortum omnis vitae*). A bride's family contributed a dowry (*dos*) for the marriage. The groom's family also contributed marriage gifts (usually equivalent to the *dos*). The intent of the man and woman to create a marriage was essential. Often a dowry served as evidence of such intent (making clear that the couple did not intend merely a concubinage). There were certain formal methods of creating a dowry. There were also certain procedures that had to be followed in the event that later the wife's father or the wife, herself, wished to sue for the return of the dowry (*actio rei uxoriae*). One of the principal results of a valid Roman marriage was that the couple's children were considered legitimate and they were under the *patria potestas* of their *paterfamilias* (*i.e.*, typically, the father, grandfather, or great-grandfather).

Roman law only recognized marriage as valid when it was between Roman citizens or a union between a Roman citizen and a citizen of a state having a right of intermarriage with Rome. Slave marriages were not regarded as legal. Plebeians were not permitted to marry Patricians until the passage of the *lex Canuleia* in 445 B.C. The Emperor Augustus (27 B.C.–14

---

67. *See infra* § 12.07[B].
68. *See infra* § 12.05[E].

A.D.) forbade senators—and their descendants—from marriage with freedmen (and freedwomen) and actresses.

Certain blood relatives were legally prohibited from intermarriage. The proximity of relationship that was impermissible vacillated as the societal mores and expectations of the Roman people changed over the years. In early law, second cousins were prohibited from intermarriage. But by the late Republic (*i.e.*, 150–27 B.C.), even first cousins were allowed to marry one another. During most periods, uncles and nieces could not marry nor could great-uncles marry their great-nieces. Still, the Emperor Claudius (41–54 A.D.) had the law changed so that he could marry his niece, Agrippina. Thus, for a brief period afterwards, such a union was considered legal. A Roman girl had to be at least twelve years old to marry. It appears that many girls had not yet reached puberty when they were married, and in fact, whether they had reached puberty seems to have been irrelevant. For boys, the Proculians held the view that eventually was adopted in law; namely, a boy simply had to be at least fourteen in order to marry. The Sabinian view—a view that faded—was that a boy had to have reached puberty as a precondition of marriage. The Sabinians even required that a boy undergo a physical examination as proof that he had reached puberty.

[2] TYPES OF MARRIAGE

Fundamentally, there were two recognized, legal types of Roman marriage: 1) *matrimonium cum manu* (marriage with power); and, *matrimonium sine manu* (marriage without power). Marriage *cum manu* was the older of the two. In such a marriage, the wife was considered to be living under her husband's power. A wife was subordinated to her husband. In the event that her husband, himself, still was under the power of his *paterfamilias*, then the bride also was regarded as being under the power of that superior *paterfamilias* (*i.e.*, her father-in-law). In either case, the bride's status was, legally speaking, roughly equivalent to that of being her husband's daughter. He automatically took legal ownership of any property that had previously belonged to her. People still commonly married *cum manu* in the early 1st century B.C. but the practice became the exception by mid-century. Roman law also permitted unmarried persons to live together in concubinage. We know, for example, that the emperors Vespasian and Marcus Aurelius did so.

By the time of the Twelve Tables (451/450 B.C.), the three ways in which marriage *cum manu* could be formed were already in existence: 1) *confarreatio*; 2) *coemptio*; and, 3) *usus*. *Confarreatio* was a religious ceremony that involved two priests and a ceremony with a cake of spelt—the *far* in *confarreatio*. The *confarreatio* was, as a practical matter, exclusively an aristocratic institution. *Coemptio* was marriage using an early ritualistic form of sale (*mancipatio*).[69] It was a mock sale of the bride by the *paterfamilias* to the groom. *Usus* was marriage created when a husband and wife lived together for a complete year, so long as the wife did not stay away from her husband for three consecutive nights during that year. In some respects, this type of marriage is similar to the acquisition of property by adverse possession or usucaption (*usucapio*).[70] Eventually, the law of the three nights fell into disuse by custom. Instead, a woman only came under her husband's power through the consent of her guardian. *Usus* was abolished entirely by legislation during the early Empire. Soon the other types of marriage *cum manu* had all but disappeared.

In marriage *sine manu*, the wife did not fall under the power of her husband (or his *paterfamilias*). Thus, it was a union in which the wife was not subordinated to her husband as *paterfamilias*. Instead, she remained under the power of her own *paterfamilias* (ordinarily her father or grandfather). In the event that she had been independent at the time of marriage *sine manu*, she retained her independent status even upon marriage. Interestingly, if a wife had no *paterfamilias* and the couple wished to avoid marriage *cum manu*, they could invoke the doctrine of *trinoctii absentia* (absence for three nights). In order to accomplish this, the wife moved back and lived with her previous family for three consecutive nights every year. By doing so, she avoided living with her husband continuously for an entire year (which would have resulted in marriage *cum manu*). Marriage *sine manu* was the most common type of civil marriage. By the early 2nd century B.C., marriage *sine manu* was routine.

[3] DIVORCE

During the earliest period of Roman law (*i.e.*, the Monarchy—753–509 B.C.), a husband was allowed, with impunity, to divorce his wife for three reasons: 1) if she committed adultery; 2) if she "tampered with the keys" (the presumption operating was that she had altered the household keys as a means by which a lover could enter); and, 3) if she poisoned a child. Under these three circumstances, neither she nor her father was entitled to have any of her dowry returned. If a husband divorced his wife for any other reason, the wife was entitled to one-half of her husband's property.

If the marriage had been performed with the *confarreatio*,[71] it could only be dissolved by means of a revocation ceremony, called *diffarreatio*. Otherwise, Roman marriages could be terminated without any special procedure.

---

69. For more on *mancipatio, see supra* §§ 12.02[A] and 12.02[D][1].
70. *See supra* § 12.02[D][7].
71. *See supra* § 12.03[B][2].

The most common form of divorce was done by *repudium*, which did not even require mutual consent. *Repudium* was considered a simple withdrawal of the *affectio maritalis* by the couple together (or merely one of them). Augustan legislation required seven witnesses.

In early Roman law there were stiff financial penalties for being found the guilty party in a divorce proceeding. Similarly, there were penalties if a husband or wife divorced without cause. By the late Republic, these penalties were no longer enforced. As a general rule, upon divorce, a husband was required to return most of the dowry to either the ex-wife or to her father. He was entitled to retain specified portions of it unless he was at fault in the divorce, in which case, he had to return the dowry in its entirety. As divorce law evolved during the Republic, a husband was allowed to divorce his wife for no particular reason at all. A wife was able to divorce her husband so long as she was not under his power. The Emperor Constantine (306–337 A.D.) took a dim view of divorce. He imposed rather severe penalties on spouses who divorced—except for those who divorced for what he deemed legitimate reasons. Under Justinian (6th century A.D.), there were certain legitimate reasons for which a wife could divorce her husband. If she divorced him for another reason, she surrendered all her property and was sent to a nunnery permanently. On the other hand, if a husband divorced his wife for a reason not recognized as legitimate by law, he suffered only fines.

[C] ADOPTION

There were two principal forms of adoption discussed in Justinian's *Digest*: 1) *adoptio* and 2) *adrogatio*. It was also possible to adopt by means of a will. Julius Caesar, for example, adopted Augustus in his will. *Adoptio* was the form used when the adoptee was still under *patria potestas*. The father (or grandfather) went through the formality of "selling" his son (or grandson) (*i.e.*, the adoptee) three times. That act technically freed the boy. Once freed by the triple sale, the adoptive father could secure his own *patria potestas* over the adoptee by a decree of the praetor. *Adrogatio* was the form of adoption employed in cases where the adoptee was *not* under the *patria potestas* of another.

The primary problem with *adrogatio* as a method of adoption was that, if a man was not under another's *patria potestas*, then, "if he were adopted, his family would at once die out and there would be no one to continue the family's religious rites."[72] Thus, the law developed certain prerequisites to *adroga-*

---

72. WATSON, ROMAN LAW & COMPARATIVE LAW 34.

tio. First, the prospective adopter had to be childless. He had to be unable to father children. In the absence of any extenuating circumstances, he had to be at least sixty years old. He must at least have attempted to father children if possible. The pontiffs, themselves, conducted an investigation into these matters. Then if they approved, next, the *comitia curiata*[73] (using the appellation *comitia calata* for this process) had to vote to approve the adoption.

[D] TUTORS

Boys and girls who had not reached puberty and who, for one reason or another, were not under the power of a *paterfamilias* were legally required to have a tutor to look after them and their affairs. A tutor managed his ward's affairs in the best interests of the ward. A tutor was obligated to serve at least until the ward reached puberty. Even after a girl had reached puberty and had grown to womanhood, she was legally required to have a tutor if she was *sui iuris*. Such women, however, had a certain degree of flexibility and freedom of action not possessed by their pre-pubescent analogues. There were four ways of creating a tutor, and several had specific formalities: 1) by will; 2) by law; 3) by public official; and, 4) temporary tutor. The establishment of a tutor by a will was known as a *tutor testamentarius*. There were fairly rigid formulae necessary for setting up a tutor by will. The testator was required to use specific language. A tutor could be appointed by operation of law when there was no testamentary appointment (*tutor legitimus*). This method of appointment was part of the Twelve Tables. The law favored appointment of a tutor by agnatic relationship (*i.e.,* relationship connected through men).[74] In some cases, public officials (usually a praetor and a majority of the tribunes of the plebs) could appoint a tutor. This type of tutor was called a *tutor dativus*. The appointment of a temporary tutor was a very old form used during the pendency of a dispute between the ward and the person who was his regular tutor. This may have fallen into disuse by the time of Gaius (*i.e.,* the great jurist who wrote the *Institutes* about 161 A.D.).[75]

Roman law considered tutorship a serious obligation. If appointed as a tutor, the appointee was required to fulfill his obligation to serve. There were exceptions for disqualification or for certain exemptions. But the laws regarding exemptions were long and complicated. There were a number of legal actions that a ward could bring against his tutor if he (*i.e.,* the ward) believed that the tutor had been remiss in his duties. The precise

---

73. *See supra* § 11.02[B].
74. For more on agnatic relationships, *see infra* § 12.04[B].
75. *See supra* § 10.04[A].

forms and remedies for these legal actions varied depending upon factors such as whether the tutor had been appointed by will or by operation of law, whether the ward was still under the tutor's protection, and whether the conduct complained of was alleged to have been intentional or merely negligent.

[E] CURATORS

Under the Twelve Tables, persons who were mentally incompetent had to be cared for by their closest agnatic relative, who served as a curator. The Twelve Tables also reiterated an old law that provided that a magistrate could appoint a curator for a prodigal/spendthrift who had squandered his inheritance. This law originally applied only to an inheritance by intestacy but was later amended to include a prodigal who squandered his testamentary inheritance as well. By the later Republic, youth between age fourteen (*i.e.*, the time when the tutorship over them expired) and age twenty-five were required to have a curator who managed their affairs and helped to ensure that others would not take advantage of them.

§ 12.04 INHERITANCE & SUCCESSION

[A] INTRODUCTION

Justinian's *Digest* has 50 books, and eleven of them deal with succession. The law of succession is related both to property and the methods of acquiring property. In Roman law, an heir became the owner, creditor, and debtor of a deceased's estate. As is common in modern legal systems, the ancient Romans appreciated two basic types of succession: 1) *intestate* (without a will; thereby forcing property to pass to persons and in proportions established by law); and, 2) *testate* (with a will indicating who should receive property and in what proportions). Clearly, intestate succession rules controlled long before the law recognized a person's ability to control the allocation of property by means of a will.

[B] INTESTATE SUCCESSION

In order to comprehend the workings of Roman intestate succession, it is first important to understand the distinction between two groups: the *cognati* and the *agnati*. The *cognati* were those relatives who were related by blood. The *agnati* were those relatives who were related through a male ancestor. The distinction between the concepts of *cognatio* and *agnatio* was central in determining inheritance. *Cognatio* distinguishes between direct linear and indirect linear descendants. Direct linear descendants are those on a direct originating line with one another (*e.g.,* grandparents and grandchildren). Relatives on a direct linear line are the most favored for inheritance based on *cognatio*. Indirect linear descendants are those with a common ancestor (*e.g,* brother and sister). In an inheritance system based on *cognatio*, indirect linear descendants have fewer rights than direct descendants (sometimes they get no inheritance at all).

In terms of inheritance in the absence of a will, the Twelve Tables showed a preference for agnates, those related to a deceased through males. Roman succession law slowly, step-by-step, evolved towards a system based on blood relationship (*i.e.,* as opposed to agnatic relationships). Praetors' edicts amended the law as did statutes in the mid-2nd century A.D. Under Justinian's *Novellae* (which superseded the *Institutes* — which had retained some of the agnatic elements of the Twelve Tables and other prior law), blood relationship became the cornerstone of intestate succession. Thus, although early in the Roman legal development of succession, the laws preferred the *agnati*, later, the law shifted to prefer *cognati*.

As part of their law of inheritance,[76] the Romans also developed the notion of degree of kinship. In order to determine degrees of kinship, one must simply count the number of births necessary to get from one person to the other. For example, a mother and child are in the "first degree" — because they are only one birth (or "step") removed from one another in descent. A grandfather and grandchild are in the "second degree" because they are two births (or "steps") removed. In the examples just given, it only takes one birth to get from a mother to her child (the child's birth), but two births are required in order to get from a grandparent to a grandchild (the birth of the grandparent's immediate offspring — a son or daughter — and then the birth of his or her child — the grandchild).

By the time of Justinian in the 6th century A.D., the laws of the praetor (*i.e.,* the praetorian order of succession) established a fixed order of preference for inheritance. Most modern legal systems today (except Muslim) use basically the same scheme. In the *Corpus Iuris Civilis*, the order of intestate succession was as follows. The first rank in line to inherit were the *liberi* (literally "children"). These ordinarily were the children and grandchildren.

---

76. This was also relevant for marriage law. *See supra* § 12.03[B][1].

Typically, children inherited equal shares (*per capita*) and the grandchildren inherited on the basis of *ius representationis*, the right of representation, from their parents (also known as *per stirpes*, "through the stem"). For example, if a *paterfamilias* had three sons at the time of his death, each son took one-third of his father's estate (*per capita*). But, now assume that each son himself had two sons as well (*i.e.*, that would make a total of six grandsons). If each of the original three sons was alive when the *paterfamilias* died, the grandchildren took nothing at that time. But, if, for example, before the *paterfamilias* died, one of his three sons had predeceased him, then each of the dead son's surviving sons (*i.e.*, the *paterfamilias'* grandchildren by his deceased son) would take one-half of the one-third to which his father would have been entitled, had he lived. In such a case, then, each of those two grandsons would take one-sixth of the *paterfamilias'* estate by *ius representationis* (*per stirpes*). This principle still operates today in many legal systems (*e.g.*, French and German law). Second in line were the *legitimi*. These were usually the parents, grandparents, brothers, and sisters (in that order). These were the closest relatives, who excluded the remoter relatives in succession. The parents were deemed closer relatives than grandparents and also closer than brothers and sisters. Third were the *cognati*. In particular, this group consisted of any other blood relatives who were not included in the *legitimi* (*e.g.*, any half-brothers or half-sisters). The fourth rank of heirs was the husband or wife of the deceased — last in line to inherit. To summarize, then, in Justinian's *Novellae*, the order of intestate succession is as follows: 1) male and female descendants (offspring taking their deceased parent's share); 2) ascendants (*e.g.*, parents and grandparents); 3) full brothers and sisters; 4) if there were no full siblings, half-brothers and half-sisters; 5) all other blood relatives. Husbands and wives succeeded one another. If all else failed, the deceased's property escheated to the State.

[C] TESTATE SUCCESSION

The Twelve Tables make it clear that wills were an accepted means for transferring property to heirs even in the 5th century B.C. In early law, there were two distinct types of wills. The *testamentum comitiis calatis* required public approval by the *comitia calata*,[77] and could only be made on either March 24 or May 24. The *testamentum in procinctu* was the type of will that a soldier could make when he was part of an army that was prepared to march. A *testamentum in procinctu* could be made orally and did

---

77. *See supra* § 11.02[B].

not require any specific formalities. Soldiers' wills enjoyed a number of legal exceptions. For example, a soldier was permitted to name foreigners as heirs and legatees. But a soldier's will was only valid for one year after discharge. The Twelve Tables mention a later form of will known as *testamentum per aes et libram* ("will by means of bronze and a scale"). This type of will is clearly adapted from sale of *res mancipi* by *mancipatio*.[78] It was the conventional will in the late Republic and then throughout the Empire. There were certain requisite elements: 1) five witnesses; 2) another person to hold the scale; 3) the presence of the *familiae emptor* ("buyer of the family", *i.e.*, the person to whom the estate would eventually be transferred); and, 4) specific prescribed declarations of transfer made by both the testator and the *familiae emptor*. Ordinarily the witnesses, scale holder, and *familiae emptor* affixed their seals to the document. Augustus (27 B.C.–14 A.D.) made codicils, "informal additions to wills," enforceable. And, finally, in the 5th century A.D., the "tripartite will" became popular. The three "parts" were: 1) there had to be seven witnesses; 2) each witness had to affix his seal to the document; and, 3) the testator had to sign the document.

A person had to have capacity to make a will (*testamenti factio*) in order for his will to be considered valid and effective. Males had to be at least fourteen years old and females had to be twelve.[79] Generally speaking, a testator was required to be a Roman citizen who was *sui iuris* (*i.e.*, not under the *patria potestas* of another).[80] Until the mid-2nd century A.D., there were complicated restrictions on the ability of women to make wills. After that time, a woman could be a valid testatrix with the consent of her *tutor*.[81]

There are certain elements commonly found in ancient Roman wills. To be a valid will, the document had to name an heir and the heir had to be a Roman citizen, unless the heir was a slave—in which case the will's provisions had to free the slave. Roman law required precise language in a will to create an heir. There were two acceptable patterns. If the testator, for example, wanted someone named Marcus to be his heir, in order to be valid, the will had to state either, "Let Marcus be my heir" or "I order Marcus to be my heir." The clause creating the heir usually came first in the will because anything that preceded it was deemed invalid. The *lex Voconia* (169 B.C.) established that the wealthiest class of Romans could not appoint a woman as heir. By the Empire (27 B.C.–mid-5th century A.D.), *fideicommissa* (trusts)—which from the time of Augustus forward gained increas-

---

78. *See supra* §§ 12.02[A] and 12.02[D][1].
79. These were the same ages required prior to marriage. *See supra* § 12.03[B][1].
80. *See supra* § 12.03[A].
81. See supra § 12.03[D].

ing validity—provided effective mechanisms to obviate the *lex Voconia*. Trusts also gave a testator a way to leave property to a foreigner. Occasionally an heir would have predeceased the testator or would refuse his inheritance. Whether an heir could legally refuse an inheritance was an important issue, because heirs inherited the debts of the testator as well as his assets. Thus, Roman testators often included in their wills several persons designated as *substitutii* (*i.e.*, substitute heirs). The *substitutii* were added to take an inheritance in the event that heirs named either refused or had predeceased the testator. Although there were some restrictions, it was, as a rule, possible to disinherit sons, daughters, and other descendants in one's will. A Roman testator could disinherit persons who otherwise would have been heirs, and it was common for a will to include a clause saying "and let all others be disinherited." But eventually, by the early Empire, a person who was disinherited could contest the will on grounds that s/he had been disinherited by an undutiful (*inofficiosi*) will. These cases were tried by the *centimuiri*.[82] If the plaintiff won, s/he received that which would have been his/her intestate portion of the decedent's estate. Other clauses commonly found in Roman wills relate to: 1) the manumission of slaves; 2) the appointment of tutors for children; 3) the creation of legacies (*i.e.*, bequests of specific property or specific rights to individuals); and, 4) the establishment of trusts (*fideicommissa*).

There were three categories of heirs under Roman law: 1) *necessarii* (slaves who were not allowed to refuse their inheritance); 2) *sui et necessarii* (persons who passed from the *potestas* of the testator to their own [*i.e.*, they gained their independence] upon the testator's death, *e.g.*, the testator's sons,); and, 3) *extranei* (all others). The *heredes necessarii* were the testator's slaves who were manumitted by the will. They were obliged to accept what was given to them; they could not refuse acceptance. The *sui et necessarii heredes* were those who had been under the testator's *potestas* (power) at the time of his death. For example, children, grandchildren, and wives (*in manu*). The third type of heir, the *extraneus heres*, was one who, in order to accept his legacy, had to do so in the presence of a Roman magistrate.

Roman inheritance involved the acceptance of both rights and also duties. Heirs were required to pay the debts of the deceased even if the property of the deceased was insufficient to cover those debts. Thus, creditors of the testator became creditors of the heirs. Because an heir would inherit debts, Justinian's approach was to grant the named heir (*i.e.*, an *extraneus* not a *necessarius*)—before deciding whether to accept or decline as heir—

---

82. *See supra* § 11.03[B].

the opportunity to request an inventory of the testator's estate. In that way, before making a commitment, an heir could ascertain whether there would be sufficient funds to pay the testator's debts.[83] In one sense, then, since a potential heir was unlikely to accept an inheritance in a case where a testator's property was insufficient to cover his outstanding debts, the practical result was that a deceased's debt liability was limited to the value of his property.

A legatee had to be a Roman citizen. In early Roman law, specific language was necessary to create a valid legacy. The *senatus consultum Neronianum* (64 A.D.) significantly relaxed the interpretation for legacies. Justinian tore down the remaining barriers, in effect, lending validity to virtually any form of legacy.

§ 12.05 CRIMINAL LAW

[A] CRIMINAL LIABILITY & ELEMENTS OF CRIME

Roman law considered that children under the age of seven were incapable of conceiving *dolus* (criminal intent). Therefore, they could not be criminally liable. Similarly, between age seven and puberty, Roman law considered a child's inability to conceive of *dolus* as a rebuttable presumption. In like manner, the insane were treated as incapable of being criminally liable. Roman magistrates with *imperium* were insulated from criminal liability while they were in office.

Dolus (criminal intent) was ordinarily a required element of any crime. Modern legal systems typically refer to this element as *mens rea* (a guilty mind). In addition to *dolus*, an *actus reus* (criminal act) was an essential element for a crime in Roman law. An *attempt* to commit a criminal act could also constitute an *actus reus*. Treasonous speech could constitute an *actus reus*, as could defamatory speech and certain other false communications (such as perjury, forgery, and false pleadings). Women, minors, and those who lived in the country were usually held to a lesser standard than others. The law presumed that they simply could not conform their conduct to the higher standards of adult men who lived in Rome. The jurists Labeo and Paul explained that accomplices (*socii*) could be liable for criminal acts along with the principal who actually committed a crime. Accomplices ordinarily received the same punishment as the actual perpetrator.

---

83. The heir had to begin the inventory within 30 days and had to complete it within 90.

[B] HOMICIDE

Prior to the Twelve Tables (451/450 B.C.), there may have been a very old rule regarding homicide which stated that if the killing was accidental, the killer was required to perform some sort of religious atonement but could not receive the death penalty. In order to effectuate this rule, special magistrates, called *quaestiones paricidii*, were appointed to determine whether a death was caused intentionally or accidentally. Supposedly the king Numa Pompilius (the legendary second king of Rome, *c.* 715–673 B.C.) enacted that death was the penalty for premeditated homicide. In the Republic the death penalty was usually inflicted by decapitation by axe or later by sword.

In 81 B.C., Sulla's *lex Cornelia de sicariis et veneficis* established a *quaestio perpetua* (*i.e.,* permanent court) designed to handle murder trials. The praetor, or judge, supervised the jury in cases involving a murder that had been committed within one mile of Rome. The law also criminalized the act of carrying weapons with the intent to kill or steal. The *lex Cornelia de sicariis et veneficis* could be used as both a peacekeeping measure and a statutory basis for prosecuting murder. But throughout the Republic, Roman law ordinarily treated murder as a matter to be addressed by the victim's *paterfamilias* not necessarily by the State. Presumably, the victim's *paterfamilias* did his best to track down the murderer and then accused him. The most probable person to accuse another of murder (*i.e.,* to serve as prosecutor) was the victim's father, husband, or brother. As a general rule, only male citizens could instigate murder charges. The most common exception to this rule was made for a woman when the victim was her parent or child. But in any case the action was, by and large, originally private.

According to the jurist Paul, the *lex Cornelia*, in addition, punished those who possessed, sold, or made a poison with intent to murder, and also punished anyone whose false testimony caused another's death. Paul wrote: "A murderer is someone who kills a man with any kind of weapon or causes death."[84] Before long, the *lex Cornelia* was applied to common murder— not only murder associated with public violence. Generally speaking, however, suicide was not a criminal act. Those from the upper classes who were convicted under this law, received capital punishment. Death by crucifiction or being thrown to wild animals was the punishment for the lower classes.

One of the essential elements of murder was intent. Thus, neither the insane nor minors could be guilty of murder since the law presumed them

---

84. ROBINSON, CRIMINAL LAW 42–43 (Citing and quoting Paul's Sententiae 5.23.1-2).

incapable of having legal intent. But there was a distinction between intent and even "gross carelessness." An absence of premeditation might serve as a mitigating circumstance.

The *lex Pompeia* (55 B.C.) was the first statute that criminalized parricide (murder of close relatives) as an offense distinct from ordinary murder. This law defined the relationships that encompassed parricide. In addition to the obvious—killing one's parent—the Romans also treated the murder of a grandparent, sibling, cousin, aunt or uncle, and patron as parricide. The punishment for parricide was usually either death or banishment. It was also common for a person convicted of parricide to forfeit his property. There was a particularly cruel punishment, called the sack (*culleus*), that was sometimes administered in the case of someone who murdered either a parent or grandparent. By the end of the 3rd century A.D., burning alive or mauling by wild animals was used instead. Much later in the Empire (*i.e.*, in the time of the Christian emperors), the *culleus* again became fashionable. And, in fact, to increase the suffering of the convicted parricide, assorted deadly animals were inserted into the sack as well.

Abortion was treated as a crime insofar as the death of the fetus was considered a crime against the woman's husband. The law presumed that a married woman might take poison to induce abortion, hoping to hide an adultery or to deprive her husband of an heir. The punishment was exile. Since abortion was, therefore, deemed a violation against the husband, it was, apparently, legal for an unwed woman to induce abortion.

Because slaves were considered property, in early Roman law, murder did not apply to the killing of a slave. At some point, possibly in the late Republic, murder of a slave became cognizable. Ultimately, in the Empire, even the killing of one's own slave was criminalized.

Roman law recognized certain affirmative defenses to murder. For example, self-defense and defense of a family member (even from sexual assault) were valid excuses. In addition, killing a military deserter was considered justifiable homicide. A father was barred from killing a son unless he first accused him and had a hearing with the Urban Prefect.

[C] THEFT CRIMES

The Twelve Tables punished the cutting of another's fruiting trees as a kind of crime. Forced labor was the penalty for the less privileged citizens, while the *honestiores* (*e.g.,* army veterans) merely paid a fine. Also in the Twelve Tables, the death penalty was imposed both for arson and for theft of crops at night (burglary). It was during the Empire that Romans began treating theft in general more as a crime than as a tort. During the Empire (27 B.C.–mid-5th century A.D.), ordinarily a victim of theft had a choice of bringing either a criminal action or a civil action. In Republican Rome (509–27 B.C.), the *tresviri capitales* routinely handled cases involving theft, and in the Empire, it was the Prefect of the Night Watch (*Praefectus Vigilum*).

Abigeatus (rustling) was a specific subspecies of theft. Both the type of animal stolen and the number of animals stolen were factors that could turn simple theft into *abigeatus*. According to Paul, the theft of one stallion, or two mares or oxen, or ten sheep or goats, or five pigs constituted rustling. Forced labor was a common penalty. But a rustler could receive a more harsh penalty—such as work in the mines or even death—if he acted as part of a hired band, was armed, or was a recidivist. The Emperor Hadrian (117–138 A.D.) made *abigeatus* a capital offense in Spain.

The *Praefectus Vigilum* had charge of burglary, arson, mugging, theft, and the resale of stolen goods on the black market. Roman law had special names for certain types of thieves. For example, *effractores* were burglars who broke into apartments, and *saccularii* were thieves who slit pockets and purses to empty their contents. Particular thieves, called *expilatores,* who ransacked homes in the countryside, were considered especially blameworthy. These thieves usually were punished with forced labor. According to the jurist Paul, thieves often received forced labor as a penalty. Some were beaten first. Convicted burglars frequently were beaten and then also sent to the mines. It was a praetor's edict that established the delict *rapina* (*vi bonorum raptorum*), theft with violence. *Rapina* was, in a number of respects, treated as a crime. For *rapina* a thief had to pay multiple damages—four-times the amount stolen.[85]

Roman law had an action for conduct that was, essentially, looting in the wake of a natural disaster like fire, shipwreck, or a collapsed building (*de incendio ruina naufragio rate nave expugnata*). If a complainant brought his action within one year, the criminal was liable for four-times the value of what he stole or damaged. For a suit brought after one year, the fine was only the value of the stolen or damaged property. If, on the other hand, the culprit, instead of merely being opportunistic, deliberately set a fire as a stratagem for stealing goods, he faced capital punishment if his crime was in the city, and faced work in the mines, forced labor, or banishment if he had targeted a rural farm or villa.

Those who bought or otherwise received stolen goods, knowing them to have been stolen ("fencing") were treated just the same as thieves. Harbor-

---

85. *See also infra* § 12.06[B][3].

ing thieves was also a criminal offense. Interestingly, Roman law considered that a person who harbored a relative should not be treated as harshly. The relationship, therefore, served as a mitigating circumstance.

[D] VIS

The Romans treated *vis* ("force/violence") as a special kind of crime. *Vis* included conduct such as armed robbery, battery, and sedition. Late in the Classical period (*i.e.*, 3rd century A.D.), two separate kinds of *vis* were recognized, public and private. Public *vis* included offenses committed by public officials (*e.g.*, killing, torturing, or beating a citizen), and private *vis* involved violent crimes perpetrated by private individuals. Brandishing a weapon in a threatening manner could constitute *vis* in certain social contexts. Although the penalty for *vis* was usually capital punishment or exile, there were a number of instances in which lesser punishments were applied. If the *vis* involved abduction of a freeborn woman, in addition to a death penalty, the offender's property was confiscated. Roman law used the concept of *vis* in a very broad sense to include many kinds of criminal conduct. But, in particular, physical and sexual assault (including abduction)—motivated either by political advancement, sexual desire, or profit—were also considered forms of criminal *vis*.

[E] SEXUAL CONDUCT

[1] ADULTERY & *STUPRUM*

Before the time of Augustus (27 B.C.–14 A.D.) Roman law treated adultery basically as a private matter. In the Republic (509–27 B.C.), it was considered justifiable for a husband to kill or beat his wife's paramour when caught in *flagrante delicto*. Republican law provided that the husband would divorce his wife and that he would keep the dowry. In about 18 B.C., Augustus spearheaded legislation that functionally criminalized adultery. The *lex Iulia de adulteriis coercendis* established a permanent court, the *quaestio perpetua de adulteriis*. In order for adultery to occur, the female involved had to be a "respectable married woman" and the man had to be someone who was not her husband. According to Ulpian, to be found guilty, the accused must have acted *sciens dolo malo* ("knowingly and with malicious intent").

The crime of *stuprum* occurred when a man, acting *sciens dolo malo*, had sexual relations with a "respectable" unmarried girl or woman, or a respectable man or boy. Under the *lex Iulia*, both abduction and rape fell within the scope of criminal *stuprum*, and both were punished with death. Justinian's Code makes it clear that an unwilling victim was not guilty of either adultery or *stuprum*.

Schoolbooks often make much of the paterfamilias' *ius occidendi* ("the right of killing"). Technically, a *paterfamilias* was entitled to put family members to death at his discretion.[86] But even by the late Republic, ordinarily fathers only used the *ius occidendi* just after a child was born (*i.e.,* his decision to accept or reject the child). Augustus' *lex Iulia*, however, granted a *paterfamilias* authority to kill his own daughter if she were caught committing adultery *in flagrante delicto* either in his house or the house of his son-in-law. It was considered homicide if the *paterfamilias* killed the lover but not his daughter. The law made divorce compulsory when a wife was caught in the act. The husband was also obligated to initiate criminal charges against his wife.

Even though a man was capable of committing adultery (*e.g.,* when a married man had sex with a married "respectable" woman), the *lex Iulia* did not give the man's wife authority to charge him with adultery. She could, however, initiate divorce proceedings against him.

When charges were brought for adultery, slaves were usually questioned as part of the evidence taken against the accused. The *lex Iulia* provided extraordinarily stiff financial penalties for adultery. A woman's paramour paid a fine amounting to one-half of his patrimony and he was thereafter no longer able either to make a will or to take anything pursuant to someone else's will. An adulteress paid a fine of one-third of her patrimony and also forfeited one-half of her dowry. In addition to these fines, a later version of the law confined adulterous lovers to different islands.

[2] INCEST

Not only were sexual relations between a parent and a child considered incest but also marriage between persons whose family relationship was considered too close (*i.e.,* marriage was permitted by persons no more closely related than first cousins—the fourth degree).[87] The Emperor Claudius (41–54 A.D.) had special legislation passed that permitted him to marry his brother's daughter (*i.e.,* his niece). Even a marriage between tutor and pupil was considered incest. There were various penalties possible for incest, ranging from death by crucifixion and banishment to more moderate punishments.

---

86. *See supra* § 12.03[A].
87. *See supra* § 12.03[B].

[3] LENOCINIUM, PROSTITUTION, & HOMOSEXUAL ACTIVITY

The *lex Iulia* also created a statutory basis for the crime known as *lenocinium*. In simple terms, *lenocinium* was any conduct that facilitated sexual crime (*e.g.,* adultery and *stuprum*). For example, a husband who was aware of his wife's adultery but failed to divorce her or to take appropriate legal steps was, himself, guilty of *lenocinium*. Friends of adulterous lovers who kept the secret were also culpable under this law. This was especially true if the friends secured money or gifts as "hush money." Interestingly, *lenocinium* even applied to a man who married a woman who had, at some earlier date, been convicted of adultery or *stuprum*. Organized prostitution was, literally speaking, *lenocinium* under the *lex Iulia*. However, ordinarily the *leno* ("pimp") was punished with only infamy (*infamia*—*i.e.,* a formal loss of reputation and certain rights[88]).

Roman law treated homosexual conduct as criminal only in narrowly defined circumstances. If a man raped or seduced another male (adult or minor) he was guilty of *stuprum*. In order for the act to be considered criminal, the victim must have been "freeborn" (*i.e.,* neither a slave nor a freedman). Otherwise, sex between a man and a male slave or a male prostitute was not criminal. Roman law did not treat lesbian sex as wrongful in any manner. In the Classical period (1st century B.C.–3rd century A.D.), convicted homosexual rapists received death sentences. A willing, passive partner paid one-half of his property as a fine, and any will that he made was declared invalid. Justinian's *Institutes* assigns death as the penalty for homosexual *stuprum*.

[F] INIURIA

It is possible that Sulla was responsible for establishing a permanent court regarding *iniuria* but we cannot be certain. Sulla was responsible for the *lex Cornelia de iniuriis*, a law that created what amounted to a criminal cause of action against persons for hitting others or for forcefully breaking into another's home. Roman law also treated *iniuria* as a kind of tort (delict).[89] We really are uncertain of the subtle distinctions that differentiated criminal *iniuria* from *iniuria* as an *obligatio ex delicto*. From our ancient sources (*e.g.,* Gaius) it appears that the two operated in a parallel, non-exclusive fashion.

---

88. *See* J.A. CROOK, Law and Life of Rome, 90 B.C.–A.D. 212 83–85 (1967).
89. For more about torts and delicts, *see infra* § 12.06.

Any injury to one's reputation, dignity, honor, or bodily integrity was classified under *iniuria*. *Iniuria* applied to a variety of offensive conduct. For example, daubing excrement on a person and the deliberate contamination of a water supply were considered types of *iniuria* that warranted severe penalties. If an alleged defamatory statement were proved true, that truth operated as a defense to *iniuria*. Fines, beating, and flogging were common punishments imposed for *iniuria*. Apparently, the severity depended, in part, upon the status of the perpetrator, and, in part, upon the perceived outrageousness of the conduct involved.

[G] CRIMES AGAINST THE STATE

[1] PERDUELLIO & MAIESTAS

In the Classical period (1st century B.C.–3rd century A.D.), the most commonly used term for treason was *maiestas* (short for *crimen laesae maiestatis*). *Perduellio* is a term that also refers to treasonous conduct, but it was a term used more in the earlier Republic. Clearly one could be guilty of *vis*, *res repetundae* (extortion),[90] and *maiestas* for the same act. According to the jurist Paul, *maiestas* included a number of illegal activities: armed assault on the State; gathering soldiers or conducting warfare without the State's permission; and, desertion. The giving of any assistance to an enemy (*e.g.*, supplying information, selling goods, providing shelter) constituted treason as well. Ulpian makes it clear that conspiring to kill a magistrate or other public official was treasonous. In 103 B.C., the *lex Appuleia* established the first permanent court dedicated to accusations related to treason. As part of his court revamping, Sulla (82/81 B.C.) appended additional measures to address *maiestas* in the provinces. The most common penalties for *perduellio* during the Republic were death or exile. In the Classical period, although it was possible to receive a milder punishment if the circumstances warranted it, *maiestas* was routinely punished with the combination of execution (often by crucifixion) and forfeiture of one's property to the State.

[2] RES REPETUNDAE

The *lex Calpurnia* (149 B.C.) criminalized *res repetundae* (extortion) by provincial governors. Other legislation—probably passed in the latter half of the 2nd century B.C.—broadened the definition of extortion to include losses not just by Roman citizens but losses suffered by allies and foreigners

---

90. *See infra* § 12.05[G][2].

as well. In time, in addition to treating improper gain by provincial governors themselves as *res repetundae*, Roman law also punished others working for or in association with provincial governors for extortion (even the wives of provincial governors). *Res repetundae* included within its scope a variety of activities, such as accepting bribes or special favors, trading for personal profit, and any other conduct that allowed a person to reap individual gain by virtue of his office. By the last century of the Republic, banishment was the most common punishment for *res repetundae*. In the Empire both banishment and execution are attested as penalties.

[3] PECULATUS & DE RESIDUIS

The jurist Paul describes the crime *peculatus* (a kind of embezzlement) as defined by the *lex Iulia*, as any wrongful appropriation, diversion, or conversion of sacred, religious, or public funds. *Peculatus* included taking the spoils of war (since such plunder technically belonged to the Roman people). What we ordinarily think of as embezzlement (*i.e.,* the unlawful appropriation of money that has been entrusted) is closer to the Roman crime of *de residuis*. Another fundamental difference is that in *peculatus* the embezzler never has the right to possession of the money (or property) whereas in *de residuis* he did, at one point at least, have lawful possession. The punishment for *peculatus* was usually banishment and (in the Empire) confiscation of the offender's property. The customary penalty for *de residuis* was to pay a fine.

[4] AMBITUS

Ambitus was criminal conduct related to elections, such as bribery and other types of electoral corruption. *Ambitus* is well attested as a crime even in the early Republic, and we know of trials in the *quaestio de ambitu* in the late 2nd century B.C. There was quite a bit of legislation concerning *ambitus* in the last half century of the Republic. As the law developed, even activities such as staging gladiatorial contests and giving lavish banquets were considered to come within the scope of *ambitus*. The commonest punishments for *ambitus* were fines and a loss of status (*e.g.,* expulsion from the Senate).

[5] COUNTERFEITING & FORGERY

Sulla's legislation (82/81 B.C.) created a permanent court that dealt with forgery of money and forgery of wills (*falsum*). In the Empire (27 B.C.–mid-5th century A.D.), the *cognitio* procedure saw to it that the concept of forgery was broadened.[91] Eventually any intentional alteration of a

---

91. See *supra* § 11.03[C] regarding *cognitio* procedure.

formal document was considered forgery. Sulla was responsible for the *lex Cornelia nummaria*, the earliest Roman statute to criminalize the counterfeiting of money. According to Ulpian's account, Sulla's law prohibited the unsanctioned manufacture of silver coins as well as the purchase or sale of coins that were made to look like silver (but which were, in truth, some cheaper metal substitute). By the early 4th century A.D. the Romans had passed legislation that expanded counterfeiting to include copper money as well as silver. Paul specifically notes that coins might be "counterfeited" in a number of creative ways: *lavaverit* ("washed"), *conflaverit* ("melted"), *raserit* ("shaved"), *corruperit* ("sheared"), *vitiavert* ("adulterated"). Ulpian explains that counterfeiters tried to simulate gold coins by rubbing or washing fakes with an artificial gold color or they attempted to shave traces of metal from otherwise legitimate gold coins.

The penalties for counterfeiting silver or copper coinage depended, to a great extent, on the counterfeiter's social class. Free men were usually banished (to distant islands during the Empire) and forfeited their property. Lower classes were either condemned to work in the mines or crucified, and slaves were executed. If, on the other hand, the counterfeiting involved gold coins, even upper class citizens could be sent to die by wild animals or, in special circumstances, burning, and slaves were executed by either burning or crucifiction.

[H] MISCELLANEOUS CRIMES

[1] STELLIONATUS

One of the more interesting crimes was *stellionatus* (acting like a lizard). There do not appear to have been specific elements necessary for proof of *stellionatus*. Rather, it seems to have been a general concept that was related to fraud. According to Paul, it involved one person convincing another to give him property. For example, pledging property that belonged to someone else was *stellionatus*. Also, an imposter who posed as another person (and thereby profited) was guilty of *stellionatus*. Presumably, any conduct that was dishonest or fraudulent (but that did not fit neatly into another defined criminal category) could be dealt with as *stellionatus*.

[2] KIDNAPPING

Kidnapping (*plagium*) was treated as a crime. A late Republican statute, the *lex Fabia* (63 B.C.), criminalized the sale of a Roman citizen, freedman, or slave who belonged to someone else. Indeed, this was simply a kind of kidnapping. If the buyer knew that the object of the sale was actually a free citizen, he also was liable as a criminal for kidnapping. On the other hand, a good faith purchaser of someone else's slave could not be criminally liable. Depending on the individual factors present in a kidnapping case (and the particular period of legal history), the penalty might be death. But we know that not all kidnappings were punished by death. Some kidnappers were fined. In the Empire, members of the upper classes were fined as much as half of their property. Lower classes guilty of kidnapping were sometimes crucified and sometimes sent to work in the mines.

[3]   SALE OF RUNAWAY SLAVES

Criminals guilty of trading in runaway slaves were usually punished with fines. Near the end of the Republic, one of the praetor's edicts transformed the delict of slave corruption into a criminal act as well.[92] The criminal penalty for slave corruption was twice the value of the slave. Nevertheless, the civil aspects of this wrong continued to dominate.

[4]   CASTRATION & CIRCUMCISION

A person guilty of castrating another received capital punishment. Slaves were the most common victims. Interestingly, the Emperor Hadrian (117–138 A.D.) broadened the ban on castration to include circumcision within its scope as well. Later, the Emperor Antoninus Pius (138–161 A.D.) made an exception regarding circumcision for the Jews.

[5]   GAMBLING

Certain Republican laws prohibited gambling (at least outside of the family). Even the Senate resolved to forbid gambling but, in the same way that office pools thrive during NCAA March Madness in the United States, a fair amount of informal wagering seems to have prospered in ancient Rome as well.

[6]   CRIMES RELATED TO RELIGION

Although the Romans resisted the infiltration of foreign religions, legally, at least, they were reasonably tolerant. They drew the line, however, at the human sacrifice involved in Druidism. The extent to which Christianity was illegal is the subject of robust historical debate. Clearly there were persecutions under Nero (54–68 A.D.) and other emperors in the early Empire. But it is doubtful that Christianity was "illegal" *per se* under Roman criminal law.

---

92. *See infra* § 12.06[B][6].

Roman law did treat circumcision of non-Jews as a criminal offense,[93] but Imperial Roman law dealt with Jews and Jewish religion itself with a considerable degree of tolerance. For example, Jews were allowed to worship on their Sabbath and they did not have to sacrifice to the State gods of Rome. But Christians were prohibited from converting to Judaism and Christians and Jews were not allowed to intermarry.

§ 12.06 TORTS (OBLIGATIONES EX DELICTO & OBLIGATIONES QUASI EX DELICTO)

[A] CLASSIFICATION: THE LAW OF OBLIGATIONS

In a very basic sense, there were essentially two methods of acquiring things in Roman law: 1) by succession; and, more importantly, 2) by an *obligatio*. Although the law of *obligationes* (obligations) is not commonly used in the terminology of English Common Law, it is still conventional in the Civil Law countries of continental Europe. In the United States lawyers speak of torts and contracts, but in most European legal systems, these are lumped together in the law of "obligations."

Generally speaking, an *obligatio* in Roman law entailed some relationship between two persons in which one was a creditor and the other a debtor. The legal relationships that gave one person the right to require any performance of any sort from the other were *obligationes*. According to one definition in Justinian's *Digest*, a creditor had the right to require a debtor to perform any one of three tasks: 1) *dare* (to give); 2) *facere* (to make or do); and, 3) *praestare* (to give to the creditor that which the debtor has produced).[94]

The Roman jurists who compiled Justinian's *Institutes* categorized *obligationes* into four groups: 1) *obligationes ex contractu* (obligations arising from contract); 2) *obligationes ex delicto* (obligations arising from delict); 3) *obligationes quasi ex contractu* (obligations as if arising from contract); and, 4) *obligationes quasi ex delicto* (obligations as if arising from delict). For purposes of our study, we will consider *obligationes ex delicto* and *obligationes quasi ex delicto* as part of the body of tort law.[95] Similarly, we will

---

93. *See supra* § 12.05[H][4].
94. For example, this would occur when a publisher contracts with an author to write a book and then transfer the manuscript to the publisher.
95. This not because the analogy is perfect, but because it is adequate for our purposes.

consider *obligationes ex contractu* and *obligationes quasi ex contractu* as part of the law of contracts.[96]

[B] OBLIGATIONES EX DELICTO (DELICTA)

[1] INTRODUCTION

Although the Roman law of delict is analogous in some respects to modern tort law, (*i.e.*, civil wrongs), merely translating the Latin term *delictum* as a "tort" is, strictly speaking, unsatisfactory. In many respects the Roman *delictum* was closer to either crime or an intentional tort. Damages for delicts were usually punitive. The Romans thought of a delict as any violation of legal prohibitions that caused a negative result. As is true with tort law today, however, there is no one, all-encompassing definition for delict. Rather, there are distinct types, individual delicts. Gaius and Justinian, in their *Institutes*, address four delicts: 1) *furtum* (theft); 2) *rapina* (robbery with violence); 3) *damnum iniuria datum* (property damage); and 4) *iniuria* (personal injury).

[2] FURTUM (THEFT)

The Twelve Tables differentiated between *furtum manifestum* and *furtum nec manifestum*. This distinction is basically the difference between whether a thief is caught in the act or not. The penalty for *furtum manifestum* was to be beaten and then the perpetrator was handed over to the victim of the theft as a slave or bondsman. In addition, the thief was required to pay quadruple damages (*i.e.*, four-times the value of the objects that he had attempted to steal). A slave who was found guilty of *furtum manifestum* was first beaten and then executed by hurling him from the famous Tarpeian Rock. According to the Twelve Tables, when someone discovered a thief red-handed at night, he was entitled to kill him on the spot. By the time of Hadrian (117–138 A.D.), summary execution in this manner was considered illegal only if the death was later deemed unwarranted.

The Twelve Tables permitted someone who accused another of *furtum* to search the accused's house to look for the stolen property. The accuser was required to search practically naked (save for a loincloth) so that he, himself, could not later be accused of planting the allegedly stolen property by hiding it under a garment. This ritualistic search was called *lance et licio*. If the accuser discovered stolen property in this manner, the theft was considered *manifestum*. If the accused refused to permit the *lance et licio*, his penalty was to pay quadruple the value of the goods alleged to have been stolen.

---

96. *See infra* § 12.07.

The Roman jurists debated the nature of the *actus reus* ("wrongful conduct") that was necessary as an element of *furtum*. Did a person have to actually remove the thing (*res*) or was merely touching the *res* sufficient to constitute the requisite *actus reus*? This, in turn, sparked a debate as to whether the taking of only a small portion of a bulk constituted a theft of the whole or whether it really should be considered merely a theft of that portion taken. For example, was the taking of a few sips of wine or a few grains of wheat the taking of the entire cask or bushel? The debate was lively but never satisfactorily resolved by the jurists.

[3] RAPINA (ROBBERY WITH VIOLENCE)

Rapina was identified as a separate wrong about 76 B.C., after the civil war. As a penalty, a convicted robber paid his victim quadruple damages. Oddly, most scholars believe, however, that the victim was not also entitled to have his property returned to him.

[4] DAMNUM INIURIA DATUM (PROPERTY DAMAGE)

In 287 B.C., the *concilium plebis* enacted the *lex Aquilia*, the principal Republican statute that dealt with property damage. There were three main sections, or chapters, of the *lex Aquilia*: 1) relating to the killing of slaves and herd animals; 2) relating to debtors who defrauded their creditors; and, 3) relating to other general property damage.

In chapter one, the law addressed situations where a person intentionally or negligently killed either a slave or herd animal. Some of the animals that came within this statute were horses, mules, sheep, goats, and pigs. In order for a cause of action to be viable, the death had to have been the result of a direct cause. For example, if A's cart ran over B's pig, A would be liable. But if an axe fell off of A's cart and B's pig came along later and tripped over it resulting in the swine's death, A would not be liable, because the death was indirect. Nevertheless, a praetor could interpret this rule broadly if he felt that justice would be served in any given case. If found liable, the defendant had to pay the owner the highest value of the slave or animal during the previous year.

Chapter two was intended to deal with special situations involving fraud in a creditor-debtor relationship. Later, the contract known as *mandatum*[97] rendered this section obsolete.

In chapter three, the law dealt with property damage that was: 1) direct (like the damage in chapter one); 2) intentional or negligent; and, 3) caused

---

97. *See infra* § 12.07[E].

by burning, snapping, or breaking (*urere, frangere, rumpere*). If found liable, the defendant had to pay the amount of damage incurred as assessed up to thirty days after the incident.

[5] INIURIA (PERSONAL INJURY)

The Twelve Tables had three provisions that dealt with *iniuria*. The first established that, if a person's limb were actually destroyed, the injured party and the wrongdoer should try to reach a monetary settlement; but if they could not, the injured party was entitled to seek revenge. The second provided that when a person suffered a broken bone as a result of another's wrongdoing, the injured party was entitled to 300 asses[98] if he was a free man and 150 asses if he was a slave. The third provision gave an action for 25 asses for all lesser injuries. Aulus Gellius (*c.* 130–180 A.D.) tells the story of a wealthy Roman who used to walk around town accompanied by a slave who held a bag of coins. The man simply smacked any person whom he pleased and then instructed the slave to give his victim 25 asses. If a plaintiff sued for *iniuria* and lost, he had to pay the defendant 10% of the value of the claim. Presumably, this rule discouraged the bringing of frivolous lawsuits.

In the 3rd century B.C., praetors included a law of *iniuria* in their edicts and gradually transformed the law. Under the praetors' edicts, judges determined damages on a case by case basis rather than having damages that were fixed by statute. In addition, praetors expanded the law of *iniuria* to include intangible as well as tangible injuries. For example, certain insults and verbal abuse intended to disgrace or dishonor others were interpreted as forms of *iniuria*.

[6] MISCELLANEOUS DELICTS

Other major delicts included the following:

1) About 80 B.C. the praetor named Octavius issued an edict that dealt with extortion.

2) In 66 B.C. Aquillius Gallus issued an edict on fraud that actually related to fraud in a contract context only. In the Empire, Labeo redefined fraud more broadly to include non-contractual fraud as well.

3) Another edict created an action known as *actio servi corrupti*. This action concerned situations where a person influenced another's slave in a negative manner.

---

98. An as was the principal bronze coin and monetary unit in the Republic.

4) There were a number of other miscellaneous actions that dealt with the use of and damage to agricultural property.

[C] NOXAL LIABILITY & LIABILITY FOR DAMAGE CAUSED BY ANIMALS

The concept of noxal liability operated to limit liability for a father or a slave owner—for injuries caused by a son or slave—to the amount of the value of the son or slave. If a son or slave caused damage to another, the father/master retained the option of paying the claim up to the value of the son/slave. If the claim was worth more than the son/slave, the father/master, then, had the option of merely turning the son/slave over to the victim, as full payment.

Under the Twelve Tables, an animal's owner was liable for damage caused by the animal. The owner, though, was not liable in cases where someone provoked the animal. If, however, the amount of damage was greater than the beast's value, then the owner could opt, instead, simply to turn over the animal. Aediles issued special edicts regarding damage done by wild animals that were being kept near a road in preparation for gladiatorial combat.

[D] OBLIGATIONES QUASI EX DELICTO (QUASI DELICTS)

Justinian, but not Gaius, categorized four separate actions that he labeled as *quasi ex delicto* (as if arising from delict). It is difficult to isolate a common thread that unites the *obligationes quasi ex delicto*. In some respects these quasi delicts—at least three of the four—are similar to some modern torts in which American law imposes liability as a matter of vicarious liability (*e.g.*, liability imposed on employers due to injuries caused by employees). But the oldest, "the judge who made the case his own" (*iudex qui litem suam fecit*), does not involve the principle of vicarious liability. One common characteristic, however, may be that each quasi delict, apparently, imposed liability without reference to fault. In other words, the Roman law concerning *obligationes quasi ex delicto* imposed liability in circumstances where modern law imposes strict liability (*i.e.*, liability imposed without regard to "fault"). The following were the four most prominent quasi delicts: 1) *actio de rebus effusis vel deiectis* ("an action relating to things which have been poured out or thrown out"); 2) *actio de posito et suspenso* ("an action relating to something that has been placed or hung out"); 3) *iudex qui litem suam fecit* ("a judge who has made a case his own"); and lastly, 4) an action relating to *nauta, caupo, stabularius* (for owners of a ship, inn, or stable).

1) *Actio de rebus effusis vel deiectis* was an action against the owner of premises from which things were thrown or poured onto a street. This action gave passers-by redress for damage caused by the things that were thrown or poured from a structure.

2) *Actio de posito et suspenso* was an action against the owner of a structure when an obstruction was suspended or otherwise placed in such a way that it injured passers-by.

3) *Iudex qui litem suam fecit* occurred when a judge rendered an incorrect decision or otherwise wrongfully damaged a litigant (*e.g.*, if the judge imposed damages outside of the scope of those provided in the praetor's formula).

4) There was also strict liability imposed on those in charge of a ship, inn, or stable for damages caused to persons or their property on the ship, at the inn, or in the stable.

§ 12.07 TRADE, CONTRACTS & COMMERCIAL LAW

[A] INTRODUCTION

All school children are familiar with the vast extent of the Roman Empire. Its size and importance are well known. There is little doubt that sophisticated laws of contract and commercial law were necessary for the economic growth of such an empire. Even as early as the Etruscan period in the 6th century B.C., Rome was known for its vibrant trade and commerce.

As was noted, the Roman law relating to contracts, *obligationes ex contractu*, was actually a sub-part of the Roman law of *obligationes*.[99] A contract to an ancient Roman was altogether a different notion from what it has become in Anglo-American Common Law. A Roman contract was any agreement expressed in the appropriate form (of course there also had to be some cause or purpose). In early Roman law, without the proper form, there was no contract. Unlike modern legal systems, Roman contract law was not based upon a general, abstract theory of contract. Instead, the Romans recognized a number of types of individual contracts. In order to be valid, an agreement had to be fashioned using one of these types, employ-

---

99. *See supra* § 12.06[A].

ing either an established pattern of words and conduct or, in the alternative, relating to a specific purpose.

Both Gaius and Justinian arranged contracts into four categories: 1) real; 2) verbal; 3) literal; and, 4) consensual. We shall examine these in a slightly different order: 1) verbal; 2) literal; 3) real; and, 4) consensual. In addition, we shall consider a fifth group that has come to be known as "innominate."

[B] VERBAL CONTRACTS

Verbal contracts existed well before the end of the *legis actio* period[100] but had long since lost their prominence by the time of Justinian (482–565 A.D.). These contracts were those executed orally. But the law strictly delineated the precise words that were required. The parties had to say a scripted formula of words in order for a verbal contract to be valid. If the parties failed to utter the proper words in the proper sequence at the proper time, the contract was void. *Stipulatio* (also known as *sponsio*) is the earliest known of the verbal contracts in Roman Law. The Twelve Tables make it clear that *stipulatio* was enforceable. *Condictio* was the name of the cause of action that a plaintiff brought for breach of *stipulatio*. Originally, only Roman citizens could conclude a contract by *stipulatio*. It became available to foreigners, however, by the Empire (27 B.C.).

Stipulatio required a very rigid verbal formula. It demanded that both promisor and promisee meet face to face to create their contract by means of an oral exchange in a prescribed formulaic pattern of question and answer. The promisee had to begin by asking the promisor a question using the Latin verb (second person singular, present active indicative) *spondesne*? (*Spondesne* to do such and such?—"Do you promise on your oath to do such and such?"). The promisor, playing his role, had to respond to the promisee's question using the same verb, but in the first person singular, present active indicative, *spondeo* (*Spondeo* to do such and such—"I promise on my oath to do such and such"). As the law evolved, other verbs were eventually accepted as valid in addition to *spondere*. But the essence remained the same; the promisor's answer to the promisee's question had to be a mirror image in order to meet the strict rules of contract by *stipulatio*. In time, a number of the formal requirements slackened. Ultimately, although this was certainly not required, it became commonplace for parties to chronicle their *stipulatio* in written form (*i.e., cautio*).

---

100. This period of Roman legal procedure came to a close about the end of the 3rd century B.C. *See supra* § 11.03[A].

One of the truly remarkable features of *stipulatio*—at least in early Roman law—was that once made, it was virtually indestructible. To be sure, there were some circumstances that would make a purported *stipulatio* void. For example an agreement to do something that was immoral, illegal, or impossible was invalid. In addition, a *stipulatio* promising performance either by or for a third party was similarly invalid. But, otherwise, even if a promise had been coerced by fraud or threats of violence, a contract of *stipulatio* was considered iron-clad.

Eventually, praetors took measures to alleviate some of these injustices during the final half-century of the Republic. For example, the praetor Octavius (80 B.C.) granted a cause of action (*metus causa*) that exacted quadruple damages to the victims of *stipulatio* by extortion. Similarly, he granted such victims a valid affirmative defense (*exceptio metus*) in cases where they were sued for breach of contract. Aquillius Gallus (66 B.C.) took corresponding steps for persons who had been lured into a *stipulatio* by fraud. He provided a cause of action (*actio de dolo*) for which he allowed compensatory damages. And, as was the case with Octavius' measures for extortion, Gallus allowed an affirmative defense for contracting parties who had entered a *stipulatio* due to fraud (*exceptio doli*).

[C] LITERAL CONTRACTS

The literal contract is curious, indeed. We have a number of these contracts from the ruins of Pompeii. The Roman head of the household kept an account book. By recording transactions in this ledger, a literal contract was presumed to have been made. In several respects, the literal contract appears to have been a type of memorandum that was meant to formalize and amend an already existing debt. The detailed steps necessary for the creation of a literal contract were as follows. The *paterfamilias*, the creditor, wrote two records in his ledger: 1) He fictitiously indicated that his debtor had paid a certain debt; and, 2) He fictitiously indicated that he had made a loan to his debtor. It is possible that this was similar to our modern concept of "novation". We can only assume that the debtor agreed to the literal contract in exchange for a different interest rate or a longer period in which to repay the debt.

[D] REAL CONTRACTS

Real contracts were agreements that entailed one person (call him A) delivering a *res* (hence the appellation "*real*" from the Latin word *res*, "thing") to another (call him B). In simple terms, then, the agreement became binding when one party transferred an object to another. Basically, the agreement in each real contract was that B promised to return to A either the *res* itself or an equivalent *res*, depending upon which particular type of real contract was used. There were four kinds of real contracts: 1) *mutuum*; 2) *commodatum*; 3) *depositum*; and, 4) *pignus*.

In a contract of *mutuum*, one party gave either money or fungible goods (*i.e.*, goods that may be substituted for one another without significant impact) to another. The recipient then used the money or goods. His obligation was to return the equivalent amount of money or goods (*i.e.*, not the same exact money or goods that were loaned at the outset). *Mutuum* was a unilateral contract that bound the person who borrowed the money or goods. In short, *mutuum* was a loan of one or more fungible goods. For example, *mutuum* was convenient when grain or money was the subject *res*. The creditor did not care whether he received the exact grain or money in return. He only cared that he receive its equivalent. The creditor in a *mutuum* actually transferred ownership (*i.e.*, *dominium*) of the *res* to the debtor. Thus, many legal historians characterize *mutuum* as a loan for consumption.

Commodatum was a gratuitous loan.[101] Unlike *mutuum* the debtor did not receive actual ownership of the subject *res*. He simply was given the right to use it (*i.e.*, *usus*)[102], not to consume it. Thus, *commodatum* was similar to *mutuuum* in some respects (*i.e.*, a loan of goods) but ordinarily the borrower was obligated to return the thing, itself, not merely its equivalent, at the end of the contract. So, only *res quae usu non consumatum*[103] could be the object property of a contract of *commodatum*. In modern law, we might characterize this as a bailment for the benefit of the bailee.

Depositum differed from *commodatum* in that it was a delivery intended to benefit the depositor (bailor), not the depositee (bailee). The depositee was not permitted to use the thing deposited. He merely kept it for the depositor and returned it. *Depositum*, therefore, was a gratuitous loan for safekeeping. Again, like *commodatum*, ownership did not pass from bailor to bailee.

Pignus was a very old type of real security (a pledge).[104] In *pignus* the creditor transferred merely possession (*i.e.*, *detentio*) of the collateral to his debtor and he (*i.e.*, the debtor) retained ownership (*i.e.*, *dominium*) of it.

---

101. It was essential that it was gratuitous or else the contract would be considered a contract for the hire of a thing (*locatio conductio rei*). *See infra* § 12.07[E].
102. *See supra* § 12.02[E].
103. *See supra* § 12.02[B].
104. *See infra* § 12.07[I].

[E] CONSENSUAL CONTRACTS

The Roman consensual contracts exhibit the practical common-sensical penchant of the ancient Romans. There was no specific formula required (*e.g.*, as in the case of the *stipulatio*) for these contracts—no formalities. The good faith agreement of the parties was really all that was necessary. The four consensual contracts that Roman law admitted were: 1) *emptio venditio* (purchase and sale); 2) *locatio conductio* (renting and hiring); 3) *societas* (partnership); and 4) *mandatum* (mandate: grant and acceptance of a gratuitous commission). We do not know what praetor or praetors first recognized consensual contracts as valid and binding agreements. But Roman commercial law greatly benefitted from this innovation.

Emptio venditio was a contract for purchase and sale. It occurred simply when a seller transferred something to a buyer for a sum of money. The two indispensable ingredients needed for a contract of *emptio venditio* were an agreement as to the subject matter (*res*) and a stipulated price. It was routine, though not a legal requirement, for the buyer and seller either to reduce their agreement to writing or to conclude the contract in the presence of witnesses. Justinian altered the contract of *emptio venditio* in the following manner. If the parties agreed to put their contract in writing, then either party was entitled to withdraw unless the buyer had given an *arra* (deposit/earnest money). If the buyer backed out after he had given the seller an *arra*, then he forfeited it. On the other hand, if the seller was the one who withdrew, then he was obligated to give the buyer double the amount of the *arra* that had been given. This particular rule was similar to our modern liquidated damages (*i.e.*, an amount of money stipulated in a contract that a party promises to pay in the event of breach).

If the parties were mistaken about the *res*, it was possible for one of the parties legally to avoid the contract. For example, suppose a buyer agreed to buy a statue on the assumption that it was made of gold. If it turned out to be bronze, instead, the mistake was probably sufficiently significant to permit him to avoid the purchase.

The majority view (the Proculian view in this case) was that the price for *emptio venditio* had to be paid in coined money in order to be valid. The Sabinian view allowed for a contract of sale when the parties actually contemplated an exchange of goods (barter). The price had to be certain—not dependent upon future events. For example, the price could not be next week's market price. In addition, the price had to be a real price, not merely a sham amount used to mask what would have otherwise been a gift.

Locatio conductio was a contract of renting and hiring for money. The parties had to agree on both the subject matter and the price. There were three types of *locatio conductio* contracts: 1) *locatio conductio rei* (which involved the rental of a thing or land);[105] 2) *locatio operis faciendi* (which involved contracting for completion of a job—*i.e.*, work to be done—or the creation of a designated outcome for a fee, *e.g.*, constructing a building, washing clothes, providing medical care); 3) *locatio conductio operarum* (which was rental of services—usually relatively menial tasks that involved little, if any, independent judgment).

Societas was the Roman partnership or joint venture. And *mandatuum* was a originally any gratuitous service performed in response to another's request.[106]

[F] INNOMINATE CONTRACTS

There was a separate group of Roman contracts that did not fit neatly into any of these four categories. These came to be known as *innominate* (*i.e.*, without a name). Nevertheless, the law recognized that they created binding relationships (and in fact some did have names). This ultimately became a very large group. Three innominate contracts (that actually had names) are worth mentioning: 1) *permutatio* (analogous to barter); 2) *aestimatum* (analogous to a conditional sale); and, 3) *transactio* (analogous to a settlement in lieu of legal process).

[G] CONTRACT DAMAGES

Some Roman contracts included a *sanctio* (sanction) actually written into the text. This was generally analogous to liquidated damages in modern contract law. Similarly, it will be recalled that the consensual contract *emptio venditio* imposed a type of liquidated damages when the buyer gave a deposit (*arra*).[107] Otherwise, a *sanctio* could result from non-performance or improper performance of a contract. If the parties themselves failed to include a *sanctio*, the Roman law of contract presumed that the breaching party would compensate the injured party for two types of damages: 1) *damnum emergens* (damage suffered as a consequence of breach, *e.g.*, expenses for the decreased value of the property); and, 2) *lucrum cessans* (lost profit). A breaching party had to pay both of these types of damages. But in order to recover damages, a plaintiff was required to prove that the defendant had breached

---

105. This could also include the hiring and rental of slaves.
106. In later Roman law, the person who performed the service was permitted to receive compensation.
107. *See supra* § 12.07[E].

(*i.e.*, that the defendant was guilty, *culpa*). There were different degrees of *culpa*; for example, *culpa lata* (broad guilt) and *culpa levis* (slight guilt). Even *culpa levis* made a breaching party liable for *damnum emergens*. But if a breacher was found to be *culpa lata*, he was liable for both *damnum emergens* and *lucrum cessans*.

Culpa lata was, in some respects, similar to the modern "reasonable person" standard; disregard of the vigilance which would be observed by any *paterfamilias*. *Culpa levis*, however, was analogous in many respects to a "very careful person" standard; disregard of the vigilance which would be observed by a *diligentissimus paterfamilias* (a very careful *paterfamilias*).

[H] OBLIGATIONES QUASI EX CONTRACTU

In Roman Law quasi contract bore certain similarities to the notion of quasi contract in English and American Common Law. Although Justinian's laws discuss six different varieties, two examples should suffice to give a sense of the principles involved.

1) *Condictio indebiti per errorem soluti* was an action available when a person lost ownership of something (usually money) under conditions where the law considered that it would be unjust for him to be incapable of recovering it or its value. Essentially this happened whenever something belonging to one person passed into the hands of another in circumstances in which the latter ought not to be able to retain it. We might say that the latter had been unjustly enriched and that the former should be entitled to have the value returned to him.

2) *Negotiorum gestio* occurred when one person provided a service to another, even though the beneficiary had neither requested nor authorized the service. If performed in appropriate circumstances and in good faith, the party who conferred the benefit was entitled to reasonable compensation. A standard example of *negotiorum gestio* occurred when a landowner was absent for a period of time and his property had fallen into disrepair. In these circumstances, another person was allowed to enter and make the necessary repairs. Ordinarily, a person was legally permitted to step in and take charge of another's affairs only: 1) if the owner could not manage his own affairs—due to certain obstacles; 2) if no other person was authorized by the owner to manage his affairs; and, 3) if immediate measures were not employed, the owner would have suffered more substantial damage than he would otherwise. In such circumstances, although there was no agreement, an *obligatio quasi ex contractu* was created, and the owner was legally required to pay a reasonable fee to the person who performed the services (the *gestor*).

[I] REAL SECURITY

Very early in their history, the Romans practiced the custom of taking collateral (real security) for loans. *Fiducia* was probably the first type of real security legally recognized in ancient Rome. *Fiducia* was accomplished by an actual transfer of ownership (*dominium*). In other words, the debtor actually transferred ownership of the collateral to his creditor. *Fiducia* was doubly burdensome for a debtor since, because he no longer owned the collateral, he was unable to take out a second mortgage using the same collateral. Obviously, if the collateral were *res mancipi*, the method of transfer was *mancipatio* or *in iure cessio* (for intangible *res mancipi*).[108] For *res nec mancipi*, transfer was usually effected by *in iure cessio*.[109] This was a great deal for creditors, who could simply keep the security if the debtor failed to repay the loan. A creditor could sell the security and pass good title to it, since he was, in fact, the owner. In many instances, however, a creditor allowed his debtor to retain possession of the collateral during the pendency of the *fiducia*. If, on the other hand, the creditor had possession of it and refused to return it after the debtor had repaid the debt, the debtor was entitled to a legal action against the creditor, called *actio fiduciae*.

Another truly antique type of real security was *pignus*.[110] The principal distinction between *pignus* and *fiducia* is that in *pignus* the debtor transferred merely possession (*detentio*) of the collateral to his creditor; but unlike the case with *fiducia*, he (*i.e.*, the debtor) retained *dominium*, ownership of it.[111]

The third kind of real security, *hypotheca*, was common by about 150 B.C. *Hypotheca* merely created a right in the creditor to claim the collateral in the event that the debtor defaulted on his loan. Thus, the creditor did not obtain either ownership, *dominium* (as was the case with *fiducia*) or possession, *detentio* (as was the case with *pignus*) of the collateral.

[J] BUSINESS ENTITIES

In modern law, especially with the rise of capitalism in the 19th century A.D., the recognition of legal entities, or juridical "persons" has become important. One aspect of legal entities that is crucial is the fictitious separation of the entity from the individuals involved in it (*e.g.*, the insulation

---

108. *See supra* §§ 12.02[D][1] and 12.02[D][3].
109. *See supra* § 12.02[D][3].
110. *See supra* § 12.07[D].
111. *See supra* § 12.02[C].

from liability for capital investors). This separation was actually an ancient Roman concept. In Roman law, there were a number of recognized legal entities. Technically speaking, at least four types of things were characterized as separate legal entities in Roman law: 1) the property of the Roman State (or the *Populus Romanus*); 2) the *Fiscus* (treasury); 3) *municipii* (local governments); and, 4) a *societas* (an entity that arose when two or more people combined their efforts into a joint enterprise — like building a ship to transport goods).[112] The notion of the separation of corporate responsibility from personal responsibility evolved in dealing with the *societas*.

[K] TAXES

Romans paid taxes on such diverse things as the sale of slaves, prostitution, urine (gathered from public toilets), importation of goods, and inheritance. Augustus (27 B.C.–14 A.D.) was responsible for a 5% estate tax (with exceptions only for very small estates and only for very close relatives who were heirs. The *siliquae* was a tax on the sale of goods. In order to fund the Roman army, the middle class paid high taxes. By the latter part of the 2nd century A.D., the tax burden had become extreme.

§ 12.08 CHAPTER SUMMARY

[A] PERSONAL STATUS

There were three types of status that affected an individual's legal capacity (*caput*) most significantly: 1) citizenship (*civitas*); 2) freedom (*libertas*); and, 3) family (*familia*). Roman citizens — a group which by 212 A.D. included all adult males living in the Empire — enjoyed three important rights: 1) the right to governmental office (*ius honorum*); 2) the right to marry another citizen (*ius connubium*); and, 3) the right to participate in commercial and property transactions (*ius commercium*). The Roman notion of *caput* (legal capacity) encompassed what scholars today characterize as both "legal capacity" (*i.e.*, the legal capacity that one possesses merely by birth) and also "dispositive capacity" (*i.e.*, the capacity that one acquires). It was possible (for example, as a result of criminal punishment or marriage) for a Roman citizen to suffer a reduction in his/her personal status (*capitis deminutio*). In extreme cases, a citizen might lose all citizenship rights, while in others, he might be only partially disenfranchised (*i.e.*, losing only certain rights).

---

112. *See supra* § 12.07[E].

Roman law considered slaves as property. It was not until the Empire that laws restrained a master's freedom to punish or even to kill a slave at will. As a rule, an individual became a slave as a result of being a prisoner of war, as a result of birth, as a result of debt, or as a result of criminal punishment. Generally speaking, the child of a slave was also considered a slave. But, eventually, the law allowed that, if the mother had been free at any time during her pregnancy, then her child was considered free, not slave. Because many slaves served in responsible positions, Roman law permitted them to enter into valid contracts, on the presumption (basically a legal fiction) that their conduct created a "natural obligation" (*obligatio naturalis*). Ordinarily, a master was legally responsible for damage caused by his slaves. But a slave who served in a position of responsibility was not kept on a short leash; rather he was usually given a stipend of money by his owner (*peculium*) that he used virtually as his own.

Manumitted slaves (*libertini*) acquired both freedom and a limited form of Roman citizenship. A master could manumit a slave either legally by formal means (*e.g.*, by will, *manumissio censu, manumissio vindicata*) or extralegally by informal means (*e.g.*, by letter or declaration in the presence of witnesses). Although freedmen had some citizenship rights (*e.g.*, a limited *ius commercium*), they could neither marry a Roman citizen nor hold public office until the time of Justinian in the 6th century A.D.

[B] PROPERTY

Roman jurists classified property by creating numerous dualistic categories. Gaius said that all property was either under divine law or human law. These categories were further subdivided as well. Gaius also classified property as tangible and intangible—a classification which dictated the means by which any given property legally could be transferred from one person to another. It was also Gaius who classified property as either *res mancipi* or *res nec mancipi*. This classification also dictated the potential legal means of transfer (*i.e.*, the formalistic *mancipatio* was the only valid method for transferring *res mancipi*, such as slaves, oxen, horses, real property, and the praedial servitudes). By the time of Justinian, however, this distinction was no longer meaningful. Other property dualisms recognized by Roman jurists include: 1) things in economic circulation *vs.* those not in economic circulation (*res in commercio/res extra commercio*); 2) movables *vs.* immovables (*res mobiles/res immobiles*); 3) unique things *vs.* fungibles (*species/genera*); 4) things consumed by use *vs.* things not consumed by use (*res quae usu consumatum*/*res quae usu non consumatum*); 5) things that could be divided and maintain their basic character *vs.* those that could not.

Roman law distinguished several kinds of legal title. The three most important are: 1) *dominium* (basically equivalent to what we today call ownership); 2) *possessio* (control of a thing — though not necessarily *physical* control — coupled with a belief that one owns the property in question); 3) *detentio* (control of a thing not believing that one owns it).

Certain types of property could only be transferred, legally at least, in certain ways. For example, *res mancipi* (*e.g.*, Italic land, slaves, cattle, horses, mules, donkeys, and the four praedial servitudes; namely, *iter, actus, via,* and, *aquaeductus*) could only be transferred by *mancipatio* — a method of transfer that required specific formalities, including five witnesses, a scale, and certain formulaic statements made by the transferee. Property transferred by *mancipatio* came with an automatic warranty of title. For *res nec mancipi, traditio* — a means of transfer requiring physical delivery of the object, the intent of the transferor to transfer, and the intent of the transferee to accept — was the most widespread and practical method of property transfer. As the law evolved, the Romans validated three "soft" versions of *traditio* which, for a number of practical reasons, relaxed the requirement of actual, physical delivery: 1) *traditio longa manu* ("delivery" by providing access); 2) *traditio brevi manu* ("delivery" which has already occurred); and, 3) *constitutum possessorium* ("delivery" to occur in the future). *In iure cessio* — a form of conveyance somewhat similar to a pre-arranged quiet title action before a magistrate — was used both for *res mancipi* and *res nec mancipi* (especially for intangibles). Romans could acquire ownership (*dominium*) of an object either that had never been owned by another (*res nullius*) or that had been abandoned (*res derelictae*) simply by taking physical control of it (*occupatio*). Similarly, landowners and discoverers could acquire rights in treasure that had been found (*thesauri inventio*). *Specificatio* was a unique means of gaining ownership that arose when someone created an object that was completely new (*nova species*) from materials that someone else initially owned (*e.g.*, a sculpture created by an artist made from a stone owned by another). Under Justinian, the creator of the new thing — not the owner of the original thing — was considered the owner of the new object only if it was impractical or impossible to return it to its original state (in which case the creator had to compensate the original owner for the value of the raw material). Roman law granted ownership, by *accessio*, to the owner of a principal object when another accessory object was incorporated into the principal thing in such a way that the two became inseparably merged (*e.g.*, writing on a parchment). But it was not always easy to determine which thing should be considered the principal and which the accessory. *Usucapio* was the Roman method of acquiring property roughly analogous to modern law's adverse possession. To obtain ownership by *usucapio*, a person had to maintain *possessio* (*i.e.*, good faith possessory control) of land for two years or of other types of property for only one year.

As early as the Twelve Tables, Roman law recognized certain servitudes that were, in a number of respects, analogous to what modern law calls easements appurtenant (*i.e.*, easements dependent on a relationship to land itself). The four oldest servitudes were the so-called praedial servitudes: 1) *via* (the general right of passage through a neighbor's property); 2) *iter* (the right to walk through a neighbor's property); 3) *actus* (the right to drive animals through a neighbor's property); and, 4) *aquaeductus* (the right to conduct water from one's own property across a neighbor's property). Eventually, Roman jurists also acknowledged personal servitudes (similar to modern easements in gross), such as *usus fructus* (the right to use another's property and its fruits), *usus* (the right to use another's property but not its fruits); and *habitatio* (the right—for life—to live in another's house).

[C] FAMILY

In a Roman family, one individual was the *paterfamilias* (typically the father/husband) who controlled the legal rights and affairs of his family members. A Roman *paterfamilias* held the *patria potestas* (father's power) over all his subordinate family members. *Patria potestas* gave a father/*paterfamilias* tremendous control over the lives of his subordinates. Augustus granted a limited degree of freedom to sons who were in the army; permitting them to control the assets that they obtained through military service (*peculium castrense*).

Before the Empire, it was usually the *paterfamilias* of the groom and the *paterfamilias* of the bride who fashioned an agreement for marriage. It was common for the bride's family to contribute a dowry (*dos*) and for the groom's family to contribute marriage gifts of an equivalent amount. The offspring of a valid marriage between Roman citizens were considered both legitimate and Roman citizens as well. As a rule, girls had to be at least twelve to marry and boys had to be at least fourteen. Roman law did prohibit marriage between close relatives (but the proximity of the barred relationships varied throughout Roman history).

The two recognized, legal types of marriage were *matrimonium cum manu* (marriage with power), the older of the two, and *matrimonium sine manu* (marriage without power). When a woman married *cum manu*, she legally became subject to her husband's authority (having essentially the same legal status as a daughter). There were three principal kinds of marriage *cum manu*: 1) *confarreatio* (involving a religious ceremony); 2) *coemptio* (fundamentally an old ritualistic form of sale); and, 3) *usus* (resulting from continuous cohabitation for a year). By the Empire, marriage *sine manu* (allowing a wife to retain independent legal status) became the more common type of civil marriage.

During the Monarchy (753–509 B.C.), a husband was entitled to divorce his wife, with impunity, if she committed adultery, "tampered with the keys," or poisoned a child. The most common means of divorce was a rather simple repudiation (*repudium*), which did not even require mutual consent. Although in early Roman law a husband or wife could be penalized for initiating divorce without cause, as the law evolved, divorce without cause became common and legally accepted without penalty. As a rule, upon divorce a husband had to return most of the dowry.

Adoptio was the form of adoption that Romans used when the adoptee was still under the *patria potestas* of his *paterfamilias*. *Adoptio* employed the machinery of an artificial triple sale to make the adoption possible. *Adrogatio* was the procedure reserved for adoptees not under *patria potestas*. Because of the likelihood of extinguishing an entire family, the pontiffs and the *comitia curiata* had to approve any adoption done through *adrogatio*. A person had to be both childless and also incapable of fathering children in order even to be considered eligible to adopt by *adrogatio*.

Boys and girls who had no *paterfamilias*, and who had not yet reached puberty, were legally required to have a tutor to take care of them and to manage their affairs. A tutor could be appointed by a will, by a public official, or one could be appointed as a temporary tutor. A ward could bring legal action against a tutor who mismanaged his duties. Curators were appointed both for the mentally incompetent as well as for prodigals who squandered their inheritance.

[D] INHERITANCE & SUCCESSION

Roman law acknowledged two basic types of succession: 1) intestate (without a will; thereby forcing property to pass to persons and in proportions established by law); and, 2) testate (with a will indicating who should receive property and in what proportions). Roman inheritance law depended, to a great degree, on the distinction between cognatic relationships (family related by blood) *versus* agnatic relationships (family related through a male ancestor). Although the earliest laws of intestate succession (*i.e.*, principles established in the Twelve Tables) favored agnatic relationships, in time laws gradually came to favor cognatic ones. Intestate succession generally preferred relatives who were close in terms of degrees (*i.e.*, in terms of the number of births necessary to go from one person—ordinarily the deceased—to another—ordinarily the putative heir). As established under Justinian, the order of intestate succession was as follows: 1) children and grandchildren (*liberi*); 2) parents, grandparents, brothers and sisters (*legitimi*); 3) any other blood relatives who were not included among the *legitimi* (*cognati*); and, 4) the spouse of the deceased.

Roman law admitted a number of different forms of wills: 1) *testamentum comitiis calatis* (requiring public approval on specified days); 2) *testamentum in procinctu* (an oral will made by a soldier preparing for battle); 3) *testamentum per aes et libram* (the conventional will of the late Republic and Empire—requiring certain formalities, such as witnesses, scales, and a "buyer"); 4) the tripartite will (requiring seven witnesses, seals, and the testator's/testatrix's signature). A girl, by age twelve, and a boy, by age fourteen, could make a valid will provided that s/he was a Roman citizen and not under the *patria potestas* of another. Provisions commonly found in a Roman's will are: 1) appointment of an heir (using very precise wording); 2) appointment of *substitutii* (in the event that the named heir could not or would not serve); 3) disinheritance; 4) manumission of slaves; 5) appointment of a tutor; 6) creation of a legacy; and, 7) establishment of a trust. There were three categories of heirs under Roman law: 1) *necessarii* (slaves, who were not allowed to refuse their inheritance); 2) *sui et necessarii* (persons who passed from the *potestas* of the testator to their own [*i.e.*, they gained their independence upon the testator's death]); and, 3) *extraneii* (all others). Because a testator's heirs inherited his debts along with his assets, Justinian's laws permitted an *extraneus* to take an inventory prior to deciding whether to accept or decline an inheritance (*i.e.*, giving him the opportunity to determine whether the estate had funds sufficient to pay the testator's debts). Early laws rigidly controlled the means by which a testator could create a legacy, but later laws under Nero and Justinian relaxed these restrictions.

[E] CRIMINAL LAW

Roman law assumed that infants and insane persons were incapable of possessing criminal intent (*dolus*). Both criminal intent and a criminal act (*actus reus*) were considered standard, essential elements of any crime. Some evidence suggests, before the Twelve Tables, that an accidental homicide was punished by religious atonement, not the death penalty. In 81 B.C., Sulla established a permanent court to hear homicide cases, but the responsibility for prosecuting such a case continued to fall upon the victim's *paterfamilias*, not the State. Sulla's law, the *lex Cornelia*, brought within its scope both murder by poison and murder by means of a weapon. But intent was an element necessary to convict for murder, and absence of premeditation could serve as a mitigating circumstance. The *lex Pompeia* (55 B.C.) addressed parricide (murder of a close relative), which resulted in severe punishments such as forfeiture of property, banishment, and/or death by burning, by wild animal, or by enclosure in a sack (*culleus*). Abortion was considered a crime against a woman's husband (*i.e.*, either as a means to conceal an adultery or as a way to deprive the husband of an heir). Although early Roman law did not consider the killing of one's slave as murder (because a slave was considered mere property), by the Empire such an act was criminalized as murder. Self defense, defense of a family member, and the killing of a military deserter were all considered justifiable excuses that absolved a slayer of murder charges.

The Twelve Tables punished certain types of theft with forced labor or fines, but inflicted the death penalty in the case of arson and burglary of crops. *Abigeatus* (rustling) was treated as an extremely serious offense. During the Republic the *tresviri capitales* ordinarily adjudicated theft cases, while in the Empire it was the Prefect of the Night Watch. In addition to the garden variety thief, officials brought to justice a variety of thieves who had distinctive names: apartment burglars (*effractores*); purse cutters (*saccularii*); and those who ransacked country homes (*expilatores*). Romans usually punished thieves with forced labor in the mines and/or beatings. Special theft laws punished looters, persons who knowingly bought or otherwise received stolen goods, and persons who harbored thieves.

Vis—both public and private—was considered a unique kind of crime that encompassed a vast array of criminal conduct, typically characterized by threats, force, and violence. Acts such as armed robbery, battery, sedition, violent threats, and certain kinds of sexual assault constituted forms of *vis*.

Early Roman law treated adultery as a private matter which a husband vindicated, but Augustus (27 B.C.–14 A.D.) made it a crime and established a permanent court to hear adultery cases only. Roman law imposed severe financial penalties for adultery. Both conduct that we today would classify as seduction and conduct that we would classify as rape (*i.e.*, sex without consent involving an unmarried victim) the Romans called by the name *stuprum*. Under Augustus' law, a father was given legal authority to kill his own daughter if she were caught *in flagrante delicto* either in his house or in the house of his son-in-law. Not only were sexual relations between a parent and a child considered incest but also marriage between persons whose family relationship was considered too close (*e.g.*, marriage was permitted by persons no more closely related than first cousins—the fourth degree). The crime of *lenocinium* was any conduct that facilitated a sexual crime—such as adultery or *stuprum*—(*e.g.*, knowing about but not disclosing an adultery). Homosexual relations between men were considered criminal (*i.e.*, *stuprum*) only in cases were the victim was "freeborn".

Sulla's *lex Cornelia de iniuriis* created what was essentially a criminal cause of action against persons for hitting others or for forcefully breaking into another's home. Other types of *iniuria* that, in context, strike modern readers as having more in common with crimes than torts include: 1) an injury to reputation, honor, or bodily integrity; 2) defiling another with excrement; and, 3) deliberate contamination of a water supply.

Roman law recognized several crimes that were committed against the State. *Perduellio* and *maiestas* are the terms used by the Romans of the Republic and Empire, respectively, to refer to various acts that constituted treason (*e.g.*, armed assault on the State, assisting an enemy, conspiracy to murder a public official). The Romans usually punished *res repetundae* (extortion) by provincial governors and their accomplices with banishment. Banishment was also the normal punishment for *peculatus*, embezzlement of State-owned funds. Persons found guilty of *ambitus* (*i.e.*, criminal conduct related to elections, such as bribery and other types of electoral corruption) were usually disciplined with fines and a loss of status. Roman law punished counterfeiting and forgery severely (*e.g.*, with banishment, forced labor, crucifiction, burning, mauling by wild animals).

Criminal law also penalized a number of acts which do not fit neatly into other categories. For example, *stellionatus* was a crime associated with several kinds of ill-defined fraudulent practices. *Plagium* was the Roman crime analogous to kidnapping. And it was illegal to sell a runaway slave. As a rule, castration was a crime and, by the time of Hadrian (117–138 A.D.), circumcision also was forbidden. Laws designed to curb gambling existed but were not as effective as the senate had intended. The Romans—and to a limited extent Roman law—treated Druidism and Christianity rather harshly. They dealt with Judaism, on the other hand, with comparative leniency; allowing Jews, for example, to practice circumcision and to worship on the Sabbath.

[F] TORTS

The civil law countries of continental Europe have adopted the Roman law classification that includes the law of obligations—roughly equivalent to what Anglo-American lawyers refer to as both contracts and torts. An *obligatio* (obligation) in Roman law created a legal relationship that made one person a debtor and the other a creditor. Justinian's *Institutes* classify obligations into four groups: two that are analogous to categories of modern contract law and two that are analogous to modern tort law.

The closest Roman law classification to what American lawyers call torts was the group called *obligationes ex delicto* (delicts). But to be more precise this group bears strong similarities to intentional torts and some crimes (theft, violent robbery, property damage, personal injury). The Romans subdivided theft (*furtum*) into *furtum manifestum* (caught in the act) and *furtum nec manifestum* (all other thefts). The Twelve Tables permitted an accuser to search an accused thief's home, looking for stolen goods (*lance et licio*). Roman jurists debated the philosophical distinctions of the requisite *actus reus* for theft, without ever reaching any definitive conclusions. Violent robbery (*rapina*) was identified as a distinct kind of theft around 76 B.C. The *lex Aquilia* of 287 B.C. contained three principal sections: 1) laws relating the killing of slaves and herd animals (only direct not indirect); 2) laws relating to debtors who defrauded their creditors; 3) and, 3) laws relating to other general property damage (direct, negligent, intentional, burning, snapping, breaking). The laws governing personal injury (*iniuria*) awarded money damages to victims. The Twelve Tables, generally speaking, established fixed damage amounts, whereas the praetors later modified *iniuria* to provide damages on a case by case basis (including cases involving intangible injuries such as insults). Roman law also recognized delicts dealing with matters such as extortion, fraud, corruption of slaves, and injuries to agricultural property. Although a father was generally liable for damage caused by his son, a master was generally liable for damage caused by his slave, and an owner was generally liable for damage caused by his animal, the concept of noxal liablity allowed that if the amount of liability exceeded the value of the son, slave, or animal, then the father, master, or owner could merely surrender the son, slave, or animal instead of paying. Generally speaking, both vicarious liability and strict liability appear to have been common features of the actions that the Romans called *obligationes quasi ex delicto*: 1) an action relating to things which have been poured out or thrown out; 2) an action relating to something that has been placed or hung out; 3) a judge who has made a case his own; and, 4) an action relating to a ship, inn, or stable.

[G] TRADE, CONTRACTS & COMMERCIAL LAW

The robust nature of Rome's economic growth influenced development of contract and commercial law. Roman contract law (a sub-part of the law of obligations) did not ripen into a general theory of contract but rather developed as a number of discrete types of individual contracts; each requiring for validity either specific language coupled with specific conduct or a relationship to a specific purpose. Roman contracts may be categorized into five basic types: 1) real; 2) verbal; 3) literal; 4) consensual; and, 5) "innominate".

Verbal contracts—the oldest recognized Roman contracts—required that the promisor and promisee say aloud a scripted formula of words. The earliest verbal contract was the *stipulatio* (also known as *sponsio*) in which the promisee asked the promisor to make his promise using the Latin verb, *Spondesne?* And the promisor responded by making that exact promise, *Spondeo.* Because obligations created by contracts formed by *stipulatio* were originally considered unshakable, praetors inevitably excused and provided redress for parties who had entered into such contracts due to extortion or fraud.

The head of a Roman household created a literal contract when he recorded a particular kind of memorandum in his ledger.

Several types of real contracts could be created when one party delivered an object (usually personal property) to another. Roman law had four of these real contracts—which required the transferee later to return either the thing delivered or its equivalent: 1) *mutuum* (a loan of fungibles); 2) *commodatum* (a temporary loan permitting the bailee merely to use the object); 3) *depositum* (a temporary loan for safekeeping); and, 4) *pignus* (a delivery of collateral as security for a debt).

The law—thanks no doubt to praetors' innovations—permitted four kinds of consensual contracts (*i.e.,* contracts that demanded no formalities but merely the good faith agreement of the parties): 1) *emptio venditio* (purchase and sale); 2) *locatio conductio* (renting and hiring); 3) *societas* (partnership); and, 4) *mandatum* (a grant and acceptance of a gratuitous commission).

Among the most important of the innominate, or miscellaneous, contracts were *permutatio* (barter), *aestimatum* (conditional sale), and *transactio* (settlement).

Occasionally parties to a written contract included a provision (*sanctio*) stipulating liquidated damages, but if they did not, in the event of breach, the breaching party was ordinarily liable for damage suffered as a consequence of the breach (*damnum emergens*) and/or lost profit (*lucrum cessans*).

The law of *obligationes quasi ex contractu* imposed an obligation to pay for a benefit conferred (*e.g.,* services rendered) or to return money or property in circumstances where the beneficiary would be unjustly enriched if he were permitted to retain the money, property, or benefit without payment.

There were several variations of contractual real security. The contract known as *fiducia* allowed a debtor to transfer ownership (*dominium*) of a collateral to his creditor. But the law also permitted a debtor—through a contract called *pignus*—to transfer merely possession (*detentio*) not ownership of a collateral to his creditor. Beginning about 150 B.C., a third type of real security, *hypotheca*, granted a creditor the right to seize the collateral in the event that the debtor defaulted.

There were at least four legal/business entities recognized: 1) *Populus Romanus* (any property of the Roman State); 2) *fiscus* (treasury); 3) *municipii* (local governments); and, 4) *societas* (partnership/joint venture). The State assessed taxes on the sale of goods, slaves, prostitution, imports, and inheritance.

Further Reading

Early Mesopotamian Law

Bottéro, Jean, *The "Code" of Hammurabi*. (ch. 10 in MESOPOTAMIA: WRITING, REASONING, AND THE GODS (Zainab Bahrani and Marc Van De Mieroop trans., 1982)).

Driver, G. R., and Miles, John C., THE BABYLONIAN LAWS (Vol. I: Legal Commentary 1952).

Ellickson, Robert C., and Thorland, Charles DiA., *Ancient Land Law: Mesopotamia, Egypt, Israel*, 71 CHICAGO-KENT L. REV. 321 (1995).

Finkelstein, J.J., *The Goring Ox: Some Historical Perspectives on Deodands, Forfeitures, Wrongful Death and the Western Notion of Sovereignty*, 46 TEMPLE L.Q. 169 (1973).

_____, *The Laws of Ur Nammu*, 22 J. CUNEIFORM STUDIES 66 (1969).

Greengus, Samuel, *Legal and Social Institutions of Ancient Mesopotamia*. In 1 CIVILIZATIONS OF THE ANCIENT NEAR EAST 469 (Jack M. Sasson ed., 1995).

_____, *The Old Babylonian Marriage Contract*, 89 J. AMERICAN ORIENTAL SOC. 505 (1969).

Lafont, Sophie, *The Ancient Near Eastern Laws: Continuity and Pluralism*. IN THEORY AND METHODS IN BIBLICAL AND CUNEIFORM LAW 91 (Bernard M. Levinson ed., 1994).

Oppenheim, Leo A., *The Seafaring Merchants of Ur*, 74 J. OF THE AMERICAN ORIENTAL SOC. 6 (1954).

Renger, Johannes M., *Institutional, Communal, and Individual Ownership or Possession of Arable Land in Ancient Mesopotamia from the End of the Fourth to the End of the First Millennium B.C.*, 71 CHICAGO-KENT L. REV. 269 (1995).

Roth, Martha T. *Gender and Law: A Case Study from Ancient Mesopotamia*. In GENDER AND LAW IN THE HEBREW BIBLE AND THE ANCIENT NEAR EAST (Victor H. Matthews, Bernard M. Levison, and Tikva Frymer-Kensky eds., 1997).

_____, Law COLLECTIONS FROM MESOPOTAMIA AND ASIA MINOR (1995).

_____, *Mesopotamian Legal Traditions and the Laws of Hammurabi*, 71 Chicago-Kent L. Rev. 13 (1995).

Sasson, Jack M. *King Hammurabi of Babylon*. In 2 CIVILIZATIONS OF THE ANCIENT NEAR EAST 901, (Jack Sasson., ed., 1995).

Veenker, Ronald A., THE OLD BABYLONIAN JUDICIARY AND LEGAL PROCEDURE, Unpublished Ph.D dissertation, Hebrew Union College-Jewish Institute of Religion (Cincinnati, OH) (1967).

_____, *An Old Babylonian Legal Procedure for Appeal: Evidence from the tuppi lā ragāmim*. HEBREW UNION COLLEGE ANNUAL (1974).

VerSteeg, Russ, EARLY MESOPOTAMIAN LAW (2000).

Westbrook, Raymond, *Biblical and Cuneiform Law Codes*, 92 REVIEW BIBLIQUE 248 (1985).

_____, *Cuneiform Law Codes and the Origins of Legislation*, 79 ZEITSCHRIFT FÜR ASSYRIOLOGIE UND VORDERASIATISCHE ARCHÄOLOGIE 201 (1989).

_____, OLD BABYLONIAN MARRIAGE LAW (1988).

_____, *Slave and Master in Ancient Near Eastern Law*, 70 CHICAGO-KENT LAW REV. 1631 (1995).

_____, *Social Justice in the Ancient Near East*. IN SOCIAL JUSTICE IN THE ANCIENT WORLD 149 (K.D. Irani and Morris Silver eds., 1995).

Yoffee, Norman, *Context and Authority in Early Mesopotamian Law*. (ch. 5 in POLITICAL ANTHROPOLOGY (1988)).

Law in Ancient Egypt

Allam, Schafik, *Egyptian Law Courts in Pharaonic and Hellenistic Times*, 77 J. EGYPTIAN ARCHAELOGY 109 (1991).

_____, *Women as Owners of Immovables in Pharaonic Egypt*. In WOMEN'S EARLIEST RECORDS FROM ANCIENT EGYPT AND WESTERN ASIA 123 (Barbara S. Lesko ed., 1989).

Bedell, Ellen, CRIMINAL LAW IN THE EGYPTIAN RAMESSIDE PERIOD (Brandeis University, Ph.D. Dissertation) (1973).

Edgerton, William E, *The Nauri Decree of Seti I: A Translation and Analysis of the Legal Portion*, 6 J. NEAR EASTERN STUD. 219 (1947).

Eyre, Christopher J., *Crime and Adultery in Ancient Egypt*, 70 J. EGYPTIAN ARCHAEOLOGY 92 (1984).

_____, *Peasants and "Modern" Leasing Strategies in Ancient Egypt*, 40 J. ECONOMIC & SOCIAL HIST. ORIENT 367 (1997).

_____, *The Adoption Papyrus in Social Context*, 78 J. EGYPTIAN ARCHAEOLOGY 207 (1992).

_____, *The Market Women of Pharaonic Egypt*. In LE COMMERCE EN ÉGYPT ANCIENNE 173, (Nicolas Grimal and Bernadette Menu eds., 1998).

Hoch, James, and Orel, Sara, *Murder in Ancient Egypt*. In DEATH AND TAXES IN THE ANCIENT NEAR EAST 87 (Sara Orel ed., 1992).

Janssen, Jac, *Rules of Legal Proceeding in the Community of Necropolis Workmen at Deir el-Medina*, 32 BIBLIOTHECA ORIENTALIS 291 (1975).

Johnson, Janet H., *The Legal Status of Women in Ancient Egypt*. In MISTRESS OF THE HOUSE MISTRESS OF HEAVEN: WOMEN IN ANCIENT EGYPT 175 (Anne K. Chapel and Glenn E. Markoe eds., 1996).

Katary, Sally L.D., LAND TENURE IN THE RAMESSIDE PERIOD (1989).

Lorton, David, *Legal and Social Institutions of Pharaonic Egypt*. In 1 CIVILIZATIONS OF THE ANCIENT NEAR EAST 345 (Jack M. Sasson ed., 1995).

McDowell, Andrea, JURISDICTION IN THE WORKMEN'S COMMUNITY OF DEIR EL-MEDINA (1990).

_____, *Legal Aspects of Care of the Elderly in Egypt to the End of the New Kingdom*. In THE CARE OF THE ELDERLY IN THE ANCIENT NEAR EAST 199 (Marten Stol and Sven P. Vleeming eds., 1998).

Mattha, Girgis, THE DEMOTIC LEGAL CODE OF HERMOPOLIS WEST (1975, preface, additional notes, and glossary *by* George R. Hughes).

Manning, J.G., *Demotic Egyptian Instruments of Transfer as Evidence for Private Ownership of Real Property*, 71 CHICAGO-KENT L. REV. 237 (1995).

Menu, Bernadette, *Women and Business Life in the First Millennium B. C.* In WOMEN'S EARLIEST RECORDS FROM ANCIENT EGYPT AND WESTERN ASIA 193 (Barbara S. Lesko ed., 1989).

Pestman, Pieter Willem, MARRIAGE AND MATRIMONIAL PROPERTY IN ANCIENT EGYPT (1961).

_____, *The Law of Succession in Ancient Egypt*, 9 STUDIA ET DOCUMENTA AD JURA ANTIQUI PERTINENTIA 58 (1969).

Pflüger, Kurt, *The Edict of Horemhab*, 5 J. NEAR EASTERN STUD. 260 (1944).

Phillips, Jacke, *Tomb-robbers and their Booty in Ancient Egypt*. In DEATH AND TAXES IN THE ANCIENT NEAR EAST 157 (Sara Orel ed., 1992).

Shupak, Nili, *A New Source For the Study of the Judiciary and Law of Ancient Egypt. "The Tale of the Eloquent Peasant"*, 51 J. NEAR EASTERN STUD. 1 (1992).

Théodorides, Aristide, *The Concept of Law in Ancient Egypt*. In THE LEGACY OF EGYPT 291 (J.R. Harris ed., 2d ed. 1971).

VerSteeg, Russ, LAW IN ANCIENT EGYPT (2002).

_____, *Law in Ancient Egyptian Fiction*, 24 GA. J. INT'L & COMP. L. REV. 37 (1994).

Ward, William A., *Some Aspects of Private Land Ownership and Inheritance in Ancient Egypt, ca. 2500–1000 B. C.* In LAND TENURE AND SOCIAL TRANSFORMATION IN THE MIDDLE EAST 63 (Tarif Khalidi ed., 1984).

Warburton, David A., STATE AND ECONOMY IN ANCIENT EGYPT: FISCAL VOCABULARY OF THE NEW KINGDOM (1997).

Wilson, John A., *Authority and Law in Ancient Egypt*, Supplement to 40 J. AM. ORIENTAL SOC. 1 (1954).

Law in Classical Athens

Annaoutoglou, Ilias, ANCIENT GREEK LAWS (1998).

____, ANCIENT GREEK LAWS: A SOURCE BOOK (1998).

Aristophanes, WASPS (David Barrett, *trans.* 1964).

Bonner, Robert, LAWYERS AND LITIGANTS IN ANCIENT ATHENS (1927).

Bonner, R.; Smith, G., THE ADMINISTRATION OF JUSTICE FROM HOMER TO ARISTOTLE (1930–38).

Calhoun, G. M., THE GROWTH OF CRIMINAL LAW IN ANCIENT GREECE (1927).

Carawan, Edwin, RHETORIC AND THE LAW OF DRACO (1998).

Carey, Christopher, TRIALS FROM CLASSICAL ATHENS (1997).

Cartledge, Paul; Todd, Stephen; Millett, Paul (eds.), NOMOS: ESSAYS IN ATHENIAN LAW, POLITICS AND SOCIETY (1990).

Cohen, David, LAW, VIOLENCE AND COMMUNITY IN CLASSICAL ATHENS (1995).

Foxhall, L; Lewis, A. (eds.), GREEK LAW IN ITS POLITICAL SETTING (1996).

Gagarin, Michael, DRAKON AND EARLY ATHENIAN HOMICIDE LAW (1981).

____, EARLY GREEK LAW (1986).

Havelock, Eric, THE GREEK CONCEPT OF JUSTICE: FROM ITS SHADOW IN HOMER TO ITS SUBSTANCE IN PLATO (1978).

Harrison, A.R.W., THE LAW OF ATHENS (1968).

Johnstone, Steven, DISPUTES AND DEMOCRACY: THE CONSEQUENCES OF LITIGATION IN ANCIENT ATHENS (1999).

MacDowell, Douglas, ATHENIAN HOMICIDE LAW IN THE AGE OF THE ORATORS (1963).

____, THE LAW IN CLASSICAL ATHENS (1977).

Otswald, Martin, FROM POPULAR SOVEREIGNTY TO THE SOVEREIGNTY OF LAW: LAW, SOCIETY AND POLITICS IN FIFTH-CENTURY ATHENS (1990).

Sealey, Raphael, THE JUSTICE OF THE GREEKS (1994).

____, WOMEN AND LAW IN CLASSICAL GREECE (1990).

Todd, S.C., THE SHAPE OF ATHENIAN LAW (1993).

Law in Ancient Rome

Bauman, Richard, CRIME AND PUNISHMENT IN ANCIENT ROME (1996).

Crook, J.A., LAW AND LIFE OF ROME, 90 B.C.–A.D. 212 (1967).

Furguson, Carr, *A Day in Court in Justinian's Rome: Some Problems of Evidence, Proof, and Justice in Roman Law*, 46 Iowa L. Rev. 732 (1961).

Gardner, Jane, FAMILY AND FAMILIA IN ROMAN LAW AND LIFE (1998).

____, WOMEN IN ROMAN LAW AND SOCIETY (1991).

Ioffe, Olympiad, ROMAN LAW (1987).

Johnson, David, ROMAN LAW IN CONTEXT (1999).

Justinian, THE DIGEST OF ROMAN LAW: THEFT, RAPINE, DAMAGE AND INSULT (C.F. Kolbert, *trans.* 1979).

Kunkel, Wolfgang, AN INTRODUCTION TO ROMAN LEGAL AND CONSTITUTIONAL HISTORY, 2d. ed. (J.M., Kelly, *trans.* 1973).

McGinn, Thomas A., PROSTITUTION, SEXUALITY AND THE LAW IN ANCIENT ROME (1998).

Nicholas, Barry, AN INTRODUCTION TO ROMAN LAW (1962).

Riggsby, Andrew, CRIME AND COMMUNITY IN CICERONIAN ROME (1999).

Robinson, O. F., THE CRIMINAL LAW OF ANCIENT ROME (1995).

____, THE SOURCES OF ROMAN LAW: APPROACHING THE ANCIENT WORLD (1997).

Tellegen-Couperus, Olga, A SHORT HISTORY OF ROMAN LAW (1990).

Thomas, J.A.C., TEXTBOOK OF ROMAN LAW (1976).

Watson, Alan, ROMAN LAW & COMPARATIVE LAW (1991).

____, THE DIGEST OF JUSTINIAN (1998).

____, THE SPIRIT OF ROMAN LAW (1995).

Wolff, Hans Julius, ROMAN LAW: AN HISTORICAL INTRODUCTION (1951).

Index

Papyrus Salt, 172
Papyrus Turin 1977, 172
Papyrus Westcar, 169
paragraphē, 210–211, 222
parent(s), 11, 17, 35, 47–48, 53–54, 96,
    156–157, 159, 184, 225–226,
    237–238, 240, 262–263, 265, 298,
    304, 330, 362
partners, partnership(s), 16, 89, 99,
    169, 353–354, 366–367
pʿt, 141
paterfamilias, 306, 322–325, 327,
    330, 334, 338, 351, 355, 360–361,
    363
patria potestas, 322–323, 326, 331,
    360–362
patrician, 271, 283, 290
patron, 229, 271, 303, 309, 335
Paul, 277. See also Paulus
Paulus, 277–278. See also Paul
peasant(s), 113–116, 143, 153, 165
peculatus, 297, 341, 364
peculium, 308, 322–323, 358, 360
peculium castrense, 323, 360
Peikharu, 133, 146
Peiraeus, 213, 258–259
Peloponnesian War, 197, 225
penalty, penalties, 8–10, 26, 29–31,
    44–45, 54–56, 60–70, 72–73,
    75–78, 80, 86–87, 90–91, 95–98,
    123, 133, 135, 140, 161–163,
    165–170, 179, 185, 193–195, 209,
    214, 218–220, 222, 225–227,
    231–232, 248–249, 251, 259, 264,
    296–297, 326, 334–343, 345–346,
    361–363. See also punishment(s)
Pennestytauy, 135
Pentoere, 147
Pepi I, 121–122, 136, 168, 185
per capita, 240, 330
Per Formulam, 288, 291–292, 299
per stirpes, 240, 262, 330
perduellio, 340, 364
peregrini, 303
perfume, 79
Pericles, 215, 225–226, 260
perjury, 9, 30–31, 68, 97, 134–135,
    140, 162, 164, 173, 216, 220, 223,
    299, 333. See also false testimony

permutatio, 354, 366
Persian Gulf, 79
persona alieni iuris, personae alieni
    iuris, 305–306, 322
persona sui iuris, 305, 322
personal injury, 8, 12–13, 21, 27, 71,
    73–74, 254, 283, 345, 347, 365
personal property, 8, 14, 21, 81,
    142–143, 150, 158, 176–177, 228,
    230, 233–234, 247, 257, 261, 306,
    315–316, 321, 345, 360, 365–366
personal status, 33, 44, 72, 94, 141,
    182, 225, 260, 303, 357
pharaoh(s), 104–106, 108, 111,
    113–114, 116–117, 119–124, 126,
    128–129, 133, 136–139, 142–145,
    151, 153, 162–163, 165–168,
    170–173, 179
phasis, 238, 259, 265
Philolaos, 193
philosophy, 19, 110–111, 189, 200,
    282, 285
Phoenicia, 173
phratries, 230
Phreatto, 246, 263
phylae, 226
physician, 77, 244. See also doctor(s)
Pi-Raʿmesse, 135
pig, 61–62, 346
pignus, 352, 356, 366–367
pinakion, 215, 223
plagium, 342, 364
plaintiff(s), 28–29, 82, 128, 130–132,
    136, 140, 146–147, 172, 195,
    203–204, 206–210, 219–222, 233,
    248, 250–252, 254–255, 258, 287,
    291–293, 299–300, 332, 347, 350,
    354
Plato, 189, 197–201
Plautus, 294
plebeian, 271, 275, 290–291, 299
plebiscita, plebiscites, 289–291, 299
Plutarch, 194, 226, 271
Pn-ʿnḳt, 172
Polemarch, Polemarchus, 210–211,
    213, 222, 228–229
police, 30–31, 105, 124–125, 130, 164,
    166, 171, 173, 229, 242
polis, 196, 201

usus fructus, 147–148, 160, 183, 307, 321, 360
uzubbûm, 53

Valentinian III, 278–279, 284
vandalized, vandalism, 133, 172, 185
verbal (contracts), 350, 366
verdict(s), 6, 26–28, 113, 161, 195, 214–215, 247, 295
veterinarian(s), 77, 93, 97
via, 74, 310, 314, 320–321, 359–360
vicarious liability, 229, 348, 365
violence, 8, 78, 89, 91, 155, 190, 205–206, 239–240, 248–251, 294, 334, 336–337, 345–346, 351, 363. *See also* vis
vis, 294, 337, 340, 363. *See also* violence
vizier, 104, 106, 110–112, 114, 116–120, 122–124, 126–133, 135, 137, 139, 147–148, 158, 160, 168, 177, 183–184
volunteer prosecutor, 205, 221, 238

wages, 11, 13, 91–93, 99
wagon(s), 11, 92
wall, 46, 67–68, 152, 194, 321
war, warfare, 16, 35, 40, 44, 66, 84, 94–95, 143, 163, 182, 197, 225–226, 229, 249, 261, 266, 305–307, 340–341, 346, 358
ward, 144–145, 149, 177, 238, 262, 327–328, 361
wardum, wardu, 11, 33
warranty, 15, 45, 84–85, 176, 178, 315, 359
water, 9, 28, 52, 65–66, 69–70, 75, 111, 114–115, 148, 164, 208, 222, 232, 258, 261, 297, 310, 321, 340, 360, 364
wealth, 59, 113, 142, 153, 155, 158–159, 199, 201, 228, 296, 298
wealthy, 14, 20, 259–260, 266, 347. *See also* rich, upper class
weights and measures, 7, 259, 265
Weni, 122, 136, 168

Wernero, 127
widow, 8, 49, 53, 55–58, 61, 96, 111, 113, 127, 240, 306
wife, wives, 8–10, 12, 15, 25, 39–40, 46–53, 56–59, 61, 65–66, 77, 91, 95, 97, 115, 142, 152–159, 169–170, 175, 183–185, 225, 236–237, 249, 261–262, 271, 297–298, 306, 321–326, 330, 332, 337–339, 341, 361
Wilbour Papyrus, 145–146, 149–151, 183
William the Conqueror, 287
wine, 79, 150, 346
witchcraft, 30, 69, 97
witness(es), 9, 14–15, 27, 29–31, 39, 52, 63–64, 68, 80–81, 83, 94, 98, 125, 127, 133–136, 138, 140, 142, 145, 149, 159, 176, 178, 196, 207, 209–210, 216–217, 220, 223, 234, 241–242, 247, 256, 265, 289, 293, 296, 298–301, 309–310, 314, 326, 331, 353, 358–359, 362
woman, women, 10, 15–16, 19, 21, 23, 34–37, 45, 50–53, 56–61, 65–66, 68–70, 73, 80–81, 87, 90–91, 94, 97–98, 103, 108, 117, 120, 127, 133–135, 137, 139, 142, 145, 152–160, 165, 169–172, 175–176, 181, 183–184, 196, 217, 223, 225–228, 234–237, 247–250, 259, 261, 264, 273, 305–306, 323, 325, 327, 331, 333–335, 337–339, 360, 363
wood, 173, 218, 223, 272. *See also* lumber, timber, trees
wool, 37, 79, 81, 92
writ, 287

xenika, 258
xenodikai, 212–213, 222

Zaleucus, 193
Zeno, 282, 285